Islamic Law and International Commercial Arbitration

T0295943

This book examines the intersection between contemporary International Commercial Arbitration and *Shari'a* law in order to determine possible tensions that may arise between the two systems. It develops evidentiary and procedural rules under *Shari'a*, as well as examining the consequences of stipulating qualifications of arbitrators based on gender and/or religion. The author extensively analyses the prohibition against interest (*riba*) and uncertainty (*gharar*) under *Shari'a* and its impact on arbitration agreements, arbitral awards and public policy. The book also explores the prohibition against *riba* in light of international conventions, such as the *United Nations Convention on Contracts for the International Sale of Goods*. Case studies in the book include the Asian International Arbitration Centre, formerly the Kuala Lumpur Regional Centre for Arbitration, and the International Islamic Centre for Reconciliation and Arbitration, as well as the 'Shari'a Standards' developed by the Accounting and Auditing Organization for Islamic Financial Institutions.

The book will be a valuable resource for academics, students and practitioners working in the areas of Islamic law and the Islamic finance industry.

Maria Bhatti is a lawyer and academic in Australia. She is currently teaching at University of Technology of Sydney Law School and was previously teaching at Monash Law School. She completed her PhD from Monash Law School, and her Bachelor of Laws and Masters of Law from the University of Melbourne.

Islamic Law in Context
Series Editor:
Javaid Rehman
Brunel University, UK

The Islamic Law in Context series addresses key contemporary issues and theoretical debates related to the Sharia and Islamic law. The series focuses on research into the theory and practice of the law, and draws attention to the ways in which the law is operational within modern State practices. The volumes in this series are written for an international academic audience and are sensitive to the diversity of contexts in which Islamic law is taught and researched across various jurisdictions as well as to the ways it is perceived and applied within general international law.

Woman's Identity and Rethinking the Hadith
Nimat Hafez Barazangi

Changing God's Law
The Dynamics of Middle Eastern Family Law
Edited by Nadjma Yassari

Applied Family Law in Islamic Courts
Shari'a Courts in Gaza
Nahda Shehada

Islamic Law and International Commercial Arbitration
Maria Bhatti

For more information about this series, please visit: www.routledge.com/Islamic-Law-in-Context/book-series/ISLAMLAWCXT

Islamic Law and International Commercial Arbitration

Maria Bhatti

Routledge
Taylor & Francis Group

LONDON AND NEW YORK

First published 2019 by Routledge

2 Park Square, Milton Park, Abingdon, Oxfordshire OX14 4RN

52 Vanderbilt Avenue, New York, NY 10017

Routledge is an imprint of the Taylor & Francis Group, an informa business

First issued in paperback 2020

British Library Cataloguing-in-Publication Data
A catalogue record for this book is available from the British Library

Library of Congress Cataloging-in-Publication Data
Names: Bhatti, Maria.
Title: Islamic law and international commercial arbitration /
    Maria Bhatti.
Description: Abingdon, Oxon ; New York, NY : Routledge, 2019. |
    Based on author's thesis (doctoral – Monash University, 2017)
    issued under title: The application of shari°a in contemporary
    international commercial arbitration. | Includes bibliographical
    references and index.
Identifiers: LCCN 2018027453 | ISBN 9781138604254 (hardback)
Subjects: LCSH: International commercial arbitration. | Arbitration
    and award (Islamic law)
Classification: LCC K2400 .B548 2019 | DDC 347/.09—dc23
LC record available at https://lccn.loc.gov/2018027453

ISBN: 978-1-138-60425-4 (hbk)
ISBN: 978-0-367-49698-2 (pbk)

Typeset in Galliard
by Apex CoVantage, LLC

This book is dedicated to the unconditional love and support of my parents, Dr Ishaq Bhatti and Mrs Asma Bhatti.

Contents

Arabic translation, transliteration and dates

This book uses a simple method to transliterate Arabic terms. Dots and macrons on or below letters have not been used (i.e., ī, ṣ or ū). The symbol ʿ has been used to signify the Arabic letter *ʿayn* in the middle of the word (i.e., *Shariʿa*) and the symbol ʾ has been used to signify the Arabic letter *hamza* in the middle or end of a word (i.e., *Ibraʾ* and Qurʾan). However, ʿ and ʾ have not been used if they occur in the beginning of words.

Apart from the glossary below, italics have been used for most Arabic words, except for commonly used terms such as: hadith, Qurʾan, schools of thought (i.e., Hanbali, Hanafi . . . etc.).

This book refers to years in the Common Era (CE) and provides the year of death for prominent people in Islamic history.

The translation of Arabic terms is the author's, unless indicated otherwise in the footnotes.

Glossary of basic Arabic terms

Arabic term	Definition provided in this book
Adala	Morally righteous character.
Ahl al-ra'y	Rationalist school.
Aqidah	Creed, or system of religious belief.
Al-kutub al-arba'a	'The four books.' Relied upon by *Shi'a* Muslim, which contain hadith.
Allah	The Arabic name for one God.
Amarat	Indications or textual indications (also known as *dalalat*).
Bai bi-thamin ajil	Deferred payment financing.
bay al-inah	Sale with immediate repurchase.
Caliph	Leader of an Islamic state, political entity.
Caliphate	A political-religious State where Islam is implemented.
Dalalat	Indications or textual indications (also known as *amarat*).
Darura	Necessity.
Dhimmi	Non-Muslims protected under *Shari'a* (usually Christians and Jews who are referred to as the 'people of the book' in the Qur'an).
Diwan al-Mazalim (or *Al Mazalem*)	The Board of Grievances. A regulatory body in Saudi Arabia, which was created to deal with the heavy caseload of Saudi courts.
Diya	'Blood money' or financial compensation provided to the victim (in cases of wounding) or their family (in homicide).
Fatwa (pl. fatawa)	An Islamic legal ruling.
Fiqh	Islamic jurisprudence or the understanding of Islamic law.
Gharar	*Risk/uncertainty.*
Ghayr lazim	Not binding.
Hadd	'Limit or prohibition.' Refers to serious crimes under Islamic law.
Hadith (*pl.* ahadith)	Traditions or reports – a record of the Prophet Muhammad's actions and sayings.
Hakam	Arbitrator (also known as a *muhakkam*).
Halal	Permissible in Islamic law.
Hanafi school	Sunni school of thought (*madhab*) named after Islamic jurist Abu Hanifa Nu'man ibn Thabit (d. 767 CE).
Hanbali school	Sunni school of thought (*madhab*) named after Islamic jurist Ahmad ibn Muhammad ibn Hanbal (d. 855 CE).

(*Continued*)

Arabic term	Definition provided in this book
Haram	Forbidden in Islamic law.
Hakkama	Turning back from wrongdoing. Root word for *tahkim*, *hakam* and *muhakkam*.
Hukm (pl. Ahkam)	Rulings or directions through which Islamic law is understood.
Ibra'	Rebate.
Ijara	Leasing.
Ijma	Consensus.
Ijtihad	The use of independent thinking or reasoning by jurists to apply Islamic legal theory and develop new laws or find solutions to problems.
Ijtihad jama'i	Collective *ijtihad* –when Islamic jurist consult each other when applying Islamic legal theories to develop new laws or find solutions to problems.
Imam	The religious-political leader of the *Shi'a* community; or the leader of a congregational prayer for all Muslims regardless of the sect.
Istihsan	Juristic preference or equity.
Jahada	Striving, self-exertion.
Ja'iz	Permissible.
Kalam or Ilm al Kalam	Islamic theology.
Madhab	School of religious law or thought.
Majmu al-Fatawa al-Kubra	The Great Compilation of Religious Rulings.
Malki school	Sunni school of thought (*madhab*) named after Islamic jurist Malik ibn Anas al-Asbahi (d. 795 CE).
Maslaha	Public interest. A source of Islamic jurisprudence through which juristic preference or equity (*istihsan*) is exercised if an issue is not clearly dealt with by primary sources.
Maqasid al-Shari'a	The higher objectives or aims/purposes of *Shari'a*. *Maqasid al-Shari* refers to the objectives of *Shari'a* which relate to worship of God, as outlined in the *Shari'a*.
Maqasid al-Mukallaf	*Maqasid* refers to higher objectives/purposes and *al-mukallaf* refers to 'the competent or an accountable person' (literally meaning 'the taxpayer' in Arabic). In this book, *maqasid al-mukallaf* refers to the worldly objectives of *Shari'a*.
Medjella	The first codification of the *Shari'a* (based on the Hanafi school) under the Ottoman Empire.
Mudaraba	Trustee finance.
Mufti	Muslim legal scholar who may issues *fatwas*.
Mujtahid	An Islamic scholar, or a person who exercises *ijtihad*.
Mulgha	Discredited.
Murabaha	Cost plus financing.
Mursala	Undetermined.
Musharaka	Equity participation.
Mutawwi'a	Religious Police.
Qadi	Judge.
Qiyas	Analogical reasoning – one of the sources of Islamic law.

Arabic term	Definition provided in this book
Qisas	Retaliation. In *Shari'a*, crimes where the victim is allowed to 'retaliate' include homicide and wounding.
Qur'an	The final scripture, believed to be word of God, revealed to the Prophet Muhammad and the primary source of *Shari'a*.
Ra'y	Personal reasoning.
Riba al-jahilliya	*Riba* practiced during 'the age of ignorance' (pre-Islamic period).
Riba al-nasiah	*Riba* by way of deferment.
Sahih	Valid or correct.
Salafism	An ideology which stems from sunni Islam and advocates a return to the practices of the original followers of Islam.
Salafs	Original followers of Islam.
Salam	Advance Purchase.
Shafi'i school	Sunni school of thought (*madhab*) named after Islamic jurist Muhammad ibn Idris al-Shafi'i (d. 820 CE).
Shari'a	Literally 'the road' or 'the way' – refers to Islamic law and jurisprudence as derived from the Qur'an, hadith etc.
Shi'a	A major religious-political group in Islam. They believe that Ali, the Prophet Muhammad's son-in-law, was the first *caliph* after the Prophet Muhammad's death and that Ali's direct descendants are the rightful successors.
Shura	Consultation. As per Islamic law, scholars consult each other when formulating decisions impacting the public.
Sira	The Prophet Muhammad's biography.
Sulh	Conciliation.
Sunna	The normative behaviour of the Prophet Muhammad, as recorded in the hadith.
Sunni	The major denomination in Islam. Sunni Muslims consider themselves to be people of the community and the *sunna*.
Tahkim	Arbitration.
Takaful	Mutual insurance which is *Shari'a*-compliant.
Taqlid	To follow. In Islamic jurisprudence, to follow an established doctrine.
Tawarruq	A sale contract through which a buyer purchases a commodity from a financial institution and repays the institution on a deferred payment basis.
Ulama	Muslim scholars – often referred to by Sunni Muslims as those that transmit religious knowledge.
Urf	Custom.
Usul-ul fiqh	Sources or roots of Islamic jurisprudence; Islamic legal theory.
Wahabbism	An ideology or political movement within Islam, based on the teachings of Muhammad bin Abd al-Wahhab (d. 1791 CE).
Zaahir	Outward meaning (in the context of textual interpretations).

1 Introduction

I Introduction

> [*The Sheikh, an*] *absolute, feudal monarch . . . administers a purely discretion-*
> *ary justice with the assistance of the Koran; and it would be fanciful to suggest*
> *that in this very primitive region there is any settled body of legal principles appli-*
> *cable to the construction of modern commercial instruments.*[1]

This book addresses whether *Shariʿa* or Islamic law (defined in Chapter 2) is a
predictable, enforceable and comprehensive body of law which can be applied
to contemporary international commercial arbitration matters ('contemporary
ICA'). The hypothesis tested in this book is that *Shariʿa* can effectively apply to
and harmoniously exist with contemporary ICA if: firstly, its rules on arbitration
are thoroughly codified; and secondly, if there is mutual respect and recognition
between *Shariʿa* and contemporary ICA.

The first part of this chapter explains the development of contemporary ICA
and the need for arbitration that caters for *Shariʿa*. Subsequently, this chapter outlines the methodology used in this book and establishes how the chapters
are structured.

II Scope of this research

A Development of contemporary ICA

Historians and academics have struggled with pinpointing when the concept of
'arbitration' initially developed. For example, Lord Mustill observes that '[a]rbi-
tration has a long [p]ast, but scarcely any [h]istory . . . [t]here are none of the
grand perspectives in which modern arbitration could be viewed as the inheritor
of a continuous process of change.'[2] Some historians argue that international

---

1 *Petroleum Development (Trucial Coast) Ltd. v. Sheikh of Abu Dhabi* (1951) 19 ILR 144.
2 M. J. Mustill, 'Foreword: Sources for the History of Arbitration' (1998) 14(3) *Arbitration International* 235.

arbitration may have initially originated out of ancient Greek mythology.[3] Roebuck observes that the earliest evidence of arbitration could be from the poems of Homer and Hesiod.[4] There are also historical accounts of arbitration taking place in ancient Rome.[5] Historians report that '[t]he bulk of ancient Greek arbitration was inspired by disputes over territorial boundaries, possession or use of territory, and breached treaty obligations.'[6] One example that is often provided is from the Greek writer of the second century, Pausanias,[7] who relates that arbitration was used to resolve disputes between people belonging to the Greek region called Messenia (the Messenians) and the Spartans.[8] On the other hand, Fraser argues that this story is probably fabricated and that the first case of European arbitration actually took place in 650 B.C.E in a dispute between two cities, Adnors and Chacis. This case concerned the ancient city of Acanthus, and it was resolved by independent Greek citizens known as the Parians, Samians and Erythraens.[9] Commercial arbitration can also be traced back to ancient Egyptian civilisations.[10]

In China, arbitration has also been traced back to 2100–1600 B.C.E and it became even more popular after Confucian ideologies began influencing China, because Confucius was a strong advocate of resolving disputes through arbitration as opposed to litigation.[11] Similarly, arbitration can also be traced back to ancient India.[12] In fact, Taniguchi uses Japan as an example of a country in which, until 1868, law was not practiced due to the emphasis on conciliation, which he observes was common in Asian cultures.[13] This is also true in the Islamic world,

3 Kaja Harter-Uibopuu, 'Anthropological and Historical Foundations: Ancient Greek Approaches Toward Alternative Dispute Resolution' (2002) 10 *Williamette Journal of International Law & Dispute Resolution* 47, 48–52; see also Henry King and Marc Leforestier, 'Arbitration in Ancient Greece' (1994) 49(3) *Dispute Resolution Journal* 38; Derek Roebuck, *Ancient Greek Arbitration* (The Arbitration Press, 2001).

4 Roebuck, above n 3, 51.

5 See generally, Louise E. Matthaei, 'The Place of Arbitration and Mediation in Ancient Systems of International Ethics' (1908) 2(4) *The Classical Quarterly* 241.

6 King and Lefrostier, above n 3, 40.

7 W. L. Westermann, 'Interstate Arbitration in Antiquity' (1907) 2(5) *The Classical Journal* 197, 199 n 2.

8 Ibid. 199.

9 Henry S. Fraser, 'Sketch of the History of International Arbitration' (1926) 11(2) *Cornell Law Review* 179.

10 See generally, Derek Roebuck, 'Sources for the History of Arbitration: A Bibliographical Introduction' (1998) 14(3) *Arbitration International* 237; Margit Mantica, 'Arbitration in Ancient Egypt' (1957) 12 *Arbitration Journal* 155.

11 Simon Greenberg, Christopher Kee and Romesh Weeramantry, *International Commercial Arbitration: An Asia-Pacific Perspective* (Cambridge University Press, 2010) 1–8.

12 See generally, Nagendra Singh, 'The Machinery and Method for Conduct of Inter-State Relations in Ancient India' in Yôrām Dinštein and Mala Tabory (eds), *International Law at a Time of Perplexity: Essays in Honour of Shabtai Rosenne* (Martinus Nijhoff Publishers, 1989) 845.

13 See generally Yasuhei Taniguchi, 'Is There a Growing International Arbitration Culture? An Observation from Asia' in Albert Jan van den Berg (ed), *International Dispute Resolution: Towards an International Arbitration Culture* (Kluwer Law International, 1998) 31.

due to the fact that *Shari'a* encourages resolving disputes through conciliation, as will be discussed in more detail in the next chapter.

There are also many examples of inter-state arbitration in Europe during the Middle Ages and arbitration was also employed during the 15th and 16th centuries to resolve border disputes arising from colonisation.[14] However, Born notes that while international arbitration began to decline during the 16th, 17th and 18th centuries,[15]

> [b]y the end of the 19th century, proposals for more universal and binding state-to-state arbitration mechanisms emerged with greater frequency, often supported by religious and pacifist groups. Capturing the moral roots of such proposals, Andrew Carnegie famously remarked that "[t]he nation is criminal which refuses arbitration."[16]

This book will provide a comparative analysis between contemporary ICA and *Shari'a* (as defined and discussed in Chapter 2). Contemporary ICA refers to the contemporary legal framework for international commercial arbitration as developed in the 19th and 20th centuries. Greenberg, Kee and Weeramantry note

> [t]he seeds of international commercial arbitration as we know it today were sewn in the late 19th and 20th centuries as a response to growing international trade, mainly in Europe, and the desire for an internationally enforceable, commercially sensible mechanism to resolve disputes.[17]

For example, by the 20th century, most of the important international rules, treaties and conventions governing international commercial arbitration had been developed. More specifically, this book will refer to the following:

- The New York Convention of 1958 ('*New York Convention*');
- The United Nations Commission on International Trade Law Arbitration Rules ('*UNICTRAL Rules 2010*') adopted in 1976 and revised in 2010;
- The United Nations Commission on International Trade Model Law on International Commercial Arbitration ('*UNCITRAL Model Law*') adopted in 1985 and amended in 2006;
- The United Nations Convention on Contracts for the International Sale of Goods ('*CISG*') adopted in 1980.

For this reason, commentators such as Shalkany argue that '[a]s a technocratic mechanism of dispute settlement, with a particular set of rules and doctrines,

14 Greenberg, Kee and Weeramantry, above n 11, 4.
15 Gary Born, *International Commercial Arbitration* (Kluwer Law International, 2nd ed, 2014) 12. See also Greenberg, Kee and Weeramantry, above n 11, 4.
16 Born, *International Arbitration* 2nd edition, above n 15, 12.
17 Greenberg, Kee and Weeramantry, above n 11, 6.

international commercial arbitration is a product of this century.'[18] Taniguchi also opines that the *New York Convention* and the *UNCITRAL Rules 2010* have contributed to

> a distinct "commercial arbitration culture" in the West, and through the reception of the western legal system by the non-western world, arbitration has become a legitimate method of dispute resolution virtually everywhere in the world with a varying degree and scope of its application.[19]

Since the early 1990s, most Arab countries moved towards modernising their arbitration legislation and codifying laws and regulatory systems regarding commercial arbitration.[20] An increasing number of Arab states (as well as Iran and Malaysia) have also chosen to draft their arbitration laws modelled on the *UNCITRAL Model Law*. This includes countries such as Bahrain, Egypt, Jordan, Oman, Tunisia, Kuwait and the UAE.[21] On the other hand, Saudi Arabia, one of the main case studies examined in this book, has only recently decided to model its arbitration regime on the *UNCITRAL Model Law*. As will be discussed in more detail in the next chapter, the Saudi government introduced the new *Saudi Arbitration Law 2012*[22] and the new *Saudi Enforcement Law 2013*[23] (collectively referred to in this book as the '*new Saudi Arbitration laws*'). The new *Saudi Arbitration Law 2012* replaces the old *Arbitration Regulation of 1983* ('*Saudi Arbitration Law 1983*')[24] and the *Implementation Rules* of the previous *Saudi Arbitration Law 1983*[25] ('old *Implementation Rules 1985*') (collectively

---

18 Amr A. Shalakany, 'Arbitration and the Third World: A Plea for Reassessing Bias Under the Specter of Neoliberalism' (2000) 41(2) *Harvard International Law Journal* 419, 430; Tariq Hassan, 'International Arbitration in Pakistan: A Developing Country Perspective' (2002) 19(6) *Journal of International Arbitration* 591.

19 Taniguchi, above n 13, 32.

20 Lara Hammoud and Sami Houerbi, 'ICC Arbitration in the Arab World' (2008) 25(2) *Journal of International Arbitration* 231, 235.

21 Ibid. 235.

22 Royal Decree No. M/34 (legislation date 16 April 2012, published in the official Saudi Gazette (Um Al-Qura) on 8 June 2012 and came into effect on 9 July 2012). For an Arabic and English translation, [Law Firm, Alsulaim Alawaji & Partners Law Firm in partnership with Jones Day, trans]. English translation also available online, 'New Saudi Arbitration Act Issued on 16 April 2012' (2012) 4(3) *International Journal of Arab Arbitration* trans, 141–160. See generally, Saud Al-Ammari and Timothy Martin, 'Arbitration in the Kingdom of Saudi Arabia' (2014) 30(2) *Arbitration International* 387.

23 Royal Decree No. M/53 (legislation date 3 July 2012, published in the official Saudi Gazette (Um Al-Qura) on 31 August 2012 and came into effect on 27 February 2013). See also Al-Ammari and Martin, above n 22.

24 Royal Decree No. M/46 (legislation dated 25 April 1983). For an English translation, see Pieter Sanders (ed), 'Arbitration Regulation of Saudi Arabia' (1984) 9 *Y.B. Comm. Arb* (Kluwer Law International) 316–318.

25 Resolution No. 7/2021/M (legislation dated 27 May 1985 and published in the official Saudi Gazette (Um Al-Qura) on 28 June 1985). English translation in Albert Jan van den Berg (ed), 'Saudi Arabian Arbitration Regulation' (1986) 11 *Y.B. Comm. Arb* (Kluwer Law International) 370–377.

referred to as the '*old Saudi Arbitration laws*') which will also be considered in this book by way of comparison. One of the aims of the new arbitration laws in Saudi Arabia is to align with international standards and ensure enforcement of foreign arbitral awards, and the following chapters discuss whether it is possible to achieve these objectives. Saudi Arabia's first arbitration centre, the Saudi Centre for Commercial Arbitration (SCCA) was also recently established by the Saudi Cabinet Decree dated 15 March 2014 'in order to further enhance both local and foreign investment in the Kingdom' of Saudi Arabia.[26] The *SCCA Rules 2016* are based on the *UNCITRAL Rules 2010* and came into effect recently on 31 July 2016.[27] This book does not examine this centre because it has only recently been established (it was formally established in 2016, despite being introduced by Saudi law in 2014). Commenting on these recent developments in Saudi Arabia, Nesheiwat and Al-Khasawneh observe that the *new Saudi Arbitration laws* are:

> still untested, as no major awards have yet been brought for enforcement, and there are still major issues keeping people away from Saudi dispute resolution, such as the lack of suitably qualified arbitrators, the lack of a professional lawyers' syndicate, and the lack of arbitration centers in Saudi Arabia. More importantly, the court system requires a major overhaul and a codified civil transactions law (even one based on *Shari'a*), in addition to accurate reporting of Saudi court jurisprudence.[28]

Although this book does not provide a detailed analysis of the arbitration system in the following countries, by way of comparison, it will briefly analyse the application of *Shari'a* in specific jurisdictions from the Middle Eastern and North African region ('MENA region'), such as Egypt, Saudi Arabia, Kuwait, the United Arab Emirates, Qatar, Bahrain and Oman, as well as Iran. The reason why these countries have been examined as case studies in this book is due to the historical or current application of *Shari'a* in the respective jurisdictions, or the availability of ICC decisions from certain countries, such as Iran. This will be explored in more detail in the following chapters.

Since the international community has become more globalised, this has encouraged countries to establish international and domestic legal frameworks which support international commercial arbitration as a legal mechanism through which international commercial disputes are resolved.[29] It is due to this growing global consensus on international arbitration that many countries from the

---

26 Saudi Centre for Commercial Arbitration, *About SCCA* <http://sadr.org/en/about-2/organization>.

27 Saudi Centre for Commercial Arbitration, *Arbitration Rules* <http://sadr.org/en/adr-services-2/arbitration-2/rules/>. Due to the recent introduction of the *SCCA Rules 2016*, this book only briefly examines these rules.

28 Faris Nesheiwat and Ali Al-Khasawneh, 'The 2012 Saudi Arbitration Law: A Comparative Examination of the Law and Its Effect on Arbitration in Saudi Arabia' (2015) 13(2) *Santa Clara Journal of International Law* 444, 465.

29 Charles Brower and Jeremy Sharpe, 'International Arbitration and the Islamic World: The Third Phase' (2003) 97 *The American Society of International Law* 643, 647.

MENA Region have also ratified the *New York Convention*. These countries include: Algeria, Bahrain, Djibouti, Egypt, Jordan, Kuwait, Lebanon, Mauritania, Morocco, Oman, Palestine, Qatar, Saudi Arabia, Syria, Tunisia and the UAE.[30] Iran and Malaysia are also signatories to the *New York Convention*. Another example of international cooperation in the region is the ratification of the *Riyadh Convention on Judicial Cooperation*, which was agreed upon in 1983 between the members of the Arab League. This convention allows for mutual recognition and enforcement of judgements and awards between Algeria, Bahrain, Djibouti, Iraq, Jordan, Kuwait, Lebanon, Libya, Mauritania, Morocco, Oman, Palestine, Qatar, Saudi Arabia, Somalia, Sudan, Syria, Tunisia, the UAE and Yemen.[31]

The growing number of countries acceding to the *New York Convention* makes it extremely significant, and one of the most widely accepted conventions governing international commerce.[32] As will be discussed in more detail in Chapter 8 on *Shari'a* public policy and the recognition and enforcement of foreign arbitral awards, one of the principal obligations of the convention is to recognise and enforce foreign arbitral awards as if they were domestic judgements. Furthermore, since contemporary ICA is a well-recognised international dispute settlement mechanism, it is beneficial for countries in the MENA region to ratify international conventions and adopt international model laws, because it increases foreign direct investment.[33] Ismail reports that:

> [m]ost private foreign entities which have huge investments in the Middle East and North Africa are investors from developed countries. These investments are generally in infrastructure, telecommunications, oil and gas, energy sectors and tourism etc. Statistics show that the total value of projects in the Middle East region is USD 2.288 billion. It also shows that other projects may not be disclosed.[34]

However, in order to narrow the scope of this book, international investment arbitration governing investor-state dispute resolution including bilateral investment treaties (BITs), the International Centre for Settlement of Investment Disputes (ICSID) and ICSID Convention and Rules, will not be examined in detail.[35] Instead, this book will briefly examine the *IBA Guidelines on Conflicts*

---

30 New York Arbitration Convention, *The New York Arbitration Convention on the Recognition and Enforcement of Foreign Arbitral Awards 10 June 1958* <www.newyorkconvention.org/countries>.

31 Dubai International Financial Centre Courts, *Enforcement Guidelines* (3 January 2016) <http://difccourts.ae/enforcing-difc-court-judgments-and-orders-outside-the-difc1/>.

32 Brower and Sharpe, above n 29, 647.

33 Mohamed Ismail, *International Investment Arbitration* (Taylor and Francis, 2013) 52.

34 Ibid.

35 See generally, Tarek Badawy, 'The General Principles of Islamic Law as the Law Governing Investment Disputes in the Middle East' (2012) 29(3) *Journal of International Arbitration* 255; Lafi Daradkeh, 'Commercial Arbitration Under Investment Treaties and Contracts: Its Importance and Danger in the Arab World' (2013) 27 *Arab Law Quarterly* 393.

of Interest 2014 ('IBA Guidelines'),[36] *International Bar Association Rules on the Taking of Evidence in International Arbitration 2010* ('*IBA Rules*')[37] and the *Chartered Institute of Arbitrators Protocol for the Use of Party-Appointed Expert Witnesses in International Arbitration* ('*CIArb Protocol*')[38] in Chapter 5. Chapter 7 will note institutional arbitration in the *Rules of the London Court of International Arbitration* ('*LCIA Arbitration Rules 2014*')[39] and the *World Intellectual Property Organisations Arbitration Rules*.[40] These rules will be briefly examined in the context of comparing the procedures and interest provisions of *Shariʿa* arbitration-based arbitral rules and laws, which will be introduced in Chapter 2.

During the late 19th century and early 20th century, various arbitration centres were also established, and this book will briefly discuss the *LCIA Arbitration Rules 2014*, the LCIA having been created in 1892. The rules published by the International Chamber of Commerce ('*ICC Rules 2012*') will also be discussed, as well as cases from the ICC, which was established in 1919, and the ICC International Court of Arbitration ('ICC Court') established in 1923. The development of international commercial arbitration in the 20th century also led to the establishment of a number of new arbitration centres in the Muslim world, including the Euro-Arab Chambers of Commerce, Asian International Arbitration Centre ('AIAC'), formerly known as the Kuala Lumpur Regional Centre for Arbitration ('KLRCA'), the Cairo Regional Centre for International Commercial Arbitration, Bahrain Chamber for Dispute Resolution ('BCDR'), Gulf Cooperation Council Commercial Arbitration Centre, Dubai International Arbitration Centre, Abu Dhabi Commercial Conciliation and Arbitration Centre and the International Islamic Centre for Reconciliation and Arbitration ('IICRA').[41] As discussed in the next chapter, this book will be focusing on AIAC, IICRA and arbitration guidelines contained in the '*Shari'a* Standards' developed by the

---

36 International Bar Association, *Guidelines on Conflict of Interest in International Arbitration*, adopted 23 October 2014, <www.ibanet.org/Publications/publications_IBA_guides_and_free_materials.aspx>.

37 International Bar Association, *International Bar Association Rules on the Taking of Evidence in International Arbitration 2010*, adopted 29 May 2010, <www.ibanet.org/Publications/publications_IBA_guides_and_free_materials.aspx>.

38 Chartered Institute of Arbitrators, *Protocol for the Use of Party-Appointed Expert Witnesses in International Arbitration*, adopted September 2007, <www.ciarb.org/docs/default-source/ciarbdocuments/international-arbitration-protocols/partyappointedexpertsinternationalarbitration.pdf?sfvrsn=8>.

39 London Court of International Arbitration, LCIA Arbitration Rules (effective 1 October 2014) <www.lcia.org/Dispute_Resolution_Services/lcia-arbitration-rules-2014.aspx>.

40 World Intellectual Property Organisation, *World Intellectual Property Organisation Arbitration Rules* (effective 1 June 2014) <www.wipo.int/amc/en/arbitration/rules/>.

41 In 2018, the Kuala Lumpur Regional Centre for Arbitraiton rebranded and renamed itself as the Asian International Arbitration Centre. For more information, see Asian International Arbitration Centre, i-Arbitration <www.aiac.world/Arbitration-i-Arbitration/>. See generally, Elana Levi-Tawil, 'East Meets West: Introducing Sharia into the Rules Governing International Arbitrations at the BCDR-AAA' (2011) 12 *Cardozo Journal of Conflict Resolution* 609.

Accounting and Auditing Organization for Islamic Financial Institutions ('*AAO-IFI Standards*').[42]

B Growth of the Islamic finance industry and the need for Shariʿa-compliant arbitration

'*Shariʿa*-compliant arbitration,' as the term suggests, can be defined as arbitration which is compliant with *Shariʿa* (as discussed in Chapter 2).[43] In fact, the term *Shariʿa*-compliant is used to describe Islamic banking and finance transactions, contracts or products that do not invest in industries forbidden by *Shariʿa* (such as the alcohol, pornography, gambling and prostitution industries) and also avoid *riba* (interest) and/or *gharar* (risk/uncertainty).[44] Most Islamic financial institutions have *Shariʿa* Supervisory Boards (SSBs) or *Shariʿa* Advisory Councils (SACs) that regularly audit Islamic banking and finance products in order to ensure that they are *Shariʿa*-compliant.[45] Similarly, in Chapter 5, this book will discuss the appointment of experts from SSBs or SACs in the context of *Shariʿa*-compliant arbitration. More broadly, this book will also assess whether *Shariʿa*-compliant arbitration is possible and the impact of *Shariʿa* on choice of law, arbitrability and validity of arbitration agreement, composition of the arbitral tribunal, evidence and procedure, arbitral awards and public policy matters in arbitration.

In the following chapters, this book will argue that *Shariʿa*-compliant arbitration is not only possible, but is also significant, and should be further developed because the international nature of commercial arbitration suggests that contemporary ICA should cater for global cultures and religions. Furthermore, as discussed later, the growth of the Islamic finance industry could possibly increase the demand for *Shariʿa*-compliant arbitration. Although the banking and finance industry have previously been reluctant to utilise arbitration to resolve their

---

42 Accounting and Auditing Organization for Islamic Financial Institutions (AAOIFI), *Shariʾah Standards* (Dar Al Maiman, 2015). See generally, Adel Mohammed Sarea and Mustafa Mohd Haefah, 'Adoption of AAOIFI Accounting Standards by Islamic Banks of Bahrain' (2013) 11(2) *Journal of Financial Reporting and Accounting* 131; Scott Anderson, 'Forthcoming Changes in the Shariʾah Compliance Regime for Islamic Finance' (2010) 35 *The Yale Journal of International Law* 237.

43 For more information on the concept of Shariʿa compliance in the context of Islamic banking and finance products, see Mohamad Akram Laldin, 'Shariʾah – Non-Compliance Risk' in Rifaat Ahmed Abdel Karim and Simon Archer (eds), *Islamic Finance the New Regulatory Challenge* (John Wiley & Sons Singapore, 2013) 240–243; Andrew White and Chen Mee King, 'Legal Risk Exposure in Islamic Finance' in Simon Archer and Rifaat Ahmed Abdel Karim (eds), *Islamic Finance: The New Regulatory Challenge* (John Wiley & Sons, 2013) 225; Humayon Dar and Umar Moghul, *The Chancellor Guide to the Legal and Sharia Aspects of Islamic Finance* (Harriman House, 2010); Anderson, above n 42. Cf Kilian Balz, *Sharia Risk? How Islamic Finance Has Transformed Islamic Contract Law* (Islamic Legal Studies Program Harvard Law School, 2008).

44 *Gharar* and *riba* will be further explained in Chapter 6.

45 Maria Bhatti, 'Taxation of Islamic Finance Products' (2015) 20(2) *Deakin Law Review* 264, 265–266.

disputes, Hanefeld observes that '[t]oday, the traditional reluctance towards arbitration in the banking and finance industry is less prevalent. Instead, there is an increasing demand to have recourse to arbitration.'[46] Shehabi also observes that 'the push to embrace alternative dispute resolution in the financial services sectors has been most pronounced on a transnational level, where the benefits most strong outweigh the negatives of non-court dispute resolution services.'[47] This book will also argue that an increase in *Shari'a*-compliant rules and *Shari'a* qualified arbitrators will also contribute towards increasing competition in the contemporary ICA market and thus, facilitate economic development. Finally, *Shari'a*-compliant arbitration will cater to countries, such as Saudi Arabia, where public policy is based on *Shari'a*. However, as will be argued in this book, *Shari'a* does not exist in a vacuum and in order to effectively apply, there must be mutual recognition and respect between contemporary ICA and *Shari'a*.

As will be discussed further in Chapters 2 and 6, Islamic banking and finance is based on rules derived from *Shari'a* and this often raises complications due to the various interpretations regarding the prohibition against *riba* and *gharar*, including decisions as to whether and how *Shari'a* should be implemented. The subjective nature of the term '*Shari'a*-compliant' will be examined further in this book. Arbitration rules considered *Shari'a*-compliant by one expert may be viewed as contradicting the *Shari'a* according to other experts. It is this subjective and fluid nature of *Shari'a* that this book analyses in the context of contemporary ICA. This book discusses the different interpretations of *Shari'a* from a theoretical and practical perspective by providing case studies with reference to how *Shari'a* is implemented by countries, international financial institutions and arbitration centres.

Interestingly, unlike *Shari'a*-compliant arbitration, the Islamic banking and finance industry has flourished since the late 20th century. Most academics and historians observe that the contemporary Islamic banking and finance industry emerged in the 1960s and 1970s as a result of the establishment of Islamic banks, such as Mit Ghamr in Egypt and the increasing oil revenue flowing into countries such as Saudi Arabia, Kuwait, UAE, Iran, Iraq and Qatar.[48]

---

46 Inka Hanefeld, 'Arbitration in Banking and Finance' (2013) 9 *NYU Journal of Law and Business* 917. The International Chamber of Commerce (ICC) is about to launch a new report titled 'Financial Institutions and International Arbitration'. See ICC, *ICC Commission Report: Financial Institutions and International Arbitration* (2016) <www.iccwbo. org/Training-and-Events/All-events/Events/2016/ICC-Commission-Report-Financial-Institutions-and-International-Arbitration/>.

47 Faris Shehabi, 'Resolving Shariah Disputes – Navigating the Governing Law' (2015) 12(2) *Transnational Dispute Management* 1, 6; see also, The Panel of Recognised International Market Experts in Finance <www.primefinancedisputes>; The International Swaps and Derivatives Association, 2013 ISDA Arbitration Guide <https://www2.isda.org/attach ment/...==/ISDA_Arbitration_Guide_Final_09.09.13.pdf>.

48 Abdullah Saeed, *Islamic Banking and Interest* (Brill, 1996) 9–10; Tariq Alrifai, *Islamic Finance and the New Financial System: An Ethical Approach to Preventing Future Financial Crises* (Wiley, 2015) 101–103.

These countries began investing in Islamic banks and the topic of Islamic finance was discussed at a number of conferences, such as the First International Conference on Islamic Economics in Makkah in 1976 and the Conference of Finance Ministers of Islamic Countries in Karachi (1970).[49] The Islamic Development Bank was also established in 1975 as a result of these conferences and was funded an amount of approximately US$2 billion by leading oil exporters of the Gulf.[50] Following the establishment of the Islamic Development Bank, the following Islamic banks were also founded: Dubai Islamic Bank (1975), Faisal Islamic Bank in Egypt (1977), Faisal Islamic Bank of Sudan (1977) and Kuwait Finance House (1977).[51] Saeed also observes that many Muslim governments became shareholders in Islamic banks and that '[g]rowing confidence in Islamic banking may mean more accommodation of Islamic banks, even by the so-called secular governments of the Muslim countries.'[52] Therefore, as will be discussed in later chapters, even though most Muslim countries do not completely prohibit *riba* and/or *gharar*, they still invest in and promote Islamic banking and finance which, as discussed later, has become a lucrative industry. In order to expand their global business and investment opportunities, the United Kingdom and Australian governments have also shown interest in the Islamic banking and finance market and the United Kingdom has issued a number of Islamic bonds (*sukuk*) as well as establishing Islamic banks such as Al Rayan Bank (previously known as the Islamic Bank of Britain).[53]

The International Monetary Fund Report released in April 2015 and titled 'Islamic Finance: Opportunities, Challenges and Policy Options,' indicates that Islamic finance assets have doubled since 2003 when they were estimated at US$200 billion to US$1.8 trillion at the end of 2013.[54] The Thomson Reuters Islamic Finance Development Report 2015 ('Thomson Reuters Report') further notes that in 2014, global Islamic finance assets were worth $1.814 trillion and that '[t]he value of assets in the Islamic finance sector is expected to increase by 80 per cent over the next five years, reaching $3.24 trillion by 2020.'[55] The Thomson Reuters Report also reports that there are approximately 1,143 Islamic finance institutions worldwide including 436 Islamic banks or windows, 308 *takaful* (*Shari'a*-compliant insurance) institutions and 399 Islamic financial and investment companies.[56] The majority of Islamic finance assets, according to the Thomson Reuters Report, are held by Saudi Arabia, Malaysia, Iran and the

49 Ibid.; Alrifai, 102.
50 Ibid.; Saeed, above n 48, 11.
51 Ibid. above n 48, 14.
52 Ibid. 14.
53 See generally, Bhatti, above n 45. Al Rayan Bank, *About Us* <www.alrayanbank.co.uk/useful-info-tools/about-us/>.
54 International Monetary Fund Report, *Islamic Finance: Opportunities, Challenges and Policy Options* (2015) <www.imf.org/external/pubs/ft/sdn/2015/sdn1505.pdf> 11–13.
55 Islamic Corporation for the Development of the Private Sector (ICD) – Thomson Reuters, *Islamic Finance Development Report 2015: Global Transformation* (2015) <www.zawya.com/mena/en/ifg-publications/241115073158K/> 6.
56 Ibid. 6.

UAE.[57] A report by Ernst and Young in 2016 also shows that Saudi Arabia and Malaysia (two of the main case studies in this book) are the market leaders in the GCC and Asia-Pacific region respectively.[58] A report by Standard & Poor's Rating Services titled, 'Islamic Finance Outlook 2016 Edition' compares asset growth between Islamic and conventional banks from 2008 to 2014, and suggests that Islamic banks in the GCC are also growing at a faster pace than conventional banks between 2008 and 2014 2).[59] Consequently, Ayub observes that:

> Islamic principles of economics and finance . . . have already proved their ability to attract policymakers and practitioners from all over the world to develop the edifice of an efficient financial a system. . . . Islamic finance has been developing so vigorously that it has evolved from a nascent industry to a global market, where Muslim and non-Muslim are working together and learning from each other for the development of relevant products and services.[60]

In addition, according to the Pew Research Centre report published in 2015, the Muslim population is increasing and it projects that 'by 2050 there will be near parity between Muslims (2.8 billion, or 30% of the population) and Christians (2.9 billion, or 31%), possibly for the first time in history.'[61] Muslims are also projected to be the largest religious group in the Asia-Pacific region by the year 2050.[62] In 2016, US exports to Saudi Arabia have been valued at approximately $13 billion[63] and exports to the UAE are estimated at $16 billion (US dollars).[64] The European Union exports to Saudi Arabia were valued at approximately €40 billion for 2015 and have been exponentially increasing since 2009.[65] European exports to the UAE are estimated at approximately €48 billion.[66]

57 Ibid.
58 Ernst & Young, *World Islamic Banking Competitiveness Report 2016* (2016) <www.ey.com/ Publication/vwLUAssets/ey-world-islamic-banking-competitiveness-report-2016/$FILE/ ey-world-islamic-banking-competitiveness-report-2016.pdf> 11.
59 This is despite the fact that the net profits in Islamic banks have recently been slower. See Standard & Poor's Ratings Services: McGraw Hill Financial, *Islamic Finance Outlook 2016 Edition* (2016) <www.spratings.com/documents/20184/86966/Islamic_Finance_Out look_2016_v2/4d9d6fd9-3b11-4ae2-9168-13ee2543b73b> 40.
60 Muhammad Ayub, *Understanding Islamic Finance* (Wiley, 2007) 15.
61 See Pew Research Center, *The Future of World Religions: Population Growth Projections, 2010–2050* (2015) <www.pewforum.org/files/2015/03/PF_15.04.02_ProjectionsFull Report.pdf>.
62 Ibid.
63 United States Census Bureau, *U.S. Trade in Goods with Saudi Arabia* (2016) <www.census. gov/foreign-trade/balance/c5170.html>. Interestingly, in 2015, US exports to Saudi Arabia were valued at approximately $19 billion.
64 Ibid. In 2015, US exports to the United Arab Emirates were valued at approximately $23 billion.
65 European Commission, *Trade in Goods with Saudi Arabia* (2016) <http://trade.ec.europa. eu/doclib/docs/2006/september/tradoc_113442.pdf>.
66 European Commission, *Trade in Goods with United Arab Emirates* (2016) <http://trade. ec.europa.eu/doclib/docs/2006/september/tradoc_113458.pdf>.

Arguably, due to the rise of the Islamic banking and finance industry, globalisations of world economies and the growth of the Muslim population, the global market demand for *Shari'a*-compliant arbitration may also increase.[67] This is because arbitration is often preferred over litigation because it provides parties with procedural flexibility, neutrality, finality, privacy and efficiency.[68] Furthermore, as discussed further below, many international institutions, practitioners and academics have shown interest in the development of *Shari'a*-compliant arbitration in order to provide customers with holistic *Shari'a*-compliant services as the Islamic finance market grows.[69] Despite this, as discussed at length in this book, the only *Shari'a*-compliant arbitration rules currently available are provided by the IICRA[70] and the *Rules* developed by the AIAC[71] (and brief arbitration guidelines contained in the *AAOIFI Standards*,[72] as discussed in the next chapter).[73] Interestingly, some practitioners, such as Craig Shepherd of Herbert Smith in Dubai, also note that '[t]here is no actual need for specialized Islamic centers . . . [c]urrent international arbitration law is adequate. But it's always good to have more, and to have specialization, as it will increase efficiency and speed of dispute resolution.'[74] However, Rajoo, the director of the AIAC argues that:

> [t]he Islamic world has not really explored international commercial arbitration, and after a certain point, there is a dichotomy between a religious and secular disputes system. In all honesty, business people do not want to go to

67 Jonathan Lawrence, Peter Morton and Hussain Khan, 'Resolving Islamic Finance Disputes' *K & L Gates* (online), 23 September 2013 <www.klgates.com/files/... d738.../Dispute_Res olution_in_Islamic_Finance.pdf>; 'Islamic Arbitration: A Healthy Debate,' *Islamic Finance News* (online), 6 February 2013 <http://islamicfinancenews.com/news/islamic-arbitration-healthy-debate>; 'Dispute Resolution: The Final Piece of the Puzzle' *Islamic Finance News* [Supplements] 7 November 2012 Expanded Academic ASAP; Alex Saleh and Riza Ismail, 'The Choice of Law and Dispute Settlement Resolution in Islamic Cross Border Finance Transactions,' *Islamic Finance News* (online), 25 May 2011 <http://islamicfinancenews.com/news/choice-law-and-dispute-settlement-resolution-islamic-cross-border-finance-transactions>.

68 Born, above n 15, 73–89; Lawrence, Morton and Khan, above n 67.

69 See generally, Hakimah Yaacob, 'Towards Our Own Lex Mercatoria: A Need for Legal Consensus in Islamic Finance' (2014) 22 *Pertanika Journal of Social Sciences and Humanities* 257. Cf Tun Abdul Hamid Mohamad and Adnan Takic, 'Enforceability of Islamic Financial Contracts in Secular Jurisdictions: Malaysian Law as the Law of Reference and Malaysian Courts as the Forum for Settlement of Disputes' (ISRA Research Paper No. 33, 2012).

70 For a copy of the rules, see IICRA, 'Chart and Arbitration and Reconciliation Procedures' <iicra.com/admin/download.php?file_name=arb.pdf&content_type=>.

71 For a copy of the most recent i-Arbitration Rules developed by the KLRCA, see Kuala Lumpur Regional Centre for Arbitration, 'KLRCA Arbitration Rules (Revised 2013)' (2013) <http://klrca.org/rules/arbitration/>.

72 AAOIFI, above n 42.

73 See also Ruba Abdel Halim, 'DIAC Discusses the Launch of an Islamic Arbitration Window' *Zawya* (online), 8 February 2016 <www.zawya.com/story/DIAC_discusses_the_launch_of_an_Islamic_Arbitration_Window-ZAWYA20160208120400/>.

74 'Islamic Arbitration: A Healthy Debate' above n 67.

the *Shari'a* court, and prefer a legal secular system . . . [w]ith the KLRCA *i-Arbitration Rules*, there is now an option for a dispute resolution mechanism that is *Shari'a*-compliant, thereby putting the last block in place for a complete *Shari'a*-compliant transaction.[75]

This argument will be explored further in the following chapters of this book.

The need for a separate *Shari'a*-compliant arbitration option was also discussed at a meeting in 2016 by the Board of Trustees of the Dubai International Arbitration Centre ('DIAC') when they announced a proposal for establishing an 'Islamic arbitration' window.[76] One of the reasons why DIAC is interested in Islamic arbitration is 'to meet the demand of growing Islamic economy users and to promote Dubai Government's initiative of making Dubai the global capital of Islamic economy.'[77] Nonetheless, further details were not provided as to how this Islamic arbitration window would be set up and whether *Shari'a*-compliant rules would be formulated.

The Dubai International Financial Centre ('DIFC') has also indicated its desire to tap into the Islamic finance market and become a 'hub for *Shari'a*-compliant finance.'[78] Regardless, the *Arbitration Law 2008* offered by the DIFC is based on the *UNCITRAL Model Law* and does not mention *Shari'a*. The DIFC also offers curial courts for DIFC-seated arbitrations of which Michael Hwang is the Chief Justice. Hwang explains that he also acts as the nominal head of the DIFC Arbitration Institute ('DAI').[79] Therefore, the DIFC Courts provide an alternative to the national Dubai courts, which are governed by UAE federal laws on arbitration (Chapters 5 and 6). However, despite the international recognition of DIFC courts and the DIFC's interest in Islamic finance, the centre also does not offer *Shari'a*-compliant arbitration rules. Alex Saleh, a partner at Al Tamimi in Kuwait, observes that:

I am not aware of any arbitration tribunals solely handing *Shari'a* matters. I tend to use the DIFC-LCIA rules. And while there are not specific Shariah components to it, I can make sure that the arbitrators chosen have a *Shari'a* compliant background or qualification.[80]

The Sharjah International Commercial Arbitration Centre also does not offer any *Shari'a*-compliant rules. Nonetheless, the list of arbitrators prepared by the Sharjah International Commercial Arbitration Centre includes well-known experts in *Shari'a*

75 'Dispute Resolution: The Final Piece of the Puzzle,' above n 67.
76 'DIAC Discusses the Launch of an Islamic Arbitration Window,' above n 73.
77 Ibid.
78 Dubai International Finance Centre, 'DIFC Authority Releases Updated Version of Guide to Islamic Finance' *Dubai International Finance Centre* (online), 20 July 2009 <www.difc.ae/news/difc-authority-releases-updated-version-guide-islamic-finance>.
79 Michael Hwang, 'Commercial Courts and International Arbitration – Competitors or Partners?' (2015) 31(2) *Arbitration International* 193, 202.
80 'Islamic Arbitration: A Healthy Debate' above n 67.

and arbitration, such as Ibrahim Hassan Almulla and Dr Nailah Obaid.[81] Similarly, the International Islamic Mediation and Arbitration Centre ('IMAC') was established by the Arab Chamber of Commerce & Industry on 31 July 2008 in Hong Kong.[82] IMAC does not offer *Shari'a*-compliant arbitration rules; however, the arbitrators listed on its website appear to have experience in *Shari'a* and arbitration.

The Qatar International Court and Dispute Resolution Centre (QICDRC) also plans to tap into the Islamic finance market by offering Islamic dispute resolution services. In 2012, the Chief Executive Officer of QICDRC, Robert Musgrove, stated:

> [w]e are currently looking at the possibility of resolving Islamic finance disputes by setting up dispute resolution mechanism. To this objective we started a joint feasibility study with QICCA (Qatar International Chamber of Commerce Arbitration) last month . . . [w]ith the increasing popularity of Islamic finance funds and schemes globally and specifically in the GCC, it would be ideal to have a mechanism in place to resolve disputes that would arise.[83]

However, to date, the QICDRC also does not offer *Shari'a*-compliant arbitration rules, nor does the Qatar Financial Centre or QICCA.[84] Consequently, one of the aims of this book is to provide guidance to international institutions in relation to developing *Shari'a*-compliant arbitration rules by examining possible tensions that may arise between *Shari'a* and contemporary ICA, and by providing reform proposals which aim to harmonise the two systems.

III Limitations, gaps in research, methodology and structure of the book

This book contains sources and information relevant until November 2016. The research does not address the general effectiveness of the Saudi arbitration

---

81 Thomsons Reuters Zawya, 'The Sharjah International Commercial Arbitration Centre Approves the Operational Plan for 2016 and Its List of Arbitrators' *Zawya* (online), 19 January 2016 <www.zawya.com/story/The_Sharjah_International_Commercial_Arbitration_Centre_approves_the_Operational_Plan_for_2016_and_its_List_of_Arbitrators-ZAWYA20160119135617/>.

82 International Islamic Mediation and Arbitration Centre (IMAC), *IMAC: About Us* <www.arabcci.org/IMAC_aboutus.htm>.

83 The Peninsula Qatar, 'Qatar International Court Plans Expansion' *The Peninsula Qatar* (online), 4 July 2012 <www.thepeninsulaqatar.com/news/qatar/199730/qatar-international-court-plans-expansion>; 'Islamic Arbitration: A Healthy Debate' *Islamic Finance News* (online), above n 67.

84 See Qatar International Court and Dispute Resolution Centre, *The Qatar Financial Centre Civil and Commercial Court Regulations and Procedural Rules 2010* <www.qicdrc.com.qa/sites/default/files/s3/wysiwyg/qfc_civil_and_commercial_court_regulations_date_of_issuance_15_december_2010_0.pdf>. See also Vineeta Tan, 'World Nations Turn to Islamic Arbitration Services as Shariah Finance Goes International' *Islamic Finance News* (online), 29 June 2016 <http://islamicfinancenews.com/news/world-nations-turn-islamic-arbitration-services-shariah-finance-goes-international-0>.

system. Instead it analyses the effectiveness of *Shari'a*'s application if Saudi law is chosen as the governing law or if arbitral awards are enforced in Saudi Arabia. This book relies on published arbitral awards and case law to support some of its conclusions; however, it is also important to understand that such data is limited due to the confidential status of certain arbitral awards,[85] and the lack of transparency regarding case law in many of the jurisdictions examined.[86] As will be explained in detail in subsequent chapters, the author has relied on case law which has been translated into English by Kluwer Arbitration and other reputable publishers. Also, due to the author's limited ability to translate case law and other references in Arabic and Malay, there may be other sources which have not been translated into English that are not referred to in this book. However, the author has a basic knowledge of the Arabic language and an attempt has been made to translate Arabic legislation into English through a professional translator or Arabic-speaking lawyers from the Middle East.

Furthermore, as discussed in the previous section, despite the demand for *Shari'a*-compliant arbitration, only two well-known institutions have developed arbitration rules which address *Shari'a* matters. Similar to the arbitral institutions discussed in the previous section, academics and commentators have argued that dispute resolution in *Shari'a* matters is important. For example, Aida Maita opines that there needs to be 'universal standardization and codification of Shari'a that could be easily applied to govern Islamic financial dealing internationally.'[87] Similarly, White observes:

> [i]n tandem with the exponential growth of Islamic finance, there is emerging a still nascent but fast growing movement from existing conventional dispute resolution practices (especially litigation) towards reviving a classical Islamic dispute resolution process . . . this Shari'a-based form of ADR not only provides desperately needed subject matter expertise in Islamic finance dispute resolution, but at the same time accommodates Islamic legal values and traditions in resolving the disputes that inevitably arise in the context of Islamic finance.[88]

Despite this demand and interest in *Shari'a*-based arbitration, the current research on arbitration does not analyse contemporary arbitral rules and law, such as the

---

85 See generally, Leon E. Trakman, 'Confidentiality in International Commercial Arbitration' (2002) 18(1) *Arbitration International* 1; Michael Hwang and Katie Chung, 'Defining the Indefinable: Practical Problems of Confidentiality in Arbitration' (2009) 26(5) *Journal of International Arbitration* 609; Steven Kouris, 'Confidentiality: Is International Arbitration Losing One of Its Major Benefits' (2005) 22(2) ibid., 127.

86 See Chapter 8 for more information in relation to the limited case law available.

87 Aida Maita, 'Arbitration of Islamic Financial Disputes' (2014) 20 *Annual Survey of International & Comparative Law* 35, 64. See generally, Andrew White, 'Dispute Resolution and Specialized ADR for Islamic Finance' in David Eisenberg and Craig Nethercott (eds), *Islamic Finance: Law and Practice* (Oxford University Press, 2012) 306.

88 White, 'Dispute Resolution and Specialized ADR for Islamic Finance' above n 87. See also, Andrew White and Chen Mee King, above n 43, 225.

i-Arbitration Rules developed by the AIAC in 2012 and the recent *Saudi Arbitration Law* introduced in 2012 (Chapter 2). Nor does it analyse the interaction between the various interpretations of *Shari'a* in the context of contemporary ICA. There have been, for example, a number of books addressing arbitration under classical Islamic jurisprudence by using Arabic primary sources, such as commentary of historical Islamic scholars.[89] In comparison, this book limits its analysis on the impact of the four schools of jurisprudence recognised by Sunni Muslims[90] (known as the *Hanbali, Maliki, Shafi'i* and *Hanafi* schools) in the context of contemporary ICA. This book uses different case studies, such as the *new Saudi Arbitration laws* and the *i-Arbitration Rules*, as well as the *CISG* and *IBA Rules*. Therefore, this book does not aim to provide detailed research, based on classical Islamic texts, in relation to the rules of arbitration under classical *Shari'a*, as this research is already available. In contrast, as noted previously, the hypothesis of this book examines the possible application of *Shari'a* in contemporary ICA and in light of recently introduced arbitral laws and rules. Therefore, as discussed in the next chapter, it is important to note that this book approaches *Shari'a* through a Western lens as opposed to a classical *Shari'a* perspective.

Other books, such as Abu Sadah's PhD thesis, discuss the potential harmonisation of international commercial arbitration law in the Middle Eastern region from a contractual and theoretical perspective.[91] Similarly, Mary Ayad discusses the potential of creating a harmonised international commercial arbitration code in the Middle East region by examining civil law, common law and *Shari'a* law in the context of arbitration.[92] This book does not propose a

---

89 For a detailed discussion on Islamic jurisprudence in the context of the old Saudi Arbitration Law 1983, see Mohammed Al Jarba, *Commercial Arbitration in Islamic Jurisprudence: A Study of Its Role in the Saudi Arabian Context* (PhD Thesis, Aberystwyth University, 2001). Similarly, Abuhimed analyses the procedural rules under the old Saudi Arbitration Law of 1983. See Fahad Ahmed Mohammed Abuhimed, *The Rules of Procedure of Commercial Arbitration in the Kingdom of Saudi Arabia (Comparative Study)* (PhD thesis, The University of Hull, 2006). Al Suhaibi discusses Islamic law, the old Saudi Arbitration Law 1983 and the UNCITRAL Model Law in the context of contemporary ICA by examining classical Islamic law and the Saudi Arbitration Law of 1983. See Abdulrahman A. I. Al-Subaihi, *International Commercial Arbitration in Islamic Law, Saudi Law and the Model Law* (PhD thesis, The University of Birmingham, 2004).

90 As explained in detail in the next chapter, Sunni Muslims constitute the largest denomination of Islam. Other sects of Islam and schools of thoughts will be noted in the next chapter.

91 Muhammad Abu Sadah, *International Contracting and Commercial Arbitration: An Analysis of the Doctrine of Harmonisation and Regionalism with Special Reference to the Middle East Region* (PhD thesis, Cardiff University, 2006).

92 See Mary Boulos Ayad, *A Proposal to Guide Future Draft Art: Provisions for a Model Harmonised International Commercial Law Code (HICALC) in the Middle East and North African or a Uniform Arab Arbitration Law* (PhD thesis, Macquarie University, 2012). See also Mary Ayad, 'Harmonisation of International Commercial Arbitration Law and Sharia: The Case of Pacta Sunt Servanda vs Ordre Public: The Use of Ijtihad to Achieve Higher Award Enforcement' (2009) 6 *Macquarie Journal of Business Law* 93 Mary Ayad, 'Towards a Truly Harmonised International Commercial and Investment Arbitration Law Code (Hicialc): Enforcing Mena-Foreign Investor Arbitrations via a Single Regulatory Framework: A New Map for a New Landscape' (2010) 7 *Macquarie Journal of Business Law* 285.

harmonised arbitration law for the MENA region, nor does it investigate common law and civil law systems. On the other hand, this book addresses whether various interpretations of *Shari'a* can apply to and co-exist harmoniously with contemporary ICA, and whether this would require a comprehensively codified and standardised model of *Shari'a* arbitration rules available for use institutionally and internationally, by parties to incorporate into their agreements. Furthermore, this book argues that in order for *Shari'a* to effectively apply and be recognised internationally, countries where public policy is based on *Shari'a* should also recognise international norms and conventions. Mutual respect and recognition between contemporary ICA and *Shari'a* is significant in order to create an effective system of arbitration, which is internationally accepted and enforceable.

This book uses a normative analysis and comparative approach when addressing whether *Shari'a* can effectively apply to contemporary ICA and if so, how this can be achieved. The reforms proposed in this book are aimed at harmonising *Shari'a* and contemporary ICA by taking into consideration efficiency, fairness and the international commercial market, which also consists of alternative financial systems, such as Islamic banking and finance.

Therefore, Chapter 2 attempts to define *Shari'a* by explaining the theological interpretations of Islamic law and its application on arbitration in the contemporary world. This chapter will indicate that in order for *Shari'a* to be recognised as an effective body of law, its multidimensional interpretations must be understood.

Chapter 3 will further address whether *Shari'a*, as a body of religious law that is subject to a variety of interpretations, is likely to be enforced as the governing law in secular countries. The case study used in this chapter will be England because it is a jurisdiction where the applicability of a national or religious law, such as *Shari'a*, has been discussed by English courts.

In Chapter 4, the strict requirements under classical *Shari'a* regarding the composition of the arbitral tribunal will be contrasted with contemporary ICA standards. More specifically, this chapter will examine whether parties to arbitration proceedings have the autonomy to stipulate qualifications based on gender and/or religion when selecting their arbitrator/s.

The evidence and procedural rules governing arbitration under classical and contemporary *Shari'a* rules will be analysed in Chapter 5. This chapter will compare *Shari'a*-based arbitration rules with contemporary ICA rules, such as the *IBA Rules* and the *UNCITRAL Rules 2010*. This chapter also makes recommendations in relation to the reform of existing *Shari'a*-based arbitration rules in order to ensure the rules are comprehensively codified in accordance with the overall objective of this book.

Chapters 6 and 7 discuss the prohibition of *riba* (interest) and *gharar* (risk or uncertainty) under *Shari'a*. After explaining the concepts of *riba* and *gharar*, as well as the different interpretations of this prohibition under *Shari'a*, Chapter 6 will discuss the impact of *riba* and/or *gharar* on arbitrability and arbitration agreements if parties select a governing law or arbitration rules based on or influenced by *Shari'a*. Chapter 6 will also show the significance of codified *Shari'a* arbitration rules or a *Shari'a* model law which countries, such as Saudi Arabia, could adopt in order to create a consistent framework to address issues raised by the above-mentioned prohibitions.

Following from this discussion, Chapter 7 will provide an extensive analysis on whether the prohibition against *riba* and the award of interest on arbitral awards creates tension between *Shari'a* and contemporary ICA. The *CISG* will be used as a case study in this chapter to assess whether the provision on interest contained in this convention means that contemporary ICA may not take *Shari'a* into consideration in certain situations. If *Shari'a* is not taken into consideration by international conventions, then this will impact on the analysis within this book as to assess whether *Shari'a* can be an internationally recognised body of law to govern arbitration proceedings.

Chapter 8 will discuss the impact of *riba* in the context of enforceability of arbitral awards in countries where *Shari'a* influences public policy due to Art. V(2)(b) of the *New York Convention*. This chapter will use the following countries as case studies: Egypt, Saudi Arabia, Kuwait, the United Arab Emirates, Qatar, Bahrain and Oman. Therefore, Chapters 7 and 8 both discuss the intersection between interest and arbitral awards. Chapter 7 considers whether international conventions, such as the *CISG*, take into consideration the prohibition of *riba* in the context of arbitral awards, while Chapter 8 discusses whether arbitral awards containing *riba* may be enforced in certain countries where *Shari'a* may influence public policy.

2 The theoretical and practical framework for *Shari'a* arbitration[1]

I Introduction

It is important to discuss the theological foundations and historical development of *Shari'a* in order to better comprehend the application of *Shari'a* in contemporary ICA. This chapter will begin by providing an overview of the theological foundations of *Shari'a*, the development of arbitration (*tahkim*) rules under the four schools of Islamic jurisprudence and the eventual codification of arbitration rules under the Ottoman Empire. It will then provide an overview of how *Shari'a* is implemented in the contemporary world and discuss the possible implications of applying a multidimensional body of law, such as *Shari'a*, to contemporary ICA.

II Theological foundations of *Shari'a*

Muslims believe that the Prophet Muhammad is the last prophet or messenger of Islam. Historically, according to Sunni Islamic teachings, it was only after the Prophet Muhammad's death that Islamic jurisprudence (*fiqh*) was formulated, under the Abbasid Caliphate in the eighth and ninth centuries.[2]

This book generally focuses on the Sunni approach and interpretation of *Shari'a*. Sunni Islam is the largest denomination of Islam and the term sunni is derived from the understanding that Muslims are the 'people of the community' who follow the *sunna*, which is the normative behaviour of the Prophet Muhammad including his actions and sayings.[3] Sunni Muslims believe that the first leader (caliph) for Muslims after the Prophet Muhammad was the Prophet's father-in-law, Abu Bakr.[4] Sunni Islam can be contrasted with Shi'a[5] Islam because Muslims from this major religious-political group believe that Ali, the Prophet Muhammad's son-in-law, was the first caliph after the Prophet Muhammad's

---

1 An amended form of this chapter is forthcoming in *Wisconsin International Law Journal*, Volume 35, Issue 4.
2 Joseph Schacht, *An Introduction to Islamic Law* (Oxford University Press, 1964) 69–71.
3 Abdullah Saeed, *The Qur'an: An Introduction* (Routledge, 2008) 241.
4 See Sunni Islam (Oxford University Press, 2016) <www.oxfordislamicstudies.com/article/opr/t125/e2280?_hi=2&_pos=2>.
5 Also spelt as Shi'ite. Individually referred to as Shi'i. For consistency, this book will use the spelling Shi'a, except when a reference adopts an alternative spelling.

death and that Ali's direct descendants are the rightful successors.[6] The word Shi'a is derived from *Shi'at Ali*, meaning 'partisans of Ali.'[7] The Twelver Imam Shi'a Muslims constitute approximately 10–15% of the Muslim population, and there are three main subsects of Shi'a Muslims. These include Zaydis who follow Zayd Ibn Ali ibn al-Husayn (d. 740 CE), the Ismailis (named after Imam Isma'il ibn Jafar (d. 755 CE)) and the Ithna Asharias (Twelvers Imam Shi'as).[8] The Twelvers Imam Shi'as are the largest group, and recognise 12 Imams who they believe are divinely guided.[9] Most Atharis and Ismailis follow the Ja'fari school of thought.[10]

By the tenth century, certain Islamic scholars[11] had come to an agreement that their religious rulings were complete, and there was no longer a need to exercise independent reasoning (*ijtihad*)[12] to develop the established laws and therefore, Muslims should follow the views established by the *Hanbali, Maliki, Shafi'i* and *Hanafi* schools of jurisprudence.[13] These four schools of jurisprudence heavily influence the rules governing arbitration under Islamic jurisprudence, which I will refer to in my book as 'classical *Shari'a.*'

On the other hand, as explored below, other scholars believed that Islamic jurisprudence could be further developed through the exercise of independent reasoning (*ijtihad*). This included scholars from Shi'a Islam who generally follow the Ja'fari school of thought as well as Taqi al-Din Ahmad Ibn Taymiyya (d. 1328 CE) ('Ibn Taymiyya') and Muhammad Ibn Abd al-Wahhab (d. 1791 CE) ('Ibn Abd al-Wahhab'), who heavily influenced *Shari'a* as implemented in Saudi Arabia.[14] As discussed further below, many contemporary Islamic scholars also utilise principles

---

6 See generally, Shii Islam (Oxford University Press, 2016) <www.oxfordislamicstudies.com/article/opr/t125/e2189?_hi=26&_pos=238#>; Saeed, above n 3, 240.

7 Ibid.

8 Ibid.

9 Ibid.

10 Ibid.

11 As will be discussed in this chapter in more detail, Hallaq notes that the Islamic scholars who advocated blind imitation (taqlid) over independent reasoning (ijtihad) include 'traditionalists' who take a literal interpretation of religious texts as opposed to the right of people to interpret texts according to their own independent reasoning. This included scholars such as Dawud al-Zahri. See Wael Hallaq, 'Was the Gate of Ijtihad Closed?' (1984) 16(1) *International Journal of Middle East Studies* 3, 7–10.

12 The process of ijtihad has also been defined by Hallaq as 'the maximum effort expended by the jurist to master and apply the principles and rules of usul al-fiqh (legal theory) for the purpose of discovering God's law.' Hallaq also argues that the 'gates of ijtihad' were never closed and that ijtihad remained an essential part of Sunni Islam. Wael Hallaq, above n 11.

13 See Ijtihad (Oxford University Press, 2016) <www.oxfordislamicstudies.com/article/opr/t236/e0354>
    Schacht, above n 2; Esther van Eijk, 'Sharia and National Law in Saudi Arabia' in Jan Michiel Otto (ed), *Sharia Incorporated* (Leiden University Press, 2010) 139, 23; Hamza Yusuf, *Shaykh Murabtal Haaj's Fatwa on Following One of the Four Accepted Madhhabs* <http://shaykhhamza.com/transcript/Fatwa-on-Following-a-Madhab>.

14 See generally, Taqi al-Din Ahmad Ibn Taymiyyah (Oxford University Press, 2016) <www.oxfordislamicstudies.com/article/opr/t125/e959>; Muhammad Ibn Abd al-Wahhab (Oxford University Press, 2016) <www.oxfordislamicstudies.com/article/opr/t125/e916?_hi=0&_pos=16>.

such as 'contextual *ijtihad*' and the concept of public interest (*maslaha*) to argue that *Shari'a* has the ability to evolve and adapt to the society and context in which it is implemented. Therefore, classical *Shari'a* may also vary if independent reasoning (*ijtihad*) is utilised by a *mujtahid* (Islamic scholar who can exercise *ijtihad*).

Furthermore, in contemporary domestic legal systems, *Shari'a* is used (to varying extents) as a source of law,[15] in conjunction with the civil and/or common law tradition depending on the jurisdiction. Literally, *Shari'a* means 'the way,' or 'the clear path,' which Muslims should follow in order to be guided rightly.[16] Many Muslims view *Shari'a* as the embodiment of the 'Divine Will,' and God is seen as the 'supreme legislator' whose laws sanctify human life.[17] The majority of Muslims believe that the primary sources of *Shari'a* include the Qur'an and hadith. The Qur'an is the final book which Muslims believe is the word of God as revealed to the Prophet Muhammad, and is the primary source of *Shari'a*, as explained later.[18] The hadith are records of the Prophet Muhammad's actions and sayings (*sunna*), and were gathered into written collections in the eighth and ninth centuries.[19] The *sira* refers to the Prophet's biography. The hadith, *sunna* and *sira* provide Muslims with a living example or role model to follow.[20] Although both Sunni and Shi'a Muslims believe in the Qur'an as the primary source of *Shari'a*, Shi'a Muslims believe in different collections of hadith (which are not explored in this book), narrated by the *Imams*[21] and their companions in four books known as *al-kutub al-arba'a*.[22] It is also noted that some Muslims, often referred to as Qur'anists, do not accept *Shari'a* as a body of law based on the hadith and the established schools of thought (as discussed further later), because they argue that *Shari'a* was formulated many years after the death of the Prophet Muhammad. This is not a major sect of Islam, but an interpretation of Islam where the Qur'an is the only primary source.[23]

---

15 For example, the implementation of laws and regulations by a government into a legal system is known as qanun, whereas Shari'a is a more complex body of law as further explained in this chapter. See generally Qanun (Oxford University Press, 2016) <www.oxfordislamic studies.com/article/opr/t125/e1917>.

16 Mohammad Hashim Kamali, *Shari'ah Law: An Introduction* (Oneworld Publications, 2008) 14.

17 Ibid. 14.

18 Saeed, *The Qur'an: An Introduction*, above n 3, 239.

19 See generally, Jonathan Brown, *Misquoting Muhammad: The Challenge and Choices of Interpreting the Prophet's Legacy* (OneWorld Publications, 2015).

20 Jamila Hussain, *Islam: Its Law and Society* (The Federation Press, 3rd ed, 2011) 36; Wael Hallaq, *A History of Islamic Legal Theories: An Introduction to Sunnī Uṣūl Al-Fiqh* (Cambridge University Press, 1997) 10.

21 The religious and political leader of the Shi'a community, but also refers to the leader of a congregational prayer for all Muslims regardless of the sect. See Saeed, above n 3, 237.

22 Wael Hallaq, *Shari'a: Theory, Practice, Transformations* (Cambridge University Press, 2009) 116–117; Saeed, above n 3, 199–200.

23 See Edip Yuksel, Layth Saleh al-Shaiban and Martha Schulte-Nafeh, *Quran: A Reformist Translation* (Brainbow Press, 2007); Jane Smith and Yvonne Yazbeck Haddad, *The Oxford Handbook of American Islam* (Oxford University Press, 2014) 150–153. For a detailed discussion on the different textual interpretations in Islam, see Abdullah Saeed, *Reading the Qur'an in the Twenty-First Century: A Contextualist Approach* (Routledge, 2014).

The concept of *Shari'a*, however, is wider than the Western definition of 'law' because it is adopted in everyday life, governing matters such as personal hygiene, food, family relations and dress code.[24] The Arabic term is '*din-wa-dunya*,' which means that Islam should act as a permanent guide to all aspects of life.[25] However, Hallaq argues that *Shari'a* should not be understood through Western linguistics, such as the European concept of 'law.' He argues that:

> the very use of the word law is . . . problematic; to use it is to project, if not to superimpose, on the legal culture of Islamic notions saturated with the conceptual specificity of nation-state law, a punitive law that, when compared to Islam's jural forms, lacks . . . the same determinant moral imperative.[26]

Consequently, for the purposes of this book, *Shari'a* is recognised as a multidimensional and complex body of law that is understood and implemented through Islamic jurisprudence (*fiqh*) based on the Qur'an and the hadith, as explained earlier. Ramadan further elaborates on the definition of *fiqh* and its relationship with *Shari'a* by explaining that:

> [f]iqh represents the product of human thought and elaboration on it; more precisely [f]iqh is the state of judicial reflection reached by Muslims scholars at a certain time and in certain context in light of their study of the *Sharia*, and as such [f]iqh, while remaining faithful to the function and purpose of *Sharia*, has to be dynamic, in constant elaboration since evolution is the defining character of our world.[27]

The perspective that *Shari'a* is an adaptable and evolving body of law in light of *fiqh*, will be discussed in further detail as follows.

The Qur'an and hadith are not legal manuals and instead, provide indications (*dalalat* or *amarat*) directing an Islamic scholar to the causes (*ilal*) of the rulings (*ahkam*).[28] Therefore, an Islamic scholar who is qualified (see below) to practice *ijtihad* (*mujtahid*), ascertains *Shari'a* rules through using certain legal principles[29] such as analogy or precedent (*qiyas*) and if no precedent is found, through

---

24 Hussain, above n 20, 90.
25 Mohamed Al Awabdeh, *History and Prospect of Islamic Criminal Law with Respect to the Human Rights* (PhD thesis, The Humboldt University of Berlin, 2005), Chapter 2 <http://edoc.hu-berlin.de/dissertationen/al-awabdeh-mohamed-2005-07-07/HTML/chapter2.html>.
26 Hallaq, above n 22, 2–3.
27 Tariq Ramadan, 'Ijtihad and Maslaha: The Foundations of Governance' in M. A. Muqtedar Khan (ed), *Islamic Democratic Discourse: Theory, Debates, and Philosophical Perspectives* (Lexington Books, 2006) 3.
28 Hallaq, above n 11, 4–5.
29 The principles through which Shari'a is derived is known as *usul-al-fiqh*: roots (*usul*) of jurisprudence (*fiqh*). *Usul-ul-Fiqh* is also known as legal theory.

consensus (*ijma*'), which refers to a consensus on legal matter among scholars of *Shari'a*.[30] This concept of consensus (*ijma*') as a source of *Shari'a* is based upon the hadith of the Prophet Muhammad, in which he states, 'my community shall never agree on error.'[31]

Other sources of *Shari'a* include the writings of jurists and schools of law (*madhabs*, plural *madhahib*).[32] A legal school (*madhab*) in *Shari'a* refers to a body of doctrine that was taught by a leader, or imam, who must be a leading *mujtahid* (one who is capable of exercising independent reasoning or *ijtihad*).[33] According to various Islamic scholars, a *mujtahid* must be qualified to perform *ijtihad* (independent reasoning as opposed to following a precedent) and there-fore, requires additional qualifications. Traditionally, to be considered 'qualified' required a broad knowledge of least 500 verses of the Qur'an which refer to the legal issue, an understanding of all the hadith (including the ability to differen-tiate and ascertain the authenticity of the hadith), and a knowledge of all legal commentary on the hadith.[34] The *mujtahid* must also have a deep knowledge of the Arabic language in order to understand metaphorical and other linguistic nuances in the classical Arabic used in the Qur'an.[35] Furthermore, the *mujtahid* must also understand the context of Qur'anic revelations (including abrogated verses), and a detailed understanding of *usul-ul fiqh* and legal opinions, which have been established by *ijma*' (consensus).[36] A *mufti* or 'jurisconsult' who issues *fatwas* (legal expert opinion) must also have the same qualifications as a *mujtahid*, with the additional requirement that the community must consider a *mufti* a devout Muslim of 'just character.'[37] This is relevant because in the contemporary Islamic finance market, the *Shari'a* experts who sit on advisory boards in Islamic financial institutions are generally *muftis* as there is a debate among Islamic scholars as to whether *ijtihad* (independent reasoning) can be practiced and therefore, whether *mujtahids* exist (see Chapters 6 and 7 for more detail).

Although many schools of thought developed after the eighth century, the four most influential Sunni schools of thought discussed in this book are known as the Hanbali, Maliki, Shafi'i and Hanafi schools, named after and influenced by the works of Ahmad ibn Hanbal (d. 855 CE), Malik ibn Anas al-Asbahi (d. 795 CE), Muhammad ibn Idris al-Shafi'i (d. 820CE) and Abu Hanifah Nu'man ibn Thabit (d. 767 CE). Other schools of thought include the Ja'fari, Zaydi, Ibadi and

30 Seyyed Hossein Nasr, *The Heart of Islam* (HarperCollins, 2004) 121; Hallaq, above n 22, 98.
31 Ibid.; Hallaq, above n 22, 101.
32 Hussain, above n 20, 39. For a more complex definition and discussion of madhabs, see Wael Hallaq, *An Introduction to Islamic Law* (Cambridge University Press, 2009) 60–63.
33 Kamali, above n 16, 68.
34 Hallaq, above n 32, 110–111.
35 These qualifications were articulated by classical Islamic scholar, Al-Ghazali (d. 1111CE); how-ever, Hallaq argues that these preconditions are flexible. See generally, Hallaq, above n 11.
36 Hallaq, above n 32, 110–111.
37 Ibid. 111.

Isma'ili schools.[38] The Ja'fari, Zaydi and Isma'ili schools of thought are followed by certain Shi'a Muslims. The Ibadi school of Islam is practiced in Oman and Zanzibar, and stems from a political movement which arose in the eighth century as a separatist movement during the rule of the Abbasids.[39] There are also various Sunni schools of theology and creed, which still influence the main schools even though they are largely extinct, such as the Ash'ari, Mu'tazilite, and Zahirite schools.[40] It is also important to note that within one school of thought, scholars may hold different views; however, this book will be referring to the view that is generally practiced by the school (often referred to in classical *Shari'a* as the '*mashhur*' or 'widespread' opinion)[41] and any alternative perspectives held by certain scholars will be expressly noted as a minority view.

Depending on the school of thought, other sources (or roots) of jurisprudence (*usul-ul-fiqh*) include equity or juristic preference (*istihsan*),[42] custom (*urf*) and public interest (*maslaha*)[43] when making *Shari'a* rulings.[44] As discussed further later, the extent to which Islamic scholars should rely on independent reasoning (*ijtihad*) and *maslaha* or follow doctrine (*taqlid*) when deducing *Shari'a*, is also subject to differences of opinion. The next section will discuss arbitration (*tahkim*) under classical *Shari'a* by focusing on the four main Sunni schools, these being the Maliki, Hanafi, Hanbali and Shafi'i schools.

III Arbitration (*Tahkim*) under classical *Shari'a*

Arbitration has long-established religious and cultural roots in the Middle East, pre-dating the advent of Islam.[45] Arbitration under *Shari'a* is known as *tahkim*, derived from the verbal noun of the Arabic word *hakkama*. *Hakkama* means 'the turning of a man back from wrongdoing.'[46] An arbitrator is known as a *hakam* or *muhakkam*.[47] *Tahkim* existed in pre-Islamic Arabia as a method of resolving

---

38 See Albert Hourani, *A History of the Arab Peoples* (Faber and Faber, 2005) 39–40. This book also does not discuss the Ismaili, Druze, Qur'anist and Ahmadi movements. For a detailed discussion of these movements, see Smith and Haddad, above n 23, 139–154.

39 Hourani, above n 38, 39–40.

40 Amongst others. See Hallaq, above n 20, 135–143.

41 Ibid. 163.

42 Hallaq defines istihsan as 'reasoning that presumably departs from a revealed text but leads to a conclusion that differs from one reached by means of qiyas.' See, Hallaq, above n 22, 107. See also Saeed, above n 3, 238.

43 Saeed defines maslaha as 'a principle of Islamic jurisprudence that allowed jurists to exercise discretion or juristic preference (istihsan) in matters that were not clearly covered by a textual source.' See Saeed, above n 3, 238. See also, Hallaq, above n 22, 109.

44 Nasr, above n 30, 121.

45 Shaistah Akhtar, 'Arbitration in the Islamic Middle East: Challenges and the Way Ahead' (2008) *International Comparative Legal Guides* 11 <www.iclg.co.uk/index.php?area=4&show_chapter=2201&ifocus=1&kh_publications_id=83>.

46 Mahdi Zahraa and Nora Abdul Hak, 'Tahkim (arbitration) in Islamic Law Within the Context of Family Law Disputes' (2006) 20(1) *Arab Law Quarterly* 2, 3.

47 Ibid. 3.

disputes over property, succession or torts.[48] The appointed arbitrator (*hakam*) was required to be a reputable man known to a community, who was considered an expert in settling disputes.[49] When the *hakam* agreed to arbitrate, the parties involved provided security in order to ensure compliance, because the decision of the *hakam* was enforceable but not final.[50] An Arab historian from the tenth century, Al-Yaq'oubi, observes that:

> [a]s a result of not having religions or laws to govern their lives, pagan Arabs used to have arbitrators to settle their disputes. So when they [had] a conflict regarding blood, water, grazing or inheritance they used to appoint an arbitrator who carried the characters of honour, honesty, old age and wisdom.[51]

Many Islamic concepts of arbitration were derived from pre-Islamic practices, such as the concept of placing the burden of proof on the Plaintiff.[52] During this time, dispute resolution occurred in a holistic way and focused on creating a form of compromise between the parties rather than making a binding, enforceable decision.[53] Therefore, the traditional role of judges was to create harmony between parties, resolve differences and conflicts in order to enable the parties to continue with their normal course of business.[54]

Under *Shari'a*, matters may be resolved through *tahkim* or *sulh* (amicable settlement or conciliation). However, arbitration and conciliation differ under *Shari'a* due to the following three factors. Firstly, *sulh* can be attained by parties with or without the involvement of others.[55] On the other hand, *tahkim* requires a third party. Secondly, the agreement under *sulh* is not binding unless it is taken before the court, whereas *tahkim* is generally considered binding without court intervention (according to most Islamic jurists). Thirdly, parties can only resort to *sulh* if the dispute has already occurred, whereas *tahkim* can address both existing and prospective disputes.[56] However, as discussed in more detail later, some Islamic opinions differ on whether an agreement under *tahkim* is binding or not, and whether *tahkim* can apply to prospective disputes. During the Prophet Muhammad's time, this commitment to the arbitral process continued and was actually emphasised. The Prophet played a prominent role in acting as an arbitrator and promoted the application of arbitration, which was often used to resolve

---

48 Arthur Gemmell, 'Commercial Arbitration in the Middle East' (2006) 5 *Santa Clara Journal of International Law* 169, 173.
49 Ibid.
50 Ibid.
51 Abdulrahman Yahya Baamir, *Shari'a Law in Commercial and Banking Arbitration: Law and Practice in Saudi Arabia* (Ashgate, 2010) 45.
52 Ibid. 47.
53 Nudrat Majeed, 'Good Faith and Due Process: Lessons from the Shari'ah' (2004) 20(1) *Arbitration International* 97, 106.
54 Ibid. 106.
55 Zahraa and Abdul Hak, above n 46, 8.
56 Ibid. 8.

disputes involving goods and chattels.[57] Arbitration was explicitly revealed for family disputes in the following verse:

> If you [believers] fear that a couple may break up, appoint one arbiter from his family and one from hers. Then if the couple want to put things right, God will bring about a reconciliation between them.[58]

This verse was interpreted by Hanbali scholar, Muwaffaq al-Din Ibn Qudama (d. 1223 CE) in his book *al-Mughni* as requiring arbitrators to act as judicial officers, but also act as agents of the parties.[59] Arbitration is also supported by the actions of the Prophet Muhammad because he acted both as an arbitrator, and as a party accepting the decision of an arbitrator. The normative behaviour of the Prophet Muhammad is referred to as *sunna*, including his sayings, implicit approvals and deeds, which is recorded in hadith and as noted, is one of the sources of *Shari'a*.[60] It is also reported that the Prophet Muhammad always preferred conciliation and arbitration over litigation.[61] According to Gemmel, '[i]n fact, for a Muslim, arbitration carried with it no better imprimatur than that given to it by the Prophet himself.'[62] The continuous participation and commitment of the Prophet to the arbitral process has led many scholars to refer to him as the 'exemplary standard for the independence of arbitrators.'[63] For example, the first treaty to ever be signed during the Prophet's time was the Treaty of Medina, which was signed in 622 CE between Muslims, non-Muslims, Arabs and Jews, and which called for all disputes to be resolved through arbitration.[64] Furthermore, the Prophet Muhammad was chosen to act as an arbitrator in conflicts between Arab and Jewish tribes.[65]

Another important arbitration that took place in early Islamic history was that between Ali bin Abi Talib (who was the fourth *caliph* or head of the Islamic state between 656 and 661 CE) and Mu'awiyah b. Abi Sufyaan (the governor of Syria and founder of the Ummayad dynasty). After the death of the third *caliph* in 656 CE, there was a dispute as to whether Ali or Mu'awiyah should be the successor. It is reported that Ali and Mu'awiyah were on the way to fighting a battle to

---

57 Faisal Kutty, 'The Shari'a Factor in International Commercial Arbitration' (2006) 28 *Loyola of Los Angeles International and Comparative Law Review* 565, 598.

58 Trans. M. A. S. Abdel Haleem, *The Qur'an* (Oxford University Press, 2004) (Chapter 4, Verse 35).

59 Baamir, above n 46, 49. See generally, Ibn Qudama, Muwaffaq al-Din (Oxford University Press, 2016) <www.oxfordislamicstudies.com/article/opr/t125/e953>.

60 Saeed, above n 3, 241.

61 Baamir, above n 46, 51.

62 Gemmell, above n 48, 173.

63 Nudrat Majeed, 'Investor-State Disputes and International Law: From the Far Side' (2004) 98 *American Society of International Law Proceedings* 30, 32.

64 Aseel Al-Ramahi, 'Sulh: A Crucial Part of Islamic Arbitration' (Working Paper # 12, London School of Economics and Political Science, 2008) 14.

65 Mohammed Abu-Nimer, 'A Framework for Nonviolence and Peacebuilding in Islam' (2000–2001) 15 *Journal of Law & Religion* 217, 247.

decide this, when Mu'awiyah proposed an arbitration: 'I wish to choose a man amongst my men and you choose a man amongst yours so that both of them settle the dispute between us and make their award in compliance with the provisions of the Holy Book.'[66]

Ali consented to the arbitration and it took place in front of 400 witnesses.[67] It was the first formal Islamic arbitration agreement, and through analogical reasoning (*qiyas*), it extended the Qur'an's directive of arbitration in family disputes (mentioned above) to the political arena.[68] According to the arbitrator's decision, Ali and Mu'awiyah both surrendered their power, and the Muslim community was given the power to decide their leader. Following the award, Mu'awiyah was proclaimed the *caliph* of Jerusalem.[69] This seemingly peaceful arbitration, however, paved the way for the ensuing Sunni-Shi'a division in Islam.[70]

However, despite the significant historical role of arbitration during the time of the Prophet Muhammad, a smooth transition to the modern arbitration framework has not occurred. One reason for this is that there are different approaches to arbitration within Islam based on the different schools of thought within the Sunni branch of Islam, as well as the different approaches arising out of the Sunni-Shi'a division within Islam.[71] The next sections discuss the concept of arbitration under the four Sunni schools of jurisprudence and the *Medjella*, which is the codification of the Hanafi school of thought during the Ottoman Empire.

A *Hanafi school*

Abu Hanifa Nu'man ibn Thabit (d. 767 CE) ('Abu Hanifa') is the founder of the Hanafi School. The Hanafi School of thought had a huge influence during the Ottoman Empire and in 1869, the Ottoman Turks began to codify Hanafi ideologies in a body of law known as the Medjella, as discussed further later.[72] Abu Hanifa emphasised personal opinion (*ra'y*) and reasoning by analogy (*qiyas*).[73] He also recommended the use of *istihsan* (equity) and *ijma'* (consensus); however, Qur'an and hadith were given priority over *usul ul-fiqh*.[74] *Urf* (custom) was only referred to as a residual source after the use of the above-mentioned sources of *Shari'a*.[75] A merchant by occupation, Abu Hanifa contributed to the development

---

66 Abdel Hamid El Ahdab and Jalal El Ahdab, *Arbitration with the Arab Countries* (Kluwer Law International, 2011) 16.
67 Majeed, above n 63, 102.
68 El Ahdab and El Ahdab, above n 66, 16.
69 Majeed, above n 63, 102.
70 Kutty, above n 57, 509.
71 Gemmell, above n 48, 174.
72 Kutty, above n 57, 598; Samir Saleh, *Commercial Arbitration in the Arab Middle East: Sharī'a*, Syria, Lebanon and Egypt (Hart Publishing, 2006) 8.
73 Kamali, above n 16, 70; Saleh, above n 72, 8.
74 Ibid.
75 Ibid.

of law regarding commercial transactions (*mu'amalat*).[76] This school of thought arose in Iraq and spread to Syria and Central Asia.[77] Hanafis stress the close connection between arbitration and conciliation.[78] Therefore, for Hanafis an arbitral award is similar to conciliation and has less force than a court judgement.[79] In the Hanafi school, the arbitration contract is valid (*sahih*), but not binding (*ghayr lazim*).[80] In the other three schools, contracts are *ja'iz* (permissible), which means that either party may revoke the contracts.

The Hanafi school and the *Medjella* (discussed further below), both take the view that arbitral tribunals should not be subject to a statute of limitations, unless the parties stipulate one in the contract.[81] In the case of *Saudi Basic Industries Corporation ('SABIC') v. Mobile Yanbu Petrochemical Co* ('Saudi Basic III'), SABIC claimed that Exxon and Mobil's claim was time-barred. However, in the pre-trial bench ruling, the trial judge held that the claim could not be time-barred under *Shari'a* because the property rights were eternal and could not be barred by the passage of time.[82] However, based on publicly available arbitral decisions, this issue does not often arise, presumably because most jurisdictions, including Saudi Arabia, recognise the statute of limitations.[83] Akaddaf observes that:

> Islamic legal systems are theoretically divided as to the application of a time limit within which a legal action must be brought. Some Muslim authorities claim that it is the interest of society to bar claims from being tried after a certain period of time has passed, others adopt the traditional Islamic view under which no right shall be lost by lapse of time. Such views remain only theoretical, however, and have no impact on the existing codified laws of each country.[84]

One exception is Iranian law, where following the Islamic Revolution of 1979, the existing legal system was replaced with *Shari'a*. Reference to the statute of limitations was abolished in 1982.[85] However, the argument that several claims brought before an arbitral tribunal were not time-barred due to Iranian law was rejected by the arbitral tribunal in *Aryeh v Iran*.[86] However, since the issue of

---

76 Kamali, above n 16, 70.
77 Frank Vogel, *Islamic Law and Legal System: Studies of Saudi Arabia* (Brill, 2000) 9.
78 Kutty, above n 57, 597; El Ahdab and El Ahdab, above n 66, 14.
79 Gemmell, above n 48, 176.
80 Ibid., 176.
81 Sayed Hassan Amin, *Islamic Law in the Contemporary World* (Vahid Publications, 1985) 86.
82 Saudi Basic Industries Corporation ('SABIC') v. Mobile Yanbu Petrochemical Co 866 A.2d 1 (Del, 2005) 6.
83 Fatima Akaddaf, 'Application of the United Nations Convention on Contracts for the International Sale of Goods (CISG) to Arab Islamic Countries: Is the CISG Compatible with Islamic Law Principles?' (2001) 13 *Pace International Law Review* 1, 43.
84 Ibid.
85 Ibid.
86 Aryeh v Iran, Iran-US CTR, Award No. 581=842/843/844–1, 22 May 1997.

statute of limitations rarely arises, this book will not examine the issue in further detail. Nonetheless, it is important to note that if classical *Shari'a* or Iranian law is the governing law or if arbitral awards are enforced in Iran, then parties need to stipulate whether statute of limitations apply in their contract or whether they agree to waive the application of statute of limitations.[87]

B *Maliki school*

This school was founded by Malik ibn Anas al-Asbahi (d. 795 CE) who lived most of his life in Medina and consequently relied on the consensus (*ijma'*) of the scholars living there.[88] The book, *al Muwatta*, is a compilation of the *ijma'* of the scholars, and is based mostly on the Qur'an, hadith and *qiyas*.[89] The Maliki School is predominant in Morocco, Algeria, Tunisia, upper Egypt, the Sudan, Bahrain and Kuwait. In Algeria, a draft code was prepared in French based on the Maliki teachings in 1916.[90] The Maliki jurisprudence is known as the most dynamic and comprehensive school of thought because of its emphasis on legal principles such as independent reasoning (*ijtihad*) and public interest (*istislah*).[91] In the area of arbitration, Malikis believe that the decision of an arbitrator is binding unless there is a 'flagrant injustice.'[92] Furthermore, unlike the other three schools, this school asserts that the arbitrator cannot be removed after the arbitration has been commenced.[93] The Maliki School emphasises the neutrality of the arbitration and the effect of the award is seen as limited so that it does not affect the rights of third parties.[94]

C *Shafi'i school*

This is the school that was named after its founder, Muhammad ibn Idris al-Shafi'i (d. 820) who was a student of Malik ibn Anas al-Asbahi and was also influenced by Hanafi jurists.[95] This school of thought arose in Egypt and spread to Iraq, Persia, East Africa, and certain regions of Saudi Arabia and Central Asia.[96] It became the predominant school of thought in Southeast Asia.[97] The Shafi'i theory states

---

87 Interestingly, Iranian law implements Shari'a based on Shi'a jurisprudence, which this book does not examine. For more information, see generally Nima Nasrollahi Shahri and Amir Hossein Tanhayi, 'An Introduction to Alternative Dispute Settlement in the Iranian Legal System: Reconciliation of Shari'a Law with Arbitration as a Modern Institution' (2015) 12(2) *Transnational Dispute Management.*
88 Kamali, above n 16, 73; Saleh, above n 71, 8.
89 Saleh, above n 72, 8.
90 Ibid., 8.
91 Kamali, above n 16, 73.
92 El Ahdab and El Ahdab, above n 66, 14; Kutty, above n 57, 597.
93 Gemmell, above n 48, 175.
94 Saleh, above n 72, 17.
95 Ibid., 8.
96 Vogel, above n 77, 9.
97 Ibid., 9.

that Islamic law is based on four principles, which include: the word of God in the Qur'an, the *sunna* of the Prophet Muhammad, consensus of opinion (*ijma'*) and reasoning by analogy (*qiyas*). Unlike Maliki, Shafi'i believed that authentic hadith should always be accepted and could not be invalidated on the grounds that it conflicted with the Qur'an because he believed that the hadith and Qur'an never contradicted each other.[98] In arbitration, the position of arbitrators is seen as inferior to judges and the parties may remove the arbitrator until the award is issued.[99] Shafi'i also believed that arbitration was closer to conciliation and therefore, had a less binding effect.[100] The Shafi'i school of thought resorts to arbitration as a solution only where no courts exist.[101] Arbitrators have a lesser role than judges and their appointment may be revoked. The Shafi'i school considers arbitration particularly useful during times of corruption amongst judges.[102]

D Hanbali school

The Hanbali school of law was founded by Ahmad ibn Muhammad ibn Hanbal (d. 855 CE), a student of Idris al-Shafi'i, who was an orthodox opponent of the Rationalist school (*Ahl al-ra'y*).[103] This school is the most conservative of the four schools and its teachings are based on a textual (as opposed to contextual, see discussion later) interpretation of the Qur'an, hadith and *sunna*.[104] It was one of the schools of law to be formulated and was influential in Baghdad, Damascus and the Arabian Peninsula.[105] It uncritically accepts the authenticity of the *sunna* and makes few concessions to personal reasoning (*ra'y*) or equity.[106] As will be discussed in more detail below, in the 18th century, Wahhabism, which is a puritanical movement in the Arabian Peninsula, derived its doctrine and inspiration from the Hanbalis. The Hanbali School is currently predominant in Oman, Qatar, Bahrain and Kuwait.[107] In terms of arbitration, this school of thought believes that the decision of an arbitrator has the same binding nature as a court's judgement. Therefore, the arbitrator must also have the same qualifications as a judge, and the decision carries a *res judicata* affect.[108] Saleh notes that '[t]he Hanbalis are known to be strict in religious ritual but tolerant in commercial transactions.'[109] This will be discussed in more detail with regards to the implementation of *Shari'a* in Saudi Arabia.

98   Kamali, above n 16, 75.
99   Gemmell, above n 48, 175.
100 Kutty, above n 57, 597.
101 El Ahdab and El Ahdab, above n 66, 14.
102 Ibid., 14.
103 Saleh, above n 72, 8; Gemmell, above n 48, 175.
104 Gemmell, above n 48, 175.
105 Vogel, above n 77, 10.
106 Ibid., 10.
107 Kamali, above n 16, 84.
108 Kutty, above n 57, 598; Saleh, above n 72, 17.
109 Saleh, above n 72, 9.

E *The Medjella*

The *Medjella* of Legal Provisions was the first codification of the *Shariʿa* (based on the Hanafi school) under the Ottoman Empire.[110] An entire section in the *Medjella* is devoted to arbitration, and in accordance with the Hanafi school, it is more in line with conciliation.[111] The rules of arbitration under the *Medjella* included that there was no *res judicata* effect based on the award by itself, and instead the contractual nature of the arbitration was stressed.[112] Also, the court could determine an arbitrator's award as void if the award was found to be contrary to a previously rendered court judgement.[113] An arbitrator's scope was less than that of a court, and was limited to the matters that were before the arbitrator and relating to the dispute.[114] Furthermore, according to section 1853 of the *Medjella*, 'if a third party settles a dispute without having been entrusted with this mission by the parties, and if the latter accept his settlement, the award shall be enforced . . . according to which "ratification equivalent to agency".'[115]

Consequently, a judge could annul an arbitral award if he saw fit, unlike a judgement.[116] Furthermore, as noted earlier the *Medjella* did not recognise a statute of limitations. Schacht characterises the *Medjella* as

> an experiment . . . [that] . . . was undertaken under the influence of European ideas, and it is, strictly speaking, not an Islamic but a secular code . . . not intended for the tribunals of the [q]adis, and was in fact not used [by] them . . . it contains certain modifications of the strict doctrine of Islamic law.[117]

The codification, which governed civil matters, also applied after the fall of the Ottoman Empire in the early 20th century, until countries under its rule formulated their own legal systems.[118] Due to the fact that this civil code is no longer implemented in contemporary legal systems, this book does not examine the *Medjella* in detail.

IV The implementation of *Shariʿa* in the contemporary world

Hallaq argues that various historical and political factors, such as the collapse of the Ottoman Empire and the rise of colonialism contributed to the 'structural

---

110 Gemmell, above n 48, 176; see also, El Ahdab and El Ahdab, above n 66, 16; Al-Ramahi, above n 64, 16.
111 Gemmell, above n 48.
112 Ibid., 175.
113 Ibid., 175.
114 Ibid.,175.
115 Al-Ramahi, above n 64, 16.
116 Ibid.
117 Schacht, above n 1, 92–93.
118 El Ahdab and El Ahdab, above n 66, 16.

demise of *Shariʿa*[119] in the contemporary world.[120] This is due to the historical collapse of Islamic financial foundations, the introduction of modern legal
processes due to colonialism, and the influence of commercial, civil and criminal
laws on the legal system of nation states.[121] For this reason, it is important to
understand the form or interpretation of *Shariʿa* that is being referred to in legal
systems or arbitration.

For example, *Shariʿa* is still referred to in the constitution of Egypt, Kuwait,[122]
UAE[123] and Saudi Arabia.[124] Interestingly, in Egypt, the current constitution of
2014 replaces the Egyptian Constitution of 2012 (which was enforced under the
regime of the former Islamist president, Mohammed Morsi),[125] and one of the
most controversial questions when the new constitution was being drafted was
the role of *Shariʿa*.[126] Despite ongoing political tensions in Egypt, including a
military coup which decided to strip the constitution of religious language,[127]
Art. 2 of the Egyptian constitution remained, and still states: 'Islam is the religion
of the State and Arabic is its official language. The principles of Islamic *Shariʿa*
are the main source of legislation.'[128] Therefore, the incorporation of *Shariʿa* and
the extent to which it should be adopted is often subject to controversy due to
the political climate of nation states.

Shariʿa is also mentioned in the civil and commercial codes of Jordan, Oman
and Iraq. Art. 2 of the *Jordanian Civil Code 1976* states that in the absence of
applicable law, the court should apply the principles of *Shariʿa*,[129] Art. 5 of the
Commercial Code of 1990 (Oman) states that custom applies in the absence of the

119 Hallaq, above n 22, 500.
120 Hourani, above n 38. See generally, Hallaq, above n 22.
121 Hallaq, above n 22, 500.
122 Art. 2 of the Kuwaiti Constitution states that '[t]he religion of the state is Islam and the
     Islamic Shariʿa shall be a main source of legislation.' See Kuwaiti Constitution 1962 (rein-
     stated 1992) [World Intellectual Property trans, <www.wipo.int/edocs/lexdocs/laws/en/
     kw/kw004en.pdf>].
123 Art. 7 of the UAE Constitution refers to Shariʿa as a source of legislation. See UAE Consti-
     tution (The Federal National Council Standing Orders trans, 1997). See also Sam Luttrell,
     'Choosing Dubai: A Comparative Study of Arbitration Under the UAE Federal Code of
     Civil Procedure and the Arbitration Law of the DIFC' (2008) 9(3) *Business Law Interna-
     tional* 254.
124 The Basic Law of Governance 1992 (Saudi Arabia) states that Qurʾan and sunna are the
     sole sources of law, and all regulations, laws etc. must conform to Shariʿa (Royal Embassy
     of Saudi Arabia Washington, DC trans, <www.saudiembassy.net/about/country-informa
     tion/laws/The_Basic_Law_Of_Governance.aspx>).
125 BBC News, 'Egypt Referendum: "98% Back New Constitution",' *BBC* (online), 19 Janu-
     ary 2014 <www.bbc.com/news/world-middle-east-25796110>.
126 Brown, above n 19, 5.
127 Ibid., 5.
128 Art. 2 of the Egyptian Constitution states that 'Islam is the religion of the State and Arabic
     is its official language. The principles of Islamic Sharia are the main source of legislation'.
     See Constitution of the Arab Republic of Egypt [Egyptian Government trans, <www.sis.
     gov.eg/Newvr/Dustor-en001.pdf>].
129 World Intellectual Property Organisation, <www.wipo.int/wipolex/en/text.jsp?file_id=227
     215> [Siham Barakat, Research Fellow, Australian Council for Educational Research, trans].

relevant provisions, *Shari'a* applies in the absence of customary law.[130] Likewise, Art. 1 of the Civil Codes of Egypt and Iraq stipulate that in the absence of the relevant provisions, custom applies and in the absence of customary law, *Shari'a* applies. In the absence of applicable customary law and *Shari'a*, general principles of justice apply.[131] Furthermore, Art. 1 of the Syrian and Libyan Civil Codes states:

> [i]n the absence of applicable legal provisions, the Judge shall pass judgement in accordance with the principles of Islamic law. In the absence of Islamic legal precedent, he shall pass judgement according to prevailing custom, and in the absence of precedents in customary procedure, he shall pass judgement according to the principles of natural law and the rules of equity.[132]

In the contemporary world, Islamic countries may be separated into the following groups in terms of geographic location, and the influence of *Shari'a* and secular law.[133] As will be discussed in later chapters, these categories are not mutually exclusive.

1   Middle Eastern countries influenced by the civil law tradition (e.g. Lebanon, Syria, Egypt, Algeria, Bahrain, Kuwait, Morocco and Tunisia) or the common law tradition (Sudan);
2   Middle Eastern countries heavily influenced by the *Shari'a*, which includes countries such as Saudi Arabia, Qatar, Oman and Yemen;
3   Middle Eastern countries influenced by the *Shari'a*, but have secular commercial laws. This includes Iraq, Jordan, Libya and the UAE;
4   Other countries in Western Asia, South Asia and South-East Asia such as Iran[134] and Pakistan,[135] where *Shari'a* is referred to in the constitution, and *Shari'a* courts exist independently of secular courts. The constitutions of

---

130 Omani government trans, <www.oman.om/wps/wcm/connect/7b72e2d8-ba8e-48d4-b44e-c7c3570b639b/OMAN+I+COMMERCIAL+law1.pdf?MOD=AJPERES>.
131 See Egyptian Civil Code 1948 (World Intellectual Property Organisation, <www.wipo.int/wipolex/en/text.jsp?file_id=205494> [author's trans]) and University of Minnesota Human Rights Library trans, <http://www1.umn.edu/humanrts/research/Egypt/Civil%20Law.pdf>; Iraqi Civil Code 1951 (United Nations Refugee Agency Refworld trans, <www.refworld.org/docid/55002ec24.html>).
132 See Meredith O. Ansell and Ibrahim Massaud al-Arif, *The Libyan Civil Code: An English Translation and a Comparison with the Egyptian Civil Code* (The Oleander Press, 1971). See also Syrian Civil Code 1949 (World Intellectual Property Organisation, www.wipo.int/wipolex/en/details.jsp?id=10917) [Siham Barakat, Research Fellow, Australian Council for Educational Research, trans]. For more information on Lebanon, see Florentine Sonia Sneij and Ulrich Andreas Zanconato, 'The Role of Shari'a Law and Modern Arbitration Statutes in an Environment of Growing Multilateral Trade: Lessons from Lebanon and Syria' (2015) 12(2) *Transnational Dispute Management* 1, 11.
133 See generally Kutty, above n 57, 594–595.
134 Constitution of the Islamic Republic of Iran 1979 [World Intellectual Property Organisation trans <www.wipo.int/wipolex/en/details.jsp?id=7697>].
135 Constitution of the Islamic Republic of Pakistani 1973 (International Labour Organisation, <www.ilo.org/dyn/natlex/natlex4.detail?p_lang=en&p_isn=33863>).

Indonesia and Malaysia do not refer to *Shari'a*, but independent *Shari'a* courts exist in both countries.[136]

However, as will be discussed in later chapters, it is difficult to categorise countries in terms of the influence of *Shari'a* over the legal system, because it depends on the context. For example, in various jurisdictions, *Shari'a* may strictly forbid *riba* or interest, but simple interest is still applied in the context of arbitral awards, as will be discussed in Chapter 7. On the other hand, as will be discussed in Chapter 8, *Shari'a* is rarely applied to refuse enforcement of foreign arbitral awards in the context of contemporary ICA.

V *Shari'a* arbitral rules and standards

Some case studies examined in this book include the Saudi arbitration laws, the AIAC *i-Arbitration Rules* and the *AAOFI Standards*. However, other jurisdictions such as various Middle Eastern countries and Iran will also be used comparatively as case studies when discussing arbitrability, interest and enforcement of arbitral awards. The following sections will discuss the AIAC *i-Arbitration Rules*, the *IICRA Rules*, the AAOIFI Standards, the application of *Shari'a* in Saudi and the *Saudi Arbitration Law 2012*.

A *AIAC i-arbitration rules*

The AIAC introduced *i-Arbitration Rules* (the prefix 'i' indicates compliance with *Shari'a*) in 2012 at the Global Financial Forum.[137] The *i-Arbitration Rules* are largely based on the *UNCITRAL Rules 2010* and aim to cater for *Shari'a*-based disputes in international commercial arbitration by providing a procedure through which arbitral tribunals can refer matters to *Shari'a* advisory councils.[138] According to the Director of AIAC, Sundra Rajoo:

> With the advent of globalisation and increasing cross-border transactions, the centre decided to come up with a set of rules that provide for international commercial arbitration that is suitable for commercial transactions premised on Islamic principles, and that would be recognised and enforceable internationally. Many Asian arbitration centres have their niche – for example, Hong Kong is an obvious venue for China-related disputes, and as a plural society with a majority of Muslim citizens and a regional hub for

136 See generally, Greg Fealy and Virginia Hooker (eds), *Voices of Islam in Southeast Asia: A Contemporary Sourcebook* (Institute of Southeast Asian Studies, 2006).

137 Kuala Lumpur Regional Centre for Arbitration, 'KLRCA Arbitration Rules (Revised 2013)' (2013) <http://klrca.org/rules/arbitration/>.

138 Global Arbitration Review, 'KLRCA to Unveil Islamic Arbitration Rules' *Global Arbitration Review* (online), 17 September 2009 <http://globalarbitrationreview.com/article/1031606/klrca-to-unveil-islamic-arbitration-rules>.

Islamic finance, Malaysia could be an appealing neutral arbitration forum for parties who have issues with *Shari'a* contracts.[139]

Rajoo emphasises that it is significant for contemporary ICA to be compatible with *Shari'a* so that arbitral awards are enforceable internationally. For this reason, in 2013, the AIAC revised the *i-Arbitration Rules* allowing arbitrators to award interest and refer *Shari'a* matters to any *Shari'a* advisory council (the previous *i-Arbitration Rules* limited the referral to the Malaysian *Shari'a* Advisory Council). The *i-Arbitration Rules 2018*, which came into effect on 8 March 2018, were also recently revised and have been reformed to include new sections on the joinder of parties and consolidation of arbitral proceedings.[140]

As will be discussed in later chapters, the *i-Arbitration Rules* are not entirely consistent with *Shari'a* and this is evident by the power that arbitrators are given to award interest under Rule 12(8) of the Arbitration Rules revised in 2013, which has also been adopted by the Arbitration Rules revised in 2018 under Rule 6(g). This will be discussed in more detail in Chapter 6. Furthermore, as will be discussed in Chapter 5, the *i-Arbitration Rules* also differ from contemporary ICA rules in relation to evidentiary procedures.

B *IICRA rules*

This book will also be referring to the arbitration rules established by the IICRA. IICRA was established in the United Arab Emirates (UAE) in 2005 and was operational from 2007, following the efforts of the UAE government, Islamic Development Bank and the General Council of Islamic Banks and Financial Institutions. The centre was established to facilitate the resolution of financial or commercial disputes for parties who choose *Shari'a* to govern their proceedings. *IICRA Rules* govern both conciliation and arbitration methods of dispute resolution.[141] The IICRA website notes that it is 'an international, independent, non-profit organi[s]ation, and one [of the] major infrastructure institutions of the Islamic finance industry,'[142] but as will be discussed further in Chapter 5, its rules are more suitable for domestic disputes in the UAE. Cases resolved by

---

139 Ibid.
140 Practical Law, 'KLRCA Publishes New Rules' *Practical Law: A Thomson Reuters Legal Solution* (online), 30 October 2013 <http://us.practicallaw.com/2-547-2965?q=&qp=&qo=&qe=>. This book does not delve into a discussion on these new updates. For more information, see Jones Day, 'Kuala Lumpur Regional Center for Arbitration Rebrands as Asian International Arbitration Centre' *Jones Day*, February 2018 <www.jonesday.com/Kuala-Lumpur-Regional-Centre-for-Arbitration-Rebrands-as-Asian-International-Arbitration-Centre-02–14–2018/?RSS=true>.
141 International Islamic Centre for Reconciliation and Arbitration ('IICRA'), Establishment (30 January 2013) <http://iicra.com/en/misc_pages/detail/4c855d3580>; Kabir Hassan and Mervyn Lewis, *Handbook of Islamic Banking* (Edward Elgar Publishing, 2007) 381.
142 International Islamic Centre for Reconciliation and Arbitration ('IICRA'), Who we are (30 January 2013) <http://iicra.com/en/misc_pages/detail/4c76b6d187>.

IICRA are not published and so there is limited research available in relation to the effectiveness of and demand for the *IICRA Rules*.[143]

C AAOFI standards

AAOIFI is an organisation based in Bahrain which was established in order to provide 'accounting, auditing, governance, ethics and *Shari'a* standards for Islamic financial institutions and the industry.'[144] These standards aim to provide an international and harmonised approach to accounting, auditing, governance and *Shari'a*-related issues in Islamic finance, and may be adopted by various international Islamic financial institutions, including banks, regulatory firms or international legal and accounting firms.[145] The standards are subject to review by internal AAOIFI committee or working groups.

As will be discussed in later chapters, the relevant standards for the purposes of this book are the *Shari'a* standards,[146] which address the pre-requisites required to ensure that arbitration and various Islamic finance products comply with *Shari'a*. At a conference organised by the AAOIFI, it was noted that arbitration was the preferred dispute resolution process to resolve disputes arising from the Islamic financial contracts because of the emphasis on arbitration in the Qur'an.[147]

The chairman of the *Shari'a* board of AAOIFI, Muhammad Taqi Usmani, who notes that:

> AAOIFI decided to issue *Shari'ah* standards in the same way it had issued its accounting standards, in order to provide a reference for Islamic banks financial institutions to comply with *Shari'ah* in their transactions and products and to harmoni[s]e various [f]atwas issued by different *Shari'ah* Supervisory Boards (SSBs).[148]

However, as will be discussed in Chapter 5, the standards stipulated by the AAOIFI are not agreed upon by all Islamic organisations and scholars.

VI The application of *Shari'a* in Saudi Arabia and the *Saudi Arbitration Law 2012*

As noted in the introduction of this book, the Saudi *Arbitration Law 2012* was approved by the Shura Council in Saudi Arabia on 16 January 2012 and

---

143 The author tried to interview senior executives of IICRA, but they were unable to provide detailed information about the centre.

144 Accounting and Auding Organization for Islamic Financial Institution (AAOIFI), *AAO-IFI: What We Do* (2016) <http://aaoifi.com/?lang=en> (emphasis added).

145 AAOIFI, above n 43.

146 Ibid.

147 Jasim Salim al-Shamsi, 'Restricting Resorting to [Civil] Laws in Contract [Disputes] and Accepting the Arbitration of Shari'ah Boards Instead' (The 5th Annual Shari'ah Supervisory Boards Conference for Islamic Financial Institutions, Bahrain, 19–20 November 2005).

148 AAOIFI, above n 43, 10 (emphasis added).

introduced on 16 April 2012.[149] This *Saudi Arbitration Law 2012* was published in the Official Gazette on 8 June 2012 and came into effect 30 days later.[150] Baamir notes that the *Saudi Arbitration Law 1983* reflected the views of the Hanbali school of thought, and that it was not comprehensive on various issues relating to the arbitration proceedings such as the relationship between the arbitral tribunal and parties, the seat of the arbitral tribunal and the deliverance of arbitral awards.[151] Furthermore, under the *Saudi Arbitration Law 1983*, the Saudi courts would intervene at various stages of the arbitration proceedings in order to ensure *Shari'a* compliance, including the initiation of proceedings and enforcement of the arbitral award, which resulted in a review of the entire arbitral award.[152] In contrast, the *Saudi Arbitration Law 2012* provides significant reforms to both procedural and substantive elements of Saudi arbitration, which aim to be more consistent with the *UNCITRAL Model Law*.[153] Interestingly, the *Saudi Arbitration Law 2012* also replicates the Egyptian Arbitration Law No. 27 of 1994.[154]

In addition, arbitration reforms introduced by the new *Saudi Enforcement Law 2013*[155] replaced the provisions of the 1989 Rules of Civil Procedure before the Board of Grievances.[156] As will be discussed in Chapter 8 on *Shari'a* public policy and the recognition and enforcement of arbitral awards, the role of the Board of Grievances prior to the introduction of the *Saudi Enforcement Law 2013* was to hear enforcement requests and deal with important commercial issues before Saudi courts.[157] Parties were required to make applications to seek the enforcement of foreign judgements and arbitration awards before the Board of Grievances.[158] The *Saudi Enforcement Law 2013* abandons this system by creating a specialised forum within which judgements and awards are enforced. The purpose behind the reform is to harmonise the enforcement process with international standards.

149 Nesheiwat and Al-Khasawneh, above n 29, 444; Jones Day, 'The New Saudi Arbitration Law' (September 2012) <www.jonesday.com/new_saudi_arbitration_law/>.

150 Ibid.

151 Abdulrahman Yahya Baamir, 'Saudi Arabia' in Gordon Blanke and Habib Al Mulla (eds), *Arbitration in the MENA* (Juris Publishing, 2016), SA-19.

152 Nesheiwat and Al-Khasawneh, above n 29, 446.

153 Jones Day, above n 149.

154 Baamir, above n 151, SA-21.

155 See also, Jones Day, 'The New Enforcement Law of Saudi Arabia: An Additional Step Toward a Harmonized Arbitration Regime' (September 2013) <www.jonesday.com/the-new-enforcement-law-of-saudi-arabia-an-additional-step-toward-a-harmonized-arbitration-regime-09–04–2013/>.

156 Jean-Benoît Zegers, 'National Report for Saudi Arabia (2013)' in Jan Paulsson and Lise Bosman (eds), *ICCA International Handbook on Commercial Arbitration* (Kluwer Law International, Supplement No. 75, July 2013, 1984) 1, 77; Jones Day, above n 155.

157 Ibid.

158 Ibid. See generally, David Long, 'The Board of Grievances in Saudi Arabia' (1973) 27(1) *Middle East Journal* 71; Leon Boshoff, 'Saudi Arabia: Arbitration vs Litigation' (1985) 1 *Arab Law Quarterly* 299.

Art. 2 of the *Saudi Arbitration Law 2012* states '[w]ithout prejudice to the provisions of Islamic law and the provisions of international conventions in which the Kingdom is party, the provisions of this regulation are applied to every arbitration.' In light of this provision, it is clear that Saudi Arabia is attempting to adhere to *Shari'a* while, as noted above, also trying to align itself with the *UNCITRAL Model Law*. Nesheiwat and Al-Khasawneh observe that:

> [t]he drafters of the New [Saudi] Law made a conscious decision to base it on the *UNCITRAL Model Law* in order to create a legal framework for arbitration that is more in tune with international standards. At the same time, the drafters sought to maintain the essential principles of *Shari'a* and local practice, thus creating a hybrid set of rules that simultaneously deviate from a converge with the *UNCITRAL Model Law*.[159]

On the other hand, Tarin argues that the *Saudi Arbitration Law 2012* is more compliant with *Shari'a* than the previous law whilst also being consistent with the *UNCITRAL Model Law*.[160] However, Tarin does not comprehensively address with which interpretation of *Shari'a* the *Saudi Arbitration Law 2012* is more consistent. The following chapters will examine the tension between the attempt in the *Saudi Arbitration Law 2012* attempt to align with the *UNCITRAL Model Law* and comply with *Shari'a*

Shari'a is one of the major sources of law in the Kingdom of Saudi Arabia, which is an absolute monarchy.[161] As noted earlier, Saudi Arabia does not have a constitution (other than the Qur'an and *sunna*) and instead introduced the *Basic Law of Governance* in 1992, which describes the roles and responsibilities of institutions in the country, as well as stipulating the supremacy of *Shari'a*.[162] While Art. 44 of the *Basic Law of Governance* seems to stipulate a separation of powers between the executive, judiciary and regulatory authorities, it also states that the King will have the final authority. Mallat notes that despite the introduction of the *Basic Law of Governance*, it is clear that

> [d]elegation operates vertically, through the Council of Ministers, the various ministries, and the bureaucracy. Delegation also operates horizontally, with the King appointing a number of representatives from amongst the ruling family to head the various administrative regions in the vast Kingdom.[163]

---

159 Nesheiwat and Al-Khasawneh, above n 29, 445.
160 Shaheer Tarin, 'An Analysis of the Influence of Islamic Law on Saudi Arabia's Arbitration and Dispute Resolution Practices' (2015) 26 *American Review of International Arbitration* 131, 135.
161 Eijk, above n 105, 139.
162 Ibid., 156; Chibli Mallat, *Introduction to Middle Eastern Law* (Oxford University Press, 2007) 162.
163 Ibid.

Furthermore, the supremacy of *Shari'a* is stipulated in Art. 1 of the *Basic Law of Governance*, which provides that:

> [t]he Kingdom of Saudi Arabia is a fully sovereign Arab Islamic State. Its religion shall be Islam and its constitution shall be the Book of God and the *Sunna* (traditions) of His messenger, may God's blessings and peace be upon him.[164]

Art. 7 further stipulates that the '[g]overnance in the Kingdom of Saudi Arabia derives its authority from the Book of God Most High and the *Sunna* of his Messenger, both of which govern this Law and all the laws of the State' and Art. 48 states '[t]he courts shall apply to cases before them the provisions of Islamic *Shari'ah*, as indicated by the Qur'an and the *Sunna*, and whatever laws not in conflict with the Qur'an and the *Sunna* which the authorities may promulgate.'[165]

Consequently, *Shari'a* is a primary source of law in Saudi Arabia in conjunction with Saudi law. Vogel notes that *Shari'a* is Saudi law and 'any *fiqh* opinion authoritatively rooted in the Qur'an and *sunna* is Saudi law, because it is a valid statement of *Shari'a* and Saudi law is nothing but *Shari'a*.'[166] The sources upon which courts rely when determining *Shari'a* include the Hanafi, Maliki, Shafi and Hanbali schools of law, as well as books of *fiqh* written by Islamic scholars over 14 centuries.[167] Although judges in Saudi Arabia may apply any four schools of Sunni thought, they largely look to the Hanbali School.[168] Saudi courts also heavily rely on *al-Mughni*[169] which, as discussed previously, was written by the Hanbali scholar Ibn Qudama; the views of Ibn Taymiyya (as noted earlier); Ibn Qayyim al-Jawziyya (d. 1350 CE) and Mansur bin Yuni al-Bahuti (d. 1641 CE).[170] The views of some of these Hanbali scholars will be discussed further later. Ansary notes:

> [t]o learn the law of Saudi Arabia, one turns first to the '*fiqh*', Islamic Law. In other words, one turns not to State legislation or court precedents but to the opinions, the '*ijtihad*,' of religious-legal scholars from both the past and the present who, by their piety and learning, have become qualified to interpret

---

164 World Intellectual Property Organisation trans, *Basic Law of Governance* (promulgated by the Royal Decree No. A/90 (1992) <www.wipo.int/edocs/lexdocs/laws/en/sa/sa016en.pdf>. See also Royal Embassy of Saudi Arabia Washington, DC trans, *The Basic Law of Governance* (1992) <www.saudiembassy.net/about/country-information/laws/The_Basic_Law_Of_Governance.aspx>.

165 Ibid.

166 Vogel, above n 77,8.

167 Ibid., 9.

168 Dr. Abdullah F. Ansary, 'A Brief Overview of the Saudi Arabian Legal System' (2015) <www.nyulawglobal.org/globalex/Saudi_Arabia1.html>.

169 See the following case discussed in Chapter 8: Parties not indicated, Board of Grievances of Saudi Arabia, undated 2012 (2014) 6 (2) *International Journal of Arab Arbitration* 29.

170 Vogel, above n 77,13.

the scriptural sources and to derive laws therefrom. Most of the Islamic law applied today, according to the recognized Islamic schools of law, can be found in books of '*fiqh*' that were written by Muslim scholars (*ulama*)[171] over a period of nearly fourteen centuries. Judges in Saudi Arabia consult these books (especially those considered to be the primary sources in each Islamic school of law) in order to formulate their rulings.[172]

The concept of *ijtihad* or independent reasoning, as applied by Saudi judges, will be discussed in more detail below. For the purposes of this book, it is important to understand that court precedents and State legislation are secondary to *Shari'a* in Saudi Arabia. Therefore, Saudi law does not have a system of judicial precedent, and judges have the power to apply their own interpretations to *Shari'a*.[173] As this book will contend, in areas such as the appointment of women or non-Muslims as arbitrators (Chapter 4), the prohibition against interest and uncertainty in *Shari'a* (Chapters 6 and 7), and the extent to which public policy applies in arbitration (Chapter 8), the Saudi legal system is unclear on the extent to which *Shari'a* applies especially in matters of international and domestic commercial law and this lack of clarity often impacts on the Saudi economy.

Eijk observes that '[f]or foreign investors, uncertainties surrounding the content of Saudi commercial law, especially as to its fundamental [S]hari'a component, causes various problems and insecurities. The situation is, of course, highly disadvantageous for the Saudi economy.'[174] This book will discuss the ongoing uncertainty that the lack of judicial precedent causes in the area of contemporary ICA. The lack of certainty and predictability surrounding Saudi laws is also due to the fact that Saudi Arabia is an absolute monarchy. Art. 67 of the *Basic Law of Governance* stipulates that the King and his relevant authorities can issue regulations if it is in the public interest and does not contradict *Shari'a*:

> [t]he regulatory authority shall have the jurisdiction of formulating laws and rules conducive to the realization of the well-being or warding off harm to State affairs in accordance with the principles of the Islamic *Shari'ah*. It shall exercise its jurisdiction in accordance with this Law, and Laws of the Council of Ministers and the Shura Council.[175]

---

171 Ulama or Muslim scholars are also transmitters of religious knowledge for Sunni Muslims. See Saeed, above n 3, 241.
172 Ansary, above n 168.
173 Eijk, above n 105, 161–162.
174 Ibid., 167 (emphasis added).
175 World Intellectual Property Organisation trans, *Basic Law of Governance* (promulgated by the Royal Decree No. A/90 (1992) <www.wipo.int/edocs/lexdocs/laws/en/sa/sa016en.pdf>. See also Royal Embassy of Saudi Arabia Washington, DC trans, *The Basic Law of Governance* (1992) <www.saudiembassy.net/about/country-information/laws/The_Basic_Law_Of_Governance.aspx> (emphasis added).

However, the Saudi legal system also consists of several different judicial bodies, which have been recently been subject to reform. For example, the Royal Order issued in 2015 replaces the previous judicial system in Saudi Arabia with a new court system as follows:

1   High Court
2   Court of Appeal; and
3   First Degree Courts consisting of:

    a   General Courts;
    b   Criminal Courts;
    c   Personal Status Courts;
    d   Commercial Courts;
    e   Labor Courts; and
    f   Enforcement Courts.[176]

In addition, the Saudi Arabian legal system consists of judicial bodies that exist parallel to the court system and report directly to the King, such as the Board of Grievances or *Diwan al-Mazalim* ('*Diwan*' or 'Board of Grievances'). The Board of Grievances is independent of the Ministry of Justice (which is a body that administers the above-mentioned courts) and this body was created to deal with the heavy caseload of Saudi courts.[177] It is an administrative and judicial body, which initially heard disputes to which the government or a government entity was a party. Currently, the Board of Grievances has jurisdiction to hear administrative disputes, arbitration matters and to enforce foreign judgements and arbitral awards.[178] Another independent judicial body is the Committee for the Settlement of Banking Disputes of the Saudi Arabian Monetary Agency, which was created to settle disputes in which banks are parties.[179] However, this Committee often does not adhere to strict *Shari'a* principles. Baamir notes that the contradiction between *Shari'a* and Saudi law

> has caused a great deal of uncertainty in relation to arbitration and litigation, as the teachings of *Shari'a* prohibits all forms of banking interest, conventional insurance, sales of tobacco products, and the Saudi law does not enforce this prohibition in daily life.[180]

The inconsistency regarding the application of *Shari'a* in Saudi Arabia will be further discussed in the following chapters.

---

176 Ansary, above n 168.
177 Baamir, above n 46, 22–24. Ansary, above n 168.
178 Ibid.
179 Ibid.
180 Baamir, above n 151, SA-9.

Interestingly, in 2014, a Royal Order issued by King Abdullah established a committee, consisting of Islamic experts, researchers and judicial officers, who were given the task of codifying *Shari'a* rules to aid judicial officers.[181] Ansary notes that:

> [t]he committee is required to adhere to the rules of the Islamic *Sharia'h* and follow a scientific approach in weighting the opinions of the Islamic schools of law. All the codified material must be supported by evidence from *Shari'ah* texts and the *"ijtihad"* of religious-legal scholars.[182]

The reason why this Royal Order is interesting is because through the process of *ijtihad*, Islamic scholars in Saudi Arabia often make rulings that are not based on the Qur'an, hadith or Islamic schools of law. According to Vogel,

> Saudi judges ordinarily adhere to Hanbali legal positions, but . . . they are free to adopt views from others schools, or even from outside the four schools altogether, as long as they base their view, following proper interpretive procedures, on the Qur'an and *sunna*.[183]

These interpretative procedures are criticised by commentators such as El Fadl who argues that the Saudi government justifies its legal positions on the basis of 'blocking the means to evil' and that 'the idea of preventive or precautionary measures (*al-ihtiyat*), could be exploited to expand the power of the state under the guise of protecting the *Shari'ah*.'[184] This may be evident by the *fatwas* delivered by Islamic scholars through two public agencies established by the government in 1971: (1) the Board of Senior Ulama (Islamic scholars); and (2) the Permanent Committee for Scientific Research and Legal Opinions.[185] These two institutions consist of Islamic scholars who interpret *Shari'a*, and their *fatwas* are also available on the Saudi government's online portal called, 'Portal of the General Presidency of Scholarly Research and *Ifta*.' *Ifta* refers to the declaration of a *fatwa*, which the Saudi government enforces through the Committee for Commanding Right and Forbidding Wrong or the *mutawwi'a* (religious police). People who do not abide by the religious rulings in Saudi Arabia are punished by the State.[186] For example, one *fatwa* published online states that women should not drive cars,[187] because it could lead to adultery (which is viewed as a sinful act

181 Ansary, above n 168.
182 Ibid.
183 Vogel, above n 77, 10.
184 Khaled Abou El Fadl, 'Islam and the Challenge of Democracy' (2003) *Boston Review* (online) <http://bostonreview.net/archives/BR28.2/abou.html>.
185 Muhammad Al-Atawneh, *Wahhabi Islam Facing the Challenges of Modernity* (Brill, 2010) xiv.
186 Ibid., 2.
187 Abdul-'Aziz ibn 'Abdullah ibn Baz, 'Fatwas of Ibn Baz, Volume 3' <www.alifta.com/ Search/ResultDetails.aspx?languagename=en&lang=en&view=result&fatwaNum=&Fat waNumID=&ID=218&searchScope=14&SearchScopeLevels1=&SearchScopeLevels2= &highLight=1&SearchType=exact&SearchMoesar=false&bookID=&LeftVal=0&Right

that is forbidden in the Qur'an and hadith). This *fatwa* has been implemented in Saudi law despite the fact that it is not a view shared by the majority of Muslim scholars internationally.

In fact, according to Al-Atawneh, Saudi *fatwas* are often inconsistent because '[w]hen dealing with modern innovations and political issues, Saudi Arabian muftīs are relatively open and liberal, whereas, in the realms of social norms (e.g., ritual, the status of women), they maintain a "Puritanical" Wahhabi approach.'[188] El Fadl also notes that the

> claim of precautionary measures (blocking the means) is used today in Saudi Arabia to justify a wide range of restrictive laws against women, including the prohibition against driving cars. This is a relatively novel invention in Islamic state practices and in many instances amounts to the use of *Shari'ah* to undermine *Shari'ah*.[189]

El Fadl's critique that the Saudi interpretation of *Shari'a* undermines the objectives of *Shari'a* (*maqasid Al-Shari'a*) will be discussed in more detail later.

In order to understand the Saudi interpretation of *Shari'a*, it is important to recognise the influence of two eminent Hanbali scholars in Saudi Arabia who were introduced earlier, Ibn Taymiyya and Ibn Abd al-Wahhab.[190] In 1745 CE, Ibn Abd al-Wahhab, who founded the '*Wahhabism*'[191] movement, asked the Saudi prince, Ibn Saud (d. 1765 CE) to actively reform Islamic thought in accordance with his teachings.[192] This reform, with Ibn Saud as the political leader and Ibn Abd al-Wahhab as the spiritual leader, was initially successful and spread over most of the Arabian Peninsula, but was later overthrown by the Ottoman Empire in 1819 CE.[193] However, the Wahhabi movement was revived in 1902 CE when another Saudi prince, Abd al-Aziz (d. 1953 CE) took over the Arabian Peninsula and founded the Kingdom of Saudi Arabia in 1932 CE.[194]

The newly founded modern nation of Saudi Arabia was heavily influenced by the ideas of *Wahabbism*. The ideology of *Wahabbism* is a puritanical and legalistic approach to Islam because it believes in a return to the practice of the *salaf*, the original followers of Islam, and stems from the ideology of *Salafism*, which will be explored further later. Many Sunni Islamic scholars argue that the original followers of Islam, the *salafs*, consisted of 'rightly guided successors' of the Prophet Muhammad, being the first four Sunni *caliphs*: Abu Bakr al-Siddiq (d. 634 CE), Umar al-Khattab (d. 644 CE), Uthman Affan (d. 656 CE) and Ali Abi Talib

---

Val=0&simple=&SearchCriteria=allwords&PagePath=&siteSection=1&searchkeyword=119 111109101110032100114105118105110103#firstKeyWordFound>.

188 Al-Atawneh, above n 185, xiv.
189 El Fadl, above n 184.
190 Vogel, above n 77, xv.
191 Vogel notes that the term 'wahabbism' is in fact rejected by the movement itself and is a modern terminology. See Vogel, above n 77, xvi, n 12.
192 Ibid., xv; Eijk, above n 105, 141–143.
193 Vogel, above n 77, xv.
194 Ibid., xvi.

(d. 661 CE).[195] This concept is based on the following *a*hadith,[196] in which the Prophet Muhammad said the following:

> [t]he best people are those living in my generation, and then those who will follow them, and then those who will follow the latter[197]
>
> . . . you must keep to my *[s]unnah* and to the *[s]unnah* of the *Khulafa ar-Rashideen* (the rightly guided *caliphs*), those who guide to the right way. Cling to it stubbornly (literally: with your molar teeth). Beware of newly invented matters (in the religion), for verily every *bidah* (innovation) is misguidance.[198]

Other Islamic scholars argue that the 'rightly guided' successors is a broad concept, and refers to all the Islamic scholars succeeding the Prophet Muhammad, or the companions of the Prophet Muhammad.[199] Hassim observes that '[t]he best opinion is all of the above. "Rightly guided successors" refers to the Four Caliphs first and foremost, then the remainder of the Companions, followed by the successors and scholars who observed their way in religion.'[200]

Wahabbism emphasises the primacy of the Qur'an and *sunna* when deducing *Shari'a* rules, and a rejection of certain mystical practices (i.e. rituals followed by certain branches of Sufism, such as shrine worshipping), which are considered *bidah* (innovation).[201] For example, Vogel notes that Ibn Abd al-Wahhab claimed that if the literal meaning of a hadith was valid according to Islamic scholars, then the statement in the hadith must be followed even if the four schools of thought have a different interpretation of the hadith.[202] Therefore, Wahabbis accept the Hanbali school of law only to the extent that Hanbali scholars are strictly following the Qur'an, *sunna* or hadith, legal opinion of the companions of the Prophet (and if there is a difference of opinion, whichever view is most consistent with the Qur'an and *sunna*), and if necessary, the principles of analogy (*qiyas*).[203] One of the sons of Ibn Abd Al-Wahhab states that although the Hanbali school of thought should be followed, it is unnecessary to follow a school of thought, if

---

195 This view is taken by classical Islamic scholars: al-Tahawi (d. 935 CE), al-Nawawi (1278 CE), al-Mubarakafuri (1353 CE), Ibn Abi al-Izz (1390CE), Ibn Rajab (1393 CE). See Eeqbal Hassim, *Origins of Salafism in Indonesia: A Preliminary Insight* (Lambert Academic Publishing, 2010) 11.
196 Plural of hadith.
197 Sahih Bukhari, <www.sahih-bukhari.com/Pages/Bukhari_5_57.php> (Volume 5, Book 57, Number 3).
198 Hadith Nawawi <http://sunnah.com/nawawi40/28> (Volume 40, Hadith 28) (emphasis added).
199 Hassim, above n 195, 11.
200 Ibid., 11.
201 Vogel, above n 77, xvi.
202 Ibid., 72.
203 Ibid.

there is a clear text in the Qur'an or *sunna*.[204] The Qur'an and *sunna* are considered more valid than the view of a certain school.[205]

VII Independent reasoning (*Ijtihad*) or imitation (*Taqlid*)?

As noted above, Ibn Abd al-Wahhab was heavily influenced by the prominent Hanbali scholar, Ibn Taymiyya who believed in *ijtihad* or 'independent reasoning' as a tool for interpreting the *Shari'a*, as opposed to strict adherence to doctrine (*taqlid*).[206] Ijtihad stems from the root word '*jahada*' which means 'striving, or self-exertion in any activity which entails a measure of hardship.'[207] Kamali further defines *ijtihad* as 'the total expenditure of effort made by a jurist in order to infer, with a degree of probability, the rules of *Shari'ah* from their detailed evidence in the sources.'[208] However, as will be discussed further below, the process through which *ijtihad* is used as a tool to determine rules of *Shari'a* depends on whether scholars approach *ijtihad* in a manner that is literalist or contextual.

For example, Ibn Abd al-Wahhab and Ibn Taymiyya took a literalist interpretation of the Qur'an and hadith regarding theological matters. An example of Ibn Taymiyya's literalist approach is noted in his book *Majmu al-Fatawa al-Kubra* ('the Great Compilation of Religious Rulings') in which he states:

> The way of the Salaf is to interpret literally the Qur'anic verses and hadith that relate to the Divine attributes (*ijra' ayat al-sifat wa ahadith al-sifat 'ala zahiriha*), and without indicating modality and without attributing to Him anthropomorphic qualities (*ma' nafy al-kayfiyya wa-l-tashbih*). So that one is not to state that the meaning of "hand" is power or that of "hearing" is knowledge.[209]

This literalist approach was followed by many who follow the Salafiyya movement (also referred to as the 'reformers'), which arose in the late 19th century, and which also advocated a return to the way of the original followers of Islam (*salafs*) by utilising independent thinking (*ijtihad*) and rejecting adherence to doctrine or

---

204 Ibid., 74.
205 Ibid.
206 Schacht, above n 1, 73.
207 Mohammad Hashim Kamali, *Principles of Islamic Jurisprudence* (The Islamic Texts Society, 1991) 367.
208 Ibid., 367.
209 Taqi al-Din ibn Taymiyya, *al-Fatawa Al-Kubra* (Cairo: Dar al-Kutub al-Haditha, 1966) 152 as cited in Bernard Haykel, 'On the Nature of Salafi Thought and Action' in Roel Meijer (ed), *Global Salafism: Islam's New Religious Movement* (Columbia University Press, 2009) 39. For a more detailed analysis of Ibn Taymiyya's views, see Abd Al-Rahman Ibn Al-Jawzi (trans, Abdullah Bin Hamid Ali), *The Attributes of God* (Amal Press, 2016). See also Jon Hoover, *Ibn Taymiyya's Theodicy of Perpetual Optimism* (Brill, 2007).

imitation (*taqlid*).[210] Interestingly, classical Hanafi scholars often debated matters such as whether God's attributes, as mentioned in the Qur'an, should be interpreted metaphorically or literally. One Hanbali scholar, Abd al-Rahman Ibn al-Jawzi (d. 1201 CE), argued against other Hanbali scholars by stating that God's attributes should be interpreted metaphorically.[211] Therefore, as noted previously, even within one movement or school of thought, Islamic scholars may take a different approach to matters of Islamic theology (*kalam*) and creed (*aqidah*).[212]

Although they overlap in many matters, one difference between the Salafi and Wahabbi movement is that the latter generally follow the Hanbali school of thought as well as advocating *ijtihad*. On the other hand, there is a division between the Salafis as to whether a school of law (*maddhab*) should be followed. For example, some Salafis follow the companions of the Prophet Muhammad, their successors and the founders of the four schools of thought.[213] Other Salafis believe that Ibn Taymiyya advocated the way of the original followers of Islam (*salaf*) over imitation (*taqlid*) of the four schools of thought.[214]

The argument regarding imitation (*taqlid*) or independent thinking (*ijtihad*) is important because it defines and formulates *Shari'a* rulings on matters, especially the extent to which the four schools of thought should be followed. This argument arose between the tenth and 13th centuries when Abu Hanafi, Malik, Hanbal and Shafii decided that the religious rulings were comprehensive enough and there was no longer a need to practice independent reasoning (*ijtihad*).[215] Many contemporary commentators, for example Schacht, view this era as the 'closing of the gates of *ijtihad*.'[216] Therefore, while a *mufti* (Muslim legal expert) may issue a *fatwa*, the mufti must refer to the four schools of thought when issuing an opinion as opposed to a *mujtahid* who works with the Qur'an and hadith.[217]

On the other hand, other scholars such as Hallaq argue that *ijtihad* remained an integral part of Sunni Islam, and it was only groups such as the 'people of the hadith' and 'traditionalists' who believed in strict adherence to imitation (*taqlid*).[218] Similarly, Rabb states:

> The settling of the major areas of Islamic law gave rise to the perception, prevalent among many modern Western scholars and Sunni lay Muslims, that jurists had come to a consensus that the so-called 'gate of *ijtihad*' was closed at the beginning of the tenth century. As a result, *ijtihad* had come to be thought of as the opposite of *taqlid*, rather than the two working

210 Schacht, above n 1, 74.
211 See generally, Ibn Al-Jawzi, above n 209.
212 See Hallaq, above n 20, 135–143.
213 Hassim, above n 195, 14.
214 Bernard Haykel, 'On the Nature of Salafi Thought and Action' in Roel Meijer (ed), *Global Salafism: Islam's New Religious Movement* (Columbia University Press, 2009) 45.
215 Hussain, above n 20, 46; Schacht, above n 2, 69–71.
216 Schacht, above n 2, 69.
217 Bernard G. Weiss, *The Spirit of Islamic Law* (University of Georgia Press, 1998) 135.
218 Hallaq, above n 11, 33–35.

in tandem as before. . . . However, any perception of an *absence* of or *bar* to *ijtihad* has been shown by recent scholarship to be without foundation. There exists no evidence of such a closure or even the possibility of such a closure given the diffuse nature of juristic authority. There certainly was no consensus to that effect. To the contrary, evidence shows that the practice of *ijtihad* continued throughout the centuries, as expressed through *fatwas*, commentaries and glosses on settled legal texts.[219]

Ibn Taymiyya's argument that the 'gates of independent thinking (*ijtihad*)' should remain open was also followed by Islamic scholars of the 19th century, Jamal al-Din al-Afghani (d. 1897 CE) and Muhammad 'Abduh (d. 1905 CE) from Egypt, and 20th-century scholar, Muhammad Iqbal (d. 1938 CE) and Sayyid Ahmad Khan (d. 1898 CE) from the Indian subcontinent.[220] Although these scholars agreed with the idea of *ijtihad*, they were not literalists when it came to theological matters. They were more concerned with the 'renaissance of Muslim society' and in a Muslim 'enlightenment.'[221] Saeed argues that '[f] or these scholars, the modern context demanded a reappraisal of the intellectual heritage of Muslims that required giving up the practice of blind imitation (*taqlid*), which they argued was common among Muslims of their time.'[222] Over the 20th and early 21st centuries, a number of Muslim thinkers have also applied the 'contextual approach' or 'contextual ijtihad' to interpreting the Qur'an.[223] Such scholars include Fazlur Rahman (d. 1988 CE), Muhammad Asad (d. 1992 CE) and Abdullahi An-Naim[224] who believe that the sociological and historical context of the Qur'an and hadith is significant, and therefore it should be interpreted contextually.[225]

Therefore, Saeed categorises *ijtihad* into the following methods: 'text-based' *ijtihad* being the classical approach to *ijtihad*; 'eclectic *ijtihad*' and 'context-based' *ijtihad*, which is referred to in the modern world but stems from the early Islamic period.[226] Text-based *ijtihad* or the 'textualist approach'[227] addresses new legal issues by heavily relying on principles of jurisprudence under *Shari'a* (*usul al-fiqh*) as well as the Qur'an, hadith or the view of a school of thought.[228] On

---

219 Ijtihad (2016), above n 105.
220 Hussain, above n 20, 48–49; Haykel, above n 209, 46–47; Saeed, above n 23, 21. The extent to which ijtihad was practiced by these scholars is not discussed in this book.
221 Haykel, above n 209, 46–47.
222 Saeed, above n 23, 21.
223 Ibid., 23.
224 See generally, Abdullahi An-Na'im, *Islam and Human Rights* (Ashgate Publishing, 2010); Fazlur Rahman, *Islam & Modernity: Transformation of an Intellectual Tradition* (The University of Chicago Press, 1982).
225 See generally, Saeed, above n 23.
226 Abdullah Saeed, 'Ijtihad and Innovation in Neo-Modernist Islamic Thought in Indonesia' (1997) 8(3) *Islam and Christian-Muslim Relations* 279, 282–284.
227 Saeed, above n 3, 220.
228 Saeed, above n 226, 283.

the other hand, 'eclectic *ijtihad*' does not strictly adhere to textual sources of *Shari'a* or principles of jurisprudence and therefore, can result in conclusions that are often *ad hoc*.[229] Context-based *ijtihad* or the contextualist approach[230] heavily relies on the historical context of a problem, and scholars are directed by public interest (*maslahah*).[231] Although a scholar may apply all three methodologies, Saeed gives an example of the 'neo-Modernist'[232] trend in Indonesia where scholars use context-based *ijtihad* to address modern problems.[233] As will be discussed in following chapters, the 'context-based ijtihad' approach is also evident by the views of scholars such as Abd Al-Razzaq Ahmad Al-Sanhuri (1895–1971 CE) who heavily influenced the civil codes of Egypt, Syria, Iraq, Libya and Kuwait. Arguably, Sanhuri was using a form of 'contextual ijtihad' when he reasoned that the prohibition under *Shari'a* was against compound interest as opposed to simple interest (see Chapters 6 and 7).[234] Another form of *ijtihad* is known as 'collective *ijtihad*' or *ijtihad jama'i*, which is when a collective body of *mujtahids* create a religious ruling based on the Islamic concept of consultation (*shura*).[235] Although it is beyond the scope of this book to analyse the different forms of *ijtihad* and how they are implemented, it is important to understand that *Shari'a* is a body of law subject to a variety of interpretations and has the ability to adapt to the evolutionary nature of society, which will be discussed in the next section.

VIII   Ijtihad, maslaha and maqasid al-*Shari'a*

As noted earlier, *ijtihad* is a tool of *Shari'a* through which the changing conditions of society can be addressed and contextual *ijtihad* considers the public interest or *maslaha* (also referred to as *istislah*) in order to ascertain whether a legal decision is in the interests of contemporary society.[236] Imam Malik, the founder of the Maliki school of thought, referred to *maslaha* when he had to rule on an issue which was not addressed in the Qur'an or hadith.[237] The companions of the Prophet Muhammad also referred to *maslaha* when they decided to

229 Ibid., 283.
230 Saeed, above n 3, 220.
231 Saeed, above n 226, 284.
232 "Neo-Modernist" is a term used by Saeed to identify contemporary intellectuals who advocate ijtihad, as opposed to dogmatism, believe that classical Islamic knowledge can exist in harmony with Western thought and believe in independent reasoning (ijtihad) and therefore, Islamic law should cater for modernity. See Saeed, above n 226, 284–290.
233 Examples provided is the view polygamy should no longer be permissible under Shari'a despite the consensus among the four schools of thought that it is allowed and punishments under Shari'a for criminal acts. See Saeed, above n 226, 284–290.
234 Emad H. Khalil and Abdulkader Thomas, 'The Modern Debate Over Riba in Egypt' in Abdulkader Thomas (ed), *Interest in Islamic Economics: Understanding Riba* (Routledge, 2006) 69, 73.
235 See generally, Aznan Hasan, 'An Introduction to Collective Ijtihad (Ijtihad Jama'i): Concept and Applications' (2003) 20(2) *The American Journal of Islamic Social Sciences* 26.
236 Ramadan, above n 119, 5.
237 Hallaq, above n 22, 109–110.

establish taxation regimes, prison systems and a financial currency in conquered territories because it was in the public interest, despite the fact that there were no provisions in the Qur'an and/or hadith stipulating such systems.[238] Similarly, many *ahadith*[239] are cited to support the claim that legal decisions can be made in the public interest as long as they are not contrary to provisions of the Qur'an and hadith.[240]

Two eminent classical Islamic scholars who elaborate on *maqasid al-Shari'a* and *maslaha* include Al-Ghazali (d. 1111 CE) and the Andalusian scholar, Shatibi (d. 1388 CE). Al-Ghazali wrote at length about the concept of *maslahah* in his works, *Shifa al-Ghalil* and *al-Mustasfa*.[241] Al-Ghazali defines *maslaha* as a tool through which the objectives (*maqasid*) of *Shari'a* are achieved. According to Al-Ghazali, the five objectives of *Shari'a* include preservation of religion, life, intellect, lineage and property.[242] Therefore, the concept of public interest (*maslahah*) under *Shari'a* public policy consists of higher objectives which are religious rather than secular and thus, not recognised under secular legal systems.[243]

Al-Ghazali categorises *maslaha* as follows:

1 The 'imperative' or 'necessities' (*al daruriyyat*) which includes the preservation of the five objectives or maqasid of *Shari'a*.[244] For example, *Shari'a* rules in relation to daily rituals such as prayer aim to achieve the overall objective of preserving religion, and rules regarding food and shelter aim to preserve life and intellect. Similarly, laws may be introduced if the necessities are threatened.[245]

2 Laws may also be reformed to address the needs (*al-hajiyyat*) of society in order to alleviate difficulties in the community.[246] One example is if ritual obligations under *Shari'a* are causing illness or hardship such as fasting, then an individual does not have to abide by the law.[247] Hallaq notes that '[t]hese

238 Kamali, above n 207, 267.
239 Plural of hadith.
240 For example, the following hadith: Aisha (wife of the Prophet) reports, '[w]henever Allah's Apostle was given the choice of one of two matters, he would choose the easier of the two, as long as it was not sinful to do so, but if it was sinful to do so, he would not approach it'. See Sahih Bukhari, <www.sahih-bukhari.com/Pages/Bukhari_4_56.php> Volume 4, Book 56, Number 760; The Prophet said '[t]here should be neither harming nor reciprocating harm'. See Hadith Nawawi <http://sunnah.com/nawawi40> Hadith 32; 'Muslims will be held to their conditions, except the conditions that make the lawful unlawful, or the unlawful lawful'. See Jami' at-Tirmidhi <http://sunnah.com/tirmidhi/15> Vol. 3, Book 13, Hadith 1352; see also, Kamali, above n 207, 269.
241 Kamali, above n 16, 124.
242 Ramadan, above n 119, 5; Kamali, above n 16, 125. See also Yasir Ibrahim, 'Rashid Rida and Maqasid al-Sharia' (2006) 102/103 *Studia Islamica* 157.
243 Kutty, above n 57, 602.
244 Kamali, above n 207, 271; Ramadan, above n 119, 6; Hallaq, above n 20, 168.
245 Hallaq, above n 20, 168.
246 Ibid., 168; Kamali, above n 207, 272; Ramadan, above n 119, 6.
247 Hallaq, above n 20, 168; Kamali, above n 207, 272; Ramadan, above n 119, 6.

mitigated laws are *needed* in order to make the life and legal practice of Muslims tolerable.'[248]

3   The notion of 'improvements' or 'perfecting' (*al-tahsiniyyat* and *al-kamaliyyat*) focuses on those parts of the law that perfect the customs and practices of people.[249] For example, laws in relation to charity are viewed as perfecting or improving the *Shari'a*.

Shatibi further explains *maslahah* according to how consistent it is with the foundational texts of the Qur'an and hadith.[250] If *al-maslahah* is consistent with foundational texts, it is known as *maslaha mutabara* (accredited) and if it contradicts the Qur'an or hadith, then it cannot be taken into account and is referred to as *maslahah mulgha* (discredited).[251] On the other hand, if the Qur'an or hadith are not clear on an issue then *maslahah* is classified as *mursala* (undetermined).[252] Ramadan observes that *maslaha mursala* means that scholars are able to 'use their own analysis and personal reasoning in order to formulate a legal decision in the light of the historical and geographical context, using their best efforts to remain faithful to the commandments and to the "spirit" of the Islamic legal corpus where no text, no "letter" of the Law, is declared.'[253]

Shatibi also elaborates on the definition of *maqasid al-Shari'a* in his seminal text, *Al Muwafaqat fi Usul al-Shari'a* (the Reconciliation of the Fundamentals of Islamic Law),[254] in which he notes that the concept of *maqasid al-Shari'a* can be further divided into dual objectives, depending on whether the concept of *maqasid* is explained through the perspective of God (*maqasid al-shari*), which include objectives such as worship.[255] Alternatively, *maqasid* may be viewed through the perspective of human beings (*maqasid al-mukallaf*), which include objectives relevant to life on earth such as employment and marriage; however, the objectives of God and human beings are not mutually exclusive because 'the formulation of the laws is for securing interests of the servants (human beings) in both the here[256] and the Hereafter.'[257] These objectives are further elaborated upon by Islamic scholars to include 'deeper meanings' and 'inner wisdom'[258] of the *Shari'a*, and 'the ultimate goals, aims, consequences and meanings which

---

248 Hallaq, above n 20, 168.

249 Kamali, above n 207, 272; Ramadan, above n 119, 6.

250 Kamali, above n 207, 272–273; Ramadan, above n 119, 6.

251 Ibid.

252 Ibid.

253 Ramadan, above n 119, 6.

254 Ibrahim ibn Musa Abu Ishaq al-Shatibi, *The Reconciliation of the Fundamentals of Islamic Law Volume II* (trans, Imran Ahsan Khan Nyazee trans, Garnet Publisher, 2015) [trans, Al Muwafaqat fi Usul al-Shari'a (first published 1884)].

255 Ibid., 3–4.

256 Ibid.

257 Ibid. See also, Ibid., 9–241 (elaborates on objectives and purposes related to God); 255–310 (discuss objectives of human beings).

258 Mohammad Hashim Kamali, 'Maqasid al-Shari'ah and Ijtihad as Instruments of Civilisational Renewal: A Methodological Perspective' (2011) 2(2) *Islam and Civilisational Renewal* 245, 249.

the *Shari'ah* has upheld and established through its laws and consistently seeks to realise and materialise and achieve them at all times and places.'[259] More contemporary Islamic scholars, such as Rashid Rida (d. 1935 CE)[260] and Yusuf al-Qaradawi refer to *maqasid al-Shari'a* in the contemporary context to address issues of reform and the protection of human rights, such as the rights of women, which will be discussed in the context of women as arbitrators and witnesses in further chapters.[261] Hallaq argues that Shatibi's theories on *maqasid al-Shari'a* were later used by legal reformists because

> [t]he uniqueness of Shatibi's theory, some scholars have argued, stems from the fact that Shatibi, realising the failure of law in meeting the challenges of socio-economic change in eighth-/fourteenth-century Andalusia, tried in his theory to answer the particular needs of his time by showing how it was possible to adapt law to the new social conditions.[262]

Therefore, contextual *ijtihad*, *maslaha* and *maqasid al-Shari'a* are potential reformative tools which are able to address contemporary issues which the Qur'an or hadith are unclear or silent about. However, there has been much discussion among Islamic scholars in relation to who can interpret *Shari'a*, and how rules of *Shari'a* should be interpreted.[263] Abou El Fadl accurately notes:

> Value-based assumptions are founded on normative values that the legal system considers necessary or basic. . . . Muslim jurists often asserted that the basic necessities are five essential values . . . religion, life, intellect, lineage and property . . . [t]hese were basic values or objects that the *Shari'ah* is supposed to satisfy or guard. However, this field remained underdeveloped, and the asserted values were not necessarily those actually served or protected by the juristic culture. Muslim jurists argued that the five basic values were derived solely through textual analysis, and this might explain the largely mechanical way that they asserted or defended them.[264]

For example, as noted earlier, Al-Ghazali argues that only a *mujtahid* with certain qualifications can exercise *ijtihad*. Furthermore, even when a *mujtahid* with the relevant expertise exercises *ijtihad* to come to a certain conclusion, they may

259 Muhammad al-Zuhayli, *Maqasid al-Shari'ah: Asas li huquq al-insan, Kitab al-Ummah Series No. 87* (Doha: Ministry of Awqaf and Islamic Affairs of Qatar, 2003) 7 as cited in Kamali, above n 258, 249.

260 Ibrahim, above n 242. Contra Hallaq, above n 20, 254 (Wael Hallaq argues that Rashid Rida's methodology places more emphasis on concepts of public interest (*masalaha*), necessity (*darura*) as opposed to relying on primary Islamic texts such as the Qur'an and hadith).

261 Jasser Auda, *Maqasid al-Shari'ah as Philosophy of Islamic Law: A Systems Approach* (The International Institute of Islamic Thought, 2007) 5.

262 Hallaq, above n 20, 162–163.

263 See generally, Khaled Abou El Fadl, *Speaking in God's Name: Islamic Law, Authority and Women* (Oneworld Publications, 2001).

264 Ibid., 154–155.

approach the Qur'an and hadith literally or contextually, depending on which interpretive approach they prefer, or they may have a different concept of what constitutes 'public interest.' As discussed further in this book, this is evident in the literalist way *Shari'a* is interpreted and implemented by the Saudi government and the Wahabbi movement. For this reason, contemporary scholars such as El Fadl argue that such interpretations have stagnated the classical approach to *Shari'a*, which was creative and evolutionary in nature.[265]

Hallaq also argues that the implementation of *Shari'a* is not possible in the postmodern world and that the true essence of *Shari'a* can only be understood during the period in which it was the paradigm model of law, which includes the 12 centuries until the colonialist period beginning in the 19th century.[266] He uses the example of modern day Iran where *Shari'a* is based on a Shi'i interpretation of Islam, to argue that the contemporary Islamic state has

> disfigured *Shar[i]'a*'s norms of governance, leading to the failure of both Islamic governance and modern state as political projects. Nor have the other Muslim countries fared any better, because the political organisation they adopted from – and after – colonialism has been and remains authoritarian and oppressive and because their integration of *Shar[i]'a* as a mode of governance has hardly paid anything more than lip service to the original.[267]

Consequently, there is widespread disillusionment with the 'authoritarian implementation' of *Shari'a* in Muslim nation states, such as Saudi Arabia and Iran. For this reason, it is also important to understand that the form of *Shari'a* implemented by Saudi Arabia is different to that adopted by Iran. Similarly, the *i Arbitration Rules* developed by the AIAC may have a different understanding of *Shari'a* to the AAOIFI Standards. Islamic scholars may also come to different conclusions about *Shari'a* rules as is evident from their different views on the *Shari'a*-compliant nature of certain Islamic finance products (Chapter 5).

Shari'a is subject to varying interpretation and implantation, and depends greatly on the country, the legislation, the Islamic legal scholar, the arbitrator and the disputing parties. Contemporary scholar, Jonathan Brown, examines how debates over the interpretation of *Shari'a* have existed throughout the history of Islamic civilisation, and still exist in the contemporary world, often influenced by political considerations.[268] Therefore, when analysing *Shari'a*'s application to contemporary ICA, this book argues that *Shari'a* is not stagnant but subject to a variety of different interpretations and in addition, is likely to evolve and reform through its own sources of law and legal theories such as *ijtihad*, *maslaha* and *maqasid al-Shari'a*. The idea of an evolving, as opposed to stagnant, *Shari'a* will be repeatedly mentioned in the following chapters.

265 Ibid., 16–18.
266 Wael Hallaq, *The Impossible State* (Columbia University Press, 2013) 2.
267 Ibid., 2 (emphasis added).
268 See generally, Brown, above n 19.

IX Conclusion

Shari'a is a conceptual framework for divine law and as discussed in this chapter, is applied and understood in various ways. This book refers to the term 'classical *Shari'a*' as a body of Islamic jurisprudence based on the four schools of thought. Nevertheless, as discussed earlier, there is a strong argument that *mujtahids* may also use independent reasoning (*ijtihad*) to address contemporary issues. As the following chapters will argue, since *Shari'a* is not codified and is subject to multiple interpretations, this can often cause confusion and inconsistency as to which form of *Shari'a* is applicable to contemporary ICA. This book considers whether Islamic scholars should revive and employ principles of jurisprudence (*usul ul fiqh*) such as contextual *ijtihad, maslaha* and *maqasid al-Shari'a* to further develop *Shari'a* rules on international commercial arbitration, which have the ability to be consistent with contemporary ICA principles. Due to the concept of party autonomy, parties agreeing with the approach used by Islamic scholars could choose to apply these rules if they wish to conduct their arbitration in a *Shari'a*-compliant way. This book also considers whether *Shari'a* is a body of law, which will be recognised and accommodated by contemporary ICA. The next chapter will analyse whether *Shari'a* is an effective body of law, capable of recognition by secular jurisdictions, such as the United Kingdom.

3 Conflict of laws and *Shari'a* as choice of law

I Introduction

This chapter analyses whether secular countries will recognise *Shari'a* as an effective body of law to govern arbitration. It also examines the historical approach of courts and tribunals to *Shari'a* as governing law. In order to assess the approach of secular courts to *Shari'a*, this chapter will use the United Kingdom as a case study because it is a jurisdiction that has dealt with the issue of enforcing anational law, for example in the cases *Halpern v Halpern*[1] ('*Halpern*') and *Shamil Bank of Bahrain v Beximco Pharm. Ltd*[2] ('*Beximco*'). More specifically, this chapter will critically analyse: (1) the recognition of *Shari'a* as the choice of law in arbitration agreements, including an analysis of conflict of law principles governing arbitration agreements, and (2) the choice of *Shari'a* as substantive law in contemporary ICA and the respective conflict of law principles. By using the United Kingdom as a case study, this chapter will analyse the tension between party autonomy and whether *Shari'a* is a body of law that is enforceable, predictable and consistent.

II Party autonomy and choice of law

Contemporary ICA allows parties to resolve their disputes by independent, neutral decision-makers and provides parties with autonomy and procedural flexibility. However, contemporary ICA does not exist in a legal vacuum. Arbitration may be subject to different systems of laws, rules and guidelines, or one body of law (including anational law/s) may apply to different aspects of the arbitration including the law governing the arbitration agreement and the law governing the merits of the dispute. Born refers to the latter as the substantive law,[3] and it is often referred to as the 'governing law,' 'proper law' or the 'applicable law.'[4]

---

1 [2007] EWCA Civ 291; [2008] Q.B. 195.
2 [2004] EWCA Civ 19.
3 Gary Born, *International Commercial Arbitration* (Kluwer Law International, 2nd ed, 2014) 211.
4 Nigel Blackaby, et al., *Redfern and Hunter on International Arbitration* (Oxford University Press, 6th ed, 2015) 4.

This book, however, broadly refers to 'governing law' broadly as also governing the arbitration proceedings, arbitration agreement or the law governing the recognition and enforcement of the award (depending on where the assets are held).[5] A separate legal system may also govern conflict of laws matters.[6]

In the early 1970s a distinction was made between the law applicable to the merits of the dispute and the law governing the procedure.[7] As discussed later, this distinction was recognised due to the concept of separability, which treats the arbitration agreement as independent from the underlying contract. The law applicable to the arbitration agreement, therefore, may be different to the law governing the contract.[8] For this reason, arbitrators distinguish between 'choice of substantive law, choice of procedural law, choice of a rule of conflict of laws, and choice of law to determine the validity and effect of the arbitration clause.'[9] However, it is also important to note that in conflict of law situations, it may be unclear whether procedural or substantive law should apply to the arbitration agreement. Waincymer further explains that:

> where the agreement stipulates the Seat or place of arbitration, it in turn invariably leads to the arbitration law of that Seat forming the *lex arbitri*. The agreement may also select particular arbitral rules and specify a range of other powers, rights and duties of various parties and the tribunal . . . because it forms an agreement between the parties, it will typically be contractual in nature under some substantive law of contract. At the same time, it creates the jurisdictional basis for the arbitration. Hence an arbitration agreement has a dual character. This raises challenges when it comes to interpreting the agreement where there is a need to identify the applicable law . . . [b]ecause of the dual nature, there can be no unassailable conclusion on this question, which makes tribunal discretion more problematic in the absence of direction from the parties.[10]

English commentators have also observed that

> [a]rbitration law is all about a particular method of resolving disputes. Its substance and proceeds are closely intertwined. The *Arbitration Act* contains

---

5 Alan Redfern, et al., *Redfern and Hunter on International Arbitration* (Oxford University Press, 5th ed, 2009) 165; Rachel Engle, 'Party Autonomy in International Arbitration: Where Uniformity Gives Way to Predictability' (2002) 15 *The Transnational Lawyer* 323, 328.
6 Ibid.
7 Loukas Mistelis, 'Reality Test: Current State of Affairs in Theory and Practice Relating to "Lex Arbitri"' (2006) 17(2) *American Review of International Arbitration* 155, 159.
8 Jeffrey Waincymer, *Procedure and Evidence in International Arbitration* (Kluwer Law International, 2012) 135.
9 See Case No. 5505 of 1987, Preliminary Award, Mozambique Buyer v Netherlands Seller (1988) XIII Y.B. Comm. Arb 110.
10 Jeffrey Waincymer, *Procedure and Evidence in International Arbitration* (Kluwer Law International, 2012) 130.

various provisions which could not readily be separated into boxes labelled substantive arbitration law or procedural law, because this would be an artificial division.[11]

Although this book recognises that procedural and substantive matters cannot always be clearly delineated and that jurisdictions have different views on this issue,[12] the general approach taken is similar to the *UNCITRAL Model Law*, in which arbitral proceedings are viewed as procedural as per Chapter V which, among other matters, includes the appointment of experts and evidentiary matters. Born notes that procedural issues which parties have the autonomy to determine also include 'existence and scope of discovery or disclosure, the modes for presentation of fact and expert evidence, the length of the hearing, the timetable of the arbitration and other matters.'[13] On the other hand, matters governed by substantive law are noted in Chapter VI of the *UNCITRAL Model Law*, which includes the merits of the dispute and the making of the arbitral award.

Party autonomy is crucial for the effective application of *Shariʻa*. This is because the rationale behind party autonomy is that contemporary ICA governs private disputes and therefore, parties have the autonomy to choose which laws govern one or more aspects of the arbitration.[14] Redfern and Hunter state that

> [i]t is generally recognised that parties to an international commercial agreement are free to choose for themselves the law (or the legal rules) applicable to that agreement. The doctrine of party autonomy, which was first developed by academic writers and then adopted by national courts, has gained extensive acceptance in national systems of law.[15]

More importantly for the purposes of this chapter, parties may also choose various international laws and customs as governing laws. Therefore, parties may choose *Shariʻa* in the following ways:

1   *Shariʻa* as the sole body of law governing both procedural and substantive issues;

---

11 Georgios Petrochilos, *Procedural Law in International Arbitration* (Oxford University Press, 2004) 8.

12 Waincymer, above n 10, 8–11. See generally, Alexander J. Belohlavek, Filip Cerny and Nadezda Rozehnalova, *Czech (& Central European) Yearbook of Arbitration 2013 – Borders of Procedural and Substantive Law in Arbitral Proceedings* (Juris Publishing, 2013).

13 Born, above n 3, 85.

14 Engle, above n 5, 335. See also, Mia Louise Livingstone, 'Party Autonomy in International Commercial Arbitration: Popular Fallacy or Proven Fact?' (2008) 25(5) *Journal of International Arbitration* 529.

15 Blackaby, et al., above n 4, 187.

2   a 'combined-law clause' pairing a national legal system with *Shari'a* or sub-
    jecting a national system to *Shari'a*;[16] or
3   *Shari'a* as part of a national legal system.[17]

Theoretically, the principle of party autonomy should grant parties the right to
choose *Shari'a* as their governing law in any of the above-mentioned ways. Party
autonomy, in fact, is one of the main advantages that contemporary ICA offers, as
well as striving to provide a neutral and flexible dispute resolution process, which
accommodates the commercial needs of culturally diverse parties.[18] Arts. 10, 11,
13 and 28 of the *UNCITRAL Model Law* are all examples of the autonomy parties
have to select the number of arbitrators, procedures for appointing and/or chal-
lenging arbitrators, and to select the substantive laws and seat of arbitration. Furthermore, during the drafting of the *UNCITRAL Model Law*, it was noted that:

> the most important principle on which the model law should be based in
> the freedom of the parties in order to facilitate the proper functioning of
> international commercial arbitration according to their expectations. This
> would allow them to freely submit their disputes to arbitration and to tailor
> the 'rules of the game' to their specific needs. It would also enable them
> to take full advantage of rules and policies geared to modern international
> arbitration practice as, for example, embodied in the *UNCITRAL Arbitra-
> tion Rules*.[19]

As will be discussed elsewhere in this book, if it is found that the arbitration has
not been conducted in accordance with the parties' agreement, then the arbitral
award may be set aside if Arts. II and V(1)(d) of the *New York Convention* apply,
and/or Art. 34(2)(iv) of the *UNCITRAL Model Law* is adopted. In fact, in
the 1950s, one of the main criticisms of the *Geneva Convention* was that it did
not place enough emphasis on party autonomy, and instead referred to the rules

---

16 See, e.g., *Shamil Bank of Bahrain v Beximco Pharm. Ltd.* [2004] EWCA Civ 19 (This case
    will be discussed further below). See also Sanghi Polyesters Ltd. (India) v. The International
    Investor KCSC (Kuwait) [2000] 1 Lloyd's Rep 480 (discussed in Chapter 6).
17 See, e.g., Glencore International AG v Metro Trading International Inc [2001] All ER
    (Comm) 103; Al Bassam v Al Bassam [2002] EWHC 2281; National Group for Commu-
    nications and Computers Ltd., Plaintiff, v. Lucent Technologies International Inc. 331 F.
    Supp. 2d 290 (D.N.J, 2004) (discussed further in Chapter 7); Musawi v RE International
    (UK) Ltd. & Ords [2007] EWHC 2981 (discussed further in this chapter). See also, Julio
    Colon, 'Choice of Law and Islamic Finance' (2011) 46 *Texas International Law Journal*
    411, 415; Faris Shehabi, 'Resolving Shariah Disputes – Navigating the Governing Law'
    (2015) 12(2) *Transnational Dispute Management* 1, 5–6.
18 Richard Garnett, et al., *A Practical Guide to International Commercial Arbitration* (Oceana
    Publications, 2000) 24.
19 'Report of the [UN] Secretary General: Possible Features of a Model Law on International
    Commercial Arbitration' UN Doc A/CN.9/207 (14 May 1981) XII UNCITRAL Year-
    book, 78, para 17 [emphasis added].

of procedure in the country where the arbitration took place.[20] As discussed in Chapters 1 and 2, most countries (including those countries where *Shariʿa* applies) are signatories to the *New York Convention*, and often base their laws on the *UNCITRAL Model Law*. Therefore, the concept of party autonomy, with the exceptions noted in this book, is generally accepted by both domestic and international arbitral rules and laws.

Born notes that

> [t]he parties' freedom to elect the manner in which they resolve their disputes is a basic aspect of individual autonomy and liberty, no different from the freedom to enter into contracts and other forms of association, which is properly accorded protection in almost all developed legal systems.[21]

The emphasis on party autonomy and the contractual nature of arbitration forms the basis for the 'contractualist' theory or school of thought in arbitration whereas, as discussed later, the contrasting 'jurisdictional' theory emphasises national law, the judicial nature of arbitrators and notes the limitations on party autonomy.[22] The better view is that arbitration is a hybrid in nature due to contemporary ICA's dual emphasis on party autonomy and the binding nature of arbitral awards due to the application of national laws.[23]

Regardless of how arbitration is characterised, party autonomy is also fundamental to contemporary ICA because – as opposed to litigation – it gives parties the flexibility to structure their arbitration in a manner which best suits the needs of their dispute.[24] Commentators also justify party autonomy on the basis of economic efficiency because

> individuals are assumed to be rational maximizers of their own welfare and to have idiosyncratic knowledge about their preferences unavailable to anybody else. Therefore, they do not enter a choice-of-law agreement unless they believe that it will make them better off.[25]

As will be discussed in later chapters, although from a *Shariʿa* perspective it is arguable that parties may select *Shariʿa*-based rules due to religious reasons as opposed to economic reasons, and may even be economically inefficient because

---

20 Born, above n 3, 1546.
21 Ibid., 132.
22 Ibid., 215.
23 Ibid., 215; Nathan Isaacs, 'Two Views of Commercial Arbitration' (1927) 40 *Harvard Law Review* 929, 930–940; Alan Scott Rau, 'The Culture of American Arbitration and the Lessons of ADR' (2005) 40(3) *Texas International Law Journal* 449, 451.
24 Born, above n 3, 85.
25 Giesela Rühl, 'Party Autonomy in the Private International Law of Contracts – Transatlantic Convergence and Economic Efficiency' in Eckart Gottschalk, et al. (eds), *Conflict of Laws in a Globalized World* (Cambridge University Press, 2007) 153, 177.

of the prohibition against interest in *Shariʿa*, it is also important to note that there are alternative remedies that are *Shariʿa*-compliant.

Furthermore, although this book does not delve into economic arguments, the development of *Shariʿa*-based arbitration rules including alternative *Shariʿa*-compliant remedies and arbitral institutions could potentially introduce alternatives into the contemporary ICA market, therefore increasing competition and facilitating economic development. This is because contemporary ICA and the rise of arbitral institutions and centres in the past 20 years has increased competition in relation to administrative fees paid by the parties, arbitrators chosen by the parties, international lawyers selected by parties, as well as numerous arbitration centres and rules, all of which has contributed to a competitive market in the area.[26] In fact, commentators argue that contemporary ICA is based on an 'efficient market model of dispute resolution' which applies principles of neoliberalism and free trade doctrines, as discussed in the Introduction to this book.[27] Lynch further explains that:

> [t]he "efficient market" model is exemplified by the *New York Convention* which limits state autonomy and power to regulate transactional commerce by granting commercial parties direct access to tribunals and empowering those tribunals to issue judgements which are binding within the domestic legal systems of states.[28]

However, as will be discussed later and in Chapter 8, the public policy provisions in the *New York Convention* recognise state sovereignty and therefore, contemporary ICA attempts to strike a balance between party autonomy and state sovereignty.

Due to party autonomy, before the arbitration commences, parties have the flexibility to include provisions in their arbitration agreement stipulating, for example, the form of the arbitration that takes place (ad hoc or institutional),[29] the procedure to be followed and the number of arbitrators to be appointed.[30] Even after the arbitration agreement has been drafted, the parties may also amend their arbitration agreement, as long as they do so before the

---

26 Katherine Lynch, *The Forces of Economic Globalization: Challenges to the Regime of International Commercial Arbitration* (Kluwer Law International, 2003) 21. See also Gillian Hadfield, 'The Public and the Private in the Provision of Law for Global Transactions' in Volkmar Gessner (ed), *Contractual Certainty in International Trade – Empirical Studies and Theoretical Debates on Institutional Support for Global Economic Exchanges* (Hart Publishing, 2009) 239, 251–254.
27 Lynch, above n 26, 89.
28 Ibid., 89 (emphasis added).
29 Carita Wallgren-Lindholm, 'Ad hoc Arbitration vs Institutional Arbitration' in Giuditta Cordero-Moss (ed), *International Commercial Arbitration: Different Forms and Their Features* (Cambridge University Press, 2013) 61–81.
30 See Michael Pryles, 'Limits to Party Autonomy in Arbitral Procedure' (2007) 24(3) *Journal of International Arbitration* 327, 328–333.

arbitration has commenced.[31] As will be discussed in the next chapter, parties can select their own arbitrators based on expertise and experience, a matter which is particularly relevant to arbitration conducted in accordance with *Shariʿa*, as opposed to a judge who may or may not have the relevant expertise in specific areas of specialities. Furthermore, the parties can also select specialised arbitral rules 'reflecting both commercial parties' desire for expertise and the exercise of their autonomy.'[32] Specialised arbitral rules in the context of *Shariʿa* will be discussed further below, as well as in Chapter 5. Upon commencement of the arbitration and establishment of the arbitral tribunal, the freedom of the parties may be limited because the parties often need the arbitral tribunal's consent to any further changes to the procedures outlined in their arbitration agreement.[33] The restrictions on party autonomy were also discussed when the *UNCITRAL Model Law* was being drafted. The report of the UN Secretary General noted that parties' freedom does not:

> accord absolute priority to the parties' wishes over any provision of the law. Their freedom should be limited by mandatory provisions designed to pre-vent or to remedy certain major defects in the procedure, any instance of denial of justice or violation of due process. Such restrictions would not be contrary to the interest of the parties, at least not of the weaker and disadvan-taged one in a given case. They would also meet the legitimate interest of the State concerned which could hardly be expected to issue the above guarantee without its fundamental ideas of justice being implemented.[34]

As will be discussed in more detail in the following chapters, limits to party auton-omy include the fact that the arbitration must: firstly, be valid according to the law governing the arbitration agreement; and secondly, not be contrary to public policy principles and mandatory rules.[35] For example, Art. 18 of the *UNIC-TRAL Model law* will be discussed in more detail in the next chapter because it states that parties be treated with equality, and given 'full opportunity' to present their case. Parties may also be restricted if they opt for institutional arbitration and amend the arbitral rules in a manner which is not accepted by the arbitral institution.[36]

Similarly, if parties do not provide clear directions then the arbitral tribunal must ascertain the applicable laws. For the purposes of this chapter, it is also

---

31 Ibid., 328.
32 Born, above n 3, 84.
33 Pryles, above n 30, 330.
34 Report of the '[UN] Secretary General: Possible Features of a Model Law on International Commercial Arbitration,' UN Doc A/CN.9/207 (14 May 1981) XII UNCITRAL Year-book, 78 [19].
35 See generally, Andrew Barraclough and Jeffrey Waincymer, 'Mandatory Rules of Law in International Commercial Arbitration' (2005) 6 *Melbourne Journal of International Law* 205.
36 Pryles, above n 30, 329.

important to note that the party's agreement will not be recognised if they select a governing law which is contrary to the public policy of the country in which it is enforced. For example, in the case of *Soleimany v Soleimany*,[37] the English Court of Appeal refused to enforce an arbitral award in which the contract allowed for the illegal smuggling of carpets out of Iran in contravention of Iranian law. This was despite the fact that the applicable law of the contract was Jewish law (*halakha*), and the contract was found to be valid according to the Beth Din (a Jewish court) in London. The English Court of Appeal determined the following:

> [t]he court is in our view concerned to preserve the integrity of its process, and to see that it is not abused. The parties cannot override that concern by private agreement. They cannot by procuring an arbitration conceal that they, or rather one of them, is seeking to enforce an illegal contract. Public policy will not allow it. In the present case the parties were, it would seem, entitled to agree to an arbitration before the Beth Din. It may be that they expected that the award, whatever it turned out to be, would be honoured without further argument. It may be that the plaintiff can enforce it in some place outside England and Wales. But enforcement here is governed by the public policy of the *lex fori*.[38]

Therefore, even if parties choose religious law, such as Jewish law or *Shari'a*, as the applicable law, a possible issue could include whether an arbitral award will be refused enforcement in a country where the application of religious law results in an outcome contrary to domestic public policy. Further, as examined in this chapter, another issue may be whether religious law will be recognised by secular courts as an *effective* body of law. Jewish law was recognised as the applicable law by British courts in *Soleimany v Soleimany* despite the finding of illegality. However, for various reasons discussed further in this chapter, there have been other cases, discussed later, where British courts have not recognised the application of religious law.

The balance between protecting party autonomy and the enforcement of arbitral awards was also recognised when the *UNCITRAL Model Law* was being contemplated, and the Secretary General stated:

> [i]t will be one of the more delicate and complex problems of the preparation of a model law to strike a balance between the interest of the parties to freely determine the procedure to be followed and the interests of the legal system expected to give recognition and effect thereto.[39]

---

37 [1999] QB 785.
38 Ibid., 800.
39 Report of the '[UN] Secretary General: Possible Features of a Model Law on International Commercial Arbitration,' UN Doc A/CN.9/207 (14 May 1981) XII UNCITRAL Yearbook, 78, para 21.

Renner also observes that 'limitations of party autonomy result from the fact that every legal order is deeply embedded in a historically grown conception of shared values and social order. They are based on the assumption that certain fundamental norms of society must not be left at the parties' disposal.'[40] Similarly, this chapter tries to assess if the application of *Shariʿa* in contemporary ICA achieves this balance by analysing whether: firstly, it is an effective governing law which parties may autonomously select; and secondly, in the event that parties fail to provide proper directions, whether *Shariʿa* may be selected by the arbitral tribunal as the applicable procedural or substantive law. Finally, this chapter examines whether *Shariʿa* is a body of law that will be recognised by domestic courts.

As well as respecting party autonomy, contemporary ICA aims to ensure that arbitral tribunals determine arbitral awards based on a legal system that is predictable, certain, comprehensive and commercially focused.[41] This approach ensures enforcement of the arbitral award in national courts, and increases predictability and certainty for the parties concerned. Therefore, even if parties have the autonomy to select the governing law, there may be situations where the parties have not clearly stipulated the applicable law or national courts may not recognise or may limit the party's choice of law.[42] For example, Engle notes that there may be cases where the parties select a law which is 'too foreign or difficult for proficient application in the forum's jurisdiction. Or perhaps, when applied, the chosen law will result in an arbitrary trade practice or regulation and consequently, a result unanticipated by the parties.'[43] In order to address whether *Shariʿa* is 'too foreign' and 'arbitrary' to apply to contemporary ICA or alternatively, whether it is a predictable, certain and commercially focused governing law, it is important to understand the historical attitude of tribunals and courts towards *Shariʿa*. For the purposes of this chapter, the approach of English cases in particular will be analysed as a case study because as discussed in more detail in the following sections, English courts have previously determined the issue of whether a national or religious law may be chosen by parties as the governing law. Therefore, English cases (arbitration and litigation cases) may highlight possible issues arising as a result of selecting a national and/or religious-legal systems as the governing law. Although this book focuses on arbitration, this chapter will also examine some English court cases because certain issues that arise in litigation cases, such as the issues of possible ambiguity and lack of codification, may also arise in arbitration. The following sections discuss these issues in more detail.

---

40 Moritz Renner, 'Private Justice, Public Policy: The Constitutionalization of International Commercial Arbitration' in Walter Mattlie and Thomas Dietz (eds), *International Arbitration and Global Governance: Contending Theories and Evidence* (Oxford University Press, 2014) 117, 119.
41 Born, above n 3, 2747.
42 Engle, above n 5, 335–336.
43 Ibid., 329, n 37. For example, in Syrian State Trading Org v. Ghanaian State Enterprise, ICC Case No. 4237 (1985) 10 Y.B. Comm. Arb 52, arguably the arbitral tribunal applied English law as opposed to Ghanian law because the latter was considered too foreign.

III Historical approach to *Shari'a* as the governing law

A First phase – (1945 to 1970s)

Early cases suggest that *Shari'a* was not viewed as sophisticated enough to be utilised in commercial arbitration. This is classified as the 'first phase' of the relationship between the Islamic and Western[44] world in the field of commercial arbitration by commentators Brower and Sharpe.[45] During this period, from the end of World War II until the 1970s, many nations were uninformed about the Islamic world and Islamic legal systems.[46] International arbitration in the Islamic world took place during this time because of disputes that arose out of long-term oil concessions, involving contracts, which were often concluded in circumstances described by Brower and Sharpe as 'colonial tutelage.'[47] During this period, African, Asian, Latin American and Arab nations took the view that arbitration was a 'foreign judicial institution imposed on them.'[48] In many cases, Western legal values were imposed in arbitration disputes on countries in the Middle East, which were viewed as being 'uncivilized.'

The most significant case that represents this attitude towards the Islamic world is *Petroleum Development (Trucial Coast) Ltd. v. Sheikh of Abu Dhabi* ('the Abu Dhabi Oil Arbitration case').[49] This case involved an oil concession dated to 1939, which was granted by the Sheikh of Abu Dhabi to Petroleum Development at a time when Abu Dhabi was a British protected State.[50] According to Lord Asquith, the contract had to be executed in Abu Dhabi, since it was agreed upon there and therefore, the law applicable was that of Abu Dhabi, which was based on *Shari'a*.[51] However, Lord Asquith noted that the Sheikh (leader) of Abu Dhabi was a feudal monarch who administered 'a purely discretionary justice with the assistance of the Koran; and it would be fanciful to suggest that in this very primitive region there is any settled body of legal principles applicable to the construction of modern commercial instruments.'[52] His Lordship also said that the terms of the contract 'invite, indeed prescribe, the application of principles rooted in the good sense and common practice of the generality of civilised

---

44 The term 'Western world' is used by Brower and Sharpe generally to refer to European nations, the United States of America, Australia and New Zealand. It is important to note that such terminology is subject to debate. See Samuel P. Huntington, *The Clash of Civilizations and the Remaking of World Order* (Simon & Schuster, 1996). Contra Edward Said, 'The Clash of Ignorance' (2001) 273(12) *The Nation* 11.

45 Charles Brower and Jeremy Sharpe, 'International Arbitration and the Islamic World: The Third Phase' (2003) 97 *The American Society of International Law* 643, 645.

46 Ibid., 645.

47 Ibid.

48 Redfern, et al., above n 5, 275.

49 *Petroleum Development (Trucial Coast) Ltd. v. Sheikh of Abu Dhabi* (1952) 19 *International & Comparative Law Quarterly* 247.

50 Ibid.

51 Ibid.

52 Ibid., 250–251.

nations – a sort of "modern law of nature".'[53] Although it was agreed that English municipal law was inapplicable, Lord Asquith conceded that 'some of its rules are . . . so firmly grounded in reason, as to form part of this broad body of jurisprudence' and that the principles were of 'ecumenical validity.'[54] Finally, Lord Asquith determined that the oil company had the right to extract oil from the seabed, which was adjacent to Abu Dhabi's territorial waters, but not from seabeds beyond these waters.[55]

Similar reasoning was followed in *Ruler of Qatar v International Marine Oil Company Ltd*[56] where the law of Qatar was the proper law governing the concession agreement; however, the arbitrator refused to apply the law of Qatar.[57] The reason for this was that the school of law followed in Qatar was the Hanbali School of Islamic law, which was seen as inappropriate in governing a modern oil concession agreement.[58] The arbitrator gave the following reasons for rejecting the application of *Shari'a*:

> there are at least two weighty considerations against that view. One is that in my opinion, after hearing the evidence of the two experts in Islamic law, Mr. Anderson and Professor Milliot, 'there is no settled body of legal principles in Qatar applicable to the construction of modern commercial instruments' to quote and adapt the words of Lord Asquith of Bishopstone.[59]

Therefore, the arbitrator referred to Lord Asquith's judgement in the *Petroleum Development (Trucial Coast) Ltd. v. Sheikh of Abu Dhabi* ('*Abu Dhabi Oil Arbitration case*') and further stated:

> I have no reason to suppose that Islamic law is not administered there [i.e. in Qatar] strictly, but I am satisfied that the law does not contain any principles which would be sufficient to interpret this particular contract.[60]

Such a simplistic view of *Shari'a* failed to take into account the multidimensional nature of this body of religious law as discussed in the previous chapter, as well as the extensive scholarship on finance and commerce under *Shari'a*. Furthermore, the parties' agreement stipulating the applicability of the law of Abu Dhabi and

53 Ibid.
54 Ibid.
55 (1952) 19 *International & Comparative Law Quarterly* 247, 259–261. See also Brower and Sharpe, above n 45, 644.
56 (1953) 20 ILR 534.
57 Ibid., 534–547.
58 Ibid., 534. See also Nudrat Majeed, 'Good Faith and Due Process: Lessons from the Shari'ah' (2004) 20(1) *Arbitration International* 97, 102.
59 Ibid., 544.
60 Ibid., 545. See also, *Petroleum Development (Trucial Coast) Ltd. v. Sheikh of Abu Dhabi* (1951) 19 ILR 144.

Qatar was not respected. Consequently, this contributed to the further misunderstanding of Muslim countries during this era.

This reasoning was also followed in *Aramco v Saudi Arabia*[61] ('the Aramco Award') where an arbitration took place between the government of Saudi Arabia and the Arabian American Oil Company ('Aramco') regarding the interpretation of a concession agreement made in 1933. According to the arbitration agreement, Saudi law would be the governing law in relation to matters falling within the jurisdiction of Saudi Arabia. Saudi law was further defined under Art. 4 of the arbitration agreement as a legal system based on *Shari'a* in accordance with the Hanbali school of thought.[62] However, the arbitral tribunal supported Aramco's argument that Saudi law should not be applied:

> The regime of mining concessions, and consequently, also of oil concessions has remained embryonic in Moslem law [sic] and is not the same in the different schools. The principles of one school cannot be introduced into another, unless this is done by an act of authority. Hanbali law contains no precise rule about mining concessions.[63]

Baamir comments that:

> [t]he tribunal demonstrated a lack of knowledge regarding Islamic law and denied the application of Saudi law in the dispute, claiming that Saudi law had no rules for governing concessions . . . [t]he arbitration took place at a time when there was a total lack of awareness regarding *Shari'a* law in the international legal community. Neither arbitrator was an expert in either concession agreements or *Shari'a* law.[64]

An example of the incorrect understanding of *Shari'a* applied by the tribunal, for example, was that only one school of thought can be applied by the courts. As discussed in the previous chapter, although one school may be the prevailing opinion, Saudi judicial officers also have the discretion to consider other schools of thought. In fact, scholars from the four schools of thought often consulted each other during classical times when formulating opinions, and the founder of the Hanbali school, Ahmad ibn Muhammad ibn Hanbal, was a student of the founder of the Shafi'i school, Idris al-Shafi'i.

The Aramco Award also resulted in the Saudi government mistrusting private international law. Before the Aramco Award, the Saudi government encouraged both private parties and the government to resolve international disputes through arbitration. However, the Aramco Award contributed towards the Saudi

61 *Saudi Arabia v Arabian American Oil Company (Aramco)* (1958) 27 ILR 117.
62 Ibid., 154.
63 Ibid., 163.
64 Abdulrahman Yahya Baamir, 'Saudi Arabia' in Gordon Blanke and Habib Al Mulla (eds), *Arbitration in the MENA* (Juris Publishing, 2016), SA-15 and SA-16.

government viewing the arbitration process with suspicion. For this reason, Resolution of No. 58 of 1963 was passed by the government, which prohibited the Saudi government from entering into arbitration:

> [n]o government agency shall conclude a contract with any individual, company or private organisation that includes a clause subjecting the government agency to any foreign court of law or any judiciary body. Except in concessions granted by the Government, no government agency shall accept arbitration as a means of settling disputes that may arise between it and any individual, company or private organization. The most important principle of private international law is the principle of application of the law of the place of performance; government agencies may therefore not choose any foreign law to govern their relationship with any individual, company or private organization. The above provisions shall apply to contracts concluded after the issuance of this resolution.[65]

This Resolution has been adopted by the new *Saudi Arbitration Law 2012*, under Art. 10.2 which stipulates that: '[g]overnment bodies may not agree to arbitration unless after approval of Prime Ministers, unless there is legal provision permits that.' Therefore, the mistrust created during the first phase still impacts upon contemporary ICA, consisting of the recently introduced Saudi arbitration legal regime which aims to follow the *UNCITRAL Model Law*. As will be discussed in more detail later, it is also interesting to note that arbitral tribunals have also misunderstood *Shariʿa* in the contemporary era of ICA, which can have an impact on the objective of achieving mutual respect and understanding between *Shariʿa* and contemporary ICA. In fact, the argument that classical *Shariʿa* is inconsistent with contemporary ICA standards or that it does not comprise a comprehensive body of law to govern arbitration will be further discussed throughout this book.

B Second phase – (1970s to 1980s)

The second phase is defined by Brower and Sharpe as enduring from the 1970s and until the early 1980s.[66] During this era, the Libyan government nationalised the properties of three foreign oil companies. Such nationalisations were publicly proclaimed by Colonel Muammar Abu Minyar al-Gaddafi as a reaction to the foreign policy positions taken by the United Kingdom and the United States of America.[67] The refusal of Libya to participate in such cases signifies the ideological

---

65 Resolution of No. 58 of 1963 as cited in ibid), SA-18. See also Fahad Al Dehais, 'Saudi Arabia' (20 April 2016) *Global Arbitration Review* (online) <http://globalarbitrationreview.com/chapter/1036981/saudi-arabia>.
66 Brower and Sharpe, above n 45, 644.
67 Arthur Gemmell, 'Commercial Arbitration in the Middle East' (2006) 5 *Santa Clara Journal of International Law* 169, 177.

clash between the 'developed' and 'developing' world during this era.[68] The three Libyan nationalisation cases were *BP Exploration,*[69] *TOPCO*[70] and *LIAMCO.*[71] These cases dealt with disputes over oil concessions granted by the Libyan national governments to Western oil companies. Each concession agreement included an arbitration clause, which included a choice of law provision under which the relevant international law and Libyan law would govern.[72] The three arbitrations that arose from these cases all had identical factual backgrounds, legal documents and choice of law provisions.[73]

In the *BP Exploration* case, the sole arbitrator, Arbitrator Lagergren, held that the expropriation of BP's properties and interests in Libya violated international law as well as Libyan law due to its discriminatory nature.[74] Arbitrator Lagergren was influenced by the principles of the *Chorzow Factory* case,[75] and awarded the remedy of damages in full rather than restitution, due to the unlawful nature of the expropriation.[76]

Libya was also unsuccessful in the *TOPCO* arbitration where the sole arbitrator held that Libya's expropriation was unlawful, and determined that *restitutio in integrum* was the preferred remedy under Libyan and international law.[77] The relevance of procedural law in this case was the question of choice of law, and the fact that international procedural law, rather than Libyan law, was deemed to be the appropriate law. The arbitrator held that he had general broad powers which would allow him to decide the procedural rules.[78] In the *LIAMCO* case the sole arbitrator found no 'purely discriminatory' intent under the concession agreements.[79] However, he determined that Libya was bound by its contractual obligations, and *LIAMCO* was awarded equitable compensation on the basis of lost profits.[80]

According to Arthur Gemmell, the reasoning in these cases was bewildering to Middle Eastern arbitral observers, and baffling to Western scholars, who noted several inconsistencies.[81] During the first and second phases, many in the Islamic world looked at the Western arbitral process with mistrust due to the logic and rationales that were often used in these cases. Arbitrators were often cynical of the local law, especially Islamic law, which was seen as 'uncivilized.'

---

68 Brower and Sharpe, above n 45, 646.
69 BP Exploration Co. (Libya) v Libyan Arab Republic (1979) 53 ILR 297.
70 Texas Overseas Petroleum Co. [TOPCO] v Libyan Arab Republic (1978) 17 ILM 1.
71 Libyan American Oil Co. v the Government of the Libyan Arab Republic (1981) 20 ILM 1.
72 Gemmell, above n 67, 177.
73 Ibid., 177.
74 BP Exploration Co. (Libya) v Libyan Arab Republic (1979) 53 ILR 297.
75 Factory at Chorzow (Germany v Poland) [1927] PCIJ (ser A) No 9 (July 26) 5.
76 BP Exploration Co. (Libya) v Libyan Arab Republic (1979) 53 ILR 297, 339–370.
77 Texas Overseas Petroleum Co. [TOPCO] v Libyan Arab Republic (1978) 17 ILM 1, 40–41.
78 Ibid., 20–25, 40–49.
79 Libyan American Oil Co. v the Government of the Libyan Arab Republic (1981) 20 ILM 1, 36.
80 Ibid., 44–52.
81 Gemmell, above n 67, 178.

C Third phase – (present time)

The remainder of this chapter discusses the third (and present) phase of the Islamic Middle East's relationship with international arbitration, consisting of the region's increasing recognition in international commerce as a substantial exporter, and a major area for foreign investment.[82] As discussed in Chapter 1, during this period, it is evident that the region began making efforts to expand its economic opportunities by attracting investors. As also discussed in Chapter 1, many jurisdictions provide for *Shari'a* as a source of law, despite adopting the common law or civil law tradition. For this reason, *Shari'a* may be selected to apply as the governing law of an arbitration agreement, either directly by itself, as part of a chosen national legal system or in combination with a national legal system. The global rise of Islamic finance techniques also gave rise to the choice of *Shari'a* as the governing law in commercial arbitration disputes and litigation. This raises various issues, including whether *Shari'a* can be an effective choice of law; the willingness of an arbitral tribunal to interpret *Shari'a* and apply it to arbitral awards; and whether conflict of law principles prevent *Shari'a* from being selected. All these issues will be discussed further below, using English courts as a case study. In particular, the following will be discussed: (1) *Shari'a* as the choice of law in arbitration agreements; and (2) choice of *Shari'a* as substantive law in international arbitration.

IV *Shari'a* as the choice of law governing arbitration agreements

This section addresses whether *Shari'a* is or can be a valid and effective choice of law to govern an international arbitration agreement. The law governing an arbitration agreement impacts matters such as scope, validity and interpretation of the international arbitration agreement.[83] As discussed earlier, due to the separability presumption, an arbitration agreement may be governed by a different law than that of the underlying contract.[84] Furthermore, determining the law governing the arbitration agreement can often be a complex process, as parties often fail to identify the applicable law.[85] The question as to whether *Shari'a* can be chosen as the governing law of an arbitration agreement is also the subject of debate. The validity of an arbitration agreement is crucial to the arbitration process and consequently, it is vital for parties to consider whether *Shari'a* will be recognised by arbitral tribunals and national courts as an effective body of governing law. Although there is much commentary and regulation about whether a national law can govern the merits of an arbitration dispute, the

---

82 Brower and Sharpe, above n 45, 646.
83 Born, above n 3, 471–472.
84 Ibid., 475.
85 Ibid., 472.

role of anational law as the governing law for an arbitration agreement is not as clear.[86]

For example, the *New York Convention* provides under Art. V(1)(a) that an arbitral award may be refused if 'the said [arbitration] agreement is not valid under the law to which the parties have subjected it or, failing any indication thereon, under the law of the country where the award was made.' The question of whether the 'law' referred to in this Article consists of anational law, or more specifically whether *Shariʻa* is recognised as proper 'law,' is not entirely clear. As will be discussed further, in the context of choice of substantive law, some commentators and national courts have argued that arbitral tribunals should not select non-national law unless the parties have agreed otherwise.[87] However, it has also been argued that a reference to law also includes a reference to 'rules of law.'[88] Some commentators argue that the latter rationale should also hold for the application of anational law to arbitration agreements.[89] This is further supported by the theory that parties have autonomy in international commercial arbitration to select the law governing their arbitration agreement. However, as noted previously and further discussed later, it is less clear whether religious law can govern arbitration agreements.

This lack of clarity is also evident in the English case of *Halpern*.[90] The *Halpern* case concerned an appeal from arbitration proceedings brought before a Beth Din and under Jewish law. In the appeal, Waller J considered whether Jewish law could be considered as an applicable law under English conflict of laws principles. Waller J held that Jewish law could not be expressly or impliedly chosen as the applicable law of the contract, as the parties must expressly choose the law of a country.[91] Therefore, English law was the applicable law of the contract, and Jewish law could be incorporated as an aid to interpretation.[92] As one commentator, Hook, observes,

[i]f the decision in *Halpern* is followed, any implied or express choice of anational law to govern the arbitration agreement will have to be overridden . . .

86 Maria Hook, 'Arbitration Agreements and Anational Law: A Question of Intent?' (2011) 28 *Journal of International Arbitration* 175, 180; See generally, Kilian Balz, 'Islamic Law as Governing Law Under the Rome Convention. Universalist Lex Mercatoria v. Regional Unification of Law' (2001) 6 *Uniform Law Review* 37.

87 Born, above n 3, 2663; Andreas Junius, 'Islamic Finance: Issues Surrounding Islamic Finance as a Choice of Law Under German Conflict of Laws Principles' (2006) 7 *Chicago Journal of International Law* 537; Howard Holtzmann and Joseph Neuhaus, *A Guide to the UNCITRAL Model Law on International Commercial Arbitration: Legislative History and Commentary* (Kluwer Law International, 1989) 770.

88 Hook, above n 86, 180; see also François Dessemontet, 'Emerging Issues in International Arbitration: The Application of Soft Law, Halakha and Sharia by International Arbitral Tribunals' (2012) 23 *American Review of International Arbitration* 545.

89 Hook, above n 86, 180.

90 Halpern v Halpern [2008] Q.B. 195.

91 Ibid., 205–206.

92 Ibid., 208–215.

and to arbitrarily dismiss this choice of law on the basis that arbitration agreements cannot be governed by anational law is fraught with difficulties.[93]

Other English commentators are also unclear on whether Jewish law may govern arbitration agreements in light of *Halpern*. In Dicey, Morris and Collins, it is noted that

> [p]arties are free under s 46(1)(b) to choose a non-national system to govern the substance of the contract. However, an arbitration agreement must be governed by a national legal system. This may lead to different applicable law for the arbitration agreement even where parties have made an express choice of law to govern the substantive contract.[94]

Furthermore, Merkin and Flannery's commentary on the *Arbitration Act* 1996 provides that

> [t]he parties are free to choose the applicable law to an arbitration agreement, more or less without restraint, although it must be the law of a country . . . [i]f there is no express or implied choice of law governing the arbitration agreement, the court must apply the law of the country with which the agreement has "the closest and most real connection."[95]

In the case of *Deutsche Schachtbau-und*,[96] counsel for the defendants argued that:

> enforcement of the arbitrators' award should be refused under section 5(3) of the Act of 1975 on the ground of public policy. The proper law of the contract, even if not of the arbitration agreement contained therein, was the law of R'As al-Khaimah, for the reasons stated above. Notwithstanding this, the arbitrators chose to apply, as the substantive law in the arbitration, what they described as 'accepted principles of law governing contractual relations.' This was contrary to public policy, as understood in England, for the fundamental reason that it is impossible to know what the alleged principles of

---

93 Hook, above n 86, 177. As discussed below, this case also discussed the Rome Convention and the Rome I Regulation. See Regulation (EC) No 593/2008 of the European Parliament and of the Council of 17 June 2008 on the Law Applicable to Contractual Obligations (Rome I) [2008] OJ L 177/6.

94 Professor C.G. J.Morse, Professor David McClean and Lord Collins of Mapesbury, *Dicey, Morris and Collins on the Conflict of Laws* (Sweet & Maxwell, 15th ed, 2012) 837.

95 Robert Merkin and Louis Flannery, *Arbitration Act 1996* (Informa Law, 5th ed, 2014) 208.

96 Deutsche Schachtbau- und Tiefbohrgesellschaft mbH v Ras Al Khaimah National Oil Co and another appeal [1987] 2 All ER 769. Reversed on other grounds in Deutsche Schachtbau-und Tiefbohr GmbH v Ras al Khaimah National Oil Co & Shell International Petroleum Co Ltd.; sub nom Deutsche Schachtbau-und Tiefbohrgesellschaft mbH v Ras Al Khaimah National Oil Co [1990] 1 AC 295.

law are with any precision. The arbitrators cannot therefore be regarded as having applied any law at all.[97]

Regardless, the court rejected the above-mentioned argument, and determined that application of 'accepted principles of law governing contractual relations' did not impact on the enforceability of the arbitral award in England because:

> [b]y choosing to arbitrate under the rules of the ICC and, in particular, article 133, the parties have left the proper law to be decided by the arbitrators and have not in terms confined the choice to national systems of law. I can see no basis for concluding that the arbitrators' choice of proper law, a common denominator of principles underlying the laws of the various nations governing contractual relations, is outwith [sic] the scope of the choice which the parties left to the arbitrators.[98]

It is therefore possible for parties to agree to anational law and this view was also followed by Langeley J in *Peterson Farms v. C&M*[99] who relied on s 46(1)(b) of the *Arbitration Act 1996* (UK), which states that '[t]he arbitral tribunal shall decide the dispute . . . (b)if the parties so agree, in accordance with such other considerations as are agreed by them or determined by the tribunal.' As mentioned previously, some commentators have taken a different approach to this section. Nonetheless, Born comments that:

> [a]lmost all contemporary authorities recognise the autonomy of parties to select the law applicable to the formation and substantive validity of their international arbitration agreement . . . [t]his general principle applies with particular force to international arbitration agreements, where party autonomy enjoys special status, and is confirmed by both international treaties and national arbitration legislation.[100]

Therefore, the reasoning of *Halpern* and the English commentary noting that the governing law of an arbitration agreement can only be the law of a country is unsound. Firstly, in the English jurisdiction, s 46(1)(b) the *Arbitration Act 1996* states that parties may agree to 'other considerations.' Secondly, the *Rome 1 Regulation* does not apply to arbitration agreements under Art. 1.2 (d) and therefore, the argument used by Waller J in *Halpern* that the *Rome Convention*

---

97 Deutsche Schachtbau-und Tiefbohr GmbH v Ras al Khaimah National Oil Co & Shell International Petroleum Co Ltd.; sub nom Deutsche Schachtbau-und Tiefbohrgesellschaft mbH v Ras Al Khaimah National Oil Co [1990] 1 AC 295, 302.

98 Deutsche Schachtbau- und Tiefbohrgesellschaft mbH v Ras Al Khaimah National Oil Co and another appeal [1987] 2 All ER 769, 780.

99 Hook, above n 86, 184.

100 Born, above n 3, 559.

forbids parties from choosing a law other than that of a country does not apply to arbitration agreements.

As will be discussed in more detail later, if the *Rome I Regulation* applied to the underlying contract (as opposed to the arbitration agreement) and in the event of a conflict, it was decided that the law of the contract applied to the arbitration agreement, Recital 13 of the *Rome I Regulation* may allow parties to incorporate a non-State body of law into their contracts.[101] The *Rome 1 Regulation* was passed shortly after the decision and Waller J did comment on the proposed amendment allowing for a non-State body of law (which is now Recital 13) by stating that such an amendment was unlikely to be incorporated.[102] Waller J further noted in *Halpern* that even if this amendment was incorporated 'it is difficult to think that it could go further than assist interpretation, since remedies, if they were to be effective, would have to flow from a system of law in the sense of a law of a country.'[103] This statement is unclear as it fails to address a situation where an anational body of law regulates remedies.

In summary, there are two views: (1) the view of commentators such as Merkin and Flannery[104] who believe that, according to the *Arbitration Act 1996*, the law of a country should apply to arbitration agreements, and that of Waller J in *Halpern* who argues that the *Rome I Regulation* forbids parties from choosing anational law to govern arbitration agreements and (2) the better view of commentators such as Hook,[105] who argues that anational law may apply to arbitration agreements and notes that the *Rome I Regulation* only applies to contracts, and that Recital 13 allows for the incorporation of anational law into the contract. This will be discussed in more detail in the context of conflict of law principles in the next section.

A Conflict of law principles governing arbitration agreements

The choice of law governing an international arbitration agreement is further complicated by the fact that parties often do not identify the law governing the arbitration agreement.[106] This is because international commercial contracts sometimes contain a choice of law clause which applies to the underlying contract and does not refer to the arbitration agreement separately under the doctrine

---

101 As discussed further in this chapter, there is a technical difference between incorporating State law and non-State law into a contract. See also Born, above n 3, 2758; Adrian Briggs, *Agreements on Jurisdiction and Choice of Law* (Oxford Private International Law Series, 2008) 393.

102 Halpern v Halpern [2008] Q.B. 195, 215 [39].

103 Ibid.

104 Robert Merkin and Louis Flannery, *Arbitration Act 1996* (Informa Law, 5th ed, 2014) 208.

105 Hook, above n 86, 177.

106 Born, above n 3, 490. See generally, Carlo Croff, 'The Applicable Law in an International Commercial Arbitration: Is It Still a Conflict of Laws Problem?' (1982) 16(4) *The International Lawyer* 613.

of separation.[107] As mentioned earlier in the *Halpern* case, Waller J noted that Jewish law could not be expressly or impliedly chosen by the parties according to English conflict of law principles.[108] Furthermore, according to English conflict of law principles, if parties have not expressly or impliedly agreed to the law governing the arbitration agreement, then it may be governed by the law of the place where the arbitration has a seat,[109] or the law of the underlying contract.[110] Merkin and Flannery argue that only the 'law of a country' with which parties have the closest connection should be applied in the event that there is no agreement.[111] Marc Blessing argues that any of nine potential laws could apply to an arbitration clause, including anational law.[112] Blessing contends that it is important to determine the law which is 'subjectively fair' and meets the 'objectively reasonable expectations of each of one of the parties.'[113] The problem with this approach is that it involves nuances regarding what is considered 'fair' and 'reasonable.' There is uncertainty about which approach a tribunal or court should take in determining the applicable law of the arbitration agreement. This will inevitably have an impact on whether *Shariʻa* will be chosen by a tribunal or court in the event of a conflict.

If Blessing's approach is applied, then it may be argued that *Shariʻa* may be chosen by a tribunal or court if they find that *Shariʻa* would be subjectively fair, and aligns with the reasonable expectations of the parties. On the other hand, in the context of English conflict of law principles, if the arbitration is governed by the law of the underlying contract, then Waller J's approach in *Halpern* will not recognise *Shariʻa* as the applicable law. This view was also taken in the English case of *Beximco*.[114] In the *Beximco* case, the governing law stated '[s]ubject to the principles of the Glorious *Shariʻa*, this Agreement shall be governed by and construed in accordance with the laws of England.' In an appeal to the England and Wales Court of Appeal, Justice Potter stated that:

Article 1.1 of the *Rome Convention* makes it clear that the reference to the parties' choice of the law to govern a contract is a reference to the law of a country. There is no provision for the choice or application of a non-national system of law such as *Shariʻa* law.[115]

107 Born, above n 3, 490.
108 Halpern v Halpern [2008] Q.B. 195, 210 [26].
109 Professor C. G. J. Morse, Professor David McClean and Lord Collins of Mapesbury, *Dicey, Morris and Collins on the Conflict of Laws* (Sweet & Maxwell, 15th ed, 2012) 834.
110 C v D [2007] EWCA Civ 1282, [22]; Balz, above n 86, 44.
111 Merkin and Flannery, above n 104, 208.
112 Marc Blessing, 'The Law Applicable to the Arbitration Clause and Arbitrability' in A. J. van den Berg (ed), *Improving the Efficiency of Arbitration Agreements and Awards: 40 Years of Application of New York Convention* (Kluwer Law International, 1999) 168–170.
113 Ibid.
114 [2004] EWCA Civ 19.
115 Ibid., [40].

Commentators, such as Chuah, argued that the *Beximco* case confirmed 'that the *Rome Convention* does not allow non-country specific law to be the applicable law of the contract. Parties to a contract cannot choose *Sharia* law *per se* or English law as guided by Sharia principles.'[116]

On the other hand, as noted previously, other commentators such as Hook and Born argue that this may no longer be the case, as Recital 13 of the *Rome I Regulation* clearly stipulates that '[t]his Regulation does not preclude parties from incorporating by reference into their contract a non-State body of law or an international convention.'[117] Alternatively, it may be argued that Recital 13 refers to a 'body of law' and therefore 'principles which do not constitute a body as such are not permitted.'[118] It is further argued by commentators that whether *Shari'a* constitutes a 'body of law' under Recital 13 is unclear, because the intention for this Recital was to allow the incorporation of International Institute for the Unification of Private Law ('*UNIDROIT*') *Principles of International Commercial Contracts 2010* ('UNDROIT Principles')[119] and Principles of European Contract Law[120] which are viewed as being comprehensive.[121] Therefore, initially the proposal was that the Recital should read 'the principles and rules of the substantive law of contract recognised internationally or in the community' and it was argued that religious law and *lex mercatoria* did not fit into this category.[122] However, due to uncertainty in relation to what was recognised internationally, or in the community, this proposal was dropped.[123] If Recital 13 should reflect the original intent of the former proposal, then *Shari'a* may not be considered a substantive contract law, or a body of law recognised internationally or by the community, because similar to *lex mercatoria*, it may not be viewed as being specific enough, or a set of codified law recognised by the community.[124]

Therefore, one argument is that the former proposal of Recital 13 was dropped for a reason, and the current Recital 13 has a wider ambit and subsequently, allows for non-State body of law including religious law and *lex mercatoria*.[125]

---

116 Jason Chuah, 'Islamic Principles Governing International Trade Financing Instruments: A Study of the Morabaha in English Law' (2006) 27(1) *Northwestern Journal of International Law & Business* 137, 168.

117 Born, above n 3, 2758.

118 Rob Merkin, 'The Rome I Regulation and Reinsurance' (2009) 5 *Journal of Private International Law* 69, 76.

119 International Institute for the Unification of Private Law ('UNIDROIT'), UNDROIT Principles of International Commercial Contracts 2010 <www.unidroit.org/instruments/commercial-contracts/unidroit-principles-2010>.

120 Lex Mercatoria Database, *Principles of European Contract Law* (2002) <www.jus.uio.no/lm/eu.contract.principles.parts.1.to.3.2002/>.

121 Jason Chuah, 'Impact of Islamic Law on Commercial Sale Contracts – a Private International Law Dimension in Europe' (2010) 4 *European Journal of Commercial Contract Law* 191, 195.

122 Briggs, above n 101, 393.

123 Ibid., 393.

124 Chuah, above n 121, 195.

125 Ibid., 195.

The other argument is that Recital 13 is limited to a 'body of law' which is recognised internationally and by the community, as this reflects the original intent of the recital and is consistent with Art. 1.1 of the previous *Rome Convention*, which notes that only the 'law of a country' may apply to a contract. This interpretation of the previous *Rome Convention* was applied in the cases of *Beximco*, *Halpern* and *Musawi v R.E. International (UK) Ltd.*[126] Furthermore, the purpose of Recital 13 is to support Recital 14 which allows the European Union to introduce substantive contract law such as the European Contract Law.[127] Thus, it is unclear whether the choice of *Shari'a* is permitted under Recital 13 of the new *Rome I Regulation*, especially in light of the fact that Recital 16 states that '[t]o contribute to the general objective of this Regulation, legal certainty in the European judicial area, the conflict-of law rules should be highly foreseeable.'[128] Although a strong argument may be made for Recital 13 to be interpreted to allow *Shari'a* to govern a contract because it may be classified as a non-State body of law, it may be more difficult to prove that *Shari'a* is a highly foreseeable body of law which would promote legal certainty. This issue will be discussed in more detail in the following section.

V Choice of *Shari'a* as substantive law in international arbitration

This section looks at the validity and effectiveness of *Shari'a* as the substantive law of the contract (as opposed to the arbitration agreement) in an international arbitration. Although the concept of party autonomy implies that parties may choose *Shari'a* as the law applicable to the substance of a dispute, further complexities arise in regards to whether *Shari'a* is an effective choice of law in the context of commercial arbitration. This is because the most common choice of law provision selected by parties is the law of a nation state or country.[129] Whether *Shari'a* is an effective choice of governing law is not dissimilar to the discussion in regards to the choice of *lex mercatoria*, amiable composition, or other forms of non-national law to govern the merits of a dispute.[130] In fact, the issue of whether anational law is an effective choice of law in an arbitration agreement has been the subject of much debate, and whilst European civil law countries are generally supportive of *lex mercatoria*, common law countries such as England are generally critical.[131]

For example, Lord Mustill notes that although *lex mercatoria* is generally based on sources such as general principles of law, international customs and usages, the

---

126 [2007] EWHC 2981.
127 Chuah, above n 121, 195.
128 Ibid., 195.
129 Garnett, et al., above n 18, 24.
130 Ibid., 24.
131 Richard Garnett, 'International Arbitration Law: Progress Towards Harmonisation' (2002) 3 *Melbourne Journal of International Law* 400, 411.

expansion of the international business community makes it difficult to ascertain international legal principles which are common to nation states.[132] Further, it is difficult to predict outcomes in situations where rules of *lex mercatoria* have not yet been established. Apart from these practical problems, Pryles notes the following philosophical questions regarding the *lex mercatoria*, '[f]rom where does it derive its authority? Does it have the organisation, conceptual framework and detailed rules which would be expected of a legal system?'[133]

On the other hand, proponents of the *lex mercatoria* argue that there is no reason why the rules of a governing law must be organised in an orderly legal manner, and that certain transnational laws, such as the UNDROIT Principles, may be more desirable for the parties concerned.[134] Similarly, Art. 28(1) of the *UNCITRAL Model Law* stipulates:

> The arbitral tribunal shall decide the dispute in accordance with such *rules of law*[135] as are chosen by the parties as applicable to the substance of the dispute. Any designation of the law or legal system of a given State shall be construed, unless otherwise expressed, as directly referring to the substantive law of that State and not to its conflict of laws rules.

Thus, Art. 28 provides parties with the autonomy to choose non-national laws in their choice of law agreements. This interpretation was also applied in the case of *Musawi* which applied the cases of *DST v Raknok* and *Home and Overseas Insurance Co Ltd* to state that in the context of arbitration, s 46(1)(b) of the *English Arbitration Act 1996* allowed for non-national laws.[136] It is clear that parties may choose non-national law such as the *lex mercatoria*, transnational law, and religious law such as *Shari'a* as the substantive law governing their contract. However, the following two issues arise and they will be discussed further below:

1   The role of *Shari'a* in the event that parties have not chosen the applicable law to govern the substantial dispute, and when the arbitration is subject to review by national courts; and
2   Whether *Shari'a* is an effective and advisable choice of law. Is it detailed, consistent and thorough enough to govern contemporary ICA matters? As critics of the *lex mercatoria* note, where does the legal system derive its authority and what is the conceptual framework of such a body of law? This question is extremely pertinent in the context of *Shari'a*, as various scholars have debated the answers.

132   Michael Pryles, 'Application of the Lex Mercatoria in International Commercial Arbitration' (2008) 31 *UNSW Law Journal* 319, 324.
133   Ibid., 325.
134   Ibid., 324.
135   Emphasis added.
136   Musawi v RE International (UK) Ltd. & Ords [2007] EWHC 2981, [22] [23].

A *Conflict of laws and Shariʿa as the substantive law*

In contrast to Art. 28(1) of the *UNCITRAL Model Law* which notes that parties may select 'rules of law' to govern their arbitration, Art. 28(2) stipulates '[f]ailing any designation by the parties, the arbitral tribunal shall apply the law determined by the conflict of laws rules which it considers applicable.' Some commentators have argued that this means that arbitrators may not apply non-national legal systems in the event that there is a conflict.[137] Others have argued that Art. 28(1) and Art. 28(2) should be read in harmony, thus Art. 28(2) is taken to refer to 'rules of law' and not only the law of a nation state. Arbitral tribunals should be able to apply the 'rules of law' they consider appropriate because the consequences of this would be that the tribunal is considered independent from legal systems and conflict of law rules.[138] Further, this approach would conform to the practice of international commercial arbitration, such that an arbitral tribunal typically ascertains the substantive law by direct means rather than a particular set of conflict of laws.[139] Arbitration legislation in Switzerland, Canada, India, Algeria and Lebanon has modified Art. 28(2) of the Model Law to include 'rules of law' so that arbitrators may select a non-national legal system or rules to govern a dispute if the parties are unable to reach agreement.[140]

However, countries such as the United Kingdom, Germany and Japan refuse to follow this approach, and it is argued that unlike the parties who have autonomy to select which laws or rules of law should govern the merits of the dispute, arbitral tribunals do not have the authority to select non-national law in the absence of agreement by the parties.[141] This is because a more cautious approach should be taken by arbitral tribunals in order to ensure predictability and certainty in regards to the laws selected and imposed on the parties.[142] Born makes the convincing argument that even if tribunals do have the authority to select non-national legal systems, they 'generally fail to provide predictable results, particularly insofar as complex commercial and corporate affairs are concerned.'[143]

Similarly, Redfern and Hunter argue that the choice of national law ensures foreseeability, and Poudret and Besson further observe that parties can easily identify the content of national laws.[144] Since commercial parties are reluctant to choose non-national legal systems to govern their arbitration, arbitral tribunals generally do not impose a non-national legal system in the event that there is not an agreement.[145] Furthermore, if the non-national legal system is not codified,

---

137 Born, above n 3, 2663.
138 Holtzmann and Neuhaus, above n 87, 769.
139 Ibid., 769.
140 Born, above n 3, 2664.
141 Ibid., 2663. See also, Junius, above n 87.
142 Holtzmann and Neuhaus, above n 87, 770. See generally, Junius, above n 87.
143 Born, above n 3, 2663.
144 Jean-François Poudret and Sébastien Besson, *Comparative Law of International Arbitration* (Sweet & Maxwell, 2nd ed, 2007) 576.
145 Born, above n 3, 2664.

it is difficult to ascertain which principles or rules apply.[146] It is argued that non-national legal systems may be a more effective choice of law in areas of public international law and human rights, where general principles of international law are often applied.[147] Born further states that in the commercial context, parties require well-developed commercial laws to govern the dispute in order to ensure predictability and consistency.[148] The question then becomes whether *Shari'a* is an effective choice of law which ensures foreseeability and consistency.

B Is Shari'a an effective choice of law?

As discussed previously, despite having the autonomy to choose non-national law, parties usually choose a national legal system to govern the substance of their dispute, because they prefer a governing law which is predictable, comprehensive and commercially focused.[149] Many argue that religious law such as *Shari'a* may be contradictory in specific matters and subject to various interpretations, and therefore its use in arbitration matters is fraught with uncertainty.[150] This is one of the main reasons why *Shari'a* was not recognised as the applicable law in *Beximco*.[151] It was argued by Potter J that:

> [t]he general references to *Sharia* . . . affords no reference to, or identifica-tion of, those aspects of *Sharia* law which are intended to be incorporated into the contract, let alone the terms in which they are framed . . . [t]hus the reference to the "principles of . . . *Sharia*" stand unqualified as a reference to the body of *Shari'a* generally. As such, they are inevitably repugnant to the choice of English law as the law of the contract and render the clause self-contradictory and therefore meaningless.[152]

This reasoning was followed in *Halpern* where Waller J noted that '[t]he princi-ples of the glorious *Shari'a* law' was 'a very uncertain phase' due to the fact that *Shari'a* consists of different schools of thought.[153] When the case of *Halpern* was brought before the Queen's Bench Division,[154] Clarke J recognised that Jewish law was also subject to different interpretations:

> There is a dispute as to whether there is a uniform and settled corpus of Jew-ish law. The history of the present case certainly shows that different Beth

146 Ibid., 2664.
147 Ibid., 2665.
148 Ibid., 2665.
149 Ibid., 2747.
150 Saad Rizwan, 'Forseeable Issues and Hard Questions: The Implications of U.S. Courts Recognizing and Enforcing Foreign Arbitral Awards Applying Islamic Law Under the New York Convention' (2013) 98(2) *Cornell Law Review* 493, 504.
151 See generally, Chuah, above n 116.
152 [2004] EWCA Civ 19, [52].
153 Halpern v Halpern [2008] QB 195, 213 [33].
154 Halpern v Halpern [2006] 2 All ER (Comm) 251.

Din can reach radically different views on the effect of halachah, without characterising the opposite view as invalid, and without any system of appeal; although that does not, of itself, mean that there is no such corpus.[155]

However, on appeal, Waller J further elaborated that unlike *Shari'a*, Jewish law was viewed as a 'distinct body of law' and therefore could be utilised as part of the contractual framework as an aid to interpretation.[156] Therefore, as discussed previously, religious law was not applicable in *Halpern*, and if this opinion is taken, not only will *Shari'a* be viewed as an ineffective body of law to govern arbitration proceedings, it will also not be utilised as an aid to interpretation.

Therefore, issues may arise if *Shari'a* is selected as a choice of substantive law for the contract because, due to the multiple interpretations and variations of *Shari'a*, it will be unclear to which body of law the parties are referring, and this creates uncertainty for the parties, arbitrators and potential court proceedings. It is this uncertainty that many commentators explain as the reason why *Shari'a* should not govern an arbitration. Briggs argues that whilst foreign law may also be 'incomplete' or 'under-developed,' religious 'laws' are 'inherently likely to find expression in archaic language and broad moral principles whose precise application to a modern commercial dispute is difficult.'[157] Arguably this statement by modern day British academic Briggs, which has also been applied in *Halpern* and *Beximco*, is not so different to the argument used by Lord Asquith when he argued in *Ruler of Qatar v International Marine Oil Company Ltd* that Islamic law was insufficient to be applied to modern day commercial matters. The argument that *Shari'a* is not an effective choice of law because it is 'archaic' or 'uncertain' may have imperialistic tendencies; however, this book addresses whether and how *Shari'a* can effectively apply to contemporary ICA.

Commentators have suggested various solutions. For example, Chuah argues that parties could

> adopt a clause subjecting the contract to a set of expressed terms and conditions compliant with Islamic principles, such as a code of industry practice adopted by Islamic banks, or a specific set of rules established by an individual Islamic bank.[158]

Similarly, White argues that, '[p]arties wishing to have their disputes decided in accordance with the *Shari'a* should identify in detail those aspects of the *Shari'a* that are intended to be incorporated into the contract and the terms in which they are framed.'[159] For example, the majority of cases where *Shari'a* may be chosen

155 Ibid., 71.
156 Halpern v Halpern [2008] QB 195, 213 [33].
157 Briggs, above n 101, 386.
158 Chuah, above n 116, 168.
159 Andrew White, 'Dispute Resolution and Specialized ADR for Islamic Finance' in David Eisenberg and Craig Nethercott (eds), *Islamic Finance: Law and Practice* (Oxford University Press, 2012) 327.

as the governing law will be matters where contracts are compliant with Islamic finance rules and/or where the parties are Islamic financial institutions. In such matters, parties may wish to select the *Shariʿa* arbitration rules and standards noted in Chapter 2. If an arbitration clause is properly drafted and specifically identifies the rules of *Shariʿa* which it wishes to incorporate, such as the AAOIFI, it is more likely that an arbitral tribunal or court will recognise *Shariʿa*, or at least utilise *Shariʿa* principles as an aid to interpretation. However, as will be discussed in Chapter 5, another solution is to specify in the agreement who should have the authority to interpret the relevant *Shariʿa* rules in the event of a dispute since, under *Shariʿa* law, authority is more important than the rules themselves due to the differences in interpretation under *Shariʿa* law.[160]

Therefore, even if a specific school of thought is applied and a particular set of industry standards are stipulated in a governing clause, an expert sitting on a *Shariʿa* board or *Shariʿa* advisor should also be selected to determine any differences in interpretation.[161] Unless they have *Shariʿa* expertise, judges and arbitrators may not have the experience to interpret *Shariʿa* matters as opposed to a qualified expert sitting on a *Shariʿa* advisory board. If this approach is taken, it may be argued that institutional arbitration through the AIAC applying the *i-Arbitration Rules* may be preferable to ad hoc arbitration where parties select a *Shariʿa* school of thought or the AAOIFI Standards which (as discussed in the following chapters) are not as developed as the *i-Arbitration Rules*.[162] However, *ad hoc* arbitration may be suitable in the event that the *i-Arbitration Rules* are chosen, even if the parties do not wish to conduct their arbitration through the AIAC. One benefit of conducting *Shariʿa*-compliant arbitration through the AIAC would be that the institution ensures that the arbitral awards are internationally enforceable. Nonetheless, as will be discussed in later chapters, some parties may not view *i-Arbitration Rules* as being completely *Shariʿa*-compliant, in which case they may want to amend the rules to suit their needs, and choose *ad hoc* arbitration, which would provide greater flexibility to structure the arbitration.

As discussed in Chapter 5, *Shariʿa* experts may be able to determine any differences that the parties may have in their interpretation of *Shariʿa*, and therefore, address the uncertainty that arises from the different interpretations of *Shariʿa*. As we have seen, from the cases of *Beximco* and *Halpern*, courts are also reluctant to interpret religious law in the event that an arbitration matter is subject to court proceedings. White proposes that parties draft specific dispute resolution clauses outlining which school of thought governs the arbitration clause as well as appointing intermediaries to have final authority to interpret *Shariʿa* matters with reference to 'the Qur'an, *ahadith* of the Prophet Muhammad, *fatawa*, texts

---

160 Kilian Balz, 'Islamic Financing Transactions in European Courts' in S. Nazim Ali (ed), *Islamic Finance: Current Legal and Regulatory Issues* (Islamic Legal Studies Program, Harvard Law School, 2005) 74; See generally, Khaled Abou El Fadl, *Speaking in God's Name: Islamic Law, Authority and Women* (Oneworld Publications, 2001).

161 Ibid.

162 Shehabi, above n 17.

and treatises, and industry standards promulgated by AAOIFI, IFSP and other international standard setting bodies as listed.'[163] He also proposes that a specific arbitral institution should administer the arbitration.[164] Nonetheless, as discussed, classical religious texts, such as the Qur'an and hadith, or even *fatwas* and other classical texts and treatises, are subject to different interpretations. Therefore, application of classical texts in dispute resolution clauses will lead to uncertainty. Instead, this book argues that *Shariʿa*-compliant arbitral rules, such as the IICRA or *i-Arbitration Rules*, should govern arbitration as opposed to a reference to religious texts or classical *Shariʿa*. This book will further critically analyse whether the *IICRA Rules*, AAOIFI Standards and the *i-Arbitration Rules* are comprehensive, efficient commercially focused and also, whether they are consistent with contemporary ICA standards.

VI Conclusion

Party autonomy, as a fundamental principle of contemporary ICA, should enable parties to select *Shariʿa* to govern both arbitration agreements and the merits of the dispute. The approach taken by English courts in the *Halpern* case has been heavily criticised, and is not in line with the *English Arbitration Act* and international models. However, it is important to question whether the choice of *Shariʿa* will lead to an arbitration which is commercially focused, predictable and comprehensive for the parties, arbitral tribunals and courts. Arbitral tribunals and courts generally do not impose anational systems of law on the parties in the event of a conflict, as they are generally not codified and comprehensive. In the context of Islamic finance, one can find commercially focused rules such as the *AAOIFI Standards*, which have been approved by *Shariʿa* scholars. Further, the *i-Arbitration Rules* and *IICRA Rules* may provide parties with *Shariʿa*-compliant procedural rules. Therefore, the following chapters will provide a comparative analysis of the classical *Shariʿa* rules, AAOIFI Standards, *IICRA Rules* and *i-Arbitration Rules* in order to assess whether and how *Shariʿa* can effectively apply to contemporary ICA. Whether contemporary ICA caters for *Shariʿa* will also be examined. For example, the next chapter discusses issues which may arise if classical *Shariʿa* is applied in the context of appointing arbitrator/s.

163 White, above n 159, 327.
164 Ibid., 327.

4 Composition of the arbitral tribunal

I Introduction

It is well accepted that the composition of the arbitral tribunal is highly significant, due to the influence that arbitrators have over the arbitration proceedings and arbitral award. Furthermore, most arbitral rules and legislation recognise that a person should not be precluded from acting as an arbitrator on the basis of their nationality, gender or religion.[1]

On the contrary, the view under most textual interpretations of classical *Shariʿa* is that an arbitrator must be Muslim and male.

After discussing the approach taken by classical *Shariʿa* scholars concerning the arbitrator's qualifications, this chapter will examine issues which may arise under the contemporary ICA framework in the event that the parties or arbitral rules stipulate that an arbitrator must be Muslim and/or male. In the recent case of *Jivraj v. Hashwani* [2011] UKSC 40) ('*Jivraj*'), the Supreme Court of the United Kingdom held that parties have the autonomy to agree to a clause stipulating the religious qualification of an arbitrator, and such a clause would not breach anti-discrimination legislation in the United Kingdom.

This chapter will discuss whether *Jivraj* sets an international precedent in light of anti-discrimination legislation in the United States. Secondly, this chapter will examine whether qualifications based on religion raise issues under public policy or impact on the perceived neutrality of the arbitrator through the perspective of the parties concerned. Finally, this chapter will explore whether *Jivraj* also applies to arbitration clauses, which stipulate the gender of an arbitrator, and whether gender restrictions may raise human rights concerns in light of anti-discrimination laws and other public policy considerations.

---

1 For example, as discussed further below, Art. 11(1) of the UNCITRAL Model Law states that '[n]o person shall be precluded by reason of his nationality from acting as an arbitrator, unless otherwise agreed by the parties.' Cf. Art. 6.1 of the LCIA Arbitration Rules 2014: '[w]here the parties are of different nationalities, a sole arbitrator or the presiding arbitrator shall not have the same nationality as any party unless the parties who are not of the same nationality as the arbitral candidate all agree in writing otherwise.'

II Qualifications of arbitrators under classical *Shari'a*

Classical *Shari'a* has a relatively restrictive approach regarding the qualifications of an arbitrator, because all four schools of thought take the view that an arbitrator should possess the same qualifications as a judge ('*qadi*'), which includes being capable of testifying as a witness in court.[2] Arbitrators must possess these qualifications during the course of the arbitral proceedings, otherwise there is a risk that the arbitral award will be considered void.[3] Although Islamic scholars differ on the number of qualifications that an arbitrator must possess,[4] the majority view in all four schools of thought is that the arbitrators must be extremely intelligent and able to solve intricate problems, must be free of physical and psychological incapacity which could prevent them from acting as arbitrator, must have reached an age of maturity, and should not be slaves.[5] Clearly the condition in relation to slavery is no longer relevant due to its abolition.[6] Furthermore, according to the Maliki, Shafi'i and Hanbali schools of thought, the *qadi* should possess *adala*, which is known as morally righteous conduct. This means that the *qadi* should have character considered honourable according Islamic moral values.[7] Although this is a strict condition under the Maliki, Shafi'i and Hanbali schools, the Hanafis consider the *qadi*'s honourable character as a desirable but not essential qualification, and place more emphasis on whether the final arbitral award conforms to *Shari'a*.[8] The *qadi* should also be an expert in *Shari'a* and the sources upon which Sunni scholars rely, which as noted in Chapter 2 consist of the Qur'an and hadith, as well as other sources such as *ijma* and *qiyas*.[9] According to the Maliki, Shafi'i and Hanbali schools of thought, if it is found that the

---

2 Samir Saleh, *Commercial Arbitration in the Arab Middle East: Sharī'a*, Syria, Lebanon and Egypt (Hart Publishing, 2006) 28; see also, Mahdi Zahraa and Nora Abdul Hak, 'Tahkim (arbitration) in Islamic Law Within the Context of Family Law Disputes' (2006) 20(1) *Arab Law Quarterly* 2, 14; Abdulmajed Alrajhi, 'Islamic Finance Arbitration: Is It Possible for Non-Muslims to Arbitrate Islamic Financial Disputes?' (2015) 12(4) *Transnational Dispute Management*; Abdulrahman A. I. Al-Subaihi, *International Commercial Arbitration in Islamic Law, Saudi Law and the Model Law* (PhD thesis, The University of Birmingham, 2004) 82–101.

3 Abdel Hamid El Ahdab and Jalal El Ahdab, *Arbitration with the Arab Countries* (Kluwer Law International, 2011) 36.

4 Zahraa and Abdul Hak, above n 2, 15.

5 Saleh, above n 2, 29–30; El Ahdab and El Ahdab, above n 3, 36–38; Dato' Syed Ahmad Idid and Umar A Oseni, 'Appointing A Non-Muslim as Arbitrator in Tahkim Proceedings: Polemics, Perceptions And Possibilities' (2014) 5 *Malayan Law Journal Articles* 1, 5; For a detailed analysis of the different views within each school of thought, see Abdulrahman A. I. Al-Subaihi, *International Commercial Arbitration in Islamic Law, Saudi Law and the Model Law* (PhD thesis, The University of Birmingham, 2004) 77–101.

6 However, there are different views regarding slavery under the Hanafi school of thought if the purpose of arbitration is reconciliation. See Al-Subaihi, above n 2, 78. See generally, Saleh, above n 2, 29–30; El Ahdab and El Ahdab, above n 3, 38.

7 Saleh, above n 2, 30.

8 Ibid., 30.

9 Ibid., 31.

qadi is not an expert in *Shari'a* during the course of the arbitral proceedings, then the arbitral award is considered void.[10] However, according to the Hanafi school of thought, expertise in *Shari'a* is merely desirable and a *qadi* may consult with other *Shari'a* experts in order to ensure that the arbitral award conforms to *Shari'a*.[11] The final two qualifications in relation to religion and gender will be discussed in the following sections.

A *Religion and gender restrictions under* Shari'a

As stated earlier, since an arbitrator must be able to testify in court or have the same qualifications as a *qadi*, the prevailing position according to the four schools of thought is that the arbitrator must be Muslim.[12] This is because Islamic scholars have held that a non-Muslim or *dhimmi*,[13] is not capable of testifying as a witness, and therefore incapable of acting in a judicial capacity.[14] If this approach is taken where a non-Muslim is appointed as an arbitrator in relation to a dispute between two Muslims, the arbitral award would be rendered invalid.[15] This view is accepted by the Maliki, Shafi'i and Hanbali schools of thought, and is based on a textual[16] (as opposed to contextual) and literalist interpretation of the Qur'anic verse, 'God . . . will give the disbelievers no means of overcoming the believers,'[17] which is taken to mean that a non-Muslim cannot hold a position of power over a Muslim.[18] The contemporary justification provided for this requirement is that a Muslim arbitrator will presumably have more knowledge of *Shari'a*, and an arbitrator who adheres to Islam will be more likely to meet the qualification of *adala* or morally righteous character as defined by *Shari'a*.[19] However, the Hanafi school authorises a non-Muslim arbitrator or judge to have jurisdiction over non-Muslim parties in an Islamic territory.[20] Some Hanafi scholars also argue that non-Muslims can adjudicate in financial, civil or commercial matters involving Muslim litigants.[21] This opinion is based on the rationale

---

10 Ibid., 31.
11 Ibid., 31, El Ahdab and El Ahdab, above n 3, 38.
12 Ibid., 29, El Ahdab and El Ahdab, above n 3, 36.
13 Non-Muslims, in particular Christians and Jews, are known as people who are protected under Shari'a or dhimmis. See Dhimmi (Oxford University Press, 2016) <www.oxfordislamic studies.com/article/opr/t125/e536>.
14 Zahraa and Abdul Hak, above n 2, 16; El Ahdab and El Ahdab, above n 3, 36; Saleh, above n 2, 29.
15 El Ahdab and El Ahdab, above n 3, 36.
16 See Chapter 2.
17 Trans, M. A. S. Abdel Haleem, *The Qur'an* (Oxford University Press, 2004) (Chapter 4, Verse 141).
18 Zahraa and Abdul Hak, above n 2, 16; Dato' Syed Ahmad Idid and Umar A. Oseni, 'Appointing a Non-Muslim as Arbitrator in Tahkim Proceedings: Polemics, Perceptions and Possibilities' (2014) 5 *Malayan Law Journal Articles* 1, 5.
19 Zahraa and Abdul Hak, above n 2, 16.
20 Saleh, above n 2, 28–29; El Ahdab and El Ahdab, above n 3, 37; Al-Subaihi, above n 2, 79–80.
21 Ibid.

that the Qur'anic verse requiring witnesses to be Muslim referred only to family law matters.[22]

With reference to gender requirements, generally, the Hanbali, Shafi'i and Maliki schools of thought require the arbitrator to be male.[23] However, classical scholar, Abu Ja'far Muhammad ibn Jarir al-Tabari (d. 923 CE) ('al-Tabari'), and some Shafi'i scholars, such as Ibn Abi l-Dam, support the Hanafi opinion,[24] which supports women acting as judges and arbitrators.[25] Al-Tabari initially belonged to the Shafi'i school, but later formulated his own school of thought which eventually became extinct, but was still referenced by Sunni Muslims some two centuries after his death.[26] Most Islamic scholars following the Hanafi school argue that it is permissible for women to act as judges or arbitrators because of their capacity to testify as witnesses in all matters except for those *Shari'a* matters which are considered extremely grave in nature (such as criminal and personal injury matters).[27] Therefore, under Hanafi law, women may act as arbitrators in commercial and civil matters.[28] Likewise, some early Maliki scholars did not place gender restrictions on judges; however, the majority of Maliki scholars determined that judges must be male.[29]

Nonetheless it is also important to note views that depart from classical *Shari'a* through *usul-ul fiqh* principles of *ijtihad*, *maslaha* and *maqasid al-Shari'a*, discussed in Chapter 2. There have been various Islamic movements which utilise these principles to argue that principles of *Shari'a*, such as the appointment of male arbitrators or judges, are not compatible with concepts of justice in the contemporary world. For example, El Fadl questions the very authority that classical scholars rely upon when forming their conclusions. He argues that many hadith which are relied upon by classical *Shari'a* scholars to argue that women cannot act as judges, were either revealed in a particular context or transmitted by companions of the Prophet who may have misinterpreted his sayings and actions. El Fadl observes:

> Authenticity is a part of this inquiry, but much more important is to evaluate the totality of the authorial enterprise and reach some determination as to the way and the extent to which the various authorial voices constructed and re-constructed the voice of the reported historical author (in most cases the

22 Ibid., 29.

23 Ibid., 29; Al-Subaihi, above n 2, 86–89.

24 Karen Bauer, 'Debates on Women's Status as Judges and Witnesses in Post-Formative Islamic Law' (2010) 130(1) *Journal of the American Oriental Society*, 3; Abdullah Saeed, *The Qur'an: An Introduction* (Routledge, 2008) 197–198.

25 Al-Subaihi, above n 2, 88.

26 Jonathan Brown, *Misquoting Muhammad: The Challenge and Choices of Interpreting the Prophet's Legacy* (OneWorld Publications, 2015) 192–193.

27 See generally, Zahraa and Abdul Hak, above n 2, 20; Khaled Abou El Fadl, *Speaking in God's Name: Islamic Law, Authority and Women* (Oneworld Publications, 2001) 111; Al-Subaihi, above n 2, 87–89.

28 Saleh, above n 2, 29.

29 Bauer, above n 24, 3; Fadl, 5454, 111.

Prophet or the Companion) . . . [i]t is a comprehensive inquiry into the full historical context in order to evaluate the role of the Prophet in a particular tradition.[30]

Therefore, El Fadl uses a form of contextual *ijtihad*, as further explained in Chapter 2, to approach the hadith by critically analysing the manner in which they are transmitted. Similarly, in her books *Quran and Women*,[31] and *Inside the Gender Jihad: Women's Reform in Islam*,[32] Amina Wadud advocates a contextual approach to the Qur'an which leads to harmonisation between *Shari'a* and contemporary norms of women's rights. Wadud notes that:

[t]he development of a female inclusive theory based on interpretative authority as central to a basic paradigmatic core of what is considered 'Islam' began only in the latter part of the twentieth century. Its efficacy as a form of legitimacy has helped reconstruct the exclusively male control over who determines what 'Islam' means.[33]

Similarly, in his book, *Misquoting Muhammad: The Challenge and Choices of Interpreting the Prophet's Legacy*, Jonathan Brown examines how many classical Islamic scholars have also utilised a contextual approach when interpreting hadith, which on their literal meaning may seem contrary to contemporary notions of morality and justice.[34] An-Na'im also argues for a reinterpretation of *Shari'a* that is compatible with the rights of women as understood in the contemporary context.[35] However, the approach taken by El Fadl, Wadud, Brown and An-Na'im is criticised by scholars who interpret the Qur'an and hadith literally or textually (discussed further later), as the imposition of contemporary 'Western' human rights norms to an Islamic discourse. Hashemi and Qureshi note that:

[t]oday "secular" discourses in the Muslim world are widely discredited and viewed as inauthentic. Thus, contemporary Muslim human rights scholars have attempted to anchor human rights discourses within an Islamic paradigm; that is, the universal is particularised within the dominant idiom of Muslim societies.[36]

---

30 Fadl, above n 27, 110.
31 Amina Wadud, *Qur'an and Woman: Rereading the Sacred Text from a Woman's Perspective* (Oxford University Press, 1999).
32 Amina Wadud, *Inside the Gender Jihad: Women's Reform in Islam* (Oneworld Publications, 2006).
33 Ibid., 16.
34 See generally, Brown, above n 26.
35 See generally, Abdullahi An-Na'im, *Islam and Human Rights* (Ashgate Publishing, 2010).
36 Nader Hashemi and Emran Qureshi, *Human Rights* (Oxford University Press, 2016) <www.oxfordislamicstudies.com/article/opr/t236/e0325>.

For example, when commenting on the Universal Declaration of Human Rights, the Iranian representative noted at the United Nations conferences that Iran:

> recognised no legal tradition apart from Islamic law . . . conventions, declarations and resolutions or decisions of international organizations, which were contrary to Islam, had no validity in the Islamic republic of Iran. . . . The Universal Declaration of Human Rights, which represented a secular understanding of the Judeo-Christian traditions, could not be implemented by Muslims and did not accord with the system of values recognized by the Islamic Republic of Iran.[37]

For similar reasons, Saudi Arabia also opposed the adoption of the Universal Declaration of Human Rights as well as the International Covenant on Civil and Political Rights.[38] In order to address these issues, the Organization of the Islamic Conference, an institution established in 1969, issued the 'Cairo Declaration on Human Rights in Islam' ('Cairo Declaration'), espousing its own conception of Islamic human rights that conforming to *Shari'a*, such as the concept that women are to be treated fairly, but not necessarily equal to men.[39] For example, Art. 1 notes that:

> All human beings form one family whose members are united by submission to God and descent from Adam. All men are equal in terms of basic human dignity and basic obligations and responsibilities, without any discrimination on the grounds of race, color, language, sex, religious belief, political affiliation, social status or other considerations. True faith is the guarantee for enhancing such dignity along the path to human perfection.

Furthermore, Art. 6 stipulates:

a) Woman is equal to man in human dignity, and has rights to enjoy as well as duties to perform; she has her own civil entity and financial independence, and the right to retain her name and lineage.
b) The husband is responsible for the support and welfare of the family.

However, Arts. 1 and 6 do not define 'human dignity' and nor do they state whether it is discriminatory or acceptable if women are prevented from acting

---

37 65th Meeting of the Third Committee, General Assembly UN Doc A/C.3/39/SR.65 at 95 (1984).
38 Ilhan Isik and Taobo Zheng, *Ratification of International Human Rights Treaties – Saudi Kingdom* (University of Minnesota Human Rights Library, 2010) <http://hrlibrary.umn.edu/research/ratification-saudikingdom.html>; United Nations Ethiopia, 'Universal Declaration of Human Rights Signatories' (2014) <http://unethiopia.org/universal-declaration-of-human-rights-signatories/>.
39 Organisation of Islamic Cooperation, *The Cairo Declaration of Human Rights* <www.oic-oci.org/english/article/human.htm>.

as judicial officers or arbitrators, considering this is one of the interpretations of classical *Shari'a* where a textual interpretation is followed as per the Hanbali, Shafi'i or Maliki schools of thought. Furthermore, the Cairo Declaration does not clarify whether barring non-Muslims from certain positions, such as acting as an arbitrator, is classified as discriminatory in nature. The fundamental issue, of course, is that the Cairo Declaration does not clarify which interpretation of *Shari'a* it is following and also, it is not a standard of human rights which is often implemented at the State level. Wiley notes that for an international declaration of human rights based on *Shari'a* to be effective and adopted by national law, 'the content of *Sharia[h]* must be clear, visible and certain.'[40]

As discussed previously and further in this chapter, a textual interpretation of *Shari'a* is also evident by the approach taken in countries, for example Saudi Arabia, where scholars include those who interpret the Qur'an and hadith literally using the 'textual' approach (as opposed to the 'contextual' approach), whereby the texts and linguistics used are given priority over the socio-historical context. Saeed notes:

> [f]or most textualists, the meaning of the Qur'an is static: Muslims must adapt to its meaning. This approach is prominent in much of today's literature on the Qur'an and generally well understood. In contrast, contextualist approaches are less well known and certainly much less understood than the more traditional approaches to exegesis. In general, the scholarship of contextualists is often associated with a form of Islamic reformism.[41]

Literal meanings are also referred to by Muslim legal theorists as the 'evident meaning' or *zaahir* ('outward' meaning), however, as Brown notes:

> [l]iteral meaning is also commonly understood as the meaning that makes sense to us with the least interpretive effort. Put simply, it is the first coherent meaning that comes to mind. . . . But . . . evident meaning is also subjective. It is determined by context and by a tradition of symbols and veteran assumptions.[42]

Regardless of whether such interpretations are valid or whether they should be characterised as literalist, textualist, evident or outward meanings, if interpretations lead to the application of gender requirements for arbitrators, this may raise issues in the context of contemporary anti-discrimination and human rights norms. As noted earlier, this may be the case where the Hanbali, Shafi'i or Maliki school is followed, such that women are excluded from acting as arbitrators. These issues will be analysed and discussed as follows.

---

40 Kit Wiley, 'Human Rights, Sharia Law and the Western Concept of Democracy' in David Claydon (ed), *Islam, Human Rights and Public Policy* (Acorn Press, 2009) 78.
41 Saeed, above n 24, 220–221.
42 Brown, above n 26, 273.

III *Shari'a* qualifications and current practice

Although gender and religious qualifications are not expressly stipulated in the domestic arbitration law of Muslim countries or *Shari'a*-based arbitral rules such as the *IICRA Rules* or *i-Arbitration Rules*, the former Saudi Arbitration law required arbitrators to be Muslim or a Saudi national and arguably, women could not be appointed as per the Hanbali interpretation of *Shari'a*.[43] Art. 3 of the old *Implementation Rules 1985* stated the following:

> The arbitrator must be a Saudi national or Muslim foreigner, chosen amongst the members of the liberal professions, or other persons. He may also be chosen amongst state officials after authorization of the supervising authority that he belongs to. Should there be several arbitrators, then the chairman must know the rules of *Shari'a*, commercial law and the customs in force in the Kingdom.

Some commentators viewed this provision as preventing the appointment of women as arbitrators if the Saudi courts chose to apply the Hanbali interpretation of *Shari'a*, or where courts upheld the argument that arbitrators must be capable of being witnesses, and women cannot be witnesses under *Shari'a* because the testimony of a woman was not equal to that of a man (the latter argument is discussed in more detail in Chapter 5).[44] On the other hand, commentators such as Mohamed Jaber Nader, argue that gender is not expressly mentioned under the old *Implementation Rules 1985*, and therefore women could technically be appointed as arbitrators.[45]

Although the *Saudi Arbitration Law 2012* does not stipulate qualifications based on religion or gender, commentators disagree in relation to whether this implies that women and non-Muslim can act arbitrators. Nesheiwat and Al-Khasawneh argue that the *Saudi Arbitration Law 2012* 'merely requires that arbitrators be of full legal capacity and of good conduct and makes no reference to gender or nationality.'[46] However, the same commentators also note that women may not enjoy full legal capacity under Saudi law, and therefore it is unclear whether women can act as arbitrators.[47] Other commentators note that an arbitrator who is Muslim and male is preferred under the new arbitration regime, due to the overriding provision under Art. 5 that the arbitration

43 El Ahdab and El Ahdab, above n 3, 643.
44 Abdulrahman Yahya Baamir, *Shari'a Law in Commercial and Banking Arbitration: Law and Practice in Saudi Arabia* (Ashgate, 2010) 81; Cyril Chern, *The Law of Construction Disputes* (Informa Law, 2010) 16; El Ahdab and El Ahdab, above n 3, 643.
45 El Ahdab and El Ahdab, above n 3, 643.
46 Faris Nesheiwat and Ali Al-Khasawneh, 'The 2012 Saudi Arbitration Law: A Comparative Examination of the Law and Its Effect on Arbitration in Saudi Arabia' (2015) 13(2) *Santa Clara Journal of International Law* 444, 451.
47 Ibid., 452.

proceedings should not contravene *Shariʿa*.[48] Although there is no case law available to substantiate the claim, they argue that Art. 5 and the application of the Hanbali school makes it possible for a Saudi court to refuse enforcement of an arbitral award where the arbitrator was not Muslim or male. Similar issues may arise under the *SCCA Rules 2016*, which do not specify gender or nationality considerations when appointing an arbitrator, but under Arts. 31 (1) and (4) state:

> (1) Without prejudice to the rules of *Sharia*, the Tribunal shall apply the rules of law designated by the parties as applicable to the substance of the dispute. Failing such designation by the parties, the Tribunal shall apply the law which it determines to be appropriate.
> (4) This set of [r]ules will apply without prejudice to the rules of *Sharia*, and any international convention(s) to which the Kingdom is a party.

Two recent developments may disprove the claim that women cannot act as arbitrators in Saudi Arabia. Firstly, women are beginning to take arbitration courses in Saudi Arabia, which suggests that women could act as arbitrators in the future as per Saudi law.[49] Alternatively, the arbitration courses may be for educational purposes only and therefore, it may still be inconclusive whether Saudi law allows for women to become arbitrators. Secondly, in a recent case reported by Almulhim on the Kluwer Arbitration Blog,[50] the first female arbitrator was appointed in Saudi Arabia to preside over a commercial dispute. When the matter was brought before the Saudi Administrative Court of Appeal in Dammam, the award was rendered final and no objections were raised in regard to the gender of the arbitrator appointed.

Almulhim comments:

> [t]he finality of this decision does not preclude the possibility that challenges might arise in the future in other cases. First, while this decision is final, it is not binding to other courts. Second, as to the first case to deal directly with the issue of female arbitrators, it might be too much to assume that all future cases will take a similar approach. Finally, there is also a question of whether any objection might be raised at the enforcement stage.[51]

48 Saud Al-Ammari and Timothy Martin, 'Arbitration in the Kingdom of Saudi Arabia' (2014) 30(2) *Arbitration International* 387, 392–393.
49 Fouzia Khan, '37 Women Complete Arbitration Course' *Arab News (Jeddah)* 31 May 2013 <www.arabnews.com/news/453495>.
50 Mulhim Hamad Almulhim, 'The First Female Arbitrator in Saudi Arabia' *Kluwer Arbitration Blog (Jeddah)* 29 August 2016 <http://kluwerarbitrationblog.com/2016/08/29/the-first-female-arbitrator-in-saudi-arabia/>.
51 Ibid.

This recent case suggests that Saudi Arabia may be aligning with contemporary ICA norms in relation to the appointment of female arbitrators. Interestingly, however, there has been much discussion in contemporary ICA about the lack of female appointments to arbitral tribunals.[52] Regardless, the above-mentioned case also suggests that the new *Saudi Arbitration Law 2012* accords with the views of contemporary ICA norms because it does not prevent women from acting as arbitrators. However, as discussed in Chapter 2, due to lack of judicial precedent in Saudi Arabia and the lack of codification of *Shari'a*, it is unclear whether judges might choose to apply a strict Hanbali approach to the *Shari'a*, preventing women from acting as arbitrators. Although Saudi Arabia is progressively aligning its arbitration laws with contemporary ICA norms, the ad hoc application of *Shari'a* by judicial officers may raise uncertainty.

International arbitral rules or domestic arbitration law preventing arbitrators from acting based on their gender, religion and/or nationality is arguably inconsistent with contemporary ICA. For example, the *Saudi Arbitration Law 2012* does not contain the following Art. 11(1) of the *UNCITRAL Model Law* which states that '[n]o person shall be precluded by reason of his nationality from acting as an arbitrator, unless otherwise agreed by the parties.' Born argues that this provision is indicative of the international consensus that nationality, gender or religious requirements contained in arbitral rules and legislation are incompatible with international arbitral procedures.[53]

Furthermore, the pro-enforcement approach and emphasis on party autonomy in Arts. II(1) and II(3) of the *New York Convention* suggests that contracting states need to give effect to the parties' agreement in relation to the composition of the arbitral tribunal, and that mandatory nationality requirements in the arbitral seat should not override party autonomy.[54] Even if one argues that Saudi Arabia could invoke public policy arguments to support their mandatory nationality or religion (and potentially gender) requirements, according to most commentators, international conventions and case law, such requirements are discriminatory in nature.[55]

---

52 See generally, Lucy Greenwood and C Mark Baker, 'Is the Balance Getting Better? An Update on the Issue of Gender Diversity in International Arbitration' (2015) 31(3) *Arbitration International* 413.

53 Gary Born, *International Commercial Arbitration* (Kluwer Law International, 2nd ed, 2014) 1739.

54 Ibid., 1741.

55 Ibid., 1742; Emmanuel Gaillard and John Savage, *Fouchard Gaillard Goldman on International Commercial Arbitration* (Kluwer Law International, 1999) 456. See also Art. III of the European Convention on International Commercial Arbitration, opened for signature 21 April 1961, 484 UNTS 364 (entered into force 7 January 1964).

Art. 14 of the *Saudi Arbitration Law 2012* states that the arbitrator must be legally competent, of good conduct and reputation, and hold a university degree in *Shari'a* or legal sciences. However, one commentator notes that:

> [a]lthough not expressly stipulated in the Regulations, in practice, it would be advisable for the chairman of the tribunal and indeed the sole arbitrator, as the case may be, to be Muslim and to have knowledge of *Shari'a* law, as well as knowledge of the laws, regulations, customs and traditions applicable in Saudi Arabia.[56]

The reason why it is important for an arbitrator to be Muslim and have knowledge of the *Shari'a* (as applicable in Saudi Arabia) is due to Art. 25 of the *Saudi Arbitration Law 2012*, which states that the arbitration procedures must not violate *Shari'a*. Furthermore, Art. 2 states that provisions of the *Saudi Arbitration Law 2012* are 'without prejudice to *Shari'a* law,' and there is no provision for waiver in the legislation. Consequently, if Saudi law is the applicable law, then *Shari'a* also applies by default. The issue is further complicated by the fact that, as discussed in Chapter 1, Saudi judges have the discretion to apply their own interpretation of *Shari'a*, which can often be *ad hoc*, because *Shari'a* has not been completely codified.[57]

Therefore, both non-compliance and compliance with *Shari'a* raise issues. If parties do not comply with the gender and/or nationality criteria and appoint a female and/or non-Muslim arbitrator, this increases the risk of non-enforcement of the foreign arbitral award in Saudi Arabia, due to overriding *Shari'a* compliance provisions. However, it is important to note that this is a risk and not definitive because the judge has discretion to apply any interpretation of *Shari'a* and as noted above, a female arbitrator was recently appointed in Saudi Arabia. Furthermore, if parties agree to appoint a non-Muslim or female arbitrator, and this agreement is not honoured due to violation of *Shari'a*, then Art. V(1)(d) of the *New York Convention* may apply:

> the composition of the arbitral authority or the arbitral procedure was not in accordance with the agreement of the parties, or, failing such agreement, was not in accordance with the law of the country where the arbitration took place.

Consequently, an arbitral award may not be enforced in a country which is signatory to the *New York Convention*, and where classical *Shari'a* does not apply. Interestingly, since Saudi Arabia is also a signatory country, arguably a strict application of *Shari'a* under the *Saudi Arbitration Law 2012* is inconsistent with the

---

56 Jean-Benoît Zegers, 'National Report for Saudi Arabia (2013)' in Jan Paulsson and Lise Bosman (eds), *ICCA International Handbook on Commercial Arbitration* (Kluwer Law International, Supplement No. 75, July 2013, 1984) 1, 24.

57 As discussed in Chapter 2, the codification of Shari'a is still in progress in Saudi Arabia.

New York Convention, because *Shari'a*, not party autonomy, is the overriding consideration under the Saudi Arbitration law.

On the other hand, Art. 10 of the *IICRA Rules* is unclear, and does not explicitly state whether the arbitrator has to be Muslim and male, stating only that '[t]he arbitrator must be of jurist [sic] or someone with cast knowledge and experience in trade, industry, finance and *Sharia'a* principles. He must be with reputed morals, and be renowned for his independence.'[58] Arguably, despite the use of a male pronoun and overall requirement for the arbitration to be *Shari'a*-compliant, there is nothing to suggest that the *IICRA Rules* require the arbitrator to be male and Muslim.

The *AAOIFI Standards* also do not explicitly mention the gender of an arbitrator. However, Section 11/1 of the *AAOIFI Standard* No. 32 on Arbitration states that arbitration proceedings should 'conform to the rules of *Shari'a*.'[59] Furthermore, Section 8 of the *AAOIFI Standard* No. 32 states: '[i]n principle an arbitrator should be Muslim. However, a non-Muslim arbitrator could be appointed when acute need so requires, in order to arrive at a *Shari'a* accepted verdict (in this regard, item 11.1 below should be observed).' Section 11.1 stipulates: '[a] valid arbitration decision should lead to a verdict that conform to the rules of the Islamic *Shari'a*.' This view is similar to the one taken by the Hanafi school of thought. Therefore, the preference under the *AAOIFI Standards* for a Muslim arbitrator (although arguably, it is not a strict requirement) does not align with international standards of neutrality and non-discrimination.

Some commentators, such as Oseni and Idid, argue that in a *Shari'a*-compliant arbitration, where the subject matter is also *Shari'a* related, the AAOIFI provision is preferred because they assume that Muslims are better qualified to assess whether the arbitration is conducted in a *Shari'a*-compliant manner.[60] However, they argue that in relation to non-*Shari'a* related matters, a non-Muslim may be appointed.[61] Another justification for the appointment of Muslim arbitrators could be that parties tend to appoint arbitrators they trust. For example, in her research, D'Silva emphasises the significance of party autonomy in the appointment of arbitrators to prove her 'gatekeeper hypothesis.' This argues that due to the private nature of contemporary ICA, 'networks of trust between individuals in international commercial arbitration necessarily function as quality assurance gatekeepers in arbitrator appointment.'[62] Her research further observes that the 'networks of trust' include community groups that share common beliefs

---

58 The consequences of these provisions will be discussed in more detail below.
59 Accounting and Auditing Organization for Islamic Financial Institutions (AAOIFI), *Shari'ah Standards* (Dar Al Maiman, 2015) 799.
60 Idid and Oseni, above n 18, 8.
61 Ibid., 9.
62 Magdalene D'Silva, 'Dealing in Power: Gatekeepers in Arbitrator Appointment in International Commercial Arbitration' (2014) 5(3) *Journal of International Dispute Settlement* 605, 611.

or nationalities, which in turn fosters mutual trust and stability.[63] On the other hand, as will be discussed further later and in Chapter 5, it is also arguable the potential for perceived or actual bias may increase in party appointments based on commonalities such as religion and culture.[64] Furthermore, the next section discusses the case of *Jivraj v. Hashwani*,[65] in order to examine whether parties can agree upon arbitrator qualifications, or whether such an agreement may be viewed as discriminatory under anti-discrimination legislation.

IV *Jivraj* – discrimination or party autonomy?

A *Factual background of Jivraj*

In 1981, Mr Jivraj and Mr Hashwani entered into a joint venture agreement relating to investments in real estate. The agreement included an arbitration clause stipulating the following under Art. 8: '[a]ll arbitrators shall be respected members of the Ismaili community and holders of high office within the community.' As discussed in Chapter 1 and in further detail below, Ismailis are a subsect of *Shi'a* Muslims.

A number of disputes occurred between the parties and in 2008, Mr Hashwani instructed his solicitor to appoint Sir Anthony Colman as the arbitrator. Since Sir Anthony Colman was not from the Ismaili community, Mr Jivraj sought to invalidate this appointment. Mr Hashwani argued that he was not bound by Art. 8 because of the *UK Employment Equality (Religion or Belief) Regulations 2003* ('*UK Regulations*'),[66] which prevented discrimination on the grounds of religion in relation to employment and occupation. He argued that although the arbitration agreement had been valid at the time it was entered into, it was now rendered void due to the *UK Regulations*, as well as the *Human Rights Act 1998*, and other public policy considerations.

B *The court of appeal's decision*

At first instance, Justice Steel of the England and Wales High Court ('EWHC') determined that the *UK Regulations* did not apply to arbitrators, because they were not employees, and therefore the arbitration clause was not discriminatory in nature. Justice Steel further determined that even if arbitrators were employees for the purposes of the *UK Regulations*, the exception under regulation 7(3)

---

63 Ibid., 616–617. See generally, Roger Cotterrell, 'Law and Culture: Inside and Beyond the Nation State' (Research Paper No 4, Queen Mary University of London of Law Legal Studies, 2009) 4; Roger Cotterrell, *Law, Culture and Society: Legal Ideas in the Mirror of Social Theory* (Routledge, 2006).

64 See also, Alexis Mourre, 'Are Unilateral Appointments Defensible? On Jan Paulsson's Moral Hazard in International Arbitration' in Stefan Michael Kröll, et al. (eds), *International Arbitration and International Commercial Law: Synergy, Convergence and Evolution* (Kluwer Law International, 2011) 381.

65 Jivraj v. Hashwani [2009] EWHC 1364; Jivraj v. Hashwani (2010) EWCA (Civ) 712.

66 Now replaced by the Equality Act 2010 (UK).

applied, because in this case the requirement for the arbitrator to be from the Ismaili community was a genuine occupational requirement.[67] His Honour also held that the arbitration clause did not breach the *Human Rights Act* 1998 (UK) or public policy considerations.[68]

The Court of Appeal reversed the decision of the EWHC, and found that arbitrators were classified as employees, and therefore the *UK Regulations* applied in this case.[69] Lord Justice Moore-Bick of the Court of Appeal stated that '[s]ince an arbitrator (or any professional person) contracts to do work personally, the provision of his services falls within the definition of "employment", and it follows that his appointor must be an employer within the meaning of Regulation 6(1).'[70] Art. 8 of the parties' arbitration agreement was viewed as being discriminatory and contravening the *UK Regulations*, because it only allowed for the appointment of Ismaili arbitrators.[71] The Court of Appeal also determined whether being a member of the Ismaili community fell under the genuine occupational requirement exception stipulated in Regulation 7(3). In relation to this issue the Court of Appeal stated:

> [i]f the arbitration clause had empowered the tribunal to act *ex aequo et bono* it might have been possible to show that only an Ismaili could be expected to apply the moral principles and understanding of justice and fairness that are generally recognised within that community as applicable between its members, but the arbitrators' function under clause 8 is to determine the dispute between the parties in accordance with the principles of English law.[72]

On this basis, the entire arbitration agreement was declared invalid and unenforceable because the requirement for an Ismaili arbitrator could not be severed from the arbitration agreement.[73] The Court of Appeal's decision raised concerns for the ICA community, because the relationship between arbitrators and the parties is generally viewed by most commentators and cases as a *sui generis* contract, as opposed to one of employment.[74] Commentators argued that the court's decision would have:

> wide-ranging effects for existing international arbitration agreements and the drafting of future arbitration clauses beyond the jurisdiction of the United Kingdom. This decision has the potential to restrict the power of parties to agree on the composition of the arbitral tribunal in a commercial contract,

---

67 Jivraj v. Hashwani [2009] EWHC 1364, 33–38.
68 Ibid., 47–71.
69 Jivraj v. Hashwani (2010) EWCA (Civ) 712.
70 Ibid., 16.
71 Ibid., 13.
72 Ibid., 29.
73 Ibid., 35.
74 Born, above n 53, 143; Gaillard and Savage, above n 55, 606.

thereby altering party autonomy, one of the fundamental principles of international arbitration.[75]

Also, the Court of Appeal's judgement could potentially impact upon arbitral rules, such as Art. 6(7) of the *UNCITRAL Rules 2010* which, as discussed in the next section, advises the appointing authority to appoint an arbitrator of a nationality other than the nationalities of the parties.[76] However, much to the relief of the ICA community, the Supreme Court reversed the Court of Appeal's decision.

C *The supreme court's decision*

The judgement of the Supreme Court overturned the decision of the Court of Appeal by finding that arbitrators were not to be characterised as employees of the parties, and that English case law distinguished between employees and independent providers of services. Lord Clarke determined that an arbitrator was 'rather in the category of an independent provider of services who is not in a relationship of subordination with the parties who receive his services.'[77] This is due to the fact that an arbitrator acts as a 'quasi-judicial adjudicator,' and must act fairly and impartially to determine the issues between the parties.[78]

Referring to the Court of Appeal's argument that the genuine occupational requirement did not apply to the arbitration clause, Lord Clarke found this approach to be 'too legalistic and technical.'[79] Lord Clarke noted the findings of Justice Steel at first instance, which provided a detailed analysis of the history and development of the Ismaili community. In his decision, Justice Steel noted that the Ismaili community followed the spiritual leader Aga Khan who had established a Constitution encouraging the resolution of disputes through arbitration and conciliation based on the Islamic tradition of *sulh* (conciliation) enshrined in the Qur'an.[80] On this basis, Justice Steel found that the provision for arbitrators to be respected members of the Ismaili community was a genuine occupational requirement. Despite Lord Clarke's conclusion that arbitrators were not employees, he found that Justice Steel was 'justified in concluding that the requirement of an Ismaili arbitrator can be regarded as a genuine occupational requirement on the basis that it was not only genuine but both legitimate and justified.'[81] The decision of the Supreme Court also confirmed the importance of party autonomy in ICA, and Lord Clarke noted in his judgement that 'one of the distinguishing

---

75 Inae Yang, 'Nurdin Jivraj v. Sadruddin Hashwani: The English Court of Appeal Erects a Regulatory Barrier to the Appointment of Arbitrators in the Name of Anti-Discrimination' (2011) 28(3) *Journal of International Arbitration* 243, 252.

76 Ashurst, *English Court of Appeal Decision: Impact on Institutional Arbitration Clauses* <www.ashurst.com/publication-item.aspx?id_Content=5436>.

77 Jivraj v. Hashwani [2011] UKSC 40, 41.

78 Ibid., 41–42.

79 Ibid., 70.

80 Jivraj v. Hashwani [2009] EWHC 1364 (Comm)) 43.

81 Jivraj v. Hashwani [2011] UKSC 40, 68.

features of arbitration that sets it apart from proceedings in national courts is the breadth of discretion left to the parties and the arbitrator to structure the process for resolution and dispute.'[82]

Since the decision of the Supreme Court largely focused on the relationship between employees and arbitrators, the extent to which parties can agree upon clauses that may be viewed as discriminatory by domestic legislation, international human rights standards and public policy is still unclear. For example, as discussed in further detail later, one commentator argues that the *Jivraj* case may not be followed in the United States, where anti-discrimination legislation applies regardless of whether an arbitrator is viewed as an employee or independent contractor.[83] Furthermore, *Jivraj* does not clarify the extent to which parties may restrict the appointment of arbitrators based on religion or gender. These issues will be discussed in more detail as follows.

D *Ad hoc arbitration and discrimination*

According to the case of *Jivraj*, parties may stipulate that an arbitrator is Muslim without breaching the *Human Rights Act 1998* (UK), the *UK Regulations* or public policy in the United Kingdom. One may also argue that the *Jivraj* case sets a precedent for the ICA community, including European jurisdictions and Australia. The extent to which international human rights treaties and conventions should be considered in arbitration is unclear. For example, Bernini notes that the history of the *European Convention on Human Rights* of 4 November 1950 'shows that it was intended to introduce international State responsibility regarding the operation of a State's court system; it was not meant to apply to private justice,'[84] and that Art. 6 of the *European Convention on Human Rights* refers to a 'tribunal established by law' as opposed to the agreement of the parties.[85] Despite this, Bernini also argues that the *European Convention on Human Rights* has applied to mandatory arbitration matters, and since mandatory and voluntary arbitration are not always easily distinguishable, it is difficult to answer whether 'in the context of the voluntary arbitration, one should fight discrimination to the point of prohibiting it *per se.*'[86] Furthermore, in *R v Switzerland*, the European Commission of Human Rights initially held that the *European Convention of Human Rights* did not apply to voluntary arbitration.[87] However,

---

82 Ibid., 61.
83 Jeff Dasteel, 'Arbitration Agreements That Discriminate in the Selection and Appointment of Arbitrators' (2012) 11(4) *Richmond Journal of Global Law & Business* 383.
84 Giorgio Bernini, 'The Parties' Right to Choose Their Arbitrator and the Prohibition Against Discrimination: An Unstable Balance: A Comment on the Judgements in Jivraj v. Hashwani' (2013) 24 *American Review of International Arbitration* 27, 40.
85 Ibid., 40, 59–60.
86 Ibid., 61.
87 R v Suisse (1987) Eur Comm HR 30 Yearbook of European Convention Human Rights 36, 42 (1992) as cited in Herman Verbist, 'Challenges on Grounds of Due Process Pursuant to Article V(1)(B) of the New York Convention' in Emmanuel Gaillard and Domenico

in subsequent decisions by the Swiss Federal Tribunal,[88] it was held that arbitral tribunals should respect Art. 6(1) of the *European Convention on Human Rights*, which stipulates the right to fair trial: 'in the determination of his civil rights and obligations or of any criminal charge against him, everyone is entitled to a fair and public hearing within a reasonable time by an independent and impartial tribunal established by law.'

On the other hand, in the United Kingdom, in the case of *Mousaka Inc v Golden Seagull Maritime Inc*,[89] Steel J of the Queen's Bench Division held that '[t]he parties have agreed to arbitrate their disputes. They have thereby largely renounced (in the interests of privacy and finality) the application of Art. 6'[90] of the *European Convention on Human Rights*.[91] Therefore, commentators suggest that 'although strictly speaking the provisions contained in the *European Convention on Human Rights* do not apply to voluntary arbitration as arbitrators in such arbitrations are not organs of the State, the provisions nevertheless have an indirect bearing on arbitration.'[92] Some commentators also argue that tribunals may apply human rights considerations in relation to due process requirements, as per the *Universal Declaration of Human Rights* and the *European Convention on Human Rights*, on the basis of transnational public policy considerations in arbitration.[93] If this approach is taken, it may raise issues, because as discussed in this chapter, the application of certain interpretations of *Shari'a* results in outcomes which may be contrary to the 'Western' concept of human rights.[94]

Furthermore, despite the case of *Jivraj*, one commentator argues that parties may still be at risk in the event that the anti-discrimination legislation in the United States applies. This is due to section 1981 of the *Civil Rights Act 1866* ('*Civil Rights Act*'), which bans ethnic or racial discrimination in relation to

---

Di Pietro (eds), *Enforcement of Arbitration Agreements and International Arbitral Awards* (Cameron, May 2008) 679, 690.

88 ATF 117 Ia 166, 30 April 1991 (Swiss Federal Tribunal); *Hitachi Ltd. v. SMS Schloemann Siemag Aktiengesellschaft*, (Swiss Federal Tribunal), 30 June 1994 reported in (1997) 1 ASA Bulletin 566; A v Union des associations europeennes de football (UEFA) (Swiss Federal Tribunal), 11 June 2001, (2001) 3 ASA Bulletin 566, 571. Cf ATF 112 Ia 166, 22 July 1986 (Swiss Federal Tribunal) as cited in Verbist, above n 87) 679, 690.

89 [2002] 1 All ER 726.

90 Ibid., 733 [25].

91 Ibid.

92 Verbist, above n 87, 691.

93 Georgios Petrochilos, *Procedural Law in International Arbitration* (Oxford University Press, 2004) 110–165. See generally, Martina Závodná, *The European Convention on Human Rights and Arbitration* (Diploma, Masaryk University, 2013/2014).

94 See Chapter 8 on a discussion on Shari'a public policy compared to transnational and international public policy. See also, Thomas Schultz, 'Human Rights: A Speed Bump for Arbitral Procedures? An Exploration of Safeguards in the Acceleration of Justice' (2006) 9(1) *International Arbitration Law Review* 8, 16; Pierre-Marie Dupuy, 'Unification Rather Than Fragmentation of International Law? The Case of International Investment Law and Human Rights Law' in Pierre-Marie Depuy, Francesco Francioni and Ernst Ulrich Petersmann (eds), *Human Rights in International Investment Law and Arbitration* (Oxford University Press, 2009) 45, 60.

all contractors, including the selection and hiring of independent contractors.[95] The *Civil Rights Act* does not apply to discrimination based on gender, religion, national origin, age or disability; however, many state and municipal laws in the United States ban discrimination based on religion, race, creed, sex, age, etc.[96] Examples include New Jersey,[97] New York,[98] and Pennsylvania,[99] which have broad anti-discrimination statutes including discrimination based on religious grounds that apply to the hiring of independent contractors.[100]

For example, Section 8.107(1) of the *New York City Administrative Code* ('*NY Human Rights Law*') prohibits discrimination on the basis of religion in the course of employment,[101] and Section 8.102(5) provides that '[f]or purposes of this subdivision . . . natural persons employed as independent contractors to carry out work in furtherance of an employer's business enterprise who are not themselves employers shall be counted as persons in the employ of such employer.'[102] Therefore, if parties agree to a provision in an *ad hoc* arbitration agreement similar to the one in *Jivraj*, and the arbitration takes place in New York under the laws of the United States, *NY Human Rights Law* may prohibit discrimination on the basis of religion, even if United States courts view arbitrators as independent contractors furthering the parties' business enterprise by acting as an arbitrator in their matter.[103] On the other hand, if the courts in the United States adopt the approach taken in *Jivraj*, then an arbitrator may be viewed as having a quasi-judicial role which does not further the interests of either party.[104]

National courts and commentators have developed various theories to understand the relationship between parties and arbitrators. The most common and accepted theory is the 'contractual theory,' since the parties and arbitrators enter into a contractual arrangement, whereby arbitrators undertake certain tasks in return for payment and specified immunities.[105] There have been international cases where the relationship has been described as an agency agreement,[106] or an

---

95 Dasteel, above n 83, 386.

96 Ibid., 386.

97 See New Jersey Statutes Annotated (N.J. Stat. Ann.) (revised 2015) § 10:5–12.

98 See New York City Administrative Code (N.Y.C. Admin. Code) (current through local law 2016/104, enacted 31 August 2016) <www.amlegal.com/codes/client/new-york-city_ny/>.

99 Pennsylvania Human Relations Act, 43 Pa. Stat. Ann. §§ 951 to 963 <www.phrc.pa.gov/Resources/Law-and-Legal/Pages/The-Pennsylvania-Human-Relations-Act.aspx#.WGQ8b1V96Uk>.

100 Dasteel, above n 83, 387–389.

101 See New York City Administrative Code (N.Y.C. Admin. Code) §8.102–207 (current through local law 2016/104, enacted 31 August 2016) <www.amlegal.com/codes/client/new-york-city_ny/>.

102 Ibid.

103 Dasteel, above n 83, 390.

104 Ibid., 390.

105 Born, above n 53, 1967.

106 Hays v. Hays, 23 Wend. 363 (N.Y. Sup. Ct. 1840). Cf Martin v. Vansant, 99 Wash. 106, 117 (Wash. 1917). See also, ibid., 1967–1968; Wesley A. Sturges, 'Arbitration – What Is It?' (1960) 35 *New York University Law Review* 1031, 1044–1045.

agreement for the provision of services.[107] Some commentators argue that the latter characterisation is wider in scope and more accurate, because arbitrators are not simply agents of the parties, but also provide expert knowledge and professional services.[108] Nevertheless, the same commentators also argue that the contractual relationship does not address the judicial function of arbitrators.[109] For example, Mustill and Boyd propose the 'status theory,' whereby arbitrators are

> clothed with the power to affect the rights, not only of the appointing party but also of his [sic] opponent: and this power continues until the reference has run its course, and cannot be withdrawn short of this, otherwise than by consent or by order of the Court.[110]

Therefore, the relationship between the parties and the arbitrators is viewed as 'quasi-judicial' in nature, and the applicable law governs the arbitrator's rights and obligations (as opposed to the contract).[111] As discussed in *Jivraj* above, the better view is that the relationship between an arbitrator and the parties is a contractual one, but should be classified as 'sue generis,' due to an arbitrator's quasi-judicial role.[112]

Dasteel argues that whether the relationship between an arbitrator and employee is classified as an 'independent contractor' or as a 'sui generis' relationship does not matter under the *Civil Rights Act* and in New Jersey, because the statutes ban discrimination regardless of how the relationship between the parties is classified.[113] Yet, as noted above, the *Civil Rights Act* is limited to claims based on ethnicity and race, but does not cover discrimination on the basis of gender and religion. Therefore, in a *Jivraj* situation in the event that the courts characterise the relationship between the parties and the arbitrators as *sue generi*, then anti-discrimination laws in New Jersey may be violated.[114]

If the courts classify arbitrators as independent contractors and the parties agree to a clause stipulating that the arbitrator must be Muslim and the arbitration is taking place in New York, there is a greater chance of the *NY Human Rights Law* applying includes discrimination on the basis of religion in the hiring of independent contractors. There is also more risk of breaching the *NY Human Rights Law* if the parties cannot show that the religious requirement is a genuine occupational requirement. Dasteel notes that this defence is more difficult to prove if the parties are not religious organisations.[115] Arguably, the *NY Human*

---

107 Gaillard and Savage, above n 55, 606 [1119].
108 Ibid., 606; Born, above n 53, 1977–1979.
109 Born, above n 53, 1977–1979.
110 Michael Mustill and Stewart Boyd, *Commercial Arbitration* (Butterworths, 2nd ed, 1989) 221.
111 Born, above n 53, 1967.
112 Gaillard and Savage, above n 55, 606: Born, above n 53, 1197, 1972–1974.
113 See, Dasteel, above n 83, 387–389.
114 See New Jersey Statutes Annotated (N.J. Stat. Ann.) (revised 2015) §10:5–12.
115 Dasteel, above n 83, 393, n 54.

Rights Law might apply to a hypothetical situation where: a non-Muslim party and Muslim party agree to arbitrate a matter in New York; the arbitration clause stipulates that the arbitrator must be Muslim; and where the subject matter of the contract is not related to religious matters. If the matter is presented before a court in the United States and arbitrators are viewed as independent contractors furthering the business of their parties through providing dispute resolution services, then the parties may be at risk of breaching the *NY Human Rights Law*. This may be the case if the arbitration is subject to the laws of the United States in a domestic arbitration matter or a non-domestic arbitration matter where the seat of arbitration is New York City.[116] On the other hand, if the parties are both of Muslim background and the subject matter relates to an Islamic finance contract, it is more likely that the exception of genuine occupational requirement would apply, because as per the reasoning applied by Justice Steel in *Jivraj*, it would be easier for the courts in the United States to accept that a Muslim arbitrator who has in-depth knowledge about *Shari'a* would be best suited to resolve Islamic finance matters between two Muslim parties.

E *Arbitral rules and qualifications based on religion*

Theoretically speaking, it may also be argued that if parties agree to the *AAOIFI Standards* to govern their arbitration agreement subject to the laws of the United States, and/or the arbitration takes place in New York, there may be a risk that the *AAIOFI Standards* themselves breach the *NY Human Rights Law*. This is because the *AAOIFI Standards* state that it is preferable for the arbitrator to be a Muslim. On the other hand, this argument is likely to fail at a practical level, because the *AAOIFI Standards* are specialised rules which apply to Islamic finance matters and thus, the genuine occupational requirement will most likely apply. As noted previously in the case of *Jivraj*, at first instance, Justice Steel held that the history and development of arbitration in the Ismaili community indicates that the group is an 'ethos based on religion' and thus a genuine occupational requirement existed.[117] Similarly, the resolution of Islamic finance disputes through *Shari'a*-based arbitration, and the encouragement within the *AAOIFI Standards* for the appointment of a Muslim arbitrator is arguably due to consideration of an 'ethos based on religion' and therefore, a genuine occupational requirement.

In the event that an arbitration clause is found to violate the anti-discrimination law in the United States, the arbitration agreement may be unenforceable, even if the anti-discrimination legislation applies to contracts as opposed to arbitration agreements specifically. The courts may determine that the entire arbitration agreement is to be considered void, or the arbitration clause in breach of the anti-discrimination legislation may be severed from the agreement.[118]

---

116 Ibid., 398.This is due to Art. V, s 1(e) of the New York Convention which notes that the country where arbitration takes place has authority over the conduct of the proceedings.
117 Jivraj v. Hashwani [2009] EWHC 1364, 45.
118 Dasteel, above n 83, 398.

F Public policy and perception of bias

Although there are no reported cases in the United States where discrimination was used as a basis for refusing enforcement on public policy grounds, it may also be possible for parties to argue that anti-discrimination legislation in the United States (if it applies to independent contractors) is part of public policy.[119] Consequently, arbitration clauses stipulating that an arbitrator must be of a certain religious background may be contrary to public policy in the United States and therefore, unenforceable under the public policy exception in the *New York Convention*. However, the public policy argument may be less likely in other jurisdictions where: firstly, anti-discrimination legislation does not apply to independent contractors; and secondly, the approach taken in *Jivraj* is followed. Justice Steel in *Jivraj* held that due to the

> plethora of statutory provisions in regards to discrimination both in the criminal and in the civil field . . . [e]ven allowing for the need to move with the times, it is inappropriate for the courts to trespass further than parliamentary intention by way of filling what is suggested as a "lacuna" under the guise of public policy.[120]

Alternatively, parties could argue that the selection of an arbitrator based on religious grounds increases the risk of the arbitral tribunal being perceived as biased.[121] This argument may be based on public policy considerations, or on one of the accepted principles of contemporary ICA, which is that arbitrators are required to be neutral, independent and impartial, as per leading international arbitration rules. According to Lew, Mistelis and Kroll, the 'magna carta' of contemporary ICA has two main principles, which includes 'due process and fair hearing' and 'the independence and impartiality of arbitrators.'[122] Although it is not explicitly stated, it is generally accepted in contemporary ICA that if an arbitrator is found to lack independence or impartiality, an arbitral award may be annulled under Art. V of the New York Convention or Art. 34(2) of the *UNCITRAL Model Law*.[123] Verbist notes that Art. V(1)(b) of the *New York Convention*:

> sanctions a violation of the right of the parties to be heard and to be treated equally, which is often referred to in common law jurisdictions as 'due process' or sometimes as 'fundamental fairness' or 'natural justice'.

---

119 Ibid., 403–404.
120 Jivraj v. Hashwani [2009] EWHC 1364, 70–71.
121 Dasteel, above n 83, 403.
122 Julian Lew, Loukas Mistelis and Stefan Michael Kröll, *Comparative International Commercial Arbitration* (Kluwer Law International, 2003) 95; See generally, Verbist, above n 87, 679.
123 Born, above n 53, 3279–3281.

As will be discussed in Chapter 8, the concept of Islamic public policy is based on similar notions within boundaries delineated by the principles of *Shari'a*. However, there is no international consensus on the definition or standard of bias required to challenge an arbitrator. Derains and Levy define independence and impartiality as follows:

> independence is the objective absence of any substantial link to any of the parties as that may alter the freedom of judgment of the arbitrator; impartiality is the subjective will not to favour any of the parties.[124]

Art. 11(2) of the *ICC Rules 2012* provides that:

> [t]he prospective arbitrator shall disclose in writing to the Secretariat any facts or circumstances which might be of such a nature as to call into question the arbitrator's independence in the eyes of the parties, as well as any circumstances that could give rise to reasonable doubts as to the arbitrator's impartiality.

A similar provision also exists under Art. 12(1) of the *UNCITRAL Rules 2010*: '[a]ny arbitrator may be challenged if circumstances exist that give rise to justifiable doubts as to the arbitrator's impartiality or independence.'

The *IBA Guidelines*[125] provide very specific situations that may raise justifiable doubts as to the arbitrator's independence and impartiality, depending on the factual scenario. For example, Art. 3.3.6 describes a scenario where a close friendship exists between the arbitrator and counsel of a party,[126] and Art. 3.5.2 notes a situation where the arbitrator holds a public opinion that has been published in a paper or speech. Similar conditions are articulated in the *AAA Code of Ethics for Arbitrators in Commercial Disputes* and *The Chartered Institute of Arbitrators Code of Professional and Ethical Conduct for Members*. Commentators also argue that certain social media etiquette, such as adding an arbitrator as a friend on LinkedIn, may also raise concerns of bias.[127] El Kosheri and Youssef note that '[i]n the world of globalised business and legal services in which

---

124 Yves Derains and Laurent Lévy, *Is Arbitration Only as Good as the Arbitrator? Status, Powers and Role of the Arbitrator* (International Chamber of Commerce, 2011) 7. See generally, Loretta Malintoppi, 'Independence, Impartiality, and Duty of Disclosure of Arbitrators' in Peter Muchlinski, Federico Ortino and Christoph Schreuer (eds), *Oxford Handbook of International Investment Law* (Oxford University Press, 2008) 789.

125 International Bar Association, *Guidelines on Conflict of Interest in International Arbitration*, adopted 23 October 2014, <www.ibanet.org/Publications/publications_IBA_guides_and_free_materials.aspx>.

126 This Art. is categorised into an 'orange list' outlining scenarios that are considered waivable if the parties are aware of the situation and agree to the appointment of the arbitrator.

127 Jean Kalicki, 'Social Media and Arbitration Conflicts of Interest: A Challenge for the 21st Century' on *Kluwer Arbitration Blog* (23 April 2012) <http://kluwerarbitrationblog.com/2012/04/23/social-media-and-arbitration-conflicts-of-interest-a-challenge-for-the-21st-century>.

international commercial arbitration operates, many, if not most, players are in some way acquainted with each other.'[128]

For this reason, Australian and English courts take a narrower approach to 'justifiable doubts,' by applying the 'real danger' test according to which

> the court should ask itself whether . . . there was a real danger of bias on the part of the relevant member of the tribunal in question, in the sense that he might unfairly regard (or have unfairly regarded) with favour, or disfavour, the case of a party to the issue under consideration by him.[129]

Australia is the first country to adopt the 'real danger' test into its legislation, and section 18A of the *International Arbitration Act 1974* states:

> (1) For the purposes of Art. 12(1) of the Model Law, there are justifiable doubts as to the impartiality or independence of a person approached in connection with a possible appointment as arbitrator only if there is a real danger of bias on the part of that person in conducting the arbitration.[130]

Another test proposed by the case of *Porter v Magill*[131] is the 'real possibility' test, which argues that the 'fair minded and informed observer' would view a real possibility of bias in the arbitrator.[132] According to Luttrell, the 'reasonable apprehension' test has a lower threshold than the real danger test because, as per the judgement of Lord Hewart CJ in *Sussex Justices*,

> [w]hile a suspicion (or apprehension) may be reasonably founded insofar as it has been formed in the mind of a person as a result of his or her exercise of the faculty of reason, the facts upon which the suspicion is based may not necessarily interact to produce the result that the apprehended outcome is a real possibility.[133]

---

128 Ahmed S. El-Kosheri and Karim Y. Youssef, 'The Independence of International Arbitrators: An Arbitrator's Perspective' (2007) *Special Supplement of the ICC Intl. Court of Arb. Bull: Independence of Arbitrators* 43, 48.

129 AT&T Corporation and another v Saudi Cable [2000] 2 Lloyd's Rep 127, 135; see also R v Gough [1993] AC 646.

130 See also, Sam Luttrell, 'Australia Adopts the "Real Danger" Test for Arbitrator Bias' (2010) 26(4) *Arbitration International* 625.

131 Porter v Magill [2002] AC 357.

132 Sam Luttrell, *Bias Challenges in International Commercial Arbitration: The Need for a "Real Danger" Test* (Kluwer Law International, 2009) 8.

133 Ibid., 39.

Therefore, the higher threshold as per the 'real danger' or 'real possibility' test is proposed in order to ensure that the removal of arbitrators or the unenforceability of arbitral awards on the basis of bias, is limited.[134]

Bias has also been further characterised as 'institutional bias' or 'systemic bias' (bias that arises from the system of arbitration). For example, Park uses the term institutional bias to argue that bias may arise if certain arbitral institutions appoint arbitrators favouring particular litigants, such as financial institutions, as opposed to consumers.[135] He further argues that arbitrators may also be accused of favouring those parties with which they have professional affiliations; for example, they may favour parties that increase their chances of reappointment.[136] Brekoulakis suggests a broader approach to bias which takes into consideration 'systemic bias' and argues that the focus of contemporary ICA law and practice has been on the conduct of arbitrators or 'apparent bias.'[137] Brekoulakis explains systemic bias as follows: '[i]f an adjudicatory system is systemically biased, the strong majority of the people selected and appointed to act as adjudicators will typically share the same values and take a similar position on fundamental legal, social, economic and political matters.'[138]

Nonetheless, he does not address how systemic bias, which is implicit and broad in nature, can be regulated. It is extremely difficult to particularise and regulate bias that is ideological and value-based. In fact, if international rules and guidelines began addressing 'systemic bias,' this may impact on *Shariʿa*-based arbitration, which is a system of arbitration founded on religious law, as opposed to the contemporary ICA system which is secular in nature (despite the fact that it may cater for religious requirements due to party autonomy) and therefore, one could argue that arbitrators may be systemically biased in favour of the contemporary ICA system. For example, in an arbitration consisting of Muslim parties, could a secular arbitrator (or a Muslim arbitrator who publicly condones secular ICA) be viewed as being systemically biased against the Muslim parties, or against the application of *Shariʿa*? Such a bias would be similar to the cases discussed in Chapter 2, being the *Abu Dhabi Oil Arbitration case*,[139] and the *Ruler of Qatar v International Marine Oil Company Ltd*.[140] Arguably, under contemporary ICA, it would be extremely difficult to prove such systemic bias due to its implicit nature, and this approach may also discourage arbitrators from acting in arbitral proceedings involving Muslim parties and/or where *Shariʿa* may apply.

134 Ibid., 8.
135 William Park, *Arbitration of International Business Disputes: Studies in Law and Practice* (Oxford University Press, 2nd ed, 2012) 41–42.
136 Ibid., 41–42.
137 Stavros Brekoulakis, 'Systemic Bias and the Institution of International Arbitration: A New Approach to Arbitral Decision-Making' (2013) 4(3) *Journal of International Dispute Settlement* 553, 560.
138 Ibid., 560.
139 *Petroleum Development (Trucial Coast) Ltd. v. Sheikh of Abu Dhabi* (1951) 19 ILR 144.
140 (1953) 20 ILR 534.

In the event that parties have not agreed upon an arbitrator, Art. 6(7) of the *UNCITRAL Rules 2010* notes that, when appointing a sole or presiding arbitrator, the appointing authority shall 'have regard to such considerations as are likely to secure appointment of an independent and impartial arbitrator and shall take into account the advisability of appointing an arbitrator of a nationality other than the nationalities of the parties.' On the other hand, Art. 6.1 of the *LCIA Arbitration Rules 2014* does not simply state that the appointing authority should 'have regard to such considerations,' but that:

> [w]here the parties are of different nationalities, a sole arbitrator or the presiding arbitrator *shall not* have the same nationality as any party unless the parties who are not of the same nationality as the arbitral candidate all agree in writing otherwise.[141]

Although these provisions apply to appointing authorities, commentators agree that the importance of an independent, neutral and impartial arbitrator is vital for the composition of an effective arbitral tribunal.[142] Does this mean that an arbitrator from the same nationality as one of the parties could be viewed as biased?

Some commentators argue that in light of Art. 11 of the *UNCITRAL Model Law*, which does not allow arbitrators to be precluded on the basis of nationality, sharing nationalities is not indicative of an arbitrator's impartiality.[143] Further, Veeder argues that the application of Art. 6.1 of the *LCIA Arbitration Rules 2014* fails to take into consideration the fact that arbitrators are already required to act impartiality under most national legal systems, such as English law, and that

> [t]he LCIA could doubtless justify its nationality discrimination in many, if not most, individual cases; but it could hardly justify such discrimination in all cases. Its blanket ban, with all discretion removed, is the prima facie hallmark of disproportion and therefore unjustifiable discrimination.[144]

Similarly, Petrochilos explains that 'no-one expects an arbitrator to leave his personal experience and beliefs at home when he sits. These are part and parcel of his professional life.'[145]

On the other hand, Lalive argues that neutrality goes further than independence or impartiality, because it is concerned with geographic and national equidistance.[146] In light of Art. 6(7) of the *UNCITRAL Rules 2010* and Art. 13(5) of

---

141 Emphasis added.
142 Born, above n 53, 1736–1737. See also Pierre Lalive, 'On the Neutrality of the Arbitrator and of the Place of Arbitration' in Eugene Bucher and Claude Reymond (eds), *Swiss Essays on International Arbitration* (Schulthess, 1984).
143 Lew, Mistelis and Kröll, above n 122, 259.
144 Veeder, 'Arbitral Discrimination Under English and EU Law' in Derains and Lévy, above n 124, 99.
145 Petrochilos, above n 93, 134.
146 Lalive, above n 142.

the *ICC Rules 2012*,[147] one can assume that neutrality may be linked with nationality, because appointing authorities are discouraged from appointing an arbitrator who shares the same nationality as one of the parties. This is because parties may assume that an arbitrator who shares the same nationality as one of the parties, also shares the country's ideology and common values.[148] Born argues:

> in practice, even if not prohibited from doing so by institutional rules, leading arbitral institutions are very unlikely to appoint a sole or presiding arbitrator with the same nationality as one (but not the other) party. Doing so violates the basic principle of international neutrality that underlies the arbitral process, particularly in the eyes of the "foreign" party.[149]

Lee also notes that the appointment of an arbitrator who is a 'neutral national' avoids the perception of bias rather than actual bias and therefore, even if an arbitrator from a third country is appointed, there is no guarantee of neutrality.[150] Lee argues that if impartiality is viewed through the lens of 'perceived bias' then other common characteristics such as religion and culture should also be taken into consideration.[151] Similarly, according to Park, one of the factors that may impact on independence includes 'links of group identification,' such as shared religion and nationality.[152]

However, if this is the case, then the appointment of a Muslim arbitrator in an arbitration impacted by *Shari'a* may be perceived as biased if one of the parties is not Muslim. Similarly, if both parties are Muslim in arbitration proceedings governed by the *i-Arbitration Rules*, and the arbitrator belongs to the same school of thought as one of the parties (e.g., Maliki school of thought), or the same sect of Islam as one of the parties (e.g., Shi'a Islam), would the arbitrator be perceived as biased by the other party? This would open a Pandora's Box, not only for *Shari'a*-based arbitration, but also generally in arbitration proceedings where arbitrators may share a certain ethnicity or political view with one of the parties. On the other hand, if the arbitrator has prejudiced views about people from other religions, nationalities or races then that could classify as 'actual bias.'[153] For example, in an English maritime decision regarding a vessel from Norway and

---

147 Art. 13(5) of the ICC Rules 2012 state: 'The sole arbitrator or the president of the arbitral tribunal shall be of a nationality other than those of the parties. However, in suitable circumstances and provided that none of the parties objects within the time limit fixed by the Court, the sole arbitrator or the president of the arbitral tribunal may be chosen from a country of which any of the parties is a national.'

148 Ilhyung Lee, 'Practice and Predicament: The Nationality of the International Arbitrator (With Survey Results)' (2007) 31(3) *Fordham International Law Journal* 603, 612.

149 Born, above n 53, 1738.

150 Lee, above n 148, 612.

151 Ibid., 616.

152 William Park, 'Arbitrator Bias' (2015) *Transnational Dispute Management* 1, 6. See generally, William Park, 'Neutrality, Predictability and Economic Cooperation' (1995) 12 *Journal of International Arbitration* 99.

153 Ibid.

Portugal, the arbitrator made the following statement, indicative of actual bias in response to one of the counsel's reference to an Italian case:

> Italians are all liars in these cases and will say anything to suit their book. The same thing applies to the Portuguese. But the other side here are Norwegians and in my experience the Norwegians generally are a truthful people. In this case I entirely accept the evidence of the master of the [the Norwegian vessel].[154]

Therefore, actual bias, as clearly evident from arbitrator's comments, can be compared to perceived bias on the basis of nationality or religion. A non-Muslim arbitrator would rarely be appointed in a specialised arbitration where parties are selecting a governing law or arbitral rules impacted by *Shari'a*, because the majority of arbitrators with *Shari'a* expertise tend to be Muslim.[155] Therefore, the idea that an arbitrator may be perceived as 'biased' because they share a common ideology is impractical when *Shari'a* has an impact upon the subject matter of the arbitration. Redfern and Hunter also argue that the concept of 'neutral nationality' could disqualify arbitrators who specialise in certain areas of law, or are fluent in the languages of one of the parties.[156] Therefore, a broad approach to 'bias' will limit the number of arbitrators that may be appointed, and may be misused by parties to unnecessarily delay proceedings. In 2001, Lord Mustill and Stewart Boyd QC noted:

> The continuing deterioration in the spirit of arbitration entails that objections are now being made on the grounds of supposed interest or bias which would never have been put forward in the past. These are, we hope and believe, largely rejected, and they serve the purpose only of wasting time and money.[157]

As discussed in this section, a broad approach to bias under contemporary ICA wields a greater impact on *Shari'a*-based arbitration, because the latter is religious in nature. Therefore, parties have even more grounds to challenge arbitrators based on perceived bias arising from the arbitrator's personal religious views, or possible systemic bias. Due to the reasons mentioned in this section, it is recommended that most jurisdictions adopt a narrow approach, such as the 'real possibility test' and the 'real danger test,' so that arbitrators are not challenged on broad systemic and ideological grounds, unless there is a real danger or real possibility of bias, and to ensure that arbitral awards are enforced internationally.

---

154 re The Owners of the Steamship Catalina and the Owners of the Motor Vessel Norma [1938] 61 Lloyd's Rep. 360.

155 However, as will be discussed in the next chapter, this may be possible in arbitration subject to i-Arbitration Rules where an arbitrator is not required to have Shari'a expertise and the Shari'a matters are referred to an expert witness.

156 Alan Redfern, et al., *Redfern and Hunter on International Arbitration* (Oxford University Press, 5th ed, 2009) 202.

157 Sir Michael Mustill and Stewart Boyd, *Commercial Arbitration: 2001 Companion Volume to the Second Edition* (Butterworths, 2001) 171.

V The limits of party autonomy – from *Jivraj* to gender restrictions

The Supreme Court in the case of *Jivraj* determined that parties had the auton-omy to stipulate the religious qualifications of an arbitrator. However, *Jivraj* does not clarify the impact of clauses where parties also stipulate the gender of the arbitrator. Requirements based on religion may be justified on the basis that in the field of specialised arbitration relating to *Shariʿa* matters such as Islamic finance, an arbitrator who is of Muslim background is more likely to have a holis-tic understanding of *Shariʿa* and be more culturally aware. Furthermore, even if the requirement of religion is found to breach anti-discrimination legislation, matters involving Islamic parties and *Shariʿa*-related matters are more likely to fall into the 'genuine occupational requirement' exception.

On the other hand, it is difficult to justify a qualification that the arbitrator must be male. According to contemporary ICA norms, gender has no impact on arbitration in the way that a qualification based on religion might. Although a woman has recently been appointed as an arbitrator in Saudi Arabia, and gender requirements are not stipulated in Saudi arbitration rules or any *Shariʿa* arbitral rules, one must be careful if an arbitration agreement states that the govern-ing law should be based on the classical Hanbali, Shafiʿi and Maliki schools of thought. In the event that a female arbitrator is appointed, one of the parties may decide to argue that the appointment was inconsistent with an interpretation that follows classical scholars from the noted schools of *Shariʿa*, on the basis of gender, as discussed earlier.

In fact, the issue of gender discrimination and arbitration under *Shariʿa* has been discussed at length in the United Kingdom in the context of domestic fam-ily law disputes, but as will be further argued later, this discussion also has an impact upon commercial matters. The issue of gender discrimination arose in the United Kingdom due to the establishment of faith-based tribunals, such as the Muslim Arbitration Tribunal dealing with domestic arbitration matters involving family law, inheritance and commercial arbitration.[158] The *Arbitration Act 1996* (UK) permits the establishment of *Shariʿa* tribunals, and therefore '[a]s long as the *Shariʿa* courts abide by the provisions set forth in the Arbitration Act, any decision made by the *Shariʿa* court becomes binding.'[159] Social commentators and British politicians have criticised religious arbitration tribunals, such as the MAT, for discriminating against women in family law matters, and it has been argued that women are placed 'in a poorer position than [they] would have been had [they] litigated under British courts.'[160] These concerns have arisen due to decisions which allegedly make it more difficult for women to obtain a divorce,

---

158 Muslim Arbitral Tribunal (2015) <www.matribunal.com>.
159 Maria Reiss, 'The Materialization of Legal Pluralism in Britain: Why Shari'a Council Deci-sions Should Be Non-Binding' (2009) 26 *Arizona Journal of International and Compara-tive Law* 739, 764 as quoted in Rebecca E. Maret, 'Mind the Gap: The Equality Bill and Sharia Arbitration in the United Kingdom' (2013) 36(1) *Boston College International and Comparative Law Review* 255, 267.
160 Ibid.

inheritance laws under which women receive less than men, and the issue of treating two female witnesses as equivalent to one male witness. The latter will be discussed further later in this book.

As a result of these concerns, on 7 June 2011, Baroness Cox of the House of Lords introduced the *Arbitration and Mediation Services (Equality Bill)*[161] to amend the *Equality Act* 2010 and the *Arbitration Act* 1996. One of the main aims of the Equality Bill is to address the issue of discrimination in private arbitration proceedings.[162] The *Equality Bill* seeks to amend the *Equality Act* 2010 by inserting in s 29 (after sub-s 10): 'A person must not, in providing a service in relation to arbitration, do anything that constitutes discrimination, harassment or victimisation on grounds of sex.'[163] Furthermore, the *Equality Bill* will amend the *Arbitration Act 1996* to include a provision under s 6A, entitled 'Discriminatory Terms of Arbitration,' which will prohibit arbitration agreements and processes from stipulating 'any other term that constitutes discrimination on the grounds of sex.'[164] Although the *Equality Bill* was introduced as a result of efforts to combat gender discrimination in the area of family law arbitration, it will also have an impact upon situations such as *Jivraj*, where parties stipulate that the arbitrator must be Muslim and male. Criteria based on gender will not only be in direct breach of the *Equality Bill* if and when it is passed, but thereafter, the amendments proposed in the *Equality Bill* could also be used to argue that the public policy of the United Kingdom views gender restrictions as discriminatory.[165]

Regardless, the *Equality Bill* has been the subject of criticism. The Islamic *Shari'a* Council's secretary, Dr Hasan, argues that Cox does not understand the complexities surrounding the *Shari'a* arbitration process, and is simply basing her opinions on common misconceptions surrounding *Shari'a*.[166] For example, the Muslim Arbitral Tribunal consults an expert panel consisting of women to ensure

161 'Bill stages – Arbitration and Mediation Services (Equality) Bill' [HL] 2014–15 (11 June 2014) <http://services.parliament.uk/bills/2014-15/arbitrationandmediationservices equality/stages.html>.
162 The Equality Bill also seeks to amend the Family Law Act 1996, Criminal Justice and Public Order Act 1994 and the Courts and Legal Services Act 1990 – this book does not deal with these amendments.
163 Arbitration and Mediation Services (Equality) Bill (11 June 2014) <www.publications.par liament.uk/pa/bills/lbill/2014-2015/0021/15021.pdf>.
164 Ibid.
165 Craig Tevendale, 'Jivraj – It's Back and This Time It's at the European Commission' (28 September 2012) *Kluwer Arbitration Blog* <http://kluwerarbitrationblog.com/2012/09/28/jivraj-its-back-and-this-time-its-at-the-european-commission/>.
166 Rebecca E. Maret, 'Mind the Gap: The Equality Bill and Sharia Arbitration in the United Kingdom' (2013) 36(1) *Boston College International and Comparative Law Review* 255, 276.

that there is no discrimination based on gender throughout the arbitration process.[167] In his second reading speech, Lord Bishop of Manchester notes that

> as currently drafted, the Bill appears to present anomalies which could create problems for those who are well aware of their rights, are independently advised and want to approach their faith tribunals for adjudication in a matter which they believe to be covered by the rules of their faith.[168]

The argument that parties should have the autonomy to subject their rights to faith-based tribunals if they are well aware of their rights is similar to the argument made in *Jivraj*. As the law currently stands in the United Kingdom, there is nothing to prevent parties from stipulating that their arbitrator should be both Muslim and male.

VI Conclusion

Due to the concept of party autonomy and the case of *Jivraj*, parties may have the autonomy to stipulate the gender and/or religion of their arbitrator/s within their arbitration agreement. However, such restrictions conflict with international norms, and as shown in this chapter, can raise issues in jurisdictions where anti-discrimination legislation extends to independent contractors such as the United States, and similar issues may arise in the United Kingdom if the *Equality Bill* is passed. Consequently, an arbitration agreement or a set of arbitral rules, guidelines or legislation which stipulates arbitrator qualifications based on gender and/or religion is inconsistent with contemporary ICA standards. This is because the latter focuses on independence, impartiality and expertise as qualifications for arbitrator. It is recommended that the *AAOIFI Standards* and the *Saudi Arbitration Law 2012* clarify the status of arbitrators who are not Muslim, and potentially clarify any gender restrictions which might apply in the event that a literal interpretation of classical *Shari'a* is followed. The objective should be to align with international standards, to ensure that arbitrators are viewed as impartial and independent (as much as possible), and to increase the likelihood of arbitral awards being enforced in jurisdictions where *Shari'a* does not apply.

---

167 Muslim Arbitral Tribunal, History (2015) <www.matribunal.com>.
168 United Kingdom, Parliamentary Debates, House of Lords, 19 October 2012, Column 1683, (Baroness Cox) <www.publications.parliament.uk/pa/ld201213/ldhansrd/text/121019-0001.htm#12101923000438>.

5 Evidence and procedure in *Shari'a* arbitration

I Introduction

This chapter critically analyses evidentiary and procedural rules under both classical *Shari'a* and contemporary *Shari'a*-based arbitration rules (for example, the *IICRA Rules* and *i-Arbitration Rules*).[1]

The chapter is divided into two sections. The first section discusses the issues which arise if classical *Shari'a* is relied upon to govern the arbitration proceedings. One such issue is the violation of procedural fairness if the tribunal applies a certain interpretation of *Shari'a* which treats the evidence of a woman differently to that of a man.

The second section of this chapter discusses whether the evidentiary procedure in relation to expert witnesses as set out in the *i-Arbitration Rules* could violate procedural fairness, and whether the *i-Arbitration Rules* provide comprehensive guidelines on the appointment of a *Shari'a* expert or SAC. Unlike the *IICRA Rules* which simply stipulate that the arbitral tribunal must have the relevant *Shari'a* expertise, the *i-Arbitration Rules* provide that in the event a *Shari'a*-related matter arises, the arbitral tribunal may decide to refer the *Shari'a* aspect of the arbitration to a *Shari'a* expert or the relevant SAC.

It will be argued that the appointment of a *Shari'a* expert or SAC by an arbitral tribunal under the *i-Arbitration Rules* is a better procedure for international commercial arbitrations dealing with complex *Shari'a*-related issues, as opposed to relying on party-appointed expert witnesses, or relying on the expertise of the arbitral tribunal under the *IICRA Rules*. However, using the *UNCITRAL Rules 2010* and *IBA Rules*[2] as a model, it will be argued that the *i-Arbitration Rules* need to be further reformed, and/or an accompanying body of guidelines needs to be drafted, in order to assist the parties and the arbitral tribunal in relation to procedures regulating the appointment of an expert witness.

---

1 See Chapter 1 for a background on the IICRA Rules and the i-Arbitration Rules.
2 International Bar Association Rules on the Taking of Evidence in International Arbitration 2010, as defined in Chapter 1.

II Evidence and procedure under classical *Shari'a* arbitration

As discussed in the preceding chapters of this book, one issue that arises out of *Shari'a*-based arbitration is that it is subject to various interpretations, and is not comprehensively codified in relation to arbitration matters. As discussed in Chapter 1, in the late 19th and early 20th centuries, *Shari'a* was codified with reference to civil law matters during the Ottoman Empire. It took the form of a legal code known as the 'Medjella of Legal Provisions,' and one section of the Medjella was dedicated to arbitration matters.[3] Although the Medjella is often referenced in terms of procedure and evidence under classical *Shari'a* arbitration,[4] it has not been developed since the 20th century, and the Medjella is no longer used in contemporary *Shari'a*-based arbitration. As discussed in previous chapters, in the context of arbitration, *Shari'a* is often referred to in general terms such as 'subject to *Shari'a* law' in the governing law clause. This was the case, for example, in the *Beximco* case, and is similarly stipulated in Art. 5 of the new *Saudi Arbitration Law 2012*. Despite such provisions, domestic law typically governs the procedure itself, which in the case of *Beximco* was English law.

Furthermore, even under the new *Saudi Arbitration Law 2012*, the evidentiary and procedural rules are generally modelled according to the *UNCITRAL Model Law*. Therefore, in the event that an arbitral tribunal was required to apply *Shari'a* to the evidence and procedure of the arbitration, they would find it difficult to precisely ascertain the applicable rules. There are certain principles, such as the prohibition against *riba* and *gharar*, which have the potential of being clarified if the parties further stipulate which industry standards are to be applied, such as the AAOIFI Standards. However, that still does not resolve the issue of how procedural and evidentiary matters which arise under arbitration may be resolved according to *Shari'a*. While the AAOIFI Standards attempt to outline an arbitration procedure, they are extremely vague and poorly drafted. For example, in relation to evidentiary matters, the AAOIFI Standards (which have been published in English by the AAOIFI) note under *Shari'a* Standard No. 32, s 10/4:

> [t]he arbitrator is not supposed to stick to the legally stipulated rules of evidence. Instead, he has the right to make use of any other evidence, provided that the acceptance of that evidence does not contradict with the rules of the Islamic *Shari'a*.[5]

---

3 Arthur Gemmell, 'Commercial Arbitration in the Middle East' (2006) 5 *Santa Clara Journal of International Law* 169, 176; see also, Abdel Hamid El Ahdab and Jalal El Ahdab, *Arbitration with the Arab Countries* (Kluwer Law International, 2011) 16; Aseel Al-Ramahi, 'Sulh: A Crucial Part of Islamic Arbitration' (Working Paper # 12, London School of Economics and Political Science, 2008) 16.

4 See El Ahdab and El Ahdab, above n 3.

5 Accounting and Auditing Organization for Islamic Financial Institutions (AAOIFI), *Shari'ah Standards* (Dar Al Maiman, 2015) 798.

This section fails to articulate the precise evidentiary principles of *Shari'a*, which must not be violated. In the next section, I will discuss the different interpretations of *Shari'a* in relation to the evidentiary testimony provided by a woman. This example will demonstrate why evidentiary rules under classical *Shari'a* are uncertain, and how a particular interpretation of classical *Shari'a* may result in the violation of procedural fairness under ICA norms.

A Procedural fairness and testimony by women under classical Shari'a

Art. 18 of the *UNCITRAL Model Law* states that '[t]he parties shall be treated with equality and each party shall be given a full opportunity of presenting his case.' This principle of equality and procedural fairness[6] is stipulated in most arbitral statutes and rules.[7] When applied, the procedural guarantee under Art. 18 may override the parties' procedural autonomy, and the arbitral tribunal's procedural discretion.[8] Therefore, Art. 18 sets an international standard guaranteeing procedural fairness and equality. Furthermore, Art. V(1)(b) of the *New York Convention* provides that an arbitral award may be not be enforced if 'the party against whom the award is invoked was not given proper notice of the appointment of the arbitrator or of the arbitration proceedings or was otherwise unable to present his case.' Although the exact meaning of procedural fairness and equality have been debated at length, Born states the following:

> the core value reflected by 'equality' of treatment is that both parties are guaranteed the same status before the tribunal. No party is entitled to, or may be given, preferential treatment, favor, or dispensation by virtue of its identity, its nationality, or other factors . . . [i]n particular, equal treatment means applying the same procedural rules and granting the same procedural rights to both parties, while ensuring that non-discriminatory or "like" opportunities and treatment are afforded to both parties.[9]

Therefore, in the event that *Shari'a* governs the arbitral procedure, it is important for parties to clarify which interpretation of *Shari'a* regarding evidentiary testimony will apply to the arbitration. This is because under some interpretations of classical *Shari'a*, the testimony of two women is considered equal to that of one man in financial matters.

---

6 Born observes that although the term 'due process' is often used to indicate the fairness and equality with which parties should be treated, it is preferable to use the term 'procedural fairness' since due process is also used to indicate domestic procedural standards. See Gary Born, *International Commercial Arbitration* (Kluwer Law International, 2nd ed, 2014) 2163.

7 Jeffrey Waincymer, *Procedure and Evidence in International Arbitration* (Kluwer Law International, 2012) 182.

8 Born, above n 6, 2164.

9 Ibid., 2174.

The law of evidence concerning financial matters under classical *Shari'a* in relation to the testimony of women is based on the following Qur'anic verse:

> Call in two men as witnesses. If two men are not there, then call one man and two women out of those you approve as witnesses, so that if one of the two women should forget, the other can remind her.[10]

According to most Islamic jurists, this Qur'anic verse supports the proposition that in financial matters,[11] two women witnesses are needed. However, Islamic scholars have debated the interpretation of this verse due to the fact that in other contexts, a woman's testimony in Islamic history was considered equivalent to that of a man. For example, as discussed in Chapter 2, the hadith is considered one of the most important sources of *Shari'a*, and was often transmitted by women. Therefore, Fadl's research divides Sunni jurists into two realms: firstly, the normative realm in which Muslim jurists recognise women as equal to men due to the transmission of hadith by women; and secondly, the legal-political realm where jurists marginalise the position of women as witnesses or judges in courts of law.[12] In particular, Fadl cites two jurists of the Hanbali school Ibn Taymiyya (who was also mentioned in Chapter 2) and Ibn Qayyim al-Jawziyya (d. 1350 CE)[13] – who focused on the credibility of the witness, as opposed to their gender. Although his approach does not lead to equality of treatment, Ibn Qayyim argued that a woman's testimony was equal to a man's testimony, as long as the judge found that she was 'intelligent and remembers and is trustworthy in her religion.'[14]

Contemporary Islamic scholars such as Muhammad Asad[15] and Ahmad Ali[16] combine the approach of Ibn Qayyim with contextual *ijtihad* to argue that the above Qur'anic verse was revealed in a cultural context where most women did not deal with commercial transactions, and therefore women required the support of other women when providing testimony. Consequently, in a society where women are just as aware and involved in commercial and financial matters as men, there is no need for a woman to be accompanied by another woman when providing testimony. In his commentary on the Qur'an, contemporary Islamic

10 Trans, M. A. S. Abdel Haleem, *The Qur'an* (Oxford University Press, 2004) (Chapter 2, Verse 282).
11 Trans, Seyyed Hossein Nasr, *The Study Quran: A New Translation and Commentary* (HarperCollins Publishers, 2015) 525–527; Mohammad Fadel, 'Two Women, One Man: Knowledge, Power, and Gender in Medieval Sunni Legal Thought' (1997) 29 *International Journal of Middle East Studies* 185, 196.
12 Fadel, above n 11, 196.
13 See generally, Abdul-Rahman Mustafa, *On Taqlīd: Ibn al Qayyim's Critique of Authority in Islamic Law* (Oxford University Press, 2013).
14 Fadel, above n 11, 198.
15 Muhammad Asad, *The Message of the Qur'an* (Gibraltar, 1980) 63.
16 Ahmed Ali, *Al-Qur'an: A Contemporary Translation* (Princeton University Press, rev. ed. 1988).

scholar, Seyyed Hossein Nasr comments that the verse refers to a specific type of financial transaction (forward sales and debts), and that it should be read in context, and in light of the fact that under *Shari'a*, women are able to own property and participate in commercial transactions:

> [i]f one reads this provision for women's testimony in light of the legally established principle upholding women's competence to own property and carry out economic transactions, it suggests that the stipulation regarding women's testimony in the present verse is particular to this circumstance and is meant to address certain social or communal difficulties a woman must face when witnessing in such a case.[17]

Therefore, Nasr views the verse as being revealed in a context where women owned property, but found it difficult to provide testimony due to the patriarchal nature of society at the time.

However, Muslim jurists in Saudi Arabia who follow the Hanbali school of thought might not adopt this view. Although it is difficult to find reported cases, Human Rights Watch has reported that a woman's testimony in Saudi Arabia is still not equivalent to a man's testimony in civil and criminal matters.[18] This is further supported by the religious views of Islamic scholars who advise the government of Saudi Arabia.[19] Regardless, the procedure for arbitration noted under the new *Saudi Arbitration Law 2012* is similar to the *UNCITRAL Model Law* and does not mention the treatment of women as witnesses.[20] It is therefore unclear whether evidentiary rules as interpreted by Islamic scholars in Saudi Arabia will apply to contemporary ICA.

Arguably such evidentiary rules may apply if the arbitration is conducted in Saudi Arabia. An alternative scenario is if parties agree that a certain interpretation of Islamic law should govern their arbitration, such as a strict application of the Hanbali school of thought, whereby the tribunal treats the testimony of two women witnesses is being equivalent to that of one man. In the event that this occurs, procedural fairness could be violated, because parties will not be accorded equal treatment if one of their witnesses is treated differently to witnesses of their opponent on the basis of gender. As discussed in the previous

---

17 Nasr, above n 11, 527–528.
18 Human Rights Watch, 'Arbitrary Detention and Unfair Trials in the Deficient Criminal Justice System of Saudi Arabia' (2010) 20 *Precarious Justice* 91 <www.hrw.org/reports/2008/saudijustice0308/saudijustice0308web.pdf>.
19 Abdullah ibn Qa'ud, et al., 'Hadith Mutawatir and Hadith-ul-Ahad, Fatwa no. 4696' <www.alifta.com/Search/ResultDetails.aspx?languagename=en&lang=en&view=result&fatwaNum=&FatwaNumID=&ID=1245&searchScope=7&SearchScopeLevels1=&SearchScopeLevels2=&highLight=1&SearchType=exact&SearchMoesar=false&bookID=&LeftVal=0&RightVal=0&simple=&SearchCriteria=allwords&PagePath=&siteSection=1&searchkeyword=119111109101110>.
20 See Art. 25 to Art. 37 of the new Saudi Arbitration Law 2012.

chapter, discrimination based on gender may also raise issues under mandatory laws of certain countries.

The next section of this chapter discusses whether it would be preferable for *Shari'a*-based arbitration to be subject to specific *Shari'a* arbitral rules, such as IICRA or the *i-Arbitration Rules* in order to ensure certainty and procedural fairness. The rules of evidence and procedure under the *IICRA Rules* and *i-Arbitration Rules* will be discussed in further detail below. More specifically, the next section will discuss whether qualified arbitrators or expert witnesses should be appointed when dealing with complex *Shari'a* matters.

III Relying on the arbitral tribunal's expertise – *IICRA Rules*

As per Arts. 9 and 10 of the *IICRA Rules*,[21] the arbitration tribunal shall consist of an odd number of arbitrators and as discussed in Chapter 4, the arbitrators must have knowledge and experience in *Shari'a*. Art. 10 also notes that:

> [t]he Centre shall have a list of a sufficient number of jurists, *Sharia'a* specialist[s], economists, trade specialists and professors of universities and institutes of higher learning etc . . . [t]he Centre can seek inspiration from proposals made by chambers of commerce and industry in the Organization of the Islamic Conference member countries and the like to prepare such a list. The parties concerned may consider such a list and select arbiters from it or elsewhere.

Further, Art. 37 of IICRA's procedural rules also state that the Arbitration Panel:

> may refer the draft ruling before it is signed . . . [by] the *Sharia* board of the Centre. The *Sharia'a* Board may introduce amendments in form on the ruling. It may also draw the attention of the Arbitration Panel to substantive issues related to Islamic *Sharia*, without any prejudice to the liberty of the Arbitration Panel in drafting the ruling.

Therefore, the *IICRA Rules* rely on the arbitral tribunal for its *Shari'a* expertise and parties *may* choose to appoint the arbitrators from a list prepared by IICRA. In the event that the arbitrators require more clarification on a matter related to *Shari'a*, they can choose to refer the matter to IICRA's *Shari'a* board. This means that the tribunal has the discretion as to whether the draft ruling should be referred to the *Shari'a* board, and even after referral, the tribunal has the liberty to accept or reject the suggestions of the *Shari'a* board. Since the tribunal has the power to reject the *Shari'a* board's views, this arguably defeats the purpose

---

21 See IICRA, 'Chart and Arbitration and Reconciliation Procedures' <iicra.com/admin/download.php?file_name=arb.pdf&content_type=>.

of *Shari'a*-compliant arbitral rules, and may even lead to a ruling that is not compliant with *Shari'a*. In such a case, the ruling would not be enforceable in Saudi Arabia (especially if the Hanbali school of thought is not applied by the tribunal, but applied by Saudi courts). However, Art. 28 of the *IICRA Rules* states:

> In all cases, the Panel shall exclude any provisions that contradict in the law [sic] that should be applied if such provisions are not in conformity with the rules of Islamic *Sharia*. The Arbitration Panel may invoke for the disputed issue whatever it deems appropriate from among the viewpoints of various schools of Islamic thought, rulings of Islamic Fiqh academies, and opinions of *Sharia* supervisory boards at Islamic financial institutions . . . [t]he Panel may choose to be guided by local international commercial rules or conventions that are not at variance [sic] with the provisions of Islamic *Sharia*.

Thus, even though the tribunal has the discretion to depart from the view of IICRA's *Shari'a* board, *Shari'a* is still an overriding consideration and according to Art. 10 of the *IICRA Rules*, the arbitrator must have knowledge of *Shari'a* principles. The *IICRA Rules* do not elaborate on which interpretation of *Shari'a* will be followed or whether an arbitrator or expert is selected from a list prepared by the IICRA.

Although relying on the tribunal's expertise may suffice in straightforward *Shari'a*-related matters, this procedure may be problematic in more complex *Shari'a* contracts. This involves matters such as the Islamic banking and finance industry, including Islamic bonds (*sukuk*), Islamic insurance (*takaful*) or as discussed later, contractual arrangements which are subject to various *Shari'a* interpretations. One way to address this issue could be to create a separate list of specialised arbitrators who are experts in complex Islamic banking and finance transactions. However, parties are limited to selecting arbitrators who meet the stipulated qualifications under Art. 10 of the *IICRA Rules*. As will be discussed in more detail below, it is difficult to find qualified arbitrators who are experts in *Shari'a* and also have experience in 'trade, industry, finance' as well as contemporary ICA. Even if parties rely on the list of arbitrators prepared by IICRA, the parties may be limited in choice, and the possibility of bias may arise due to the limited pool of arbitrators qualified in *Shari'a* matters.[22]

Finally, if the arbitrators decide to refer the matter to the IICRA *Shari'a* Board as per Art. 37, the parties will be limited to the IICRA *Shari'a* board, which is located in Dubai (UAE). *Shari'a*-based arbitration rules, such as those of IICRA, which require *Shari'a* expertise as a qualification for arbitrators, and refer matters to their own *Shari'a* board, may be suitable for parties from the UAE who are dealing with simple domestic *Shari'a*-related matters. In comparison, the *i-Arbitration Rules* are more flexible than the *IICRA Rules* and attempt to cater for international disputes. They are therefore more relevant to contemporary

---

22 The limited number of Shari'a experts will be discussed more detail below.

ICA. The expert evidence procedure under the *i-Arbitration Rules* will be discussed in more detail below.

IV Expert evidence rules under the *i-Arbitration Rules*

Compared to the *IICRA Rules*, the *i-Arbitration Rules* provide parties with autonomy to select arbitrators of their choice, and if a *Shariʿa* matter arises, it may be referred to a *Shariʿa* expert or the relevant SAC. Under the previous *i-Arbitration Rules*,[23] Rule 8[24] provided the arbitral tribunal with the discretion to refer matters to the SAC as established by the *Central Bank Act* 2009 ('CBA') of Malaysia ('Malaysian SAC').[25] According to Faris Shehabi, former Head of Legal Services at AIAC, the specific reference to the Malaysian SAC was amended so that other *Shariʿa* councils and experts could be appointed and subsequently, cater for the international market.[26] Therefore, the *i-Arbitration Rules* amended in 2013 and the more recent *i-Arbitration Rules* amended in 2018[27] state the following under Rule 11:

1   Whenever the arbitral tribunal has to:

    a)   form an opinion on a point related to *Shariʿa* principles; and

    b)   decide on a dispute arising from the *Shariʿa* aspect of the contract; the arbitral tribunal may refer the matter to the relevant Council or *Shariʿa* expert for its ruling.

2   For the purposes of paragraph 11(1) above, the relevant Council or *Shariʿa* expert shall be:

    a)   the *Shariʿa* council under whose purview the *Shariʿa* aspect to be decided falls, where there is one;[28] or

    b)   where the *Shariʿa* aspect to be decided does not fall under the purview of a specific *Shariʿa* council, a *Shariʿa* council or expert is to be agreed between the parties. Where the parties fail to agree to a *Shariʿa* council or expert, the provisions relating to experts appointed by the arbitral tribunal under Art. 29 shall apply.[29]

---

23 Kuala Lumpur Regional Centre for Arbitration, KLRCA Arbitration Rules 2012, in force on 20 September 2012, <https://lbrcdn.net/cdn/files/gar/articles/KLRCA_i-Arbitration_Rules.pdf>.

24 Ibid.

25 Or the Shariʿa Advisory Council established by the Securities Commission under the Securities Commission Act 1993.

26 Interview with Faris Shehabi, Former Head of Legal Services, Kuala Lumpur Regional Centre of Arbitration (Phone Interview, 15 May 2005).

27 Asian International Arbitration Centre, 'AIAC Arbitration Rules (Revised 2018)' (2018) <www.aiac.world/Arbitration-i-Arbitration/>.

28 S 2(a) of the i-Arbitration Rules is discussed in more detail below.

29 This section refers to 'Experts Appointed by the Arbitral Tribunal' in Art. 29 UNCITRAL Rules 2010, which will be discussed in more detail below.

It is unclear from the *i-Arbitration Rules* whether the decision to choose the SAC rests with the tribunal or the parties. Although Section 1 of Rule 11 states that the arbitral tribunal has the discretion to refer the matter to a SAC, it does not state whether the parties have a choice in deciding which SAC should be appointed. As will be discussed in more detail later, under section 2(b) of Rule 11 of the *i-Arbitration Rules*, parties have the autonomy to select a *Shari'a* council or expert if the *Shari'a* aspect of the arbitration agreement does not fall 'under the purview of a specific *Shari'a* council.' The initial selection of the *Shari'a* expert or SAC is conducted by the arbitral tribunal, and is similar to the appointment of tribunal-appointed experts, which is often preferred by civilian state courts that are more inquisitorial in nature because the role of experts is viewed as being for the benefit of the adjudicator.[30] On the other hand, common law jurisdictions like those in the United Kingdom prefer the adversarial approach where the parties' counsel must present the best possible case, and therefore also has control over the experts.[31] One of the benefits of tribunal-appointed experts is that they are viewed as being more independent than party-appointed experts, and the process is likely to be more cost effective since the tribunal or institution which appoints them can control the costs involved with expert appointment.[32] However, parties have less control over the tribunal-appointed experts, and it is also more difficult for parties to pass on information to experts.[33]

Furthermore, Kantor states that there is a 'legitimate concern that the tribunal-appointed expert will become de facto the fourth arbitrator, unconstrained by reliable scrutiny in the absence of party-appointed experts.'[34] This concern is especially relevant to *Shari'a* experts or a SAC appointed by the arbitral tribunal. For example, if the arbitration consists of a dispute which largely deals with *Shari'a*-related matters, then the decision-making process will heavily rest on the SAC even though, as discussed below, the *i-Arbitration Rules* note that the arbitral tribunal makes the final decision. Furthermore, from a sociocultural perspective, views expressed by *Shari'a* experts hold a lot of weight in Muslim communities due to the nature of religious law. This may not be an issue if both parties are of Muslim background and equally religious. However, if one party is not Muslim and the other party is, and an arbitral tribunal does not consider the views expressed by *Shari'a* experts, there is a risk that the Muslim party will raise concerns, especially if the arbitral award is not in their favour. This is because the views of the religious expert may be viewed by the Muslim party as holding more weight than any other expert evidence presented before the tribunal. This explains why the new *Saudi Arbitration Law 2012* and *IICRA Rules* both stipulate that the arbitration proceedings shall not violate *Shari'a* law. However, it is

---

30 Waincymer, above n 7, 932.
31 Ibid., 932.
32 Ibid., 934.
33 Ibid., 934.
34 Mark Kantor, 'A Code of Conduct for Party-Appointed Experts in International Arbitration – Can One Be Found?' (2010) 26(3) *Arbitration International* 323, 336.

important to note that Rule 11.8 of the *i-Arbitration Rules* has made clear that the decision of the SAC will not be binding on the arbitral tribunal:

> For avoidance of doubt, the ruling of the relevant Council or the *Shari'a* expert may only relate to the issue or question so submitted by the arbitral tribunal and the relevant Council or the *Shari'a* expert shall not have any jurisdiction in making discovery of facts or in applying the ruling or formulating any decision relating to any fact of the matter which is solely for the arbitral tribunal to determine.

This is despite the fact that under Section 56 of the CBA in Malaysia, the opinion of the SAC shall be binding on arbitral tribunals and courts. The position under the CBA is also a clear example of the weight that is typically placed on the opinions of *Shari'a* experts in Muslim communities.[35] The *i-Arbitration Rules* have departed from the CBA in order to ensure that they can be used internationally and more importantly, to be consistent with international norms; that is, the final decision must be made by the arbitral tribunal and not the expert witness. This is another example of the tension that exists between strict compliance with *Shari'a* on the one hand, and the need to comply with international standards on the other. The next section discusses the role of party-appointed experts under the *i-Arbitration Rules*.

V Party-appointed experts

As briefly mentioned previously, under Rule 11 of the *i-Arbitration Rules*, 'where the *Shari'a* aspect to be decided does not fall under the purview of the specific *Shari'a* council, a *Shari'a* council or expert is to be agreed between the parties.' Regarding matters which may fall under the purview of a specific *Shari'a* council, the commentary within the question and answer section provided by the AIAC notes:

> it is important to know the law applicable to your place(s) of business. Due to the Government regulation of the banking sector in relation to Islamic financial instruments and capital requirements, some *Shari'a* aspects may come under national laws. In Malaysia, for example Islamic banking is regulated by the Central Bank of Malaysia and the Islamic Capital Market is regulated by the Securities Commission. Both maintain *Shari'a* Advisory Councils.[36]

However, it is less clear which matters may fall within or outside the purview of a *Shari'a* council in an international setting. This is because the *Shari'a* governance

---

35 See also, Mohd Alias Ibrahim v. RHB Bank BHD & Anor [2011] 4 CLJ 654 (25 April 2011) (High Court Malaya). In this case, it was determined that the binding nature of the Malaysian SAC did not breach natural justice.

36 Asian International Arbitration Centre, Frequently Asked Questions (2018) <https://aiac.world/wp-content/i-arbitration/rules_iarb_en/PDF-Flip/PDF.pdf> 89.

structure in Middle Eastern countries is less centralised than in Malaysia, and rather than being regulated by national laws, each institution in the Middle East has its own team of *Shari'a* experts which make up a *Shari'a* Supervisory Board (SSB).[37] One of the major roles of the SSB include certifying whether financial instruments are *Shari'a*-compliant, and preparing reports ensuring that all transactions are *Shari'a*-compliant, which is then incorporated into the institution's annual report.[38]

Some leading financial institutions with well-known SSBs in the Middle East include the: Dallah al-Baraka Bank in Saudi Arabia; Kuwait Finance House; Dubai Islamic Bank; and the Islamic Development Bank in Saudi Arabia.[39] Furthermore, *Shari'a* experts may also be found at leading institutions or regulatory bodies such as the Institute of Islamic Research – Al Azhar University at Egypt, AAOIFI, Fiqh Institute or Academy of the Organisation of Islamic Conference in Jeddah and the Islamic Jurisprudence Institute of the Islamic League in Makkah.[40]

Due to the large number of *Shari'a* experts and SSBs in the Middle East, the issue that arises at an international level is not whether the relevant *Shari'a* council has expertise but, as will be discussed in further detail later, the different interpretations of *Shari'a* which are followed by the experts. The *i-Arbitration Rules* seem to encourage a more proactive arbitral tribunal, and parties only have the autonomy to choose their own expert in the event that a *Shari'a* aspect of the arbitration falls outside the purview of the relevant *Shari'a* council. This may be rare if Middle Eastern parties are involved.

Kantor notes that an approach favouring tribunal-appointed experts as opposed to party-appointed experts denies parties the opportunity to 'present an expert witness of its own choice . . . and the right to fairly present its case.'[41] Thus, the *i-Arbitration Rules* may be criticised for not providing parties with the autonomy to select their own *Shari'a* expert. On the other hand, it should be noted that despite party-appointed experts being common in ICA, they are often subject to criticism. This is due to the risk that party-appointed experts may misuse their position by advocating on behalf of the parties instead of providing impartial evidence.[42] There can also be higher costs associated with party-

37 Hichem Hamza, 'Sharia Governance in Islamic Banks: Effectiveness and Supervision Model' (2013) 6(3) *International Journal of Islamic and Middle Eastern Finance and Management* 226; Wafik Grais and Matteo Pellegrini, 'Corporate Governance in Institutions Offering Islamic Financial Services – Issues and Options' (Working Paper 4052, World Bank Policy Research, 2006) 17–21.

38 Wafik Grais and Matteo Pellegrini, 'Corporate Governance in Institutions Offering Islamic Financial Services – Issues and Options' (Working Paper 4052, World Bank Policy Research, 2006) 17.

39 Islamic Development Bank, 'Modes of Finance' (2014) <www.isdb.org/mof/index.html#p=2>.

40 Mahmoud El Gamal, *Islamic Finance: Law, Economics, and Practice* (Cambridge University Press, 2006) 32.

41 Kantor, above n 34, 336.

42 Waincymer, above n 7, 933.

appointed experts, particularly when more than one expert and/or shadow experts are appointed.[43] Another issue that may arise in the context of *Shari'a*-based arbitration is where an arbitral tribunal will have to consider which expert to rely upon, especially due to various interpretations and schools of thought to which *Shari'a* is subject.

Furthermore, in a multi-person tribunal, if one of the tribunal members has a pre-determined view on a *Shari'a* aspect of the arbitration, and each party appoints an expert who has different views, how should the tribunal determine which view to follow? Since *Shari'a*-based disputes are often theoretical in nature, it may be difficult to make an assessment based on the evidence provided by each of the parties.

One major difference between the *i-Arbitration Rules* and the *UNCITRAL Rules 2010* is that the latter makes provision for party-appointed experts, whereas the *i-Arbitration Rules* do not elaborate on party-appointed experts, other than stating under Rule 11 that parties may jointly appoint an expert if the *Shari'a* matter does not fall under the purview of a SAC.

One solution could be for the *i-Arbitration Rules* to adopt the wording of Art. 29 of the *UNCITRAL Rules 2010* as follows: '[a]fter consultation with the parties, the arbitral tribunal may appoint one or more independent experts to report to it.' As noted previously, Rule 11 of the *i-Arbitration Rules* only refer to Art. 29 of the *UNCITRAL Rules 2010* if the parties fail to agree on a *Shari'a* council or expert, and where the *Shari'a* aspect of the decision does not fall within the purview of a specific *Shari'a* council. Instead, Rule 11 should state in the beginning: '[a]fter consultation with the parties and whenever the arbitral tribunal has to. . . .' Adding provision for consultation between the parties and the tribunal may ensure that a consistent view of *Shari'a* is agreed upon.

Additionally, if the i-Arbitration wishes to provide parties with the option of appointing their own experts, the AIAC could develop guidelines similar to the *IBA Rules*[44] or the *CIArb Protocol*,[45] outlining policies and procedures for pre-hearing or 'witness' meetings. For example, Art. 5.4 of the *IBA Rules* states:

> The Arbitral Tribunal in its discretion may order that any Party-Appointed Experts who will submit or who have submitted Expert Reports on the same or related issues meet and confer on such issues. At such meeting, the Party-Appointed Experts shall attempt to reach agreement on the issues within the scope of their Expert Reports, and they shall record in writing any such issues on which they reach agreement, any remaining areas of disagreement and the reasons therefore.

---

43 Ibid., 934.
44 IBA Rules is defined in Chapter 1 and refers to the International Bar Association Rules on the Taking of Evidence in International Arbitration 2010.
45 CIArb Protocol is defined in Chapter 1 and refers to the Chartered Institute of Arbitrators Protocol for the Use of Party-Appointed Expert Witnesses in International Arbitration 2007.

Similarly, Art. 6 of the *CIArb Protocol* advises party-appointed experts to: (1) consult with each other and identify a list of issues which they are required to provide an opinion on, their agreements and disagreements (as well as a summary of the reasons for disagreement) and the methodology through which issues will be addressed; (2) provide the parties and the tribunal with a statement of the discussions; and (3) produce and exchange written expert opinions. Conferences and meetings between parties, the tribunal and experts, as well as detailed guidelines such as Art. 6 of the *CIArb Protocol*, will ensure that any differences arising out of interpretations of *Shariʿa* are acknowledged and addressed prior to producing the expert report.

Alternatively, the *i-Arbitration Rules* could adopt a hybrid solution as proposed by Dr Klaus Sachs, in order to address some of the concerns which arise from relying on either tribunal or party-appointed experts.[46] Sachs suggests that an alternative may be to have an arbitral tribunal select an 'expert team' composed of one expert from each list put forward by the parties.[47] This expert team would provide expertise to the arbitral tribunal, as well as having the duty of being independent and impartial.[48] Since the 'expert team' would consist of experts selected by both parties, it would ensure that the expert evidence is viewed as impartial, and it would also provide parties with the autonomy to select their own experts. The 'expert team' is similar to the concept of a *Shariʿa* council, except that it will comprise of experts selected by the parties, and thus the parties would be creating their own *Shariʿa* council instead of relying on an already established council. However, there is still a risk that the 'expert team' may consist of experts who have very different theoretical views. For example, even if each party prepared a list of possible experts and the arbitral tribunal then selects experts from both lists, there is still a chance that each party will only choose experts who have a particular interpretation of *Shariʿa*, which suits the respective party's case. Although the Sachs' proposal may address issues such as providing parties with the autonomy to select their own experts, agreeing upon one expert or one *Shariʿa* council is a better option, because it will most likely limit theoretical disputes on *Shariʿa* matters. This is because, as will be discussed in the next section, the *Shariʿa* scholars who make up a *Shariʿa* board are generally consistent in their views; however, the issue that arises is which SAC or *Shariʿa* expert to appoint.

VI Choice of *Shariʿa* experts or councils as expert witnesses

Rule 11 under the *i-Arbitration Rules* is also unclear on the procedure by which an arbitral tribunal is to select a *Shariʿa* expert or council. This is extremely important in situations where parties are divided on theoretical interpretations of

---

46 Klaus Sachs and Nils Schmidt-Ahrendts, 'Experts: Neutrals or Advocates' (2010) *International Council for Commercial Arbitration Conference 2010* 14, 57.
47 Ibid., 14, 57.
48 Ibid., 14, 57.

Shari'a. For example, if one party is from a country in the Middle East and the other party is from Malaysia, and they choose to subject their arbitration to the *i-Arbitration Rules,* the arbitral tribunal will have to decide whether to rely on a *Shari'a* expert from the Middle East or the Malaysian SAC. Furthermore, each *Shari'a* expert may have a different interpretation of *Shari'a* rules.[49] In particular, this section will provide examples of the different views on the following Islamic finance contracts: *bay al-inah, tawarruq* and the *ibra'* clause.

A Bay al-inah

The Islamic finance contract, *bay al-inah* or 'sale with immediate repurchase' or 'same-item sale-repurchase to circumvent the prohibition of interest-based lending,'[50] is a contract in which a seller or bank sells an item to the buyer at an agreed price (inclusive of profit) to be paid at a later date (on credit). Subsequently, the seller or bank immediately repurchases the item at a cash price lower than the agreed selling price.[51] Another form of the *bay al-inah* contract is when the seller buys an item for cash price and then sells the same item to the buyer for a higher price (inclusive of profit) on credit.[52] The difference between the prices is the profit that the bank earns.

In Arabic, *bay* means sale, and Maliki jurists further comment that *al inah* is either derived from the Arabic word *al-ain,* which means cash, or *al-annu,* which means assistance.[53] In either case, the classical *Shari'a* understanding is that *bay al-inah* is a sale through which cash is generated. Although they did not explicitly refer to the contemporary term '*bay al-inah,*' the classical jurists discussed a contract whereby an asset is sold in credit and then immediately repurchased at a different price.[54]

According to the Maliki, Hanafi and Hanbali schools of thought, this contract was not permissible because the profit earned by the seller was viewed as being equivalent to *riba* (interest).[55] For example, classical *Shari'a* scholar Ibn Rushd

---

49 See generally, Salman Khan, 'The Role of Shari'a Advisement in an Islamic Financial Institution' in Humayon Dar and Umar Moghul (eds), *The Chancellor Guide to the Legal and Sharia Aspects of Islamic Finance* (Harriman House, 2010).

50 El Gamal, above n 40, 70.

51 Securities Commission Malaysia, 'Resolutions of the Shariah Advisory Council of the Securities Commission Malaysia' (2012–2014) <www.sc.com.my/wpcontent/uploads/eng/html/icm/Resolution_SAC_2012-2014.pdf>.

52 Kabir Hassan, Rasem Kayed and Umar Aimhanosi Oseni, *Introduction to Islamic Banking & Finance: Principles and Practice* (Pearson, 2013) 90–91.

53 Amir Shaharuddin, 'The Bay al Inah Controversy in Malaysian Islamic Banking' (2012) 26 *Arab Law Quarterly* 499, 500.

54 Ibid., 500.

55 Dr. Mohamad Akram Laldin, Dr. Mohamed Fairooz Abdul Khir and Nusaibah Mohd Parid, 'Fatwas in Islamic Banking: A Comparative Study Between Malaysia and Gulf Cooperation Council (GCC) Countries' (2012) Research Paper 31 *International Shari'ah Research Academy for Islamic Finance* 1, 91; Shaharuddin, above n 53, 501; Hassan, Kayed and Oseni, above n 52, 91.

followed the Maliki school of thought and argued that the *bay al-inah* sale was a legal trick (*hilah*), in which an item was simply being exchanged for the purpose of generating profit for the seller, which was equivalent to *riba*.[56] This is the approach followed by the majority of *Shari'a* experts in the Middle East, including the SSBs at the Dallah al-Baraka Bank, Kuwait Finance House, Dubai Islamic Bank, AAOIFI, Academy of the Organisation of Islamic Conference and the Islamic Jurisprudence Institute of the Islamic League.[57]

On the other hand, Idris Shafi'i, the founder of the *Shafi'i* school, viewed the *inah* contract as acceptable in his book on jurisprudence, *Kitab Al-Umm*. Although this view was followed by early *Shafi'i* jurists such as Al-Mawardi (d. 1058 CE), later *Shafi'i* jurists such as Ibn Hajar (d. 1449 CE), Zakariya Al-Ansari (d. 1520 CE), Al Sharbini (d. 1569 CE) and Al-Ramli (d. 1595 CE) all disapproved of the *inah* sale, because the profit earned by the seller was viewed as *riba*.[58] Therefore, parties cannot simply resolve the differences of opinion regarding the *bay al-inah* contract by stipulating that the governing law of the *Shafi'i* school of thought applies, which may lead the arbitral tribunal to select the Malaysian SAC as the *Shari'a* council to provide expert evidence, since further problems may arise due to the differences that exist within the *Shafi'i* school of thought.

Interestingly, the Malaysian SAC has also struggled with the permissibility of *bay al-inah*. In 1997, the Malaysian SAC ruled that *bay al-inah* was permissible according to the *Shafi'i* doctrine.[59] The Malaysian SAC also justified the *bay al-inah* contract on the basis that it is not clearly prohibited in the Qur'an or *sunna*. Furthermore, they use the principle of *maslaha*[60] to argue that the *bay al-inah* contract is necessary in the contemporary Islamic banking system, to ensure that international commercial and business dealings can take place.[61] However, on 27 February 2014, the Malaysian SAC updated the 1997 resolution, and ruled that the *bay al-inah* contract was only permissible if the following requirements were met:

1   There are two valid and separate contracts and each contract complies with *Shari'a*.
2   The contracts should not stipulate a condition for the repurchase or resale of an asset.
3   The sale and purchase contracts are separate and thus, should be executed at different times.

---

56 Shaharuddin, above n 53, 499.
57 Hassan, Kayed and Oseni, above n 52, 90–91; Laldin, Khir and Parid, above n 55, 18–19.
58 Habib Ahmed and Nourah Mohammad Aleshaikh, 'Debate on Tawarruq: Historical Discourse and Current Rulings' (2014) 28(3) *Arab Law Quarterly* 278, 288–289; Shaharuddin, above n 53, 501.
59 Securities Commission Malaysia, 'Resolutions of the Securities Commission Shariah Advisory Council' (2004) <www.sc.com.my/wp-content/uploads/eng/html/icm/Resolutions_SAC_2ndedition.pdf>; Shaharuddin, above n 53, 508.
60 Maslaha (public interest) was discussed in detail in Chapter 1.
61 Shaharuddin, above n 53, 508.

4   The first sale contract should be concluded separately to the subsequent contract and the selling party should sign the contract before the purchasing party.

5   Once the asset is sold, the purchaser should own and possess the asset (constructively or physically).[62]

The Malaysian SAC stipulated the above-mentioned conditions in order to ensure that the profit earned by the seller or bank through a *bay al-inah* contract was distinguished from *riba*.

B *Tawarruq*

Tawarruq is another popular Islamic finance contract which has been subject to much debate. Also referred to as 'reverse murabaha,' *tawarruq* is a sale contract through which a buyer purchases an item from a financial institution and pays the financial institution on a deferred payment basis. The buyer then generates cash by selling the item to a third party.[63] Therefore, the *tawarruq* contract is similar to the *bay al-inah* contract, except that the involvement of a third party makes it more acceptable according to most *Shari'a* scholars. This is because *tawarruq* is considered permissible by most *Shari'a* bodies, such as the Malaysian SAC, AAOIFI, Dallah al-Baraka Bank, Dubai Islamic Bank and Kuwait Finance House.

One the other hand, classical Hanbali jurist Ibn Taymiyya argued that *tawarruq* was impermissible because

> [t]he precise economic substance for which riba was forbidden is present in this [*tawarruq*] contract, and transaction costs are increased through purchase and sale at a loss of some commodity. *Shari'a* would not forbid a smaller harm and permit a greater one.[64]

This view is also followed by *Shari'a* bodies in Saudi Arabia such as the Academy of the Organisation of Islamic Conference in Jeddah, Saudi Arabia ('OIC')[65] and the Muslim World League in Makkah, Saudi Arabia ('MWL'). At the 17th session of the Islamic Fiqh Council of the MWL (2003), the organisation issued a *fatwa* that *tawarruq* was not permissible under *Shari'a*, because it was viewed as being similar to the *bay al-inah* contract except that a third party was involved and therefore, the profit earned by the bank was equivalent to *riba*. Consequently,

---

62 Securities Commission Malaysia, 'Resolutions of the Shariah Advisory Council of the Securities Commission Malaysia' (2012–2014) <www.sc.com.my/wp-content/uploads/eng/html/icm/Resolution_SAC_2012-2014.pdf> 8–12.

63 Ahmed and Aleshaikh, above n 58, 288–289.

64 As reported by Ibn Qayyim Al-Jawziyya, Hanbali Jurist and student of Ibn Taymiyyah. See, El Gamal, *Islamic Finance: Law, Economics and Practice*, above n 40, 72.

65 International Shari'ah Research Academic for Islamic Finance, Fatwa in Islamic Finance <http://ifikr.isra.my/documents/10180/16168/blp-isra%20sep%20bulletin%20Tawarruq.pdf>.

it was argued by both the MWL and the OIC that in *tawarruq* and *bay al-inah* contracts, commodities are simply bought and sold to generate profit for banks, which are often equivalent to market interest rates.[66]

C *Ibra'*

The concept of an *'ibra' clause'* under Islamic banking and finance is similar to a 'rebate' under the conventional banking system. If an *ibra'* clause is included in a contract, a bank may waive some debts completely or partially in the event that customers make early settlement.[67] The SAC of Bank Negara Malaysia argues that the inclusion of an *ibra'* clause is permissible, because it protects the interests of the parties, and removes uncertainties (*gharar*) in price.[68] On the other hand, the majority of Middle Eastern *Shari'a* councils, such as the AAOIFI, Dallah al-Baraka Bank, Dubai Islamic Bank, Fiqh Institute and Kuwait Finance House, view the stipulation of *ibra'* as being similar to *riba* and hence, not permissible.[69]

D *Recommendations*

Due to the above-mentioned examples of theoretical differences amongst *Shari'a* advisory boards and the strong influence that a *Shari'a* expert will have on the final decision, it is extremely important for the arbitral tribunal to consult the parties, in order to ensure that they have input as to which SAC is chosen and are also aware of which *Shari'a* Advisory Council is chosen. Further, as will be discussed in more detail in the next section, the tribunal should ensure that the *Shari'a* advisory body is independent impartial, and has no conflict of interest with any of the parties.[70]

VII Procedure for *Shari'a* experts

Under Rule 11(2)(b) of the *i-Arbitration Rules*, Art. 29 of the *UNCITRAL Rules 2010* shall only apply in the event that parties fail to agree on a SAC or expert. Art. 29 of the *UNCITRAL Rules 2010* sets forth a procedure for experts appointed by the arbitral tribunal which includes the following: consultation with the parties prior to appointing an expert; the expert's terms of reference prepared by the arbitral tribunal; a procedure for the expert which includes submitting to the arbitral tribunal a statement of independence and impartiality; a procedure

---

66 Muslim World League Islamic Fiqh Council, *Resolutions of Islamic Fiqh Council* <http://themwl.org/downloads/Resolutions-of-Islamic-Fiqh-Council-2.pdf> 447; Dr. Sami ibn Ibrahim al Swaylim, *Tawarruq Banking Products* (Organization of the Islamic Conference – The International Islamic Fiqh Academy, 2009).
67 Hassan, Kayed and Oseni, above n 52, 119.
68 Laldin, Khir and Parid, above n 55, 28.
69 Ibid., 29.
70 Waincymer, above n 7, 941.

through which parties provide the expert with relevant information; reference to an expert report prepared by the tribunal-appointed expert; and a procedure through which parties may choose to interrogate the expert at a hearing.

The procedure set forth under Art. 29 of the *UNCITRAL Rules 2010* is consistent with international norms with regard to the procedure for expert witnesses appointed by an arbitral tribunal. A similar procedure for tribunal experts is noted in Art. 21 of the *LCIA Arbitration Rules 2014*, Art. 25 of the *ICC Rules 2012*, Art. 25 of the *International Centre for Dispute Resolution Rules 2014*, Art. 27 of the *Swiss Rules of International Arbitration 2012*,[71] Art. 25 of the *Hong Kong International Arbitration Centre Administered Rules 2013*[72] and Art. 26 of the *Arbitration Rules of the Singapore International Arbitration Centre*[73]. As will be discussed later, a more comprehensive procedure for tribunal-appointed experts and contents of the expert report is set forth under Art. 6 of the *IBA Rules*.

However, the issue that arises under the *i-Arbitration Rules* is that while Art. 29 of the *UNCITRAL Rules 2010* is referred to in the event that the parties cannot agree upon an expert, the initial referral by the arbitral tribunal to the SAC or *Shari'a* expert under Rule 11 does not stipulate a procedure similar to that of tribunal-appointed experts as contained in the above-mentioned arbitration rules. As will be argued in more detail later, it is important for the *i-Arbitration Rules* to stipulate a procedure by which a SAC or *Shari'a* expert operates and interacts with the arbitral tribunal. Further, this procedure should align with international standards in order to ensure that the arbitral tribunal is acting fairly. Waincymer notes that 'considerations of fairness can be further broken down into general principals of due process, equality of treatment, and providing each party with a sufficient opportunity to present its case.'[74] If such fairness standards are not met, the arbitral award may not be enforced in countries that are signatory to the *New York Convention* under Art. V(1)(b) which allows domestic courts to refuse enforcement of the arbitral award on the basis that parties were unable to present their case. This issue will be discussed in more detail in the following sections.

A Statement of independence and impartiality

Under Rule 11 of the *i-Arbitration Rules*, there is no provision requiring a *Shari'a* expert to submit a statement of independence to the arbitral tribunal and to the parties, as per the procedure articulated for tribunal-appointed experts under Art. 29(2) of the *UNCITRAL Rules 2010* and Art. 6.2 of the *IBA Rules*. Both sets of rules stipulate that the arbitral tribunal must appoint an independent expert witness, and this is one of the crucial differences between a party-appointed witness

---

71 Swiss Rules of International Arbitration, effective June 2012.
72 Hong Kong International Arbitration Centre Administered Arbitration Rules, effective 1 September 2008.
73 Arbitration Rules of the Singapore International Arbitration Centre (6th edition), effective 1 August 2016.
74 Waincymer, above n 7, 13. See generally, Waincymer, above n 7, 12–24.

and tribunal-appointed witness.[75] The issue of independence for party-appointed witnesses is more relevant when considering the probative value of their evidence, whereas tribunal-appointed witnesses are required to be independent from the outset, otherwise their appointment may be challenged by the parties.[76] The procedure under Art. 6 of the *IBA Rules* consists of the tribunal-appointed expert submitting to the arbitral tribunal his or her qualifications and a statement of independence from the parties, their legal advisors and the arbitral tribunal. The Arbitral Tribunal will then give the parties a chance to object to the tribunal-appointed expert's qualifications and independence within a specified time. In the event that parties wish to object after the expert witness has been appointed, Art. 6.2 of the *IBA Rules* also states that: '[a]fter the appointment of a Tribunal-Appointed Expert, a Party may object to the expert's qualifications or independence only if the objection is for reasons of which the Party becomes aware after the appointment has been made.'

However, unlike arbitrators (see Chapter 4), standards of independence required of expert witnesses are not codified, but arguably the 'justifiable doubt' standard may also be applied for expert witnesses as well as arbitrators. In the case of *Canada – Continued Suspension of Obligations in the EC-Hormones Dispute*,[77] the WTO Appellate Body noted that:

> [i]n the case of an expert, the panel should assess the disclosed information against information submitted by the parties or other information that may be available. It should then determine whether, on the correct facts, there is a likelihood that the expert's independence and impartiality may be affected, or if justifiable doubts arise as to the expert's independent (sic) or impartiality. If this is indeed the case, a panel must not appoint such person as an expert.[78]

Arguably, in the context of Islamic banking and finance, 'justifiable doubts' may arise regarding the expert's independence and impartiality in the event that the *Shari'a* expert or SAC appointed by the arbitral tribunal also serves as a *Shari'a* advisor to one of the parties to the arbitration. On the one hand, this issue may be alleviated by the fact that certain *Shari'a* governance models and domestic legislation restrict *Shari'a* advisors from advising more than one financial institution. For example, in Malaysia, the *Shari'a* advisors on the SAC are regulated by the *Central Bank Act* of Malaysia.[79] Under the governance model

---

75 Nathan D. O'Malley, *Rules of Evidence in International Arbitration: An Annotated Guide* (Routledge, 2012) 172.

76 Ibid., 172.

77 Appellate Body Report, Canada – Continued Suspension of Obligations in the EC-Hormones Dispute, WT/DS321/AB/R (16 October 2008).

78 Ibid., 256.

79 The previous Central Bank Act 1958 clearly stipulated under the s 16B(6) that a Shari'a advisor can only serve as a member of a Shari'a committee in one financial institution in the

provided by the Bank Negara Malaysia Guidelines entitled '*Shariʿa* Governance Framework,' an Islamic financial institution ('IFI'):

> shall not appoint any member of its *Shariʿa* Committee from a *Shariʿa* Committee of another IFI within the same industry. This is to ensure that the committee member would be more focused, avoiding conflict of interest and maintaining the confidentiality of information.[80]

On the other hand, there are no restrictions on the number of SACs or *Shariʿa* Supervisory Boards upon which an expert may serve in Middle Eastern countries such as Kuwait, Bahrain, UAE, Qatar or Saudi Arabia. This makes it even more necessary for a SAC or *Shariʿa* advisor to file a statement of independence where the SAC or expert is located in Middle Eastern countries in which there are no restrictions, in order to ensure internationally accepted standards are met. The recent *i-Arbitration Rules* attempt to appeal to the international market, and not just the domestic market in Malaysia.

Internationally, the shortage of qualified *Shariʿa* scholars in the Islamic banking and finance industry means that *Shariʿa* advisors often sit on numerous SACs or SSBs. This was highlighted in the context of a report titled 'Islamic Finance in the UK: Regulation and Challenges' issued by the Financial Services Authority, which noted that: '[t]he shortage of appropriately qualified *Shariʿa* scholars in the Islamic financial industry means it is common for individual scholars to hold positions on the SSBs of a number of Islamic firms.'[81] Similarly, commentators observe that:

> [t]he very same issue of conflict of interest related to concentration of a few scholars is related to the lack of standards in qualifying *Shariʿa* practitioners, as a number of scholars have risen to prominence without going through any substantive standards of scrutiny.[82]

Research conducted by Funds@Work,[83] and the online database Zawya established by Thomson Reuters, highlights the profile of several *Shariʿa* scholars who hold multiple board memberships internationally, as well as involvement in consulting firms, standard setting bodies, unions and government entities in the IBF

same industry. Although the new Central Bank Act 2009 does not have such a provision, the new Bank Negara Malaysia Guidelines have maintained this position.

80 Bank Negara Malaysia, 'Shariah Governance Framework' (2010) <www.bnm.gov.my/guidelines/05_shariah02_Shariah_Governance_Framework_20101026.pdf> 20.

81 Michael Ainley, et al., 'Islamic Finance in the UK: Regulation and Challenges' (Report, Financial Services Authority, 2007) 17.

82 Sayd Farook and Mohammad Omar Farooq, 'Shari'ah Governance, Expertise and Profession: Educational Challenges in Islamic Finance' (2013) 5(1) *ISRA International Journal of Islamic Finance* 137, 141.

83 Murat Unal, *The Small World of Islamic Finance: Shariah Scholars and Governance – A Network Analytic Perspective* (Funds@Work, 2011).

industry. For example, Zawya lists one of the most influential Islamic finance scholars, Nizam Mohammed Yacoubi ('Yacoubi'), and discloses his 98 current and former board positions.[84] Yacoubi sits on a number of SSBs, including leading Islamic financial institutions such as the Bahrain Islamic Bank, Abu Dhabi Islamic Bank (UAE), Khaleeji Commercial Bank (Bahrain), European Islamic Investment Bank (United Kingdom) and Citi Islamic Investment Bank (Bahrain). This is common for a number of well-known *Shari'a* scholars in the IBF industry such as Abdul Satar Abdul Karim Abu Ghuddah, Mohammed Ali Elgari, Abdul Aziz Khalifa Al Qassai and more.[85]

Further, in an article by Abbas, Yacoubi states that there are only 50 to 60 Islamic scholars who are qualified to advise banks on *Shari'a* matters internationally.[86] The shortage of scholars is also perpetuated by the fact that *Shari'a* advisors require extensive qualifications including knowledge of Islamic jurisprudence (*usul al-fiqh*), Islamic transaction/commercial law (*fiqh al-mu'amalat*) and conventional finance. Some countries also have National *Shari'a* Councils (NSCs); for example, Malaysian NSCs include the National *Shari'a* Advisory Council or the SAC of Bank Negara Malaysia, and the Pakistani NSC includes the National *Shari'a* Board, which operates under the State Bank of Pakistan.[87] Each NSC, SSB or SAC may have a different set of qualification criteria. For example, the Bank Negara Malaysia requires the *Shari'a* member to have knowledge on Islamic jurisprudence and Islamic commercial law.[88] On the other hand, the State Bank of Pakistan requires a *Shari'a* scholar to have the following qualifications:

- At least five years of experience in issuing religious rulings;
- Knowledge of the banking industry;
- Master's degree in Islamic education, or economics, banking and finance;
- Solvency and financial integrity; and
- Personal integrity, honesty and reputation.[89]

Abbas notes that:

> [s]cholars must be expert not only in Islamic law and Islamic banking, but also have a thorough knowledge of conventional laws and banking

84 Thomson Reuters Zawya, 'Shariah Scholars' <www.zawya.com/shariahscholars/sch_profile. cfm?scholarid=9>.
85 Unal, above n 83.
86 Mohammed Abbas, 'Shortage of Scholars Troubles Islamic Banking' (2008) *The New York Times* <www.nytimes.com/2008/01/22/business/worldbusiness/22iht-bank.4.9412578. html?_r=0&pagewanted=print>.
87 Khan, above n 49, 367.
88 Bank Negara Malaysia, 'Guidelines on the Governance of Shariah Committee for the Islamic Financial Institutions' <www.bnm.gov.my/guidelines/01_banking/04_prudential_ stds/23_gps.pdf>.
89 Islamic Banking Department of State Bank of Pakistan, 'Fit & Proper Criteria for Appointment of Shariah Advisors' (2004) <www.sbp.org.pk/ibd/2004/f%20&%20p%20test%20 for%20sa.pdf>

systems . . . [e]ven then, a scholar will only be taken seriously after years of experience, according to many of the delegates at a Bahrain conference on Islamic banking.[90]

This is clear from the qualifications of *Shari'a* experts in the field of IBF who have an international reputation.

Therefore, given the limited number of *Shari'a* scholars who are experts in the IBF industry, and the fact that many of these scholars sit on several *Shari'a* boards, the probability that parties may raise objections for lack of independence or impartiality increases. For these reasons, it is vital in a *Shari'a*-based arbitration for an expert witness to file a statement of independence and impartiality which also lists the *Shari'a* scholar's involvement in all the relevant SACs, SSBs, relevant government entities, consulting firms and standard settings bodies in the field of IBF. This will reduce the risk of a conflict arising in the future, and ensure independence of the expert witness as per international standards.[91]

B *Expert report*

Art. 6.4 of the *IBA Rules* further stipulates that the content of the report prepared by the tribunal-appointed experts[92] shall contain the expert's background, qualifications, training and experience, statement of facts on which the opinions and conclusions are based, evidence and information used in arriving at conclusions and if translated, the statement as to the language in which the report was originally prepared. Although dealing with party-appointed expert witnesses, Art. 4.4 of the *CIArb Protocol* also contains a list of matters which should be dealt with in an expert's report. Waincymer notes that:

> [b]ecause a key part of expert testimony is as to opinion, an important way to analyse its probative value is to understand the expertise of the person and the methodology and reasoning behind the conclusions . . . [t]he most significant aspect of the report is the reasoning, including any assumptions, the evidence on which it is based, degree of certainty and an explanation of why contrary opinions are not preferred.[93]

Furthermore, as will be discussed in more detail later, the preparation of an expert report is crucial to a party's right to be heard, in order to enable a party to review and challenge the expert's findings.[94]

The *Shari'a* expert's qualifications, as well as the methodology and reasoning used to arrive at a conclusion are extremely significant in the context of

---

90 Abbas, above n 86.
91 The international standards as to impartiality and 'justifiable doubts' are discussed in more detail in the preceding chapter on the Composition of the Arbitral Tribunal.
92 Art. 5.2 of the IBA Rules deals with party-appointed experts.
93 Waincymer, above n 7, 956.
94 O'Malley, above n 75, 186.

Shari'a-based arbitration for a variety of reasons. As discussed extensively in Chapter 2, *usul-ul fiqh* provides a juristic methodology through which *Shari'a* can be understood and rules can be formulated.[95] Furthermore, *usul-ul fiqh* consists of methodologies such as *ijma, qiyas, isthisan* and *maslaha*.[96] Muslim jurists distinguished between, on the one hand, an Islamic jurist who follows precedent (known as a *muqallid*) through the principle of *taqlid* (following a precedent, see Chapter 2), and on the other hand, a jurist who is able to formulate new legal doctrines known as a *mujtahid*. A *mujtahid* must be qualified to perform *ijtihad* and therefore, requires additional qualifications.

Chapter 2 also notes that a *mufti* or 'jurisconsult' issues *fatwas* based on the existing four schools of thought. One criticism often arising in the context of Islamic finance is when a *mufti* issues a legal opinion which does not follow *fiqh* methodologies. Often referred to as '*hila*' or 'strategem/device,' a Muslim jurist may issue a *fatwa* that a certain Islamic finance product is permissible, but the legal methodology through which the *fatwa* is arrived at is invalid. *Hila* is also referred to as 'trick' in the Islamic finance industry, whereby a financial product or contract is deemed permissible despite containing *riba*. Hegazy observed that '[t]he fiqh literature provides countless examples of scholars declaring their objections to the expansive spread of riba-related hiyal in their respective times.'[97] In contemporary Islamic finance, *Shari'a* scholars differ on whether certain Islamic finance products are permissible or whether a legal trick (*hila*) is being used to permit an alleged *Shari'a-compliant* contract or product, even though it contains *riba*.

Therefore, under *Shari'a* itself, the qualifications of a *Shari'a* expert and the methodology employed is extremely important. In the event that a *Shari'a* expert acts as a *mujtahid* rather than a *muqallid* and formulates a legal expert opinion (*fatwa*) without the necessary qualifications and valid methodology under Islamic law, there is a risk that the parties or the arbitral tribunal may be hesitant in accepting the opinion, or that the arbitral award may not be enforced in a country where *Shari'a* informs the public policy. Even if the arbitral award is enforceable, there is also the risk that the credibility of the relevant arbitral institution is impacted, because the *Shari'a*-based arbitral rules are not viewed as producing *Shari'a*-compliant outcomes.

Furthermore, a written expert report is vital to *Shari'a* arbitration, especially if the subject matter is a complex *Shari'a*-compliant financial agreement. The expert report will provide transparency and ensure that the parties, the arbitral tribunal and potentially any domestic court, are relying on expert evidence that is credible in the event that the *Shari'a* expert has the relevant qualifications and follows the correct Islamic methodology in arriving at their conclusion. The probative value of the expert report is one of the reasons why the *IBA Rules* stipulate standards that experts should adhere to when preparing their report. Although

95 Wael Hallaq, *An Introduction to Islamic Law* (Cambridge University Press, 2009) 75.
96 Ibid., 104.
97 Syed Nazim Ali, *Islamic Finance: Current Legal and Regulatory Issues* (Islamic Legal Studies Program Harvard, 2005) 144.

the arbitral tribunal is free to partially or completely reject the expert's findings, the probative value of the expert report will increase if the report is comprehensive.[98] For example, in the case of *Starret Housing*, the arbitral tribunal made the following comment on the expert's report:

> The material submitted by the Expert to the Tribunal is literally 'weighty.' It consists of 12 volumes, together with a descriptive transmittal letter summarizing his views. In this massive submission, the Expert set forth not only his conclusions but also cited the evidentiary support for them and described the positions of the Parties on each significant issue. He included full texts or quotations of relevant portions of the documents upon which he relied. His credibility is enhanced by his candor. Thus, where he drew inferences or made subjective judgments, he pointed them out and explained his reasons. Where he considered that he may have made a judicial interpretation, he identified the point and referred it to the Tribunal for final decision. Where he considered a matter beyond his terms of reference, he specifically called attention to it.[99]

Therefore, it is highly recommended that the AIAC develop Evidentiary Guidelines catering for *Shari'a* experts in a similar manner to the *IBA Rules*. If the arbitral tribunal decides to appoint a *Shari'a* expert, Art. 6.6 may be adopted save that the *Shari'a* Expert Report should also contain:

1   The *Shari'a* expert's background (including his/her religious background), qualifications, training and experience and in particular, whether the *Shari'a* expert is acting as a *mujtahid, muqallid, mufti* or any other particulars of his/her title.
2   The school of Islamic thought that the *Shari'a* expert is following.
3   In the event that the *Shari'a* expert is following an established Islamic legal opinion *fatwa*, the *Shari'a* expert should clarify the Islamic jurist who issued the *fatwa*.
4   As mentioned above, the *Shari'a* expert must stipulate all the relevant *Shari'a* Advisory Boards and/or relevant government entities, consulting firms, standard settings bodies in the field of IBF on which he/she is involved in order to ensure independence, impartiality and transparency.

C *Right to interrogate the expert*

The preparation of an expert's report also enables a party to review and challenge the expert's findings if they wish to do so and therefore, failure to prepare a

---

98 O'Malley, above n 75, 189.
99 Starrett Housing Corp. v. Iran [1987] 16 Iran-U.S. C.T.R (Iran-US Claims Tribunal) 269 <http://translex.uni-koeln.de/232100>

report may impact a party's right to be heard.[100] Art. 6.5 of the *IBA Rules* notes that 'any Party shall have the opportunity to respond to the Expert Report in a submission by the Party or through a Witness Statement or an Expert Report by a Party-Appointed Expert.' Art. 6.5 also makes reference to the right of parties to review any information examined by the expert, even if it was not relied upon.[101] Furthermore, Art. 26(2) provides

> [u]nless otherwise agreed by the parties, if a party so requests or if the arbitral tribunal considers it necessary, the expert shall, after delivery of his written or oral report, participate in a hearing where the parties have the opportunity to put questions to him and to present expert witnesses in order to testify on the points at issue.

A similar provision for an evidentiary hearing in which the tribunal-expert may be subject to cross-examination is stipulated in Art. 6.6 of the *IBA Rules.* If the parties are denied the opportunity to challenge the expert's findings, this may violate due process requirements under Art. V(1)(b) of the *New York Convention*, which states that an arbitral award may not be enforced if the defendant shows he/she was 'not given proper notice . . . or was otherwise unable to present his case.'

However, parties must be careful to observe the necessary time limits when exercising their rights to comment on the expert's report or seeking to cross-examine the expert witness. For example, in the case of *International Standard Electric Corporation* ('ISEC') *v Bridas Sociedad Anonima Petrolera, Indus Y. Commercial,*[102] the ICC Tribunal refused to allow the parties to cross-examine the expert witness. ISEC argued that it was denied due process under Art. V(1)(b) because 'the parties must be given the identity of the expert and the expert's opinion, as well as a meaningful opportunity to rebut that opinion,'[103] and therefore, ISEC argued, the arbitral award should be held unenforceable in the United States. This argument was rejected because no objection was raised by ISEC when the arbitral tribunal informed it of the procedure and when it agreed to pay its portion of the expert's fee. Consequently, Judge Conby of the United States District Court in New York made the following finding:

> We understand our obligation not to allow a party to impeach on later review a decision of a trial judge, or as here, an arbitral panel, where that party had full opportunity to contest it, and full notice of the vigorous argument of an adversary contesting it, and chose instead not to associate himself with the argument, and not to contest the matter. We thus find as a fact that ISEC never objected to the consultation of an expert by the panel and never demanded access to his report.

100 O'Malley, above n 75, 186.
101 Ibid. 185.
102 745 F. Supp 172 (SDNY, 1990).
103 Ibid., 179 (Conby J) (SDNY, 1990).

Accordingly, we hold that no objection to the appointment procedure used in the selection and consultation of the expert on New York law was made, that any objections ISEC in fact had were waived, and ISEC will not now be heard to complain about it.[104]

Further, in the case of *Parsons & Whittemore Overseas Co. v Societe Generale de l'Industrie due Papier (RAKTA)*,[105] *Parsons & Whittemore Overseas Co* tried to argue that its due process rights were infringed because it was unable to produce their expert witness, David Nes, as per the scheduled hearing date, because the time was not convenient for him. The arbitral tribunal argued that this did not deny *Parsons & Whittemore Overseas Co* due process, because the inability to produce a witness in time was a risk inherent in the arbitration process. Therefore, while a tribunal should ensure that due process is adhered to and parties are provided the right to challenge the findings of the expert, parties should also be aware of the need to raise due process concerns in a timely manner and ensure that this right is not waived. The *i-Arbitration Rules* do not expressly stipulate the right of the parties to interrogate the expert. Poudret and Besson note that the parties should be able to comment on the expert's report and 'several laws and sets of arbitration rules expressly grant them the right to put questions to the expert at the hearing, possible accompanied by their own experts.'[106] For this reason, Dr Thomas Klotzel, in his keynote address at the i-Arbitration Conference held by the AIAC, commented on Art. 11 of the *i-Arbitration Rules* and argued that:

> it may be wise for an arbitral tribunal to issue on a case to case basis, suitable directions in line with the procedures specified in Art. 29 (4) and (5) *UNCITRAL Rules 2010* in particular in the event that a *Shari'a* expert has delivered a ruling.[107]

A denial of certain procedural rights puts the arbitral award at risk of violating due process, provided that the parties raise their concerns in a timely manner and do not waive their right to examine expert witnesses.

VIII Conclusion

This chapter discussed the lack of clarity and codification in relation to evidentiary and procedural law under classical *Shari'a*, and the potential that certain

---

104 Ibid., 181 (Conby J) (SDNY, 1990).
105 508 F.2d 969, 975–76 (2nd Cir, 1974).
106 Jean-François Poudret and Sébastien Besson, *Comparative Law of International Arbitration* (Sweet & Maxwell, 2nd ed, 2007) 562.
107 Dr. Thomas R. Klötzel, 'Keynote Address' (Speech delivered at the i-Arbitration Conference, Kuala Lumpur Regional Centre for Arbitration, 8 May 2015) <https://youtu.be/SgzpDNDQ-cc?list=PLkdbSlXVnul0p1b_AjhF8GwGa_ddKRTuZ> 00:24:49-00:25:05.

interpretations of *Shari'a* may be inconsistent with international standards of procedural fairness. The first part of this chapter examines classical *Shari'a* in relation to the evidentiary testimony provided by a woman. It is argued that evidentiary rules under classical *Shari'a* are unclear, and how certain interpretations may violate procedural fairness under ICA norms.

This second part of this chapter argues that the IICRA and *i-Arbitration Rules* should be relied upon by parties, because they provide a more comprehensive set of arbitral rules. However, this chapter also argues that the *IICRA Rules* are better suited to parties from the UAE and when dealing with basic *Shari'a* matters. This is because under the *IICRA Rules*, the arbitrators are selected from a list prepared by IICRA, relied upon for their *Shari'a* expertise, and have the discretion to refer matters to the IICRA *Shari'a* board located in Dubai, UAE. In comparison, the *i-Arbitration Rules* cater for international disputes by providing the parties with the freedom to select any arbitrator, and the arbitral tribunal (or the parties) may refer a *Shari'a* matter to any relevant SAC or *Shari'a* expert.

Nevertheless, the *i-Arbitration Rules* require further reforms, and the AIAC should develop procedural and evidentiary rules further, so that the procedures through which an arbitral tribunal deals with conflicting *Shari'a* experts are addressed. Furthermore, in order to ensure impartiality, the rules should ensure that a statement of independence and impartiality is filed by the *Shari'a* expert or SAC. The *i-Arbitration Rules* also need to refer to the expert report itself, and ensure there are guidelines regarding the content of the expert report, and provide the parties with a right to examine and challenge the expert report if they choose to do so. These reforms will increase the probability of the arbitral award being enforced internationally, as well as conforming to international standards of equality and procedural fairness.

6 The impact of *riba* and *gharar* on arbitrability and arbitration agreements

I Introduction

This chapter discusses the prohibition against *riba* and *gharar* under *Shari'a* and its impact on arbitration agreements and arbitrability. The prohibition against *riba* and *gharar* will also be further examined in Chapter 7 in the context of arbitral awards and Chapter 8 in relation to the recognition and enforcement of arbitral awards. In comparison to Chapters 7 and 8, this chapter will provide a comparative analysis by examining the concept of arbitrability and validity of arbitration agreements in contemporary ICA and classical *Shari'a*. Contemporary case studies will further evaluate the impact of *Shari'a* on arbitrability and arbitration agreements under the UAE and Saudi arbitration law regimes, as well as the *i-Arbitration Rules, AAOIFI Standards* and *IICRA Rules*. The central question of this chapter is how the prohibition against *riba* and *gharar* impacts on arbitrability and arbitration agreements when parties choose governing law or arbitration rules based on *Shari'a*, or a national law influenced by *Shari'a* principles.

II Validity of arbitration agreements, non-arbitrability and public policy

In many jurisdictions, the non-arbitrability defence is often used to challenge an arbitration agreement on the basis that the subject matter, or certain aspects of it, should not be settled by arbitration.[1]

Although technically any matter may be subject to arbitration, the rationale behind the non-arbitrability doctrine is that matters involving 'public' rights and interests of third parties should be subject to governmental authority, and should not be resolved by private arbitration.[2] Examples of such matters include bankruptcy, trade sanctions and criminal matters.[3]

---

1 Gary Born, *International Commercial Arbitration* (Kluwer Law International, 2nd ed, 2014) 943.
2 Ibid., 944; Nigel Blackaby, et al., *Redfern and Hunter on International Arbitration* (Oxford University Press, 6th ed, 2015) 110–111; Julian Lew, Loukas Mistelis and Stefan Michael Kröll, *Comparative International Commercial Arbitration* (Kluwer Law International, 2003) 187–188.
3 For a discussion on the status of matters such as patents, trademarks, copyright, antitrust and competition laws, securities transactions, insolvency law, natural resources, corporate

Domestic arbitration laws define matters that may be arbitrable in accordance with the public policy of the State.[4] According to Bantekas '[arbitrability] itself is no doubt closely connected to the concept of public policy, which by definition is circumscribed and delineated exclusively by the internal processes of states.'[5] However, the non-arbitrability doctrine is treated differently to the public policy doctrine under the *New York Convention*. The *New York Convention* provides for the non-arbitrability defence at the enforcement stage under Art. V(2)(a), which notes that the recognition and enforcement of an arbitral award may be refused if '[t]he subject matter of the difference is not capable of settlement by arbitration under the law of that country.' Similarly, Art. 34(2) of the *UNCITRAL Model Law* considers non-arbitrability separately from public policy:

An arbitral award may be set aside by the court specified in Art. 6 only if:

(b) the court finds that:

    (i) the subject matter of the dispute is not capable of settlement by arbitration under the law of this State; or
    (ii) the award is in conflict with the public policy of this State.

Born argues that public policy and non-arbitrability are separate doctrines in that

the public policy doctrine provides that certain results reached by arbitral awards contradict public policy and cannot be recognised, while the non-arbitrability doctrine provides that the arbitral process itself cannot be used to produce a binding decision in particular cases (regardless of what its results are).[6]

On the other hand, as will be discussed in more detail below, countries such as Saudi Arabia define arbitrability by stating that matters contrary to public policy cannot be subject to arbitration.

Commentators on contemporary ICA argue that the non-arbitrability defence can be distinguished from an arbitration agreement that is considered invalid for duress or fraud.[7] Similarly, the *New York Convention* deals with the invalidity of

governance disputes, bribery and corruption, see Blackaby, et al., above n 2, 112–124. For a distinction between subjective arbitrability and objective arbitrability, see Emmanuel Gaillard and John Savage, *Fouchard Gaillard Goldman on International Commercial Arbitration* (Kluwer Law International, 1999) 313–337. See also Born, above n 1, 944.

4 Blackaby, et al., above n 2, 111.
5 Ilias Bantekas, 'The Foundations of Arbitrability in International Commercial Arbitration' (2008) 27 *Australian Year Book of International Law* 193, 195.
6 Born, above n 1, 951.
7 Loukas Mistelis and Stavros Brekoulakis (eds), *Arbitrability: International & Comparative Perspectives* (Kluwer Law International, 2009) 3–5; Born, above n 1, 944. See also, Bernard Hanotiau and Oliver Caprasse, 'Public Policy in International Commercial Arbitration' in Emmanuel Gaillard and Domenico Di Pietro (eds), *Enforcement of Arbitration Agreements and International Arbitral Awards: The New York Convention in Practice* (Cameron, May 2008) 801.

arbitration agreements as an independent ground for non-enforcement, as stipulated in Art. V(1)(a), which states: '[r]ecognition and enforcement of an award may be refused, at the request of the party against whom it is invoked, only if . . . said agreement is not valid under the law to which the parties have subjected it.' Therefore, it is possible for an arbitration agreement to be valid, yet the arbitral tribunal may nonetheless still not have jurisdiction over the subject matter of the arbitration.[8] Brekoulakis provides a hypothetical scenario in which an arbitration agreement in a contract regarding the licencing of a patent is a valid contract, despite the subject matter of patents being non-arbitrable in many jurisdictions. In the event that a dispute regarding licencing arose from the same contract, the arbitration agreement would be valid and the arbitral tribunal would have jurisdiction over any disputes which merely related to licencing.[9]

On the other hand, as will be discussed in the next section, arbitrability and the validity of an arbitration agreement overlap due to the prohibition against *riba* (interest) and *gharar* (risk/uncertainty) under classical *Shari'a*. For example, if there is an arbitration agreement in a contract regarding an interest-based financial transaction which stipulates that 'any disputes arising out of or in connection with this contract shall be settled by arbitration,' then the contract may be null and void under certain interpretations of *Shari'a* and therefore, any dispute arising out of the contract will also be non-arbitrable.[10] The next section explains how and why a contract and/or arbitration agreement may be invalid and non-arbitrable under classical *Shari'a*.

III Non-arbitrability under classical *Shari'a*

Similar to contemporary ICA, *Shari'a* considers an arbitration agreement invalid based on duress, lack of consent or non-compliance with form requirements.[11] Although this book does not delve into Islamic contractual law in detail, it is important to note that *Shari'a* does consist of various rules which govern the conditions and effects of contracts.[12] As will be discussed further below, classical

---

8 Loukas Mistelis and Stavros Brekoulakis (eds), *Arbitrability: International & Comparative Perspectives* (Kluwer Law International, 2009) 38–39.

9 Ibid., 39.

10 If the tribunal does decide to issue an arbitral award, then the award will also be against Shari'a public policy; see Chapters 7 and 8.

11 Nudrat Majeed, 'Good Faith and Due Process: Lessons from the Shari'ah' (2004) 20(1) *Arbitration International* 97, 109–111; Abdel Hamid El Ahdab and Jalal El Ahdab, *Arbitration with the Arab Countries* (Kluwer Law International, 2011) 22–23; Samir Saleh, *Commercial Arbitration in the Arab Middle East: Shari'a, Syria, Lebanon and Egypt* (Hart Publishing, 2006) 67–75; Faisal Kutty, 'The Shari'a Factor in International Commercial Arbitration' (2006) 28 *Loyola of Los Angeles International and Comparative Law Review* 565, 599–609; Chibli Mallat, *Introduction to Middle Eastern Law* (Oxford University Press, 2007) 282–287.

12 Nayla Comair-Obeid, *The Law of Business Contracts in the Arab Middle East* (Kluwer Law International, 1996) 17–18; Abdulrahman A. I. Al-Subaihi, *International Commercial Arbitration in Islamic Law, Saudi Law and the Model Law* (PhD thesis, The University of Birmingham, 2004) 66–76.

and contemporary Islamic scholars have approved specific *Shari'a*-compliant contracts, and ensured that such contracts do not consist of matters prohibited under *Shari'a*.

Classical *Shari'a* also considers matters such as family law, crimes, theft and adultery to be non-arbitrable, because they involve public rights or non-commercial matters.[13] Therefore, non-arbitrable matters under classical *Shari'a* can be categorised as follows:

1   Matters falling under the jurisdiction of religious courts, such as *hadd*[14] crimes which include theft, adultery, wine, alcohol or apostasy (depending on the school of thought).[15] Although criminal law in *Shari'a* is not within the ambit of this book, crimes are also subdivided into those involving *qisas* (retaliation) and matters related to offences against other people, such as homicide and wounding, where financial compensation known as 'blood money' (*diya*) is determined to be the proper punishment by the State.[16] This will be discussed further in the context of Saudi Arabia. Other general crime not clearly stipulated in the hadith or Qur'an are referred to as *ta'zir*, where the punishment is at the discretion of the judge[17]

2   Personal status matters such as marriage, affiliation and divorce.[18]

The third category of non-arbitrable matters under *Shari'a* include subject matters that do not comply with the rules of Islamic banking and finance, because they involve the imposition of *riba* or risk/uncertainty (*gharar*).[19] Such matters are considered non-arbitrable because transactions consisting of *riba* and/or *gharar* are prohibited (*haram*) under *Shari'a*. The rationale behind these prohibitions is articulated by Comair-Obeid:

> Islam is not a doctrine of renunciation of this world, but rather . . . a religion transmitted by the Creator through the mouth of the Prophet for the welfare of mankind. The welfare supposes improvement of the life of a man . . . [a]ll the economic activity of Islam, being submitted to the question of *halal*

13 Samir Saleh, 'The Recognition and Enforcement of Foreign Arbitral Awards in the States of the Arab Middle East' (1985) 1 *Arab Law Quarterly* 19, 29; Omar Aljazy, 'Arbitrability in Islamic Law' (2000) 16 *The Lebanese Review of Arbitration* 1, 2.

14 Hadd literally means limit or prohibition and refers to serious crimes under Shari'a. The plural is hudud. See Hadd, (Oxford University Press, 2016) <www.oxfordislamicstudies. com/article/opr/t125/e757>.

15 Saleh, above n 13, 29; Aljazy, above n 13, 2; See generally, Rudolph Peters, *Crime and Punishment in Islamic Law* (Cambridge University Press, 2005).

16 Rudolph Peters, *Crime and Punishment in Islamic Law* (Cambridge University Press, 2005) 7.

17 Ibid. 7.

18 Saleh, above n 13, 29; Aljazy, above n 13, 2.

19 Ilias Bantekas, 'Arbitrability in Finance and Banking' in Mistelis and Brekoulakis, above n 7, 307; Aljazy, 'Arbitrability in Islamic Law,' above n 13, 2; El Ahdab and El Ahdab, above n 11, 22–23; Kutty, above n 11, 604–606; Saleh, above n 13, 29.

and *haram*, what is licit and what is illicit, therefore depends on the moral and social values, which the individual must respect in his various activities.[20]

Prohibitions under *Shari'a* are broader than contemporary ICA, and include matters which do not involve public rights or non-commercial matters, yet are considered non-arbitrable. Consequently, the fact that a contract, agreement or transaction consists of *riba* and/or *gharar* renders it invalid under *Shari'a*.[21] Unlike contemporary ICA, it is difficult to envision a case in which a contract or arbitration agreement is *Shari'a*-compliant, but a dispute arises in relation to a matter prohibited under *Shari'a*. Therefore, contracts, transactions, subject matters or agreements which are not consistent with *Shari'a* may be rendered invalid, non-arbitrable and against public policy if the contract is subject to *Shari'a*. The remainder of this chapter will discuss three main principles operating under *Shari'a*, and their impact on arbitrability: (1) the prohibition against *gharar*; (2) the prohibition against *riba*; and (3) the sanctity of contracts under *Shari'a*, which means that contracts should be fair and based on mutual consent of the parties.

IV The *gharar* uncertainty

Gharar is a broad term which has been given several definitions by Islamic scholars including speculation, deception, cheating, fraud, risk or uncertainty.[22] For the purposes of this book and as will be explained in more detail, *gharar* relates to excessive uncertainty or risk by way of contract, or uncertainty relating to goods involved in a sale, the price, deliverability, dates of exchange or possession of goods. Comair-Obeid accurately notes that the risk of *gharar* often arises in relation to aleatory contracts whereby:

> the benefit for one of the parties depends on some uncertain happening making it impossible to know in advance whether there will be loss or gain. More precisely, the element of uncertainty or risk *gharar*, peculiar to the aleatory contract, is the result of the exact content of the benefits depending on some uncertain event in such a way that the loss or gain is for each contracting party a function of this event.[23]

---

20 Comair-Obeid, above n 12, 40.
21 El Ahdab and El Ahdab, above n 11, 22–23; Kutty, above n 11, 604–606; Saleh, above n 13, 29. See also the discussion on separability under the section 'The Gharar Uncertainty' below.
22 Sudin Haron and Wan Nursofiza Wan Azmi, *Islamic Finance and Banking System: Philosophies, Principles and Practices* (McGraw-Hill Education) 50–57; Mahmoud El Gamal, 'An Economic Explication of the Prohibition of Gharar in Classical Islamic Jurisprudence' (Paper presented at the 4th International Conference on Islamic Economics, Leicester, 13–15 August 2000) <www.ruf.rice.edu/~elgamal/files/gharar.pdf> 5–6; Comair-Obeid, above n 12, 57.
23 Comair-Obeid, above n 12, 55.

The rationale behind this prohibition is to protect weaker parties from exploitation in the event that there is risk of uncertainty or speculation.[24] The prohibition against *gharar* is not explicitly mentioned in the Qur'an. However, the Qur'an states: '[d]o not eat up your property wrongfully . . . intending sinfully and knowingly to eat up parts of other people's property,'[25] and 'God has allowed trade and forbidden *riba*.'[26] Classical Islamic scholar, Abu Bakr Ibn Arabi (d. 1148CE) notes in his book *Ahkam al-Qur'an* (commentary on the Qur'an) that these two verses are referring to transactions prohibited by *Shari'a*, including *gharar* and *riba*.[27] Further, the prohibition of *gharar* arises from several hadith[28] in which the Prophet Muhammad provides many examples of uncertain transactions prohibited under *Shari'a*:

> The Messenger of Allah (peace be upon him) forbade *[g]harar* transactions.[29]
> The *[g]harar* sale includes selling fish that are in the water, selling a slave that has escaped, selling birds that are in the sky, and similar type of sales. And the meaning of *[h]asah*[30] sale is when the seller says to the buyer: '[w]hen I toss the pebble at you, then the sale between you and I is final.'[31]
> [T]he Messenger of Allah, may Allah bless him and grant him peace, forbade selling fruit until it was clear of blight. Malik said, 'Selling fruit before it has begun to ripen is an uncertain transaction (*gharar*).'[32]

The risk associated with the sale of uncertain items is similar to that associated with gambling (*maysir*), which is forbidden under *Shari'a* because it is also viewed as being speculative.[33] El Gamal comments that *gharar* is similar to *maysir* because in a sale of *gharar* 'a known price is paid for a probability distribution of possible payoffs.'[34] A strict adherence to the prohibition of *gharar* and *maysir* means that '[a]ny contract containing speculation, or contract clause that turns

---

24 Ibid., 56.
25 Trans, M.A.S. Abdel Haleem, *The Qur'an* (Oxford University Press, 2004) (Chapter 2, Verse 188).
26 Ibid., (Chapter 2, Verse 275).
27 Abu Bakr Ibn al-Arabi (d. 1148), Ahkam Al- Quran (Dar al-Kitab al-Arabi, 2008) 137, 320.
28 See generally, Sunna, <http://sunnah.com/search/?q=gharar> (Vol. 5, Book 44, Hadith 4522; Vol. 3, Book 12, Hadith 2194; Vol. 3, Book 12, Hadith 1229; Book 31, Hadith 1).
29 Sunan Ibn Majah, <http://sunnah.com/urn/1265140> (Vol. 3, Book 12, Hadith, 2195).
30 The 'Hasah' Sale is a transaction practised in Pre-Islamic Arabia in which the outcome is determined through chance, such as the throwing of pebbles. See Benjamin Jokisch, *Islamic Imperial Law: Harun-al-Rashid's Codification Project* (Walter de Gruyter GmbH & Co, 2007) 133.
31 Jami' at-Tirmidhi, <http://sunnah.com/tirmidhi/14/30> (Vol. 3, Book 12, Hadith, 1230).
32 Muwatta Malik, <http://sunnah.com/urn/413240> (Book 31, Hadith 12).
33 Mahmoud El Gamal, *A Basic Guide to Contemporary Islamic Banking and Finance* (Rice University, 2000) 7.
34 El Gamal, above n 22, 6.

on the happening of a specified but unsure event is void.'[35] However, classical *Shari'a* scholars such as Taqi al-Din al-Subki (1355 CE) and Ibn Taymiyya argue that trivial forms of *gharar* (*haqir*) may be necessary and unavoidable in certain transactions, and what is prohibited is major *gharar* (*ghalaba alayhi*).[36] Major *gharar* is that which encourages corruption and 'leads to (*kawnuhu matiyyat*) dispute, hatred and devouring others' wealth wrongfully.'[37] Another issue that arises among Islamic scholars is in relation to what is classified as a major or minor *gharar*. Generally, contracts in which the price, subject, delivery, quantity or quality of the subject matter or commodities are uncertain are viewed by Islamic scholars as falling under the major *gharar* prohibition.[38] Therefore, *gharar* can be categorised into the following: (1) where the language of the contract is ambiguous; (2) if the subject matter of the sale is known but the delivery is uncertain; and (3) where the subject matter of the sale is uncertain.[39] Consequently, in order to avoid being viewed as *gharar*, the object should exist and be available, and 'the criteria of quantity, price and delay for delivery should be clearly stated.'[40]

More specifically, contemporary Islamic jurists have argued that insurance contracts constitute major *gharar* and are therefore void.[41] This is because although the insurance premium or option price is certain, the insurance payment or profit received is uncertain and therefore, void due to the principle of *gharar*.[42] The prohibition of *gharar* also vitiates contracts involving financial derivatives, forwards, future and conditional sales.[43] Ayub further notes that:

> [t]he prohibition of [g]harar requires Islamic banks not to engage in speculative trade in shares, short-selling, discounting of bills and securities or trading in unidentified items. Similarly, Islamic investment banks' involvement in IPOs of joint stock companies would require care to avoid [g]harar, as information asymmetry between the investors and promoters in the early

---

35 Kristin Roy, 'The New York Convention and Saudi Arabia: Can a Country Use the Public Policy Defense to Refuse Enforcement of Non-Domestic Arbitral Awards?' (1994) 18 *Fordham International Law Journal* 920, 947–948; Hans Vissier, *Islamic Finance: Principles and Practice* (Edward Elgar Publishing Limited, 2nd ed, 2013) 53–54.
36 The distinction between major and minor gharar was introduced by classical Islamic scholar, Ibn Taymiyya. See also, El Gamal, above n 33, 24; Frank Vogel and Samuel Hayes, *Islamic Law and Finance: Religion, Risk and Return* (Kluwer Law International, 1998) 92–93.
37 Ibid.
38 However, there are slight differences between the four schools of thought regarding the sale of subject matters which are unspecified but include a description in the contract. See, Vogel and Hayes, above n 36, 92. See also Ibrahim Warde, *Islamic Finance in the Global Economy* (Edinburgh University Press, 2000) 143; Vissier, above n 35, 52.
39 El Gamal, above n 22, 10.
40 Comair-Obeid, above n 12, 57.
41 El Gamal, above n 33, 25.
42 Ibid., 62.
43 Ibid., 8.

stages of companies' establishment may involve *[g]harar*. Trading in derivatives also involves *[g]harar* and, therefore, is a grey area for Islamic banks.[44]

Therefore, the prohibition against *gharar* may vitiate a multitude of international commercial transactions and sales, thereby limiting the range of contracts that parties may enter, and potentially placing them at a commercial disadvantage. Vogel observes:

> [t]he majority positions of classical *fiqh* seem antiethical to a great many modern financial transactions, since they presumptively ban all sales of goods not already both owned and in the possession of the seller, not to mention goods that do not yet exist . . . [o]nly Ibn Taymiyya's view approaches a modern one, and it is frequently relied on by modern scholars of Islamic banking and finance. But even his view would not countenance the conscious assumption of risk inherent in many modern financial transaction, such as derivatives or insurance, or, most of all, use of these transactions of sheer speculation.[45]

For this reason, as will be discussed further, either a flexible approach is taken towards *gharar*, or alternative transactions and sales considered permissible by most Islamic scholars have been formulated, despite the prohibition against *gharar*. An example is *salam*, which is a sale in which specified goods are purchased in advance. Therefore, the financier is paying for the commodities prior to delivery of the goods. During the life of the Prophet Muhammad, *salam* was often used in agricultural transactions where the advance payment was used by farmers to cover the cost of employing farmers, irrigations costs and other associated expenses.[46] This sale was viewed as being acceptable according to the rulings of the four schools of thought,[47] and the following hadith of the Prophet Muhammad, narrated by his cousin, Abd Allah Ibn Abbas (d. 687 CE):

> The Prophet [peace be upon him][48] came (to Medina) and he told the people (regarding the payment of money in advance that they should pay it) for a known specified measure and a known specified weight and a known specified period.[49]

In order to ensure that the *salam* transaction does not consist of *gharar*, the contract must specify the quantity and quality of goods to be supplied, the buyer

44 Muhammad Ayub, *Understanding Islamic Finance* (Wiley, 2007) 75.
45 Vogel and Hayes, above n 36, 92–93.
46 Rodney Wilson, *Legal, Regulatory and Governance Issues in Islamic Finance* (Edinburgh University Press, 2012) 74. See also As-Siddiq Muhammad Al-Amin Ad-Darir, *Gharar: Impact on Contracts in Islamic Fiqh* (Al Baraka Banking Group, 2012) 499–507.
47 Ad-Darir, above n 46, 500–507.
48 Translated by the author.
49 Sahih al-Bukhari, <http://sunnah.com/bukhari/35/5> (Volume 3, Book 35, Hadith 445). See generally, Sunna, Money in Advance <http://sunnah.com/search/?q=money+in+advance>.

must have the right to demand a surety for the goods, the legal title of the goods must not be transferred until the buyer received the goods, and the commodities specified in the contract must be deliverable.[50] The example provided by Islamic scholars (based on the hadith quoted previously) is that the goods cannot consist of fish or birds which are not yet caught:[51]

> In the contemporary IBF industry, *salam* transactions are used for short-term financing whereby a customer and bank enter into a *salam* contract for the purchase of specific goods.[52] The bank also enters into a *salam* contract with the commodity owner. The commodity owner delivers the goods to the bank at an agreed future date and subsequently, the bank provides the goods to the customer.[53]

Another permissible transaction is *ijara* (rent or lease), which consists of the transfer of a usufruct for rent or leasing.[54] There are different forms of *ijara* contracts, such as the *ijara mutahia bittamlki* (financial lease), *ijara thumma al-bay* (leasing and subsequent purchase), and *ijara mawsufa fi dhimma* (forward lease).[55] Under a basic financial lease, a financial institution purchases a commodity and then leases it to their customer.[56] The financial institution may initially purchase the commodity from the customer before leasing it back.[57] In order to avoid *gharar*, the consideration and the period of the lease should be known to the parties.[58] In addition, the financial institution remains the legal owner of the leased property, and only the usufructs are transferred to the lessee.[59] This means that the lessor bears the liabilities arising from ownership, whereas the lessee is only liable for use of the property.[60]

Also, *takaful* (mutual insurance) is a *Shari'a*-compliant alternative to conventional insurance, because the latter is believed to consist of *gharar*, *maysir* (gambling or speculation) and *riba*.[61] In Arabic, *takaful* originates from the verb *kafala* which means guarantee and security, and *takaful* refers to 'joint responsibility or guarantee based on mutual agreement.'[62] Therefore, in a *takaful* arrangement,

---

50 Wilson, above n 46, 500–507; Hassan, Kayed and Oseni, above n 51, 88–89.
51 Ibid. For a detailed explanation of the conditions, see Kabir Hassan, Rasem Kayed and Umar Aimhanosi Oseni, *Introduction to Islamic Banking & Finance: Principles and Practice* (Pearson, 2013) 88–89.
52 Ibid., 88–89.
53 Ibid.
54 Vissier, above n 35, 69.
55 Hassan, Kayed and Oseni, above n 51, 99–102.
56 Vissier, above n 35, 69.
57 Ibid., 69.
58 Muhammad Taqi Usmani, *An Introduction to Islamic Finance* (Kluwer Law International, 2002) 70–71; Ad-Darir, above n 46, 516.
59 Hassan, Kayed and Oseni, above n 51, 100; Usmani, above n 58, 70–71.
60 Ibid.
61 Hassan, Kayed and Oseni, above n 51, 291.
62 Ibid., 293; Haron and Azmi, above n 22, 437.

participants contribute money into a general fund used to help members against loss and damage.[63] Unlike conventional insurance policies, where there is a contract of sale between the buyer and seller, the participants in a *takaful* scheme are part of a structured arrangement in which they are mutually insuring each other against any losses or damages.[64] The parties are aware of the amount they have to contribute and the compensation they will receive (which also does not consist of *riba*), thus removing the element of *gharar* and *maysir*.[65] This *takaful* fund operates based on various Islamic banking and finance principles such as the *mudaraba* model.[66]

However, the prohibition of *gharar* and its contemporary application to accepted mainstream contractual transactions, such as insurance and financial derivatives, has led to inconsistency. As will be discussed in more detail, due to the economic pressures in the global economy, countries such as the UAE and Saudi Arabia tend to adopt a more liberal or more flexible approach to *gharar*, despite their adherence to *Shari'a*. It is argued by some Islamic scholars that the Islamic prohibition against *gharar*-based products and transactions should be interpreted liberally.[67] A liberal approach means that *gharar* is only prohibited when it leads to market manipulation and therefore, insurance, future sales and future derivatives may be necessary (*darura*) and in the public interest (*maslaha*).[68] Commentators argue that the concept of *gharar* should evolve, because what was considered unjust at the time of the Prophet no longer leads to iniquity, such as insurance matters.[69] Therefore, '[c]ontractual freedom is . . . once again called into question by the precepts of Islam in the domain of modern transactions, in order to ensure the balance of benefits in the name of justice and equity between the parties.'[70] As discussed in Chapter 2 and in following chapters, due to the evolving nature of concepts such as 'justice' and 'equity,' many *Shari'a* rules are being redeveloped in order to integrate harmoniously into the international commercial market.

For example, a liberal view of *gharar* that has been taken is in the area of arbitration clauses. Historically, arbitration agreements were categorised into arbitration clauses agreed to before a dispute arose, and submission agreements that were made after a dispute had arisen.[71] Many states only allowed arbitration in matters where there was an existing dispute and so only submission agreements were recognised.[72] For example, France did not recognise arbitration clauses in

---

63 Hassan, Kayed and Oseni, above n 51, 294.
64 Ibid., 295–297.
65 Haron and Azmi, above n 22, 424.
66 Hassan, Kayed and Oseni, above n 51, 302–303; Wilson, above n 46, 144.
67 Warde, above n 38, 176.
68 Ibid. See Chapter 2 for a detailed explanation of the concepts of darura and maslaha.
69 Comair-Obeid, above n 12, 64.
70 Ibid., 64.
71 Alan Redfern, et al., *Redfern and Hunter on International Arbitration* (Oxford University Press, 5th ed, 2009) 15.
72 Ibid., 19.

respect of future disputes until 1981.[73] This was also the view taken historically by Muslim jurisdictions because theoretically, an arbitration clause is void under the principle of *gharar* because it refers to a future dispute, which is unknown and speculative.[74] The Medjella, for example, only recognised an arbitration agreement if the dispute had already arisen and was clearly defined.[75]

However, this view is no longer adopted in the domestic arbitration law of countries where *Shari'a* applies, because both current and future disputes may be submitted to arbitration. The liberal approach towards *gharar* is justified by the fact that Islamic jurisprudence does not mention arbitration clauses, and the *pacta sunt servanda* principle is enshrined in *Shari'a*.[76] Therefore, arbitration clauses are considered a contractual commitment binding on parties, regardless of whether they refer to future or existing disputes.[77] This approach is also supported by classical scholars such as Ibn Taymiyya, who argues that the *gharar* principle should not restrict contractual freedom, otherwise it will result in 'blind legalism and undue obstacles to people's welfare.'[78] Despite this approach, White advises that if parties choose *Shari'a* as the governing law, parties may raise the *gharar* defence for future disputes.[79] This advice is more relevant if parties choose classical *Shari'a* rules, which are not codified, to govern their arbitration, and this book argues that such an approach should not be taken.

Unlike arbitration clauses, a major issue that arises is how courts and arbitral tribunals will ascertain whether a subject matter containing *riba* and *gharar* is arbitrable under *Shari'a*. The next section will discuss the case of *Sanghi Polyesters Ltd (India) v. The International Investor KCSC (Kuwait)* ('*the Sanghi case*'),[80] and the approach taken by domestic courts in the United Kingdom and India regarding a manufacturing contract under *Shari'a* known as *istisna*, which is generally considered acceptable by Islamic scholars despite the fact that the assets comprising the subject matter of the contract are typically still in the process of being manufactured at the time of conclusion.

---

73 K. V. S. K Nathan, 'Who Is Afraid of Sharia? Islamic Law and International Commercial Arbitration' (1993) 59(2) *Arbitration: The Journal of the Chartered Institute of Arbitrators Arbitration* 125, 131.

74 Abdulrahman Yahya Baamir, *Saudi Law and Judicial Practice in Commercial and Banking Arbitration* (PhD Thesis, Brunel University, 2008) 77–79; Andrew White, 'Dispute Resolution and Specialized ADR for Islamic Finance' in David Eisenberg and Craig Nethercott (eds), *Islamic Finance: Law and Practice* (Oxford University Press, 2012) 329; Fahad Ahmed Mohammed Abuhimed, *The Rules of Procedure of Commercial Arbitration in the Kingdom of Saudi Arabia (Comparative Study)* (PhD thesis, The University of Hull, 2006) 104–109.

75 El Ahdab and El Ahdab, above n 11, 19.

76 Bantekas, above n 19, 308.

77 Saleh, above n 11, 39.

78 Ad-Darir, above n 46, 62–64; White, above n 74, 329.

79 White, above n 74, 330.

80 [2000] 1 Lloyd's Rep 480.

A Istisna contract and enforceability

Istisna is a manufacturing contract in which the parties consist of the manufacturer of the goods, the bank, and the customer, regarding a 'made-to-order' asset to be delivered at a later date.[81] Consequently, the bank pays the manufacturer immediately or in instalments through an *istisna* contract, whilst the asset is delivered at a future date. Once the asset has been manufactured and delivered to the bank, the manufacturer is entitled to the full purchase price from the bank.[82] Thereafter, the bank provides the asset to the client, and the client pays the bank immediately or in instalments. Islamic banks often used *istisna* to enter into transactions with a manufacturer to produce and deliver goods at a future date. In order to avoid *gharar* and *riba*, the subject matter, price (including the profit rate) and delivery date must be pre-determined.[83] In the contemporary world, the *istisna* contract is typically employed in the Islamic bond (*sukuk*) industry.[84]

The *istisna* contract is more commonly advocated by Hanafi scholars, because the other schools generally cover manufacturing transactions through the *salam* and *ijara* contract.[85] The majority of Hanafi scholars argue that the parties are not bound to the contract until the goods are produced and accepted by the buyer.[86] However, the minority view is that the contract is binding on all parties, regardless of the fact that the contract has not yet been performed.[87] Conversely, the majority of Hanbali scholars do not view the *istisna* contract as *Shari'a*-compliant, because the subject matter is uncertain, and this type of contract is not mentioned in the hadith or Qur'an. Vogel and Hayes note that although *istisna* contracts 'vary from established rules, Hanafis accept *istisna* only because of long-established custom and the people's need for it. In contrast, for Hanbalis such an *istisna* is invalid. They allow buyers to achieve the desired results by other means, either by purchase of raw materials on condition that the seller manufacture them into specific goods, or buy purchase of abstractly defined goods.'[88]

Despite not being explicitly referred to in the Qur'an or the hadith, the Hanafi school considers the *istisna* contract permissible because of the concepts of *urf* (custom), *maslaha* (public interest), *darurura* (necessity) and *istihsan* (equity).[89] As discussed in Chapter 1, these concepts are generally considered sources of jurisprudence (*usul-ul fiqh*), and allow Islamic scholars to reach conclusions on issues

---

81 Hassan and Lewis, above n 232, 85–86; Ad-Darir, above n 46, 508–510; El Gamal, above n 33, 17; Vogel and Hayes, above n 36, 213.
82 Warde, above n 38, 143; Vogel and Hayes, above n 36, 146–147; Hassan, Kayed and Oseni, above n 51, 85–87.
83 Warde, above n 38, 143.
84 Hassan, Kayed and Oseni, above n 51, 87.
85 Vogel and Hayes, above n 36, 146–147; Ad-Darir, above n 46, 510–11.
86 Vogel and Hayes, above n 36, 146–147.
87 Ibid.
88 Ibid., 121.
89 Hassan, Kayed and Oseni, above n 51, 85–87; Vogel and Hayes, above n 36, 146–147; Ad-Darir, above n 46, 510–511.

that are not necessarily explicitly stipulated in the Qur'an and *Sunna*. In the case of *istisna*, an exception is made to the rule that the subject matter should already be in existence, because the manufactured commodity is known to the parties.[90] Another issue that may arise is that the pre-determined profit rate in an *istisna* contract might be benchmarked according to conventional interest rates, thus leading many scholars and commentators to argue that the *istisna* contract consists of *riba*.

For example, in the Sanghi case, Sanghi Polyesters Ltd ('Sanghi') entered into a *Shari'a*-compliant agreement with International Investor KCSC ('KCSC'). The agreement was for KCSC to advance money to Sanghi with a pre-determined 'profit rate' of 9% pursuant to an *istisna* (referred to in this case as *estisna*) agreement.[91] Sanghi failed to repay KCSC on time and KCSC claimed repayment of the money in addition to outstanding profit. The parties agreed to arbitrate the dispute and the contract stipulated that the dispute be governed by the laws of the United Kingdom, except to the extent that it conflicted with *Shari'a*, in which case, the latter would prevail. However, no particular school of thought was specified with reference to the application of *Shari'a*. On 1 March 1999, the arbitrator awarded KCSC the principal and profit claims, disallowed additional damage claims, and ordered Sanghi to pay costs.[92] Sanghi challenged the award on various grounds, in particular that the profit charged by KCSC was equivalent to interest as per the *istisna* contract and therefore, contrary to *Shari'a*. This is despite the fact that, as discussed earlier, most Hanafi scholars consider the *istisna* contract acceptable, and one of the conditions of *istisna* is that the parties agree to a pre-determined price and profit rate. This was also articulated by the arbitrator, Mr Saleh, who noted the following in his memorandum of 13 May 1999:

> The transaction was a financial transaction put together in the form of a *Shari'a* 'Estisna' contract, ie manufacture, purchase and sale of goods, referred to in the award as the Islamic financial cycle number 1. The 'Estisna' form was adopted in order to make the transaction conform with orthodox Islamic banking practice. Consequently there is nothing else to clarify beyond what has already been stated in the Award.[93]

The matter was then brought before Mr Mackie Q.C. who was sitting as the Deputy Judge of the High Court of the Queen's Bench Division. Mr Mackie did not consider it necessary to evaluate the *Shari'a* conclusions, and he ruled that Mr Saleh's award was a based on a clear and full evaluation of the effect of *Shari'a* on the transaction. Mr Mackie stated that Sanghi also shared Mr Saleh's view very shortly before the arbitration commenced.[94] Mr Mackie's role was to decide whether any serious irregularity or injustice had occurred, and in his opinion,

---

90 Hassan, Kayed and Oseni, above n 51, 85–87.
91 *Sanghi Polyesters Ltd. (India) v. Int' Investor KCSC (Kuwait)* [2000] 1 Lloyd's Rep 480, 480.
92 Ibid.
93 Ibid., 483.
94 *Sanghi Polyesters Ltd. (India) v. Int' Investor KCSC (Kuwait)* [2000] 1 Lloyd's Rep 480, 483.

Sanghi failed to indicate that there had been any serious irregularity or injustice.[95] Further, KCSC sought to also enforce the arbitral award in India. Although the District Judge in India granted the enforcement, it was also determined that KCSC would have to file a separate petition to execute the arbitral award.[96] In 2002, Sanghi appealed the decision and challenged the enforceability of the arbitral award in the High Court of Andhra Pradesh in India.[97] Again, one of the grounds upon which the award was challenged was that the '*Estisna* Agreement' was contrary to *Shari'a*. In response to this argument, the Andhra High Court noted:

> Even for the sake of argument the respondent's submission that agreement referred to under Section 48(1)(a) of the Act is the primary agreement which created the legal relationship between the parties thereto i.e., '*Estisna* agreement' in the present case and that such an agreement is contrary to the Islamic Law of *Shari'a* is to be accepted, the respondent must have proved before the court-below what exactly is the Islamic Law of Sharia and how it invalidates the '*Estisna* agreement[98] . . . [n]o such proof is placed before the Court in this regard.[99]

Therefore, the Andhra High Court found that the foreign arbitral award was in accordance with the agreement to arbitration, which was 'valid by its proper law and the award was valid and final according to the arbitration law governing the proceedings.'[100] Although the High Court of the Queen's Bench Division in England and the Andhra High Court did not analyse whether the *istisna* agreement was *Shari'a*-compliant, Mr Saleh (the arbitrator) found that the *istisna* contract was valid and arbitrable under *Shari'a*. Subsequently, Sanghi's argument that the profit rate was pre-determined and thus arguably equivalent to *riba* was rejected. The next section discusses the prohibition of *riba* under *Shari'a* in more detail.

V *Riba* or profit?

Although Islamic scholars unanimously agree that *riba* is prohibited under *Shari'a*, there is no consensus on the definition of *riba*. This theoretical uncertainty can cause confusion among parties to an arbitration agreement subject to

---

95 Ibid.
96 International Investor KCSC v Sanghi Polyesters Ltd./Civil Revision Petition Nos 331 and 1441 of 2002 (1) ALT 364; [2003] 43 SCL 271 AP <http://newyorkconven tion1958.org/index.php?lvl=notice_display&id=1371>; <http://indiankanoon.org/doc/1639330/>.
97 Ibid.
98 International Investor KCSC vs Sanghi Polyesters Ltd. [2003] (1) ALT 364, [24] <http://indiankanoon.org/doc/1639330/>.
99 Ibid., 33.
100 Ibid., 7.

Shari'a. If the subject matter concerns a *riba*-based transaction or agreement, is the matter arbitrable? Should courts consider such defences if the governing law consists of *Shari'a* principles? Which type of financial transaction, contract or agreement contains *riba*? In order to address these questions, the legal definition and nuanced interpretations of *riba* need to be understood.

The term *riba* is derived from root letters[101] in Arabic, which mean 'to grow' or 'to increase.'[102] The prohibition of *riba* arises from verses of the Qur'an[103] and the hadith[104] declaring *riba* as being an exploitative and unjust act, and contradictory to the Islamic principles of fairness and property rights.[105] Nabil Saleh provides a commonly accepted definition of *riba* being an 'illicit profit or gain resulting from an inequivalence in the counter-value of the reciprocal benefits during an exchange of two or of several articles of the same species and genus and governed by the same efficient cause.'[106] As discussed later, the hadith notes different forms of *riba* which has led Islamic scholars to categorise *riba* into the following three types: *riba al-jahilliya*; *riba al-fadl*; and *riba al-nasi'ah*.

Riba al jahilliya is *riba* that was practiced during the period of *al-jahilliya* ('ignorance') which was the pre-Islamic period (before the Prophet revealed the message of Islam). It refers to the exploitative and excessive charges to which debtors were subjected at the time of the Prophet.[107] *Riba al jahilliya* is prohibited in Qur'anic verses[108] which encourage charity and prohibit *riba* that is 'improperly gained and which represents not any work done but only a facile gain, an increase in luck, or an increment due to a delay.'[109] This type of *riba* was often contained in transactions through which the debtor would have to repay an amount, which was not only deferred but also drastically increased.[110]

The hadith is also referred to in order to define other forms of *riba*. For example, the hadith refers to *riba al-fadl*, which is the *riba* of increase or excess, and prohibits the exchange of goods from the same genus in different quantities.[111] This is based on the following hadith, '[g]old for gold, silver for silver, wheat for wheat, barley for barley, dates for dates, and salt for salt, like for like, hand to

---

101 The root letters are in Arabic are ر-ب-و ra-ba-waw.
102 The Qur'an also uses these root letters in the context of the following meanings 'to rise, to swell'; 'to raise'; 'a hillock' and 'to be greater and big'. See Abdullah Saeed, 'The Moral Context of the Prohibition of Riba' (1995) 12 *The American Journal of Islamic Social Sciences* 496, 499; Fazlur Rahman, 'Riba and Interest' (1964) 3 *Islamic Studies* 1.
103 The Qur'an, above n 25 (Chapter 2, Verses 278–279).
104 See generally, Sunna, Riba, <http://sunnah.com/search/?q=riba>.
105 Saeed, above n 900, 499.
106 Nabil Saleh, *Unlawful Gain and Legitimate Profit in Islamic Law: Riba, Gharar and Islamic Banking* (Cambridge University Press, 1986) 16.
107 See generally, Saeed, above n 900, 505.
108 The Qur'an, above n 25 (Chapter 2, Verses 275–280).
109 Comair-Obeid, above n 12, 46.
110 David Eisenberg and Craig Nethercott, *Islamic Finance: Law and Practice* (Oxford University Press, 2012) 42.
111 El Gamal, above n 731, 50–51.

hand, and any increase is *riba*.'[112] *Riba al-nasiah* is referred to as *riba* by way of deferment, because it refers to the exchange of counter-values with deferment.[113] The four schools of thought and contemporary Islamic scholars differ on the application of these two forms of *riba*.[114]

How the prohibition against *riba* relates to contemporary finance is the subject of debate among Islamic scholars and in the world of Islamic banking and finance. As will be discussed in more detail in the next chapter, some scholars argue that *riba* is defined as usury, and what is prohibited is akin to *riba al-jahilliya*, as defined earlier.[115] Similar to *gharar*, this liberal interpretation of *riba* is justified on the basis of historical context, *darura* (necessity) and *maslaha* (public interest).[116] According to this approach, what is prohibited is usury as practiced in pre-Islamic Arabia and not interest, which is considered a conventional economic practice. This view is also supported by the fact that:

> in a capitalist economy, loans appear to be the most common means of making the saver's capital fructify after all his labour and efforts to accumulate some money. The small saver has then every right to be protected against inflation and receive a just interest in return for entrusting his money to the bank, to the State or to any particular enterprise in order to conserve the purchasing power of his capital.[117]

Consequently, Islamic scholars from Egypt such as Rashid Rida, Ibrahim Zaki Badawi and Abd Al-Razzaq Ahmad Al Sanhuri[118] argued that *riba al-jahilliya* was 'manifest *riba*'[119] and therefore, prohibited. On the other hand, *riba al-fadl* and *riba al-nasi'ah* were 'hidden *riba*' and were only prohibited when they became 'manifest *riba*' or *riba al-jahilliya*.[120]

Yet, Gamal argues that 'the fact that much of the *[r]iba* which was used in pre-Islamic Arabia was indeed for commercial and business financing . . . [t]his is

112 Ibid., 50–51.
113 El Gamal, above n 33, 4.
114 For an explanation of the differences between the four schools of thought on the concept of riba, see Comair-Obeid, above n 12, 48–50.
115 See generally, Saeed, above n 900, 505.
116 These principles are discussed in more detail in Chapter 2. See also Warde, above n 38, 53.
117 Comair-Obeid, above n 12, 52.
118 See Chapter 7, Interest on Arbitral Awards. There were slight distinctions between these Egyptian scholars. Sanhuri went on to draft the Egyptian Civil Code 1948 upon which the Civil Codes of Syria, Iraq, Libya and Kuwait were based. See Khalil and Thomas, above n 325, 69–74.
119 Ibn Qayyim al-Jawziyya, the classical Hanafi jurist from the 14th century, argued that there were two types of riba: manifest riba (riba al-jahilliya or riba al-nasi'a) and hidden riba (riba al-fadl). He argued the ultimate rationale behind the prohibition of riba al-fadl was to prevent riba al-jahilliya and riba al-nasi'a. Ibn Qayyim, I'lam al Muwaqqi'in, (Vol II) 153–164 as cited in AbdulKader Thomas, *Interest in Islamic Economics: Understanding Riba* (Routledge, 2006) 61–62.
120 Khalil and Thomas, above n 325, 71.

in contrast to the European view of "usury" . . . which evokes the mental image of exploitative consumption loans.'[121] Islamic scholars who base their views on classical *Shari'a* argue that the above-mentioned *riba* refers to any increase in the amount of money returned by a borrower and therefore, all forms of *riba al-fadl* and *riba al-nasi'ah* are forbidden.[122] However, since the Qur'an prohibits *riba* but allows profit,[123] Islamic banks operate through a concept in Islam known as 'profit-and-loss-sharing' (PLS). PLS is based on concepts such as: trustee finance (*mudaraba*), equity participation (*musharaka*), cost plus financing (*murabaha*), leasing (*ijara*), advance purchase (*salam*), deferred payment financing (*bai bi-thamin ajil*)[124] and 'mark-up' methods.[125] Many proponents of the Islamic commercial system argue that in order to understand Islamic commercial transactions, it is essential to grasp that Islam, as a religion, governs all aspects of a believer's life. For example, a judicial commissioner in Malaysia states:

> [t]he secular economic principles address the problem of consumption, production and distribution. In contrast, Islamic principles forecast on the manner to eradicate poverty. Equitable distribution is one of its goals. Islam views that inequity is created by mass exploitation of resources to obtain maximum profit.[126]

As discussed in Chapter 2, Saeed interprets such statements by examining the 'neo-revivalism' movement, which began in the first half of the 20th century as a reaction to the 'excesses of secularism' in the Muslim world.[127] Others critique the Islamic banking and finance sector, and argue that various *Shari'a*-compliant products are akin to conventional finance and *hiyal* (legal tricks or stratagems) are used to frame the products as *Shari'a*-compliant.[128] An example of a *Shari'a*-compliant agreement that is often under scrutiny is *murabaha* or cost-plus sale. A basic cost-plus sale involves a customer approaching an Islamic financial institution ('IFI') and requesting that it purchase an item on behalf of the customer and in return, the IFI receives a pre-determined profit.[129] Scholars have debated how to calculate the profit margin, since the profit rate is often benchmarked in

---

121 El Gamal, above n 22, 2.
122 Warde, above n 38, 53.
123 Haleem, above n 25 (Chapter 2, Verses 275).
124 The deferred payment financing transaction (bai bi-thamin ajil) has caused some controversy in Malaysia because it is viewed as being similar to a conventional loan. See Affin Bank Berhad v Marilyn Ho Siok Lin [2006] 7 MLJ 249; Malayan Banking Bhd v Ya'kup Oje & Anor [2007] 5 CLJ 311. See also Zulkifi Hasan and Mehmet Asutay, 'An Analysis of the Courts' Decisions on Islamic Finance Disputes' (2011) 3(2) *ISRA International Journal of Islamic Finance* 41.
125 See generally, Mervyn Lewis and Latifa Algaoud, *Islamic Banking* (Edward Elgar, 2001) 4.
126 Malayan Banking Bhd v Ya'kup Oje & Anor [2007] 5 CLJ 311, [6].
127 Saeed, above n 48, 7.
128 El Gamal, above n 33, 6.
129 Saeed, above n 48, 10.

accordance with the LIBOR,[130] or regional equivalent.[131] In order for a *murabaha* sale to be *Shari'a* -compliant, the bank must have constructive possession of the commodity before selling it to the customer, the subject of sale must not be a commodity forbidden under *Shari'a*, the price (including the profit rate) should be fixed at the time of signing the contract (this ensures that *gharar* is avoided), and the sale must transfer the legal rights of the commodity to the customer.[132]

As discussed in Chapter 3, although the *Beximco* case was subject to litigation, it is interesting to note the approach taken in this case regarding the *murabaha* transaction and its possible impact on arbitration. Shamil Bank argued that Beximco failed to abide by their obligations under two *murabaha* agreements with Shamil Bank. Pursuant to the *murabaha* agreements, Shamil Bank sold goods to the defendant at a rate which included a pre-determined profit. The agreement included a governing law clause, which stated, '[s]ubject to the principles of the Glorious Sharia'a, this Agreement shall be governed by and construed in accordance with the laws of England.' Shamil Bank argued that the governing law clause meant that the agreement should be enforceable under both English law and *Shari'a*. Beximco raised the following defences:

> [o]n a true construction of the governing law clause quoted in paragraph 1 of this judgment, the *Morabaha* [sic] Agreements and the ESUAs were only enforceable insofar as they were valid and enforceable both (i) in accordance with the principles of the *Sharia* (i.e., the rules or laws of Islam) and (ii) in accordance with English law; (b) in fact, the agreements were unlawful, invalid and unenforceable under the principles of the *Sharia* in that . . . the transactions were in truth disguised loans at interest. As such they amounted to unlawful agreements to pay [r]iba and were thus void and/or unenforceable.

The unlawful nature of the agreements arose due to the existence of *riba* and so in the context of arbitration, the defence would overlap both the non-arbitrability defence and invalidity of an agreement due to illegality. The non-arbitrability defence ascertains whether the subject matter is capable of being arbitrated and in this case, the subject matter was a *murabaha* finance agreement, which was arguably not compliant with *Shari'a*. Beximco argued that the finance agreements themselves were considered invalid as 'it is uncontroversial that under Islamic law interest charged on loans by banks is [r]iba and prohibited. Equally, any agreement in which, in substance, interest is being charged upon a loan is unlawful, void and unenforceable.'[133] Furthermore, Shamil Bank had charged interest under the guise of an Islamic contract known as *murabahah* and

---

130 London Interbank Offered Rate.
131 Nethercott and Eisenberg (eds), above n 908, 193.
132 Bhatti, above n 45, 277.
133 Beximco Pharmaceuticals Ltd. & Ors v Shamil Bank of Bahrain EC [2004] EWCA Civ 19, [32].

therefore, the contract was unenforceable.[134] Arguably the preconditions for a *Shari'a*-compliant *murabaha* agreement were not met, because the advances made by Beximco were not used to purchase or lease any property and the banks were simply 'charging interest or an additional amount over and above the sums due in consideration of the giving of time.'[135]

As discussed in Chapter 3, the English Appellate Court ('the Appellate Court') decided that *Shari'a* did not replace English law in this case, but reflected the nature of the business. The Islamic financial transactions included in the contracts were not governed by two competing legal systems, but categorised as being '*Shari'a* compliant.' Therefore, the Appellate Court did not consider whether the subject matter was *Shari'a*-compliant. Colon argues that this reasoning was 'hasty,' because the Appellate Court did not consider prior negotiations of the parties, or the common practices of the Islamic financial industry. The result of the Appellate Court's reasoning 'was that the words "[s]ubject to the principles of the Glorious Sharia'a" are rendered superfluous, but Shamil bank is still left to represent itself to its British customers as an "Islamic bank".'[136]

According to Colon, the reference to *Shari'a* is to ensure that Islamic financial transactions remain *Shari'a*-compliant despite the litigation process. The reason why parties decide to deal with Islamic banks that include *Shari'a* clauses in their agreements is to ensure that they are participating in *Shari'a*-compliant deals.[137] Otherwise, they would choose to obtain finance from mainstream financial institutions.[138] Similarly, one may argue that if parties choose to subject their agreement to *Shari'a* in arbitration agreements, this implies that the *Shari'a* arbitration laws apply. If *Shari'a* prohibits interest, then an interest-based transaction cannot be arbitrable if *Shari'a* law governs the arbitration. It is arguable that if the parties in Beximco had subjected their agreement to *Shari'a* alone, the defence of non-arbitrability may have held greater weight. Similarly, the defence may hold greater weight in countries where *Shari'a* forms the basis of public policy. Whether the prohibition of *riba* and/or *gharar* has an impact on arbitrability in countries where *Shari'a* forms part of the country's legal system will be discussed in the next two sections by examining the approach taken in the UAE and Saudi Arabia.

VI The UAE's pragmatic approach

The *UAE Civil Procedure Code* ('the CPC')[139] governs arbitration proceedings in the UAE; however the CPC is currently not based on the *UNCITRAL Model*

---

134 Ibid.
135 Ibid.
136 Colon, above n 376, 427.
137 Ibid., 427.
138 Ibid., 427.
139 Federal Law No 11 of 1992 (UAE), Part 3 of Book II; Arts. 203–218 trans, Gordon Blanke and Habib Al Mulla, *Arbitration in the MENA Legislation* (Juris Publishing, 2016) (Legislation attached in accompanying disc).

Law.[140] The UAE is a civil law jurisdiction with *Shari'a* influence and as noted in Chapter 2, *Shari'a* is prescribed in the country's constitution. The UAE courts consider arbitrability as a matter of jurisdiction, and thus if a tribunal issues an award concerning a matter that is non-arbitrable, it is acting outside its scope.[141] Arbitrability is addressed by Art. 203(4) of the CPC, which states: '[a]rbitration shall not be permissible in matters, which are not capable of being reconciled.'[142] Art. 733 of the *UAE Federal Law No. 5 of 1985* ('*UAE Civil Code*')[143] further stipulates matters which are not capable of being reconciled or 'compromised':[144]

It shall not be permissible to enter into a compromise if it includes any of the following impediments:

(1) The annulment of a debt by another debt;
(2) The sale of food by way of commutative contract prior to delivery;
(3) The deferred exchange of gold against silver and vice versa;
(4) *Riba al-nasi'a* (usurious interest in consideration of the deferment of the payment of a debt);
(5) Substituting part of a deferred debt owed by a debtor in consideration of advancing the date of payment;

---

140 See generally, Luttrell, above n 214.
141 Reza Mohtashami, et al., 'United Arab Emirates' in International Bar Association (ed), *Arbitration – Country Guides* (International Bar Association, 2013) 5.
142 This is the translation provided by Dubai International Arbitration Centre, 'Arbitration in the UAE' <www.diac.ae/idias/rules/uae/>. Cf Karim Nassif, 'Arbitrability Under UAE Law' (2013) 5(1) *International Journal of Arab Arbitration* 5. The translation by Nassif states 'arbitration shall not be permissible in matters, which are not capable of compromise.'
143 UAE Federal Law No. 5 of 1985 [James Whelan (Clifford Chance) trans, The Civil Code <https://lexemiratidotnet.files.wordpress.com/2011/07/uae-civil-code-_english-transla tion_.pdf>].
144 Various civil law countries also define matters as being arbitrable if they are not subject to compromise or settlement. For example: Art. 806 of the Italian Code of Civil Procedure states as non-arbitrable 'issues of personal status and marital separation and those other disputes which may not be the subject of settlement.' See 'Italy – Arbitration (Title VIII of Book IV of the Italian Code of Civil Procedure)' <www.jus.uio.no/lm/italy.arbitra tion/806.html>; Art. 1030, para 1 of the German Civil Procedure Code, which states: '[a]n arbitration agreement concerning claims not involving an economic interest shall have legal effect to the extent that the parties are entitles to conclude a settlement on the issue in dispute.' See Trans-Lex, 'The New German Arbitration Law (English Translation' <www. trans-lex.org/600550>; Art. 1020 (3) of the Code of Civil Procedure in Netherlands: '[t]he arbitration agreement shall not serve to determine legal consequences of which the parties cannot freely dispose.' See Dutch Civil Law, 'Code of Civil Procedures' <www. dutchcivillaw.com/civilprocedureleg.htm>. See also, Mitsubishi Motors Corporation v Soler Chrysler-Plymouth Inc 723 F.2d 155, 164 (1st Cir, 1983) in which Coffin J determined: '[t]he precise question we ask is whether a matter that has been barred by unanimous judicial precedent for a decade and a half from resolution by arbitration, because of a multiplicity of solid reasons that lose no pertinence or weight in an international context, is a matter "capable of settlement by arbitration". It seems to us that "capable" means legally capable – for any matter can theoretically be arbitrated or compromised, even if the decision be to divide an infant.'

(6) The reduction of the amount of guarantee on a deferred debt owed by a debtor in consideration of accelerated payment with an increase; and

(7) A loan involving a benefit.[145]

The above non-arbitrable matters are based on the Maliki school of thought in Islamic jurisprudence.[146] It is clear from Art. 733 that *riba al-nas'ia* is non-arbitrable in the UAE. Nevertheless, the general prohibition of transactions involving *riba* seems to suggest that a contract containing *riba* is still valid as per Art. 714 of *the UAE Federal Law No. 5 of 1985*, which provides '[i]f the contract of loan provides for a benefit in excess of the essence of the contract otherwise than a guarantee of the right of the lender, such provision shall be void but the contract shall be valid.'[147] On the other hand, countries such as Jordan, Egypt and Lebanon[148] have adopted a position similar to France, where non-arbitrable matters include those involving personal status and public order.[149] Art. 733 of the *UAE Civil Code* has left personal status or public order matters open and therefore, relies on case law to ascertain matters regarding arbitrability.[150]

Tamimi distinguishes between arbitrability and public policy, by arguing that in cases involving real estate disputes, the UAE courts have ruled that the arbitral award or arbitration agreement is contrary to public policy, as opposed to stipulating that real estate disputes are non-arbitrable:

> [a]rbitrators are not prohibited from dealing with matters of public policy. However, it is prohibited for the award or the agreement to be contrary to public policy.[151]

However, an analysis of the cases seems to suggest that the concept of arbitrability and public policy overlap in the UAE. For example, in recent cases, the

---

145 UAE Federal Law No. 5 of 1985 [James Whelan (Clifford Chance) trans, 'The Civil Code' <https://lexemiratidotnet.files.wordpress.com/2011/07/uae-civil-code-_english-translation_.pdf>]. See also Nassif, above n 142, 5–9; Fiona Campbell, 'Arbitrability of Disputes: Issues of Arbitrability and Public Policy in the UAE' Al Tamimi & Co (May 2014) <www.tamimi.com/en/magazine/law-update/section-8/may-7/arbitrability-of-disputes-issues-of-arbitrability-and-public-policy-in-the-uae.html>; Sami Tannous and Seema Bono, 'International Arbitration 2016: United Arab Emirates' in Steven Finizio and Charlie Caher (eds), *International Comparative Legal Guide to International Arbitration 2016* (Global Legal Group, 2016) 464–475.
146 Nassif, above n 142, 6.
147 Ibid.
148 See Florentine Sonia Sneij and Ulrich Andreas Zanconato, 'The Role of Shari'a Law and Modern Arbitration Statutes in an Environment of Growing Multilateral Trade: Lessons from Lebanon and Syria' (2015) 12(2) *Transnational Dispute Management* 1, 11.
149 Nassif, above n 142, 6.
150 Ibid., 6.
151 Essam Al Tamimi, 'Arbitrators Dealing with Real Estate Property Disputes – Is It a Matter of Public Policy' Al Tamimi & Co (June 2014) <www.tamimi.com/en/magazine/law-update/section-8/june-6/arbitrators-dealing-with-real-estate-property-disputes-is-it-a-matter-of-public-policy.html>.

Dubai Court of Cassation has taken a literal approach to construing public order under Art. 3 of the *UAE Civil Code*. In its ruling dated 12 February 2012 and 16 September 2012,[152] this literal approach of the Dubai Court of Cassation to public order under Art. 3 led to it noting that the interim real estate matters and private ownership/circulation of wealth matters were non-arbitrable.[153] Art. 3 of the Civil Code states:

> public order shall be viewed as including such provisions relating to private status such as marriage, inheritance and lineage, as well as provisions relating to sovereignty, free trade, distribution of wealth, rules of private ownership and the other rules and foundations upon which society is based, in such a manner as not to conflict with the definitive provisions and fundamental principles of the Islamic *Sharia[h]*.[154]

Commentators argue that this approach was contrary to the ruling on 22 February 2009 because as argued by Nassif:

> the legal rules forming part of the public order, which individuals cannot depart from through agreements, are those intended to protect a political, social or economic general interest, related foundations of the society of high nature (sic) which are above the private interests of the individuals.[155]

Tamimi provides a brief overview of UAE case law, and concludes that public policy as per Art. 3 of the *UAE Civil Code*

> does not apply to real estate or property dispositions made in the private sector between private individuals . . . [w]hat is actually classified as public

---

152 Baiti Real Estate Development v Dynasty Zarooni Inc, Dubai Court of Cassation, Petition No. 180 of 2011, 12 February 2012 [Graham Lovett, Lara Hammond and Hassan Arab, Summaries of UAE Courts' Decisions on Arbitration. (ICC Publication, 2013) 116–117]; Dubai Court of Cassation, Petition No. 14 of 2012, 16 September 2012, [Graham Lovett, Lara Hammond and Hassan Arab, Summaries of UAE Courts' Decisions on Arbitration. (ICC Publication, 2013) 122–123]; see also Case No. 2847/2013 [2014] 6(4) *International Journal of Arab Arbitration* 49 (Court of Cassation of Abu Dhabi). In this case, it was determined that '[t]he contract is consensual, and the request for termination is not a matter of public order as it is not related to the rules of registration at the Land Registry of Abu Dhabi and does not concern the determination of ownership of real estate property in the Emirate or the lands that can be disposed of, or the transfer of property rules.' See generally, Al Tamimi, above n 151.
153 Nassif, above n 142, 7.
154 Ibid., 6.
155 Dubai Court of Cassation, Petition No. 280/2008, judgment dated 22 September 2009 as cited in Nassif, above n 142, 7.

policy is the country's control and regulation of its national resources not the private sector's right to transact among themselves.[156]

Nassif argues that a literal approach to public policy under Art. 3 of the *UAE Civil Code* could also mean that every transaction relating to private ownership would be non-arbitrable:

> [a] car is the subject matter of private ownership. The sale is a means of the circulation of wealth. Would this imply that the sale of a car is part of public order? Definitely not! It has no impact on society, on the economy, on politics and above all on sovereignty.[157]

Arguably, a literal interpretation of Art. 3 of the *UAE Civil Code* would also mean that public policy under Art. 3 of the *UAE Civil Transactions Code* was Islamic public policy, and therefore it must not conflict with *Shari'a*.[158] However, as will be discussed in Chapter 8, the UAE does not apply Islamic public policy as grounds of non-arbitrability, invalidity or non-enforcement in international arbitration, and generally tends to adhere to its obligations under the *New York Convention*.[159] This is largely due to the fact that Dubai is one of the major centres of international trade and commerce,[160] and due to the establishment of the Dubai International Finance Centre.[161]

Despite this pragmatic approach, legal practitioners such as Tamimi and Nassif argue that the arbitration law in the UAE needs to be reformed in accordance with the *UNCITRAL Model Law* to address various ambiguities in the current law, including the issue of arbitrability.[162] Consequently, the impact of *Shari'a* on arbitrability, validity and public policy also needs to be clarified in the UAE arbitration laws and, as will be discussed in the next section, also needs to be clarified in Saudi Arabia.

---

156 Al Tamimi, above n 151.

157 Ibid.

158 Gordon Blanke, 'Public Policy in the UAE: Has the Unruly Horse Turned into a Camel?' *Kluwer Arbitration Blog* (14 October 2012) <http://kluwerarbitrationblog.com/blog/2012/10/14/public-policy-in-the-uae-has-the-unruly-horse-turned-into-a-camel/>.

159 Mohamed Al-Nasair and Ilias Bantekas, 'Nullity and Jurisdictional Excess as Grounds for Non-Enforcement of Foreign Awards in Bahrain and the UAE' (2013) 30 *Journal of International Arbitration* 283, 285.

160 Ibid.

161 Ibid.

162 Nassif, above n 142, 9; Al Tamimi, above n 151. In Al Tamimi's article, above n 151, it is stated: 'Until the new UAE Arbitration law is promulgated (the draft is currently in an advanced stage) and until another judgment is issued by the Court of Cassation to overturn the principles mentioned above, it is likely that the lower courts in the UAE will follow the principles set out by Dubai and Abu Dhabi Court of Cassation in relation to the invalidity of sale and purchase agreements of properties in the UAE which have not been registered at the Land Registrar.'

VII The Saudi inconsistency

Regarding arbitrability, Art. 2 of the old *Saudi Arbitration Law* stated that arbitration was not permitted in the following matters:

a   In matters that were not amenable to conciliation (*sulh*); and
b   Matters relating to public policy.[163]

Similar to Saudi Arabia, many Arab jurisdictions have an arbitrability clause noting that arbitration is not permitted in matters that are not amenable to *sulh*.[164] However, Saudi Arabia has never legislated on matters related to *sulh* and thus at present the law of *sulh* is derived from *Shari'a*.[165] This standard arbitration clause arises from the concept of *sulh* under Islamic jurisprudence, which can be defined as both conciliation and mediation. As noted in Chapter 1, *sulh* is arguably the preferred dispute resolution method under Islamic classical jurisprudence, as it maintains family and community ties.[166]

Although under classical Islamic jurisprudence, family matters would have been arbitrable because they were subject to *sulh*, they have now been categorised as 'personal status' matters in all Muslim jurisdictions. In practice, the statement 'arbitration is not permissible in matters which cannot be conciliated' refers to *hudud* offences, which as discussed earlier, are committed against society as a whole and therefore, cannot be conciliated.[167] Under Islamic law, such offences include adultery, theft, rape, terrorism and other similar offences.[168] However, murder is not classified as a *hudud* offence but as noted previously, falls under the category of *qisas*.[169] This because although the punishment for murder is execution under *Shari'a* and Saudi law, the family of the victim may decide to settle the matter and get paid compensatory money (*diya*) instead of agreeing to capital punishment for the perpetrator.[170]

In the case of criminal and family law matters, the statement in relation to matters being arbitrable if they are amenable to *sulh* does not raise many issues under contemporary ICA. Similarly, commercial matters are amenable to *sulh* and therefore, arbitrable. However, as discussed earlier, there is uncertainty in regards to matters involving *gharar* or *riba*.[171] In general, Islamic scholars agree

---

163 S 1, Old Implementation Rules 1985 (Saudi Arabia).
164 For example, Art. 173 Code of Civil and Commercial Procedure No. 38 of 1980 (Kuwait) [trans (1989) 4(1) Arab Law Quarterly 25], Art. 173.
165 Abdulrahman Yahya Baamir, *Shari'a Law in Commercial and Banking Arbitration: Law and Practice in Saudi Arabia* (Ashgate, 2010) 154.
166 Aida Othman, '"And Amicable Settlement Is Best": Sulh and Dispute Resolution in Islamic Law' (2007) 21(1) *Arab Law Quarterly* 64–90, 69.
167 Baamir, above n 165, 156.
168 Ibid.
169 Ibid.
170 This is referred to as diya or blood money. See generally, Muhammad Abdel Haleem, *Criminal Justice in Islam: Judicial Procedure in the Shari'ah* (I. B. Tauris, 2003).
171 Baamir, above n 165, 158.

that matters concerning *gharar* or *riba* are not amenable to *sulh*. This is due to the following hadith: '*sulh* is permissible . . . except a *sulh* that makes haram that which is halal and halal that which is haram.'[172] This hadith means that conciliation is recommended, except in situations where something that is prohibited under *Shari'a* is ruled as being permissible after being subjected to *sulh*. However, the extent to which *sulh* was permissible in matters involving *gharar* and *riba* was the subject of legal debate under classical Islamic jurisprudence.[173] This has an impact upon banks that wish to settle disputes in Saudi Arabia through *sulh*.[174] Further, this uncertainty also arises under the public policy exception.

A Islamic public policy

Public policy in Saudi Arabia is derived from *Shari'a*, and the *Basic Law of Governance of the Kingdom of Saudi Arabia 1992* ('*Basic Law of Governance*')[175] states that the ruling regime derives power from the Qur'an and *sunna*.[176] At a theoretical level, this implies that any subject matters that are contrary to *Shari'a* are against public policy and therefore, non-arbitrable. This defence of non-arbitrability on the basis of Islamic public policy has been used historically, such that, if the subject matter of the transaction is prohibited, then the arbitration agreement is considered null and void, and the judgement or award is unenforceable.

For example, a contract in relation to the selling or purchasing of alcohol, pork and perhaps, music, may be under scrutiny.[177] This was discussed in Ruling No. 189/T/4 of 1427 AH 2007 in which a foreign judgement issued in Egypt was enforced in Saudi Arabia. In this case, the subject matter of the transaction related to music, and music containing instruments may be considered *haram* according to Islamic scholars who interpret *Shari'a* in an orthodox and literal manner. The Fourth Audit-Circuit Court of Saudi Arabia rejected the defence that the judgement should not be enforced on the basis that the subject matter was contrary to *Shari'a*.

Interestingly, the judges held that there was no *ijma*[178] among Islamic scholars in relation to the prohibition against music in *Shari'a*. As discussed in Chapter 1,

---

172 Sunan Abi Dawud, 'The Office of the Judge (Kitab Al-Aqdiyah)' <http://sunnah.com/abudawud/25/24> (Book 24, Hadith, 3587).

173 This thesis does not cover Islamic jurisprudence in relation to sulh. See generally, Othman, above n 166, 64–90.

174 Baamir, above n 165, 158–159.

175 World Intellectual Property Organisation trans, Basic Law of Governance (promulgated by the Royal Decree No. A/90 (1992) <www.wipo.int/edocs/lexdocs/laws/en/sa/sa016en.pdf>. See also Royal Embassy of Saudi Arabia Washington, DC trans, The Basic Law of Governance (1992) <www.saudiembassy.net/about/country-information/laws/The_Basic_Law_Of_Governance.aspx>.

176 Baamir, above n 165, 143.

177 Abdulaziz Mohammed A. Bin Zaid, *The Recognition and Enforcement of Foreign Commercial Arbitral Awards in Saudi Arabia: Comparative Study with Australia* (PhD Thesis, University of Wollongong, 2013) 292.

178 Consensus.

ijma is one of the methods through which *Shari'a* is understood and implemented. This can be compared with the prohibition against pork or alcohol, which Islamic scholars unanimously agree are *haram* under *Shari'a*.[179] The defence of arbitrability may also be invoked in Saudi Arabia if the transaction involves *riba* and/or *gharar*, and this will be discussed in more detail as follows.[180]

B Riba under Saudi law

After the Saudi oil boom in the 1970s, public funds were lent to individuals without charging interest, and the loan agreements were flexible.[181] The refusal of *Shari'a* courts and commercial courts, referred to in Chapter 1, to recognise the validity of interest in banking transactions led to banks experiencing various legal problems.[182] The government then decided to allow Saudi banks to charge interest on the basis of necessity, but interest was not awarded in disputes.[183] Furthermore, charging interest is governmental practice, such as the *Gas Concession Agreement 2004*[184] contains a clause for interest to be charged on the amount of the financial guarantee if there is a late payment at the rate of LIBOR plus 1%.[185] However, the Board of Grievances has been inflexible and hostile to the idea of resolving matters where the parties are banks, and refers such disputes to the Committee for the Settlement of Banking Disputes. This position is based on the legal doctrine that arbitration agreements and awards are considered illegal if the contract is void.[186] Baamir notes a number of cases in which the Board of Grievances has followed the Hanbali school of thought, and ruled that contracts relating to prohibited subject matters are considered null and void.[187] Thus, Baamir argues that the Saudi position on *riba* is 'truly vague and confusing to the extent that nobody is able to determine whether interest is legal or illegal.'[188] The status of *riba*, *gharar* and arbitrability under the new *Saudi Arbitration Law 2012* will be discussed in more detail in the next section.

C Saudi arbitration law 2012 on arbitrability

Referring to the defence of non-arbitrability, the following Articles are relevant under the new *Saudi Arbitration Law 2012*:

179 Bin Zaid, above n 177, 288.
180 El Ahdab and El Ahdab, above n 11, 633.
181 Baamir, above n 165, 168.
182 Ibid.
183 Ibid.
184 Art. 18, Gas Concession Agreement between the Kingdom of Saudi Arabia and Lukoil Overseas (Umm Alqura Gazette No. 3990/4 May 2004) as cited in Bantekas, 'Arbitrability in Finance and Banking' above n 19, 309; Baamir, Shari'a Law in Commercial and Banking Arbitration, above n 165, 169.
185 Baamir, above n 165, 169.
186 Ibid., 172.
187 Ibid., 173.
188 Ibid., 168.

a   Art. 2 of the *Saudi Arbitration Law 2012* states that arbitration is not permissible in matters related to personal status (e.g., family law matters) and issues where reconciliation is not permitted (e.g., *hudud* crimes, as defined in Chapter 6).[189]

b   Art. 5 of the *Saudi Arbitration Law 2012* states that if the parties subject their relationship to any document, the procedure and substance of the dispute must not be contrary to *Shari'a*. This Art. implies that contracts inclusive of interest are contrary to the purposes of *Shari'a*.[190]

Therefore, the position under the new Saudi law has not changed in regards to arbitrability due to Arts. 2 and 5 of the *Saudi Arbitration Law 2012*. Despite the fact that the *Saudi Arbitration Law 2012* distinguishes between international and domestic arbitration, and the fact that the new *Saudi Enforcement Law 2013* provides increasing recognition of international arbitration awards, commentators note that 'the new Enforcement law cannot guard against any public policy issues found in awards rendered by foreign arbitrators not versed in Saudi law or Islamic concepts.'[191] As the concept of public policy and arbitrability is very closely related under *Shari'a*, disputes that contain interest or speculation may come under scrutiny even under the *Saudi Arbitration Law 2012*.

Although the *Saudi Arbitration Law 2012* does not differentiate between international and domestic arbitration, subject matters containing *riba* or *gharar* may still come under scrutiny due to Art. 5 of the *Saudi Arbitration Law 2012*,[192] which as mentioned earlier, requires that if parties subject their relationship to any document, the procedure and substance of the dispute must not contravene *Shari'a*.

Under the old *Saudi Arbitration Law 1983*, the Board of Grievances would filter the enforcement orders in order to ensure *Shari'a* compliance. Therefore, banks would either choose English law or the law of New York as the proper law of the contract.[193] For example, in *Islamic Investment Company of the Gulf (Bahamas) Ltd v Symphony Gems NV*[194] ('*Symphony Gems*'), the Islamic Investment Company of the Gulf (Bahamas) Ltd ('IICG') entered into a *murabaha* contract with Symphony Gems NV ('Symphony'). The agreement under the *murabaha* contract was that IICG would purchase gems and resell them to Symphony on a cost plus mark-up basis. IICG instituted proceedings against Symphony when Symphony did not repay IICG in full. One of Symphony's defences was that

---

189   Salah Al Hejailan, 'The New Saudi Arbitration Act: A Comprehensive and Article by Article Review' (2012) 4 *International Journal of Arab Arbitration* 15, 17.

190   Jean-Pierre Harb and Alexander G. Leventhal, 'The New Saudi Arbitration Law: Modernization to the Tune of Shari'a' (2013) 30 *Journal of International Arbitration* 113, 122.

191   Jones Day, 'The New Enforcement Law of Saudi Arabia: An Additional Step Toward a Harmonized Arbitration Regime' (September 2013) <www.jonesday.com/the-new-enforcement-law-of-saudi-arabia-an-additional-step-toward-a-harmonized-arbitration-regime-09–04–2013/>.

192   Harb and Leventhal, above n 190, 122.

193   Baamir, above n 165, 173.

194   (Queen's Bench Division, Commercial Court, 13 February 2002).

the *murabaha* contract was not *Shari'a*-compliant, and that the IICG charter demanded compliance with Islamic law. Similar to the *Sanghi* case, *Shari'a* was not the governing law in this matter, but rather English law was chosen. Justice Tomlinson of the High Court of Justice Queen's Bench Division Commercial Court of the United Kingdom ('English Court') held that although the *murabaha* contract was not *Shari'a*-compliant, the matter was governed by English law and not Saudi law.[195] It was further noted by the English Court that '[t]he fact that the claimant was based in Saudi Arabia, and the offer made in that country was insufficient to bring into play the illegality principle, on the assumption that the agreement was contrary to Saudi law.'[196] Baamir assumes that Saudi law was deliberately avoided in this case so that the argument that the *murabaha* contract was contrary to *Shari'a* would not hold weight.[197]

The situation regarding the prohibition of *riba* and *gharar* in Saudi Arabia is uncertain. On the one hand, the conventional banking system in Saudi Arabia can charge interest and in the event a dispute arises, the Committee for the Settlement of Banking Disputes recognises that charging interest is necessary when settling banking disputes.[198] On the other hand, the practice of the Board of Grievances under the old *Saudi Arbitration Law 1983* has been to render arbitral awards void and refuse enforcement if they are contrary to *Shari'a* in both international and domestic disputes. Therefore, while interest is practiced and recognised in Saudi Arabia, it is against *Shari'a*, which is both the public policy of Saudi Arabia, and the overriding consideration under the *Saudi Arbitration Law 2012*. While the issue of arbitrability where the subject matter contains *riba* or *gharar* is not directly addressed in the *Saudi Arbitration Law 2012*, Art. 5 clearly stipulates that the procedure and substance of a dispute must not violate *Shari'a*. Although it is clear that subject matters containing *riba* and/or *gharar* are not arbitrable under *Shari'a*, this is not as clear under Saudi law, due to the fact that Saudi law permits interest to be awarded by the Committee for the Settlement of Banking Disputes. The contradiction between *Shari'a* and Saudi law is extremely apparent when it comes to the prohibition of *riba* and *gharar*. Saleh warns that although dealing with interest is common practice under Saudi law, 'it is merely tolerated out of necessity and under the exigencies of international business . . . [a]t any moment, the prohibition of *riba* and *gharar* may be reinstated, with full and comprehensive effects.'[199]

This causes arbitration to become a less attractive dispute resolution mechanism for domestic conventional banking, because parties would prefer to refer disputes to the Committee for the Settlement of Banking Disputes, in order to ensure that interest might be awarded.[200] However, the CSBD has been criticised

195 Ibid., 4–5.
196 Ibid.
197 Baamir, above n 165, 174.
198 Ibid., 180.
199 Nabil Saleh, above n 106, 5.
200 Baamir, above n 165, 186.

because its decisions are not binding. Furthermore, in international commercial arbitration, parties try to avoid the jurisdiction of Saudi Arabia, as was arguably the case in *Symphony Gems.* In fact, parties try to find ways to avoid Saudi law, in order to ensure that they can avoid any uncertainty in relation to the non-arbitrability of disputes involving *riba* or *gharar.*[201] As will be discussed in Chapter 7, the situation becomes more complicated when an award needs to be enforced in Saudi Arabia, but is denied enforcement due to the non-arbitrability of subject matters containing *riba* or *gharar.*

VIII *IICRA Rules, i-Arbitration Rules* and *AAOIFI Standards* for arbitration

As discussed in this chapter, the impact of *gharar* and *riba* on arbitrability and arbitration agreements is unclear, because there are differences of opinion in *Shari'a* regarding how *gharar* and *riba* are manifested in financial transactions, contracts and arbitration agreements. There is also ongoing tension in countries, such as Saudi Arabia and the UAE, between adhering to conventional financial practices and complying with *Shari'a.*

The theoretical uncertainty and lack of clarity regarding the impact of *riba* and *gharar* on arbitration agreements is also demonstrated in the *IICRA Rules, i-Arbitration Rules* and the *AAOIFI Standards.* The *IICRA Rules* do not explicitly deal with the prohibition of *riba* and *gharar,* and also do not discuss whether matters prohibited under *Shari'a* are arbitrable and if not, the impact of non-arbitrability on arbitration agreements and contracts. Although the *IICRA Rules* recognise the concept of separability under Art. 18, and also note under Art. 19 that the arbitration panel is competent to hear any disputes concerning arbitrability, there is no provision detailing the rules regarding the impact of matters prohibited by *Shari'a.* It is important to address this, because under Art. 28, the *IICRA Rules* stipulate that the applicable law must conform to *Shari'a.* Similarly, Art. 28 of the *IICRA Rules* also stipulates that the panel 'may choose to be guided by local or international commercial rules or conventions that are not at variance with the provisions of Islamic *Sharia.*' However, the *IICRA Rules* do not outline which international rules might conflict with *Shari'a.* Therefore, similar to the UAE and Saudi arbitration laws, the *IICRA Rules* stipulate conformity with *Shari'a* but provide no detailed explanation as to which interpretation of *Shari'a* they refer, nor do they stipulate the effect of non-conformity with *Shari'a.*

As discussed in the previous chapter, the *i-Arbitration Rules* provide guidelines on the appointment of *Shari'a* experts. However, they are silent with respect to the impact of *riba* and *gharar* on arbitration agreements and arbitrability. Therefore, even when *i-Arbitration Rules* apply in matters where *Shari'a* disputes arise, the *Shari'a* experts or arbitrators do not have clear guidelines in relation to the

---

201 Ibid.

definition of *riba* and *gharar*, or their effect on arbitrability and arbitration agreements. Instead, the Director of AIAC, Professor Sundra Rajoo, notes that such contractual issues should be dealt with by the agreed governing law.[202] Unless the agreed governing legal system incorporates *Shari'a*, the above-mentioned issue in regards to the prohibition of *riba* and/or *gharar* will not arise and instead, the contractual aspects of the arbitration may not be *Shari'a*-compliant, contrary to one of the goals of the *i-Arbitration Rules*.

As noted further in Chapter 9, the fact that *i-Arbitration Rules* are not wholly compliant with *Shari'a* is a factor to consider when proposing reforms, if the objective is to develop a set of arbitration rules that are both *Shari'a*-compliant and compatible with contemporary ICA norms. Another issue to consider when proposing reforms with the above-mentioned objective, is that there is also no international model law catering for *Shari'a* issues such as arbitrability (similar to the *UNCITRAL Model Law*) which can provide model provisions that countries, such as the UAE and Saudi Arabia, can adopt in *Shari'a* matters. Further, there is no convention, such as the *New York Convention* addressing *Shari'a*-related matters to which countries can become signatories. These issues will be further considered in Chapter 9.

IX Conclusion

If arbitration proceedings are subject to classical *Shari'a* and the subject matter contains *riba* and/or *gharar*, then the matter is non-arbitrable and renders the arbitration agreement void. However, the defence of arbitrability is rarely considered if an arbitration matter is brought before a secular court. One may argue that this is because secular courts cannot be expected to interpret *Shari'a*. This is a strong argument, because unlike most national arbitration legal systems, there are no codified model laws, conventions or guidelines on matters such as arbitrability under *Shari'a*. In fact, the impact of *riba* and *gharar* on arbitrability and arbitration agreements is also unclear in countries such as the UAE and Saudi Arabia, where public policy is supposedly based on *Shari'a* and overlaps with the arbitrability doctrine. Proposals for reform will be further discussed in Chapter 9 in relation to whether existing *AAOIFI Standards*, *i-Arbitration Rules* or *IICRA Rules* should be reformed to address the issues outlined in this chapter, or whether a *Shari'a* model law, guideline and/or convention should be developed for countries such as the UAE and Saudi Arabia. Further legal and policy reform is recommended in this area, in order to provide consistency and guidance during arbitration proceedings, and at the enforcement stage, for domestic and international parties, courts, arbitrators and expert witnesses involved in *Shari'a*-based arbitration.

---

202 Datuk Sundra Rajoo, 'KLRCA's New i-Arbitration Rules: Islamic Finance in the Global Commercial Arena' (2014) 6(2) *International Journal of Arab Arbitration*, 17.

7 Interest on arbitral awards and the prohibition against *riba*

I Introduction

The previous chapter analysed *riba* or interest in the context of arbitrability and validity of arbitration agreements. In comparison, this chapter will examine the lack of clarity regarding the award of interest in *Shari'a* and in contemporary ICA.

The chapter will begin by examining the prohibition of the award of interest under *Shari'a*. In particular, it will discuss how classical *Shari'a* forbids the payment of interest, even if the claimant is being awarded compensation or damages. However, the *i-Arbitration Rules* adopt a more lenient interpretation of *Shari'a*, which allows penalties for late payment (*gharamah*) and compensation (*ta'widh*), and refers to the Islamic money market set up by the Bank Negara Malaysia as a reference when calculating the rate of profit awarded, as opposed to conventional interest rates. Furthermore, the domestic law of most Muslim countries make provision for the payment of simple interest by judges or arbitrators, but generally prohibit the award of compound interest.[1]

In comparison, there is no prohibition against the award of both simple and compound interest in the field of contemporary ICA. Although the *UNCITRAL Model Law* and *UNCITRAL Rules 2010* do not stipulate the award of interest, Art. 78 of the United Nations Convention on Contracts for the International Sale of Goods ('*CISG*') makes provision for the payment of interest. Nonetheless, the *CISG* does not stipulate the calculation method, characterisation or rate at which the interest should be determined. In addition, since the method of calculating interest is unclear under the *CISG* and absent in most international arbitral rules and laws, a discussion of whether interest can be awarded on arbitral awards under *Shari'a* in light of the prohibition against *riba* adds to this existing layer of ambiguity. This chapter will also use the *CISG* as a case study to show how a uniform approach in relation to both the stipulation and calculation of interest fail to take into consideration the application of *Shari'a* in certain circumstances.

---

1 References and examples to support this statement will be provided in more detail as follows.

II Late payment award, compensation and *riba*

As mentioned in Chapter 5, the prohibition against *riba* under *Shari'a* has been subject to debate among Islamic scholars. Although both simple and compound interest is forbidden under a strict application of *Shari'a*, Arfazadeh notes that 'Sharia law offers a broad range of alternative claims or remedies that could constitute valuable substitutes for a claim of interest. Such alternative claims can take the form of damages for late payment or late performance, claims for sharing or disgorging profits made by the defaulting party, as well as other forms of penalty as provided for by contract or custom.'[2] However, there are differences of opinion about what constitutes interest even in the context of compensation, damages and late payment charges.

According to the Islamic Fiqh Academy in Jeddah,

> [i]f the buyer/debtor delays the payment of instalments after the specified date, it is not permissible to charge any amount in addition to its principle liability, whether it is made a precondition in the contract or it is claimed without a previous agreement, because it is "[*r*]*iba*", hence prohibited in *Shari'a*.[3]

Although penalty provisions may be included in financial contracts, if the penalty is in relation to a debt, then that is characterised as '*riba*.'[4] This is due to the Qur'anic verse: '[i]f the debtor is in difficulty, then delay things until matters become easier for him; still, if you were to write it off as an act of charity, that would be better for you, if only you knew.'[5]

This view is shared by Islamic scholar Taqi Usmani who argues 'there is no material difference between interest and the late payment [fee] charged as compensation.'[6] Usmani argues that in practice, the additional amount charged in the name of compensation is *riba*, because Islam does not allow for aggrieved parties to claim additional amounts from the debtor.[7] However, he argues that a penalty may be issued against the defaulting party, but the penalty amount is not compensation for the loss suffered by a party due to the lost opportunity of investing the money.[8] Usmani proposes that in order to prevent parties from

---

2 Homayoon Arfazadeh, 'A Practitioner's Approach to Interest Claims under Sharia law in International Arbitration' in Filip De Ly and Laurent Lévy (eds), *Interest, Auxiliary and Alternative Remedies in International Arbitration* (International Chamber of Commerce, 2008) 211–216, 213.

3 Islamic Development Bank and Islamic Fiqh Academy, *Resolutions and Recommendations of the Council of the Islamic Fiqh Academy 1985–2000* (Islamic Research and Training Institute, 2000) 104.

4 Ibid.

5 Trans. M. A. S. Abdel Haleem, *The Qur'an* (Oxford University Press, 2004) (Chapter 2, Verse 280).

6 Muhammad Taqi Usmani, *An Introduction to Islamic Finance* (Kluwer Law International, 2002) 57.

7 Ibid.

8 Ibid.

defaulting, the defaulting party should pay the penalty to a charitable fund established by the bank or institution. He argues that this approach is based on the principles established under the Maliki school of thought, and the proper wording of the penalty clause should be as follows:

> The client hereby undertakes that if he defaults in payment of any of his dues under this agreement, he shall pay to the charitable account/fund maintained by the Bank/financier a sum calculated on the basis of. . . % per annum for each day of default unless he establishes through the evidence satisfactory to the Bank/financier that his non-payment at the due date was caused due to poverty or some other factors beyond his control.[9]

Since Taqi Usmani is also the chairman of the *Shari‘a* board of the AAOIFI, this approach is taken by the AAOIFI under Standard No. 8 on *murabaha*, which also stipulates that the penalty should be given in charity, as per the following clause:

> It is permissible that the contract of *[m]urabaha* consists of an undertaking from the customer to pay an amount of money or a percentage of the debt, on the basis of undertaking to donate it in the event of a delay on his part in paying instalments on their due date. The *Shari‘a* Supervisory Board of the [i]nstitution [AAOIFI] must have full knowledge that any such amount is indeed spent on charitable causes, and not for the benefit of the [i]nstitution [AAAOIFI] itself.[10]

Similarly, the State Bank of Pakistan notes that:

> [i]t can be stipulated while entering into the agreement that in case of late payment or default by the client he shall be liable to pay penalty calculated at percent per day or per annum that will go to the charity fund constituted by the bank. . . . The bank can also approach competent courts for award of solatium which shall be determined by the courts at their discretion, on the basis of direct and indirect costs incurred, other than opportunity cost.[11]

Interestingly, the *SCCA Rules 2016*[12] are silent on the issue, except to note in its appendix on 'Arbitration Costs and Fees' that:

> All amounts paid on the account of the arbitration [c]osts shall be deposited with the SCCA and shall remain there until a termination order or final

---

9 Ibid., 59.
10 Accounting and Auditing Organization for Islamic Financial Institutions (AAOIFI), *Shari'ah Standards* (Dar Al Maiman, 2015) 214.
11 State Bank of Pakistan Islamic Banking Department, *Essentials of Islamic Modes of Financing* (5 October 2015) State Bank of Pakistan <www.sbp.org.pk/press/2004/Islamic_modes.pdf>.
12 Saudi Centre for Commercial Arbitration, as defined in Chapter 1. See Saudi Centre for Commercial Arbitration, Arbitration Rules <http://sadr.org/en/adr-services-2/arbitration-2/rules/>.

[a]ward is made. Amounts paid as advances on [c]osts do not yield interest for the parties, the arbitrator or the SCCA.[13]

Costs are further defined in the *SCCA Rules 2016* as including administrative fees, arbitrators' fees, expenses incurred, reasonable travel and witness expenses and 'legal and other costs incurred by the parties in relation to the arbitration to the extent that the Tribunal determines that the amount of such [c]osts is reasonable.'[14] However, the *SCCA Rules 2016* do not mention how and whether the tribunal can award interest, compensation or late payment charges on arbitral awards. The *IICRA Rules* are also silent on the issue of whether interest or alternative remedies can be awarded by tribunals.

On the other hand, this issue has been elaborated on by the *Shari'a* Advisory Council of Bank Negara Malaysia ('SAC') because in several meetings,[15] the SAC has ruled that a defaulting party may be charged a penalty under the principle of '*gharamah*,' and that the proceeds 'shall not be recognised as income. Instead, it has to be channelled to certain charitable bodies.'[16] *Gharamah* is an Arabic term defined as the penalty for late payment, and *ta'widh* means compensation for late payment.[17] The SAC considers compensation or '*ta'widh*' acceptable under *Shari'a*, based on the saying of the Prophet Muhammad that '[p]rocrastination (delay) in repaying debts by a wealthy person is injustice.'[18] This *Shari'a* resolution by the SAC further stipulates that the '[i]slamic financial institution may recognise *ta'widh* as income on the basis that it is charged as compensation for actual loss suffered by the institution.'[19] In the context of arbitration or judgement debts, the SAC notes that a '[c]ourt may impose late payment charge at the rate as stipulated by the procedures of court. However, from this rate, the judgement creditor (Islamic financial institution) is only allowed to receive compensation rate for actual loss (*ta'widh*).'[20]

13 SCCA Rules 2016, Art. 8 (appendix), 'Methods of Payment' <http://sadr.org/en/adr-services-2/arbitration-2/rules/>.
14 Ibid., Art. 1 (appendix), 'Definition of Costs' <http://sadr.org/en/adr-services-2/arbitration-2/rules/>.
15 The SAC 4th meeting on 14 February 1998, 95th meeting on 28 January 2010 and 101st meeting on 20 May 2010. See Bank Negara Malaysia: Central Bank of Malaysia, 'Shariah Resolutions in Islamic Finance' (2010) <www.bnm.gov.my/microsites/financial/pdf/resolutions/shariah_resolutions_2nd_edition_EN.pdf> 129–130.
16 Ibid., 129–130. See also Securities Commission Malaysia, 'Resolutions of the Shariah Advisory Council of the Securities Commission Malaysia' (2012–2014) <www.sc.com.my/wp-content/uploads/eng/html/icm/Resolution_SAC_2012-2014.pdf> 4–7.
17 Securities Commission Malaysia, 'Resolutions of the Securities Commission Shariah Advisory Council' (2004) <www.sc.com.my/wp-content/uploads/eng/html/icm/Resolutions_SAC_2ndedition.pdf>.
18 Sahih al-Bukhari, 'Loans, Payment of Loans, Freezing of Property, Bankruptcy' <http://sunnah.com/bukhari/43/16> (Volume 3, Book 41, Hadith 585).
19 Bank Negara Malaysia: Central Bank of Malaysia, 'Shariah Resolutions in Islamic Finance' (2010) <www.bnm.gov.my/microsites/financial/pdf/resolutions/shariah_resolutions_2nd_edition_EN.pdf> 130.
20 Ibid., 133. This resolution was made at the SAC meeting on 26 May 2005, 24 August 2006 and 30 April-1 May 2010.

In relation to the award of interest, the *i-Arbitration Rules* contain a provision under Rule 6(g) noting the following:

> [u]nless the parties have agreed otherwise, the arbitral tribunal may on any sum of money ordered to be paid by the award on the whole or any part of the period between the date on which the cause of action arose and to the date of realisation of the award:
>
> a) award a late payment charge determined by applying the principles of *ta'widh* and *gharamah*, where *ta'widh* refers to compensation or actual loss and *gharamah* refers to penalty for late payment; or
> b) in any other way that the arbitral tribunal considers appropriate, including interest.

This means that an arbitral tribunal may award a late payment charge as per the above rule as compensation for actual loss suffered by the aggrieved party. The SAC notes that:

> [t]o determine the compensation rate for actual loss (*ta'widh*) that may be applied by the judgement creditor, the SAC agreed to adopt the weighted average overnight rate of Islamic money market as a reference; and . . . [t]he total compensation charge shall not exceed the principal amount of debt. If the actual loss is less than the applicable rate for judgement in current practice, the balance shall be channelled [sic] by judgement creditor to charitable organisation as may be determined by Bank Negara Malaysia.[21]

The principle of *ta'widh* as stipulated by the SAC differs from the view of Islamic scholars such as Taqi Usmani, and scholars from the Islamic Fiqh Academy in Jeddah who, as discussed previously, argue that compensation is the same as interest. Furthermore, the *i-Arbitration Rules* provide the arbitral tribunal with the discretion to award interest if necessary, which is similar to the conventional position under contemporary ICA, for example the *CISG*, as examined further below. Similarly, a minority of Islamic scholars such as Tantawi and Wasil have issued *fatwas*, to the effect that simple interest is not *riba*, but merely a form of profit sharing of investments.[22] Nonetheless, it is unclear whether compound interest is treated as *riba*. The next section examines the approach taken by the domestic legislation of most Muslim countries, in relation to what constitutes as *riba*.

III Award of interest under the domestic law of Muslim countries

As discussed in Chapter 2, the impact of *Shari'a* on the domestic laws of a Muslim country varies depending on the nation. This section will briefly discuss

---

21 Ibid., 133–134.
22 Sina Ali Muscati, 'Late Payment in Islamic Finance' (2006) 6 UCLA *Journal of Islamic and Near Eastern Law* 47, 62.

whether interest can be awarded under the domestic laws of the following countries, which have been divided in this section into three categories. These jurisdictions will be examined in more detail as follows, including the fact that certain countries (i.e., Kuwait) may not fit exclusively into one category:

1   Countries where the commercial and civil codes have been influenced by a liberal scholarly approach to *riba*, and thus where awards of interest are permitted, including Egypt,[23] Kuwait,[24] Syria,[25] Iraq[26] and Libya.[27]

2   GCC countries where *Shari'a* has a strong influence, and the charging of interest is allowed in commercial matters, but prohibited or limited in civil matters.[28] This includes Oman,[29] UAE,[30] Bahrain,[31] Kuwait[32] and Yemen.[33]

3   Countries where the award of interest is generally prohibited, such as Saudi Arabia, Iran[34] and Qatar,[35] but in which interest may still be claimed in the

23 Egyptian Civil Code 1948 (World Intellectual Property Organisation, <www.wipo.int/wipolex/en/details.jsp?id=8362>); Meredith O. Ansell and Ibrahim Massaud al-Arif, *The Libyan Civil Code: An English Translation and a Comparison with the Egyptian Civil Code* (The Oleander Press, 1971).

24 See Kuwaiti Trade Law No. 68 of 1980 ('Kuwaiti Commercial Code') (World Intellectual Property Organisation <www.wipo.int/wipolex/en/details.jsp?id=7582) [Siham Barakat, Research Fellow, Australian Council for Educational Research, trans].

25 See Syrian Civil Code 1949 (World Intellectual Property Organisation, www.wipo.int/wipolex/en/details.jsp?id=10917) [Siham Barakat, Research Fellow, Australian Council for Educational Research, trans]. See also, Florentine Sonia Sneij and Ulrich Andreas Zanconato, 'The Role of Shari'a Law and Modern Arbitration Statutes in an Environment of Growing Multilateral Trade: Lessons from Lebanon and Syria' (2015) 12(2) *Transnational Dispute Management* 1, 11–18.

26 See Iraqi Civil Code 1951 (United Nations Refugee Agency Refworld trans, <www.refworld.org/docid/55002ec24.html>).

27 Ansell and al-Arif, above n 23, 42–43.

28 In the countries discussed in this chapter, civil matters refers to contractual and tortious claims arising between natural persons. See Chibli Mallat, *Introduction to Middle Eastern Law* (Oxford University Press, 2007).

29 Ministerial Decision 151/2002, Ministry of Commerce and Industry, 'Specifying the Interest in Consideration of a Loan or Commercial Debt' (Sultanate of Oman [Said Al Shahry Law Office and Richards Butler Law Firm, trans]); see also, Parties Not Indicated (2009) 1 *International Journal of Arab Arbitration* 245.

30 See Commercial Transactions Law (UAE) 1993 (United Arab Emirates) [Dawoud S. El Alami trans, *The Law of Commercial Procedure of the United Arab Emirates* (Graham & Trotman, 1994)].

31 Art. 81 of the Law of Commerce in Bahrain fixes interest at 7%. See Peter Ashford, *Handbook on International Commercial Arbitration* (JuristNet, LLC, 2nd ed, 2014) 354.

32 The commercial and civil code of Kuwait has also been influenced by Al-Sanhuri, so it also falls under the first category.

33 Desert Lines Project L.L.C. v The Republic of Yemen Award (ICSID Case Arbitral Tribunal, Case No. Arb/05/17, 6 February 2008) [294]. See commentary further below.

34 Iran and Saudi Arabia are examined in more detail below.

35 Kamal Sefioui, 'Qatar' (2016) *International Comparative Legal Guide to International Arbitration 2016* <www.iclg.co.uk/practice-areas/international-arbitration-/international-arbitration-2016/qatar#chaptercontent13>.

form of damages or compensation. As examined in this section, the countries do not always neatly fit into these categories.

The reason why interest is awarded under the domestic laws of Egypt, Syria, Iraq, Kuwait and Libya is due to the views of Egyptian scholar, Abd Al-Razzaq Ahmad Al-Sanhuri (1895–1971) who drafted the *Egyptian Civil Code 1948* ('*Egyptian Civil Code*') as well as significantly influencing the Civil Codes of Syria,[36] Iraq,[37] Libya[38] and the Commercial Code of Kuwait. From an Islamic perspective, Sanhuri's view on *riba* was that under *Shari'a*, *riba al-nasia* and *riba al-fadl* were prohibited in order to prevent the major prohibition, which was against *riba al-jahilliya*.[39] He argued that interest on loans were similar to *riba al-nasia* and *riba al-fadl* and therefore, they were only discouraged, in order to prevent *riba al-jahilliya*. Sanhuri argued that *riba al-jahilliya* was 'similar to what we now today call interest upon interest, or compound gain. It is when the lender claims interest independently upon interest which has accumulated.'[40] His views are reflected in the *Egyptian Civil Code* under Art. 226, which allows the debtor to pay the claimant damages including interest if there is a delay in payment, and this is despite Art. 2 of the Egyptian Constitution, which states that *Shari'a* is a principle source of law.[41] Art. 226 of the *Egyptian Civil Code* states the following:

---

36 Art. 227 of the Syrian Civil Code states: 'If the subject of the obligation is a sum of money and its value was known at the time of demand and the debtor delays to pay it, it will be obligatory to pay to the creditor a compensation for the delay with an interest of four per cent in civil matters and five per cent in commercial matters. These interest rates apply from the date of the judicial claim, if the agreement or the commercial custom, did not specify another date for entry into force; and all of this will apply unless the law stipulates otherwise.' Art. 228 stipulates: '[c]ontractors may agree on another interest rate, whether in return for delaying the payment, or in any other case where interest is required, on condition that this interest rate won't exceed nine per cent. 2. Each commission or benefit of any kind, stipulated by the creditor, if along the interest rate agreed upon, increases the maximum interest rate, it will be considered as a hidden interest and it will be subject to reduction in case it was proven that this commission or benefit is not matched by a real service that the creditor has performed, nor it's a legitimate benefit.' See Syrian Civil Code 1949 (World Intellectual Property Organisation, www.wipo.int/wipolex/en/details.jsp?id=10917) [Siham Barakat, Research Fellow, Australian Council for Educational Research, trans]. See also, See, Sneij and Zanconato, above n 25, 11–18.
37 Arts. 171 and 172 of the Iraqi Civil Code 1951 are similar to Arts. 227 and 228 of the Syrian Civil Code above, except that the maximum interest rate is 7%. See Iraqi Civil Code 1951 (United Nations Refugee Agency Refworld trans, www.refworld.org/docid/55002ec24.html).
38 Arts. 229–231 are similar to the Egyptian Civil Code – except that the Libyan Civil Code stipulates an interest rate of 10% (Art. 230) as opposed to 7% under the Egyptian Civil Code. Ansell and al-Arif, above n 23, 42–43.
39 Emad H. Khalil and Abdulkader Thomas, 'The Modern Debate over Riba in Egypt' in Abdulkader Thomas (ed), *Interest in Islamic Economics: Understanding Riba* (Routledge, 2006) 69, 73.
40 Ibid., 73.
41 Muscati, above n 22, 62. In 1985, an action was brought against Art. 226 on the basis that it violated Shari'a which was mentioned under Art. 2 of the Egyptian Constitution. The Supreme Constitutional Court held that Art. 226 was enacted before the Constitution

When the object of an obligation is the payment of a sum of money on which the amount is known at the time when the claim is made, the debtor shall be bound, in case of delay in payment, to pay the creditor, as damages for delay, interest at the rate of four percent in civil matters and five percent in commercial matters. Such interest shall run from the date of the claim in Court, unless the contract or commercial usages fixes another date.

Art. 227 further states that parties can agree on an interest rate, which should not exceed 7% as damages for delay in payment. However, Art. 232 of the *Egyptian Civil Code* prohibits compound interest and states: '[s]ubject to any commercial rules or practice to the contrary, interest does not run on outstanding interest and in no case shall the total interest that the creditor may collect exceed the amount of the capital.'

In GCC countries such as Kuwait, Bahrain,[42] Oman[43] and Yemen,[44] the prohibition of interest refers only to legal matters between natural persons and therefore, the charging of interest is allowed and regulated under the commercial code of each respective country.[45]

The position of the above-mentioned countries listed under category (2) above, may be contrasted with Saudi Arabia and Qatar under category (3), where interest is generally prohibited, but a claim for damages or compensation for late payment can be made. In relation to Qatar, Sefrioui advises:

As regards default interest (in any type of contracts [sic]), it remains prohibited under the general principle directed by the *Shari'a*. This does not mean

---

and therefore, it prevailed over Shari'a and the Constitution had no retroactive impact. This position was criticised by Islamic scholars. See Hossam A. El-Saghir, 'The CISG in Islamic Countries – The Case of Egypt' in Larry A. DiMatteo (ed), *International Sales Law – a Global Challenge* (Cambridge University Press, 2014) 505, 513; Saleh Majid and Faris Majid, 'Application of Islamic Law in the Middle East – Interest and Islamic Banking' (2003) 20(1) *International Construction Law Review* 177, 190–191.

42 Art. 81 of the Law of Commerce in Bahrain fixes interest at 7%. See Ashford, above n 31, 354.

43 Ministerial Decision 151/2002, Ministry of Commerce and Industry, 'Specifying the Interest in Consideration of a Loan or Commercial Debt' (Sultanate of Oman [Said Al Shahry Law Office and Richards Butler Law Firm, trans]). Art. 1 states: 'The interest in consideration for the procurement of a loan or commercial debt shall be assessed at a percentage of 10% unless agreed to a lower rate.' On 15/10/2008, an arbitration panel ruled in arbitration Case No. 1/2007 that the respondent pay 191,607,608 thousand riyals with an interest rate of 7% amounting to 12824.586 thousand riyals starting from 1/11/2007 till the date of rendering the award. The interest rate was upheld when the arbitral award was brought before the Court of Appeal, Commercial in Muscat. See Parties Not Indicated (2009) 1 *International Journal of Arab Arbitration* 245.

44 In Desert Lines Project L.L.C. v The Republic of Yemen Award (ICSID Case Arbitral Tribunal, Case No. Arb/05/17, 6 February 2008) [294]. In this case, the proceedings were conducted under the ICSID Arbitration Rules, and the claimant claimed for compound interest. However, the arbitral tribunal decided to award simple interest at the rate of 5% since compound interest was prohibited under Yemeni law, which was applicable to the contract.

45 Interest is also allowed in the banking and finance sectors.

that the Qatari law refuses to sanction contractual default or performance delays. Remedies are available, but in the form of a lump sum which can either be stipulated in the contract or assessed by the judge, after taking into account the damage effectively suffered by the creditor of the obligation . . . there is no interest attached to the enforcement of an award under Qatari law. Qatari Courts are generally strict in the application of this prohibition. . . . Therefore, when the enforcement of an award in Qatar is foreseeable, parties should consider casting their claim in the form of a lump sum (rather than an interest), if they have the possibility to do so. Otherwise, enforcement is likely to be rejected on the ground of public policy.[46]

By contrast with Qatar, Art. 547 of the *Kuwaiti Civil Code* states that loans shall be without interest in civil matters; however, Art. 102 of the *Kuwaiti Commercial Code* fixes interest at 7% in relation to commercial matters. Similarly, Arts. 110, 111 and 113 of the *Kuwaiti Commercial Code* permit interest in commercial matters.[47] In *ICC Case No. 5835/1999*,[48] an appeal was filed before the Kuwaiti Constitutional Court on 28 November 1992 in which the appellant claimed that Arts. 110 and 113 were unconstitutional, as they permitted interest, which was in violation of the *Shari'a* as per the constitution. The court held that Art. 2 of the Constitution allowed *Shari'a* to be a source of law, and that a legislator may also apply other sources of law, since *Shari'a* was not the only source of law. Furthermore, *Shari'a* was to be referred to as a source in the absence of express provision in the law and therefore, given that in this case express provisions existed in the form of Arts. 110 and 113, the court ruled that the provisions were constitutional.[49]

Art. 76 of the *UAE Code of Commercial Practice* also allows the award of interest at prevailing market rate, provided it does not exceed the maximum rate of 12%[50]

---

46 Kamal Sefrioui, 'Qatar' (2015) *The International Comparative Legal Guide to International Arbitration 2015* <www.iclg.co.uk/practice-areas/international-arbitration-/international-arbitration-2015/qatar#chaptercontent13>.

47 See Kuwaiti Trade Law No. 68 of 1980 ('Kuwaiti Commercial Code') (World Intellectual Property Organisation, <www.wipo.int/wipolex/en/details.jsp?id=7582) [Siham Barakat, Research Fellow, Australian Council for Educational Research, trans].

48 ICC Case No. 5835 (1999) 10(2) *ICC International Court of Arbitration Bulletin* 33.

49 See Majid and Majid, above n 41, 191; See ICC Case No. 5835 (1999) 33, 39.

50 See A1, India v B1 LLC, UAE and B2 SAL (2010) 2(3) *International Journal of Arab Arbitration* 270. In this case, a dispute arose between two Indian companies (A1 and A2), an Emirati Company (B1) and a Lebanese Company (B2). UAE Law as applicable in the arbitration between the Indian Claimant (A1) and the Emirati/Lebanese Respondents (B1 and B2). The Claimant sought interest at the rate of 12% as per Arts. 76 and 88 of the Commercial Code. The Respondents argued that according to Art. 203 of the CCP, arbitration is not permissible in matters that cannot be compromised and therefore, interest cannot be awarded. The Arbitral Tribunal found that the practice of interest in arbitration in the UAE was permitted in arbitrations taking place in Abu Dhabi. Concerning the rate of interest, the Tribunal found that there was no consensus and the rates usually varied between 4.5% and 9%. Therefore, the Tribunal determined that the Respondents pay the Claimant simple

(provided no alternative agreement is made),[51] despite the fact that *Shari'a* is a primary source of legislation in the UAE. In a case before the UAE Supreme Federal Court on 6 September 1983, the defendant refused to pay interest to the appellant bank on the grounds that interest and compound interest were prohibited under *Shari'a*. The appellant bank argued that the *UAE Code of Civil Procedures* which governed the matter at the relevant time (interest is now legislated under the *UAE Code of Commercial Practice*), allowed for the payment of interest, and that *Shari'a* only applied in the absence of express legislative provisions. Therefore, the UAE Supreme Federal Court acknowledged that the parties could agree to an interest rate, provided the parties did not agree on compound interest or the interest rate did not exceed the maximum rate allowed under UAE law, as noted previously.[52]

Furthermore, in a case determined by the Dubai Court of Cassation in 2008,[53] it was noted that an arbitral award may be set aside if it violates the public policy of the UAE, which is based on *Shari'a*, as noted in Arts. 3 and 27 of the *UAE Civil Procedure Code*, which was examined in Chapter 6 in the context of arbitrability. However, usury is only prohibited in transactions that take place between two natural people, as per Art. 409 of the *Federal Penal Code*. Further, as will be discussed further in the next chapter, in the recent case before the Dubai Court of Cassation,[54] it was determined that the UAE courts have no jurisdiction to set aside foreign arbitral awards on the basis that interest is forbidden under *Shari'a* when a corporate entity is involved.[55] Therefore, as noted above, simple interest

---

interest at the rate of 5% which was consistent with most Abu Dhabi and Dubai judgements. The interest would be due on all the monetary awards and would begin accruing from the date of the Final Award. See also Commercial Transactions Law (UAE) 1993 (United Arab Emirates) [Dawoud S. El Alami trans, *The Law of Commercial Procedure of the United Arab Emirates* (Graham & Trotman, 1994)].

51 See Federal Supreme Court Abu Dhabi, No. 245/20, 7 May 2000. In this case, it was held that parties may agree on an interest rate that exceeds 12%. See Hind Tamimi, 'Interest Under the UAE Law as Applied by the Courts in Abu Dhabi' (2002) 17(1) *Arab Law Quarterly* 50, 52.

52 Ibid., 50–53.

53 Dubai Court of Cassation, Petition No. 146 of 2008, 9 November 2008 [Graham Lovett, Lara Hammond and Hassan Arab, *Summaries of UAE Courts' Decisions on Arbitration* (ICC Publication, 2013) 94–96].

54 Dubai Court of Cassation, Petition No. 132 of 2012, 22 February 2012 [Lovett, Hammond and Arab, 124].

55 Federal Law No. 3 of 1987 ('Federal Penal Code') (UAE), Art. 409. Art. 409 of the Federal Penal Code states: 'Any natural persons who deals in usury with another natural person in any civil or commercial transaction shall be punished with imprisonment for no less than three months and with a fine no less than 2,000 Dirhams. This shall include any terms or conditions implying any express or implicit interest, commission or benefit of any kind by the creditor, when it is established that such interest, commission or benefit of any kind by the creditor, when it is established that such interest, commission or benefit does not correspondent to any lawful benefit or service rendered by the creditor. Such implicit debt or interest may be established by any means.' See Dubai Court of Cassation, Petition No. 146 of 2008, 9 November 2008 [Lovett, Hammond and Arab, 96]. See also, Richard Price and Essam Al Tamimi, *United Arab Emirates Court of Cassation Judgements: 1998–2003* (Brill, Arab & Islamic Law Series, 2005) 205; MUB Legal, 'Federal Law No (3) of 1987

is generally awarded in Muslim countries, even where the respective country's constitution makes reference to *Shari'a*.

However, on the contrary, some ICC decisions from the 1980s refused to award interest due to the application of *Shari'a*. For example, in *Parker Drilling Co. v. Sonatrach*,[56] the arbitrators refused to award interest on the basis that the ICC Rules provided parties with the autonomy to select Algerian law. The tribunal determined that the *Code of Civil Procedure 1966* (*'Algerian Civil Code'*) did not permit interest in regards to loans between individuals, but contained no such prohibition in regards to business contracts. Despite this, the tribunal held that the overarching application of *Shari'a* in the Algerian Civil Code meant that interest could not be awarded, regardless of the context.[57] This approach was also followed in the ICC case of French Contract v Ministry of Irrigation of African Country, where the arbitral tribunal noted:

> i[t] is not, however, possible in our view for the prohibition on interest to be circumvented by describing it as a claim for damages for loss of the use of the money. We accept the evidence of Dr. A that a court in country X would not uphold a claim for interest even though it was dressed up in such a way.[58]

Since the 1980s, arbitration law in Algeria has been reformed and there have been no recent ICC cases applying Algerian law in such a way so as to refuse an award of interest.[59]

The third category of countries include those which, although prohibiting awards of interest, allow compensation or damages for late payment, such as Qatar, which was mentioned earlier, and Saudi Arabia. Saudi law has been inconsistently applied in relation to the prohibition of interest. In Saudi Arabia, interest or profit is charged in the banking and finance sector, despite the fact that Saudi regulations do not expressly mention interest due to the prohibition against *riba*.

---

on Issuance of the Penal Code' <http://mublegal.com/wp-content/uploads/2014/07/Federal-law-penal-code.pdf> [Al Mubasheri, Advocates & Legal Consultancy trans].

56 ICC Case No. 4606 (1987), unreported; Cf Grove-Skanska v. Lockheed Aircraft Int'l AG, ICC Case No. 3903 (1981), unreported, cited and reported in David J. Branson and Jr Richard E. Wallace, 'Awarding Interest in International Commercial Arbitration: Establishing a Uniform Approach' (1988) 28 *Virginia Journal of International Law* 919, 933–940.

57 Ibid.

58 ICC Case No. 5277/1987 (1988) 13 Y.B. Comm. Arb 80. See also Omar Aljazy, 'Jurisdiction of Arbitral Tribunals in Islamic Law (Shari'a)' in Miguel Ángel Fernández-Ballesteros and David Arias (eds), *Liber Amicorum Bernardo Cremades* (Wolters Kluwer España, La Ley, 2010) 65, 79; Gary Born, *International Commercial Arbitration* (Kluwer Law International, 2nd ed, 2014) 3106.

59 The Code of Civil and Administrative Procedure was introduced in 2008 and replaced the Code of Civil Procedure 1966. Apart from its application in regards to the prohibition of interest, this book does not discuss international commercial arbitration under Algerian law. See generally, Abdel Hamid El Ahdab and Jalal El Ahdab, *Arbitration with the Arab Countries* (Kluwer Law International, 2011) 55–60; Nasr Eddine Lezzar, 'Algeria' in Lise Bosman (ed), *Arbitration in Africa: A Practitioner's Guide* (Kluwer Law International, 2013) 277.

Regardless, in the event that a matter regarding interest charges is brought before a judicial body, the judge has the discretion to annul the interest aspect of the contract if it is found to be '*riba*' and in violation of *Shari'a*.[60] The issue of whether interest may be awarded under Saudi law was also determined by the United States District Court in the case of *National Group for Communications and Computers Ltd., Plaintiff, v. Lucent Technologies International Inc.*[61] In this case, a Saudi-based company known as National Group contracted with Lucent Technologies regarding a project which would design, engineer and instal emergency and pay telephones in Saudi Arabia. Lucent Technologies terminated the subcontract and National Group was forced into liquidation. National Group then brought proceedings against Lucent Technologies seeking actual and expected damages. The agreement was that Saudi law would be the governing law, which meant that the United States District Court had to ascertain whether damages would be permitted under Saudi law. The district court found that expectation damages did not comply with Saudi law as they were uncertain, and therefore breached the prohibition against *gharar* as well as *riba* under *Shari'a*.[62] As discussed in Chapter 6, in *Islamic Investment Company of the Gulf (Bahamas) Ltd v Symphony Gems NV and others*,[63] the parties deliberately selected the governing law as English law, despite the fact that the claimant was based in Saudi Arabia, in order to ensure that the parties received interest payments.

This was also the position taken in the Final Ad Hoc Award of 20 November 1987,[64] where the arbitral tribunal applied Saudi law and rejected 'the part relating to interest – amounting to SR 4,212,044 – since this is charged on a basis which is not sanctioned by public law which is derived from the *Shari'a* Islamic law.'[65] Furthermore, in the case of *Midland International Trade Services Ltd and Other v Al Sudairy*,[66] the agreement between English and Saudi parties was that the Saudi company would pay interest on sums advanced, and the agreement noted that it was governed by English law 'without prejudice to the right of the third plaintiff to sue the Saudi company in Saudi Arabia.'[67] Interest was not awarded when the matter was brought before the Committee for the Settlement of Negotiable Instruments Disputes in Riyadh. Therefore, the debtor had to initiate a claim in England where the English court awarded interest.[68]

---

60 Abdulrahman Yahya Baamir, *Shari'a Law in Commercial and Banking Arbitration: Law and Practice in Saudi Arabia* (Ashgate, 2010) 167.
61 331 F. Supp. 2d 290 (D.N.J, 2004).
62 National Group for Communications and Computers Ltd., Plaintiff, v. Lucent Technologies International Inc. 331 F. Supp. 2d 290, 295 (D.N.J. 2004).
63 *Islamic Investment Company of the Gulf (Bahamas) Ltd. v. Symphony Gems NV* (unreported, Queen's Bench Division, Commercial Court, 13 February 2002).
64 Pipeline Contractor v Oil Company, Final Award (1989) 14 YBCA 47.
65 Ibid., 68 (emphasis added).
66 Midland International Trade Services Ltd. v Al Sudairy (1990) *Financial Times* as cited in Baamir, above n 60, 174.
67 Ibid.
68 Ibid.

The situation in Saudi Arabia is further complicated by ICC decisions in which interest on arbitral awards was recognised, despite the application of Saudi law. In the final award in *ICC Case No 7063 (1996)*,[69] the issue that arose was whether the claimant would be entitled to interest when recovering damages, or whether interest would be prohibited under Saudi law due to the prohibition against interest under *Shari'a*. The arbitral tribunal determined that

> anything in the nature of usury or unjust taking of interest, as well as compound interest, are barred by this doctrine under *Shari'a* law. But we do not accept that it also bars all awards of compensation for financial loss due to a party not having had the use of a sum of money to which it would have otherwise been entitled e.g. as a result of late payment.[70]

It was noted by the arbitral tribunal that modern commercial life in Saudi Arabia reflects conventional standards, and that commercial banks take and charge interest for loans. However, out of respect for *Shari'a*, the arbitral tribunal only awarded compensation at a rate reflecting annual inflation over the relevant period, being 5% per annum over 5 years, as opposed to a commercial rate of interest.[71] Consequently, the interest aspect of the arbitral award was referred to as 'compensation' at an annual inflation rate, in order to comply with *Shari'a*. This approach was also followed in the final award in *ICC Case No. 8677 (1997)* in which the arbitral tribunal noted that compensation was allowed under *Shari'a*, and that such an award was not 'interest in the technical Islamic sense relating to a contract of loan.'[72]

An interesting situation also exists in Iran where *Shari'a* was introduced after the Islamic revolution in 1979.[73] According to the *Constitution of the Islamic Republic of Iran 1979* ('the Iranian constitution'),[74] Art. 43 (5) prohibits 'causing of damage to others, monopoly, hoarding, usury and other invalid and forbidden interactions' and Art. 49 stipulates that 'The government is responsible for confiscating illegitimate wealth resulting from [u]sury.' However, a notice was issued by the Guardian Council ('the Guardian Council's Opinion'), which allowed:

> [r]eceiving interest and damages for delay in payment from foreign governments, institutions, companies and persons, who, according to their own

69 ICC Case No. 7063 (1996) 22 Y.B. Comm. Arb 87.
70 Ibid., 89.
71 Ibid., 90.
72 ICC Case No. 8677 (2009) 1 (4) *International Journal of Arab Arbitration* 333, 41.
73 See also James Fry, 'Islamic Law and the Iran-United States Claims Tribunal: The Primacy of International Law Over Municipal Law' (2002) 18(2) *Arbitration International* 105, 112–114; See generally, Nima Nasrollahi Shahri and Amir Hossein Tanhayi, 'An Introduction to Alternative Dispute Settlement in the Iranian Legal System: Reconciliation of Shari'a Law with Arbitration as a Modern Institution' (2015) 12(2) *Transnational Dispute Management*.
74 Constitution of the Islamic Republic of Iran 1979 (as last amended on July 28, 1989) [World Intellectual Property Organisation trans <www.wipo.int/wipolex/en/details.jsp?id=7697>].

principles of faith, do not consider [interest] as being prohibited, is permitted under religious [Islamic] standards; therefore claiming [and] receiving such funds is not against the constitution.[75]

Therefore, Iranian law allows interest to be received by Iranian nationals in transactions with foreigners.[76] This argument is based on the views of some Islamic scholars from the Jafari and Hanafi schools of thought, who argue that it is acceptable for Muslims to receive interest from non-Muslims; however, Muslims cannot give interest in any situation.[77]

Gotanda observes that:

> [i]t is unclear whether Iranian courts would limit the applicability of the Guardian Council's opinion to the situation specified by the Prime Minister . . . or whether they would give it broad application to allow for interest to be paid to, or received from, a foreigner when the foreign party's law does not consider the awarding of interest to be prohibited.[78]

In fact, in the final award in *ICC Case No. 7263/1996*, a dispute arose between the claimant, who was an Iranian purchaser, and the respondent, who was a U.S. supplier. In this case, the claimant sought damages in addition to compound interest, on the basis that the respondent failed to comply with its contractual obligations.[79] The respondent argued that Arts. 43 and 49 of the Iranian constitution of 1979 did not permit payment of interest. However, the claimant used the notice by the Guardian Council to argue that receiving interest and damages from foreign companies whose laws permitted interest was allowed under Iranian law. The Tribunal decided that the interpretation of the Guardian Council was 'discriminatory towards non-Iranian citizens, as they cannot claim such interest against Iranians in Iranian court.'[80] The ICC Tribunal also found that '[t]his special policy resulting in a discrimination against non-Iranians cannot be considered addressed to nor implementable by foreign and international arbitral organs and institutions, such as the present Arbitral Tribunal.'[81] Moreover, the application of the rules embodied in the Guardian Council's Opinion, being discriminatory against foreign citizens, would contradict 'the general principles of international public order which this Tribunal is bound to respect and implement.'[82]

---

75 Muscati, above n 22, 51.
76 John Gotanda, 'Awarding Interest in International Arbitration' (1996) 90 *The American Journal of International Law* 40, 49.
77 Muscati, above n 22; See generally, Sayed Hassan Amin, 'Banking and Finance Based on Islamic Principles – Law and Practice in Modern Iran' (1989) 9(1) *Islamic & Comparative Law Quarterly* 1.
78 Gotanda, above n 76, 49.
79 Final Award in Case 7263 (2004) 15 *ICC International Court of Arbitration Bulletin* 71.
80 Ibid., 122.
81 Ibid.
82 Ibid.

Interestingly enough, the ICC Tribunal not only denied the award of interest as per Iranian law, it also found that the interpretation of *Shari'a* as articulated by the Guardian Council in Iran, and as followed by scholars from the Jafari and Hanafi schools, to be inconsistent with international public policy on the grounds of discrimination. It is unclear to which 'general principles of international public order' the arbitral tribunal was referring. As discussed in previous chapters, the concept of procedural fairness and due process is embodied in Art. 18 of the *UNCITRAL Model Law* and Art. V(1)(b) *New York Convention*.[83] Furthermore, procedural fairness has been interpreted by commentators to mean that parties must be treated equally, and not given preferential treatment based on their nationality.[84] Alternatively, the arbitral tribunal could be referring to principles of transnational public policy, which will be discussed further in the next chapter.

A different approach was taken in the final award in *ICC Case No. 7373 (1997)*,[85] in which the claimant was a British company, and the defendant an Iranian corporation. The British company argued that the Iranian company failed to pay the outstanding amounts which were due as a result of the termination of a contract. In this case, the ICC tribunal found that the British company rightfully terminated the contract, and that interest should be awarded to them despite the prohibition under *Shari'a*, since Iranian law applied and in particular, Arts. 43 and 49 of the *Iranian Constitution*. The ICC Tribunal noted that:

> care should be taken in the wording of the relevant claim so as to cover compensation for loss of use of money (and not interest) and to provide proof of costs (such as the costs of borrowing money), so as to establish that the borrowing was directly mandated by, and that the loss suffered was a direct result of, the contractors' failure to receive payments when due.[86]

This argument was based on the fact that under Arts. 221 and 228 of the *Civil Code of Iran*,[87] compensation is allowed for losses. The tribunal determined that the award of interest was to compensate the claimant for loss of income that 'would have been earned by the sum of damages and are calculated from the date of loss to the date of payment.'[88] The tribunal found that interest rates reflect

---

83 As noted above, Art. 18 of the UNCITRAL Model Law states that '[t]he parties shall be treated with equality and each party shall be given a full opportunity of presenting his case.' Art. V(1)(b) of the New York Convention provides that an arbitral award may be not be enforced if 'the party against whom the award is invoked was not given proper notice of the appointment of the arbitrator or of the arbitration proceedings or was otherwise unable to present his case.'

84 Born, above n 58, 2174.

85 Final Award in Case 7373 (2004) 15(1) *ICC International Court of Arbitration Bulletin* 72.

86 Ibid., 345.

87 Civil Code of Islamic Republic of Iran [M. A. R Taleghani trans, *The Civil Code of Iran* (Rothman, 1995).

88 Final Award in Case 7373 (2004) 15(1) *ICC International Court of Arbitration Bulletin* 72, 347.

accurate compensation due to the impact that inflation may have on the value of the capital sum and the rate of return on the capital.[89] It was further observed that a failure to award interest would be unjust in international commercial relations, and that interest was commonly awarded by various arbitral tribunals in oil concessions in the Middle East, such as the Iran-U.S. Claims.[90] The tribunal relied on the decision of *McCollough & Co Inc v Ministry of Post*,[91] where the Iran-U.S. Claims Tribunal settled the matter according to the laws of Iran, and in which the rates of interest on the arbitral award varied from 6% to 14.5%. This was based on the fact that interest was awarded to compensate for delay, and that the rate must be reasonable in the circumstances.[92]

The arbitral tribunal in the *ICC Case 7373*[93] also noted that 'anything in the nature of usury or unjust taking of interest, as well as compound interest are barred by this doctrine under *Shari'a* law. But it does not accept that this doctrine also bars all awards of compensation for financial loss due to a party not having had the use of a sum of money to which it would have other been entitled e.g., as the result of late payment.'[94] Therefore, the tribunal determined that the applicable interest rate in the current case was 10% interest per annum on the principal amount. Thus, this approach was similar to that taken in the partial award in *ICC Case No. 5082/1989*, where Iranian law applied, and the arbitral tribunal found that whilst *riba* was prohibited, compensation was allowed and therefore, a fixed rate of interest was awarded at 9% per annum.[95]

In conclusion, the domestic law of most Muslim countries allows for the award of simple interest, and in the event that Saudi or Iranian law is applicable, the tribunal may still award simple interest as a form of compensation. The next section will argue that despite the flexible approach taken by tribunals when *Shari'a* forms part of the governing law, it differs from the conventional approach under contemporary ICA that a claimant should be fully compensated and awarded compound interest, if necessary.

IV The award of interest under international commercial arbitration

As will be discussed in more detail later, although both arbitral case law and arbitral law do not provide uniformity in relation to the calculation (simple or compound), characterisation (procedural or substantive), rate of interest and time from which interest should be calculated, it is well accepted that arbitral tribunals

89 Ibid.
90 Ibid., 348.
91 Iran-US Claims Tribunal, McCollough & Company, Inc. v. Ministry of Post, Telegraph and Telephone (1986) 11 IRAN-U.S. Claims Tribunal Report.
92 Final Award in Case 7373 (2004) 15(1) *ICC International Court of Arbitration Bulletin* 72, 348.
93 Ibid.
94 Ibid., 349.
95 Partial Award in ICC Case No. 5082/1980 (2004) 15 (1) *ICC International Court of Arbitration Bulletin* 63.

have the power to award interest.[96] In the case of *Islamic Republic of Iran v United States of America, Decision, IUSCT*, the arbitral tribunal defined interest as the sum of money which is awarded as 'compensation for damages suffered due to delay in payment,'[97] and noted that 'it is customary for arbitral tribunals to award interest as part of an award for damages.'[98] Arbitral tribunals may award pre-judgment or pre-award interest as part of the arbitral award, which is compensatory interest reflecting the loss suffered as a result of the time value of money.[99] On the other hand, an arbitral tribunal may award post-judgment interest or interest on an arbitral award.[100] The rationale behind the arbitral tribunal's power to award interest is to ensure the claimant is fully compensated, and to deter the breaching party from gaining any benefit from the money withheld in order to encourage efficiency and prompt settlement.[101] In the context of sales contracts, the *CISG* Advisory Council Opinion No. 14, 'Interest Under Art. 78 *CISG*' ('*CISG* Advisory Council Opinion No. 14') states that the reason why the award of interest is important is due to the time value of money.[102] Therefore, interest effectively represents compensation for the creditor for suffering a delay in payment, and moreover prevents the debtor from enjoying an unjust enrichment as a result of holding the money longer than their legal entitlement.[103]

The rate of interest awarded is also important in order to fully compensate the aggrieved party, because arbitration proceedings can often take a long time to resolve, and interest on the award may be quite substantial. For example, in the case of *Kuwait v Am Independent Oil Co.*,[104] the tribunal awarded the aggrieved party a principal amount of $83 million. The tribunal also awarded a 'reasonable rate of interest' at 7.5%, and 10% due to the level of inflation, both rates

---

96 Andrea Giardina, 'Issues of Applicable Law and Uniform Law on Interest: Basic Distinctions in National and International Practice' in Filip De Ly and Laurent Levy (eds) *Interests, Auxiliary and Alternative Remedies in International Arbitration* (Dossiers: ICC Institute of World Business Law, 2008) 131.

97 Islamic Republic of Iran v United States of America, Decision, IUSCT Case No. A19 (DEC 65-A19-FT) (1988) 13 YBCA 258, 261.

98 Ibid., 290.

99 John Gotanda, 'A Study of Interest' (Working Paper No 83, Villanova University School of Law, 2007) 1, 4; Jack Coe Jr and Noah Rubins, 'Regulatory Expropriation and the Tecmed Case: Context and Contributions' in Todd Weiler (ed) *International Investment Law and Arbitration: Leading Cases from the ICSID, NAFTA, Bilateral Treaties and Customary International Law* (Cameron, May 2005) 597, 631.

100 Ibid.

101 Gotanda, above n 99, 4.

102 CISG Advisory Council, CISG Advisory Council Opinion No. 14 – Interest Under Article 78 CISG (21 and 22 October 2013) Rapporteur: Professor Yesim M. Atamer, <www.CISG.law.pace.edu/CISG/CISG-AC-op14.html> 5.

103 Ibid.

104 Arbitration Tribunal: Award in the Matter of an Arbitration Between Kuwait and the American Independent Oil Company (Aminoil) (1982) 21 ILM 976. See also Jeffrey Waincymer, *Procedure and Evidence in International Arbitration* (Kluwer Law International, 2012) 1187; Charles Brower and Jeremy Sharpe, 'Awards of Compound Interest in International Arbitration: The Aminoil Non-Precedent' (2006) 3(5) *Transnational Dispute Management* 155, 156–157.

compounded annually, which resulted in an additional payment of $96 million. Compound interest is defined as interest which is calculated on the basis of a total amount consisting of both the principal sum and any accrued amount of unpaid interest due for each compounding period (e.g., annually).[105] Although some arbitral tribunals and national courts have historically been hesitant in awarding compound interest or 'interest on interest,' compound interest tends to be awarded in arbitration cases that take many years to resolve.[106]

An example of an arbitral tribunal's hesitancy in awarding compound interest was evident when the Iran-U.S. Claims tribunal granted simple interest but excluded compound interest, and noted that compound interest may be awarded if there are 'special reasons for departing from international precedents which normally do not allow the awarding of compound interest.'[107] Compound interest is also discouraged under the domestic law of civil law countries such as Art. 105(3) of the *Swiss Code of Obligations*, Art. 248 of the *German Civil Code*) and Art. 1154 of the *French Civil Code*, but an arbitral award of compound interest may still be enforced.[108]

However, the trend is changing, and one commentator, Gotanda, argues that

> when tribunals award interest in both international investment disputes and transnational contract disputes, they should strive to fully compensate the aggrieved party for the loss of the use of its money. In many cases then, they should award interest at a market rate and on a compound basis.[109]

Similarly, Professor F. A. Mann argues that 'compound interest may be and, in the absence of special circumstances should be awarded to the claimant as damages by international tribunals.'[110] Brower and Sharpe also agree that '[c]ompound interest has a rightful place in international arbitration, especially in the context of international commercial arbitration.'[111] Sénéchal argues that

> the adoption of compound interest reflects the majority of commercial realities, in that a loss of value incurred by a company that is active in normal

---

105 Tomas Cipras, *Financial and Insurance Formulas* (Springer Verlag, 2010) 11. See also, Natasha Affolder, 'Awarding Compound Interest in International Arbitration' (2001) 12(1) *American Review of International Arbitration* 45, 49. See generally, Branson and Wallace, above n 56; Martin Hunter and Volker Triebel, 'Awarding Interest in International Arbitration' (1980) 6(1) *Journal of International Arbitration* 7.
106 Brower and Sharpe, above n 104, 156–157. See also Waincymer, above n 104, 1187.
107 R. J. Reynolds Tobacco Company v. The Government of the Islamic Republic of Iran, Iran-US Claims Tribunal, IUSCT Case No. 35 (145–35–3) (1985) 10 Y.B. Comm. Arb 258, 260–261.
108 See InterMaritime Management SA (Switzerland) v. Russin & Vecchi (U.S.) 22 Y.B. Comm. Arb 789, 798 (1997); Hunter and Triebel, above n 105.
109 Gotanda, above n 99, 3.
110 F. A. Mann, 'Compound Interest as an Item of Damage in International Law' (1987) 21(3) *UC Davis School of Law Review* 577, 586.
111 Brower and Sharpe, above n 104, 160.

trading operations implies the loss of the use of that value. Not recognizing this reality would lead to awarding a windfall to the respondent.[112]

Furthermore, under English law, section 49 of the *Arbitration Act* 1996 states that the tribunal 'may award simple or compound interest . . . (a) on the whole or part of any amount awarded by the tribunal' or '(b) on the whole or part of any amount claimed in the arbitration and outstanding at the commencement of the arbitral proceedings but paid before the award was made.' Institutional arbitration rules, such as Art. 31 (4) *International Dispute Resolution Procedures (including Mediation and Arbitration Rules) 2014*,[113] r 26.4 *LCIA Arbitration Rules 2014* and Art. 62 *World Intellectual Property Organisation Arbitration Rules 2014*,[114] also stipulate that an arbitral tribunal may award compound interest.

If the contract is silent on the issue of the applicable rate of interest that applies in case of late payment, the arbitral tribunal may apply the substantive law applicable to the contract, law of the place of arbitration, applicable international conventions or rules of the international arbitration institution.[115] Born recommends that arbitral tribunals apply the law of the arbitral seat to the question of the arbitrator's authority to award interest, and, in regards to the awarding of interest, including applicable interest rates, the law of currency in which the award is made.[116] However, the trend in transnational contractual disputes has been to apply the applicable national law, which, as discussed previously, often results in an award of simple interest or the statutory interest rate.[117] On the other hand, arbitral tribunals in international investment generally award interest at market rates on a compound basis.[118]

The tendency of arbitral tribunals to award compound interest in international investment disputes is incompatible with the interpretation of *Shari'a* that forbids compound interest as applicable in many Muslim countries. Before the year 2000, compound interest was only awarded in two cases, these being *Atlantic Triton Co v People's Republic of Guinea*,[119] and *Southern Pacific Properties v.*

112 Thierry Sénéchal, 'Present-Day Valuation in International Arbitration: A Conceptual Framework for Awarding Interest' in Filip De Ly and Laurent Levy (eds), *Interests, Auxiliary and Alternative Remedies in International Arbitration* (Dossiers: ICC Institute of World Business Law, 2008) 219, 230.
113 International Centre for Dispute Resolution, International Dispute Resolution Procedures (Including Mediation and Arbitration Rules (effective 1 June 2014) <www.adr.org/aaa/ShowProperty?nodeId=/UCM/ADRSTAGE2020868&revision=latestreleased>.
114 World Intellectual Property Organisation, World Intellectual Property Organisation Arbitration Rules (effective 1 June 2014) <www.wipo.int/amc/en/arbitration/rules/>.
115 Giardina, above n 96, 135.
116 Born, above n 58, 3106.
117 Gotanda, above n 99, 19.
118 Ibid., 19.
119 Atlantic Triton Co v People's Republic of Guinea (ICSID Arbitral Tribunal, Case No. ARB/84/1, 21 April 1986).

Egypt.[120] This was because it was generally accepted by arbitral tribunals, and by various academics such as Marjorie Whiteman, that '[t]here are few rules within the scope of the subject of damages in international law that are better settled than the one that compound interest is not allowable.'[121] However, since 2000, arbitral tribunals in international investment disputes have generally awarded interest at market rates on a compound basis.[122] The principle that compound interest should not be awarded was overturned in the landmark decision of *Compania del Desarrollo de Santa Elena v Costa Rica* ('Santa Elena'). In Santa Elena, the arbitral tribunal determined that:

> while simple interest tends to be awarded more frequently than compound, compound interest certainly is not unknown or excluded in international law. No uniform rule of law has emerged from the practice in international arbitration as regards the determination of whether compound interest or simple interest is appropriate in any given case. Rather, the determination of interest is a product of the exercise of judgment, taking into account all of the circumstances of the case at hand and especially considerations of fairness which must form part of the law to be applied by this Tribunal.[123]

Compound interest is often awarded in order to compensate for the loss suffered by one party and therefore, can take the form of damages as opposed to contractual compound interest on the late payment of a debt 'where interest is viewed as an item of damage and its award is to compensate for the temporary withholding of money, then its measure should be the cost of such deprivation.'[124]

The calculation of interest is also not clearly stipulated in international conventions such as the *CISG, North American Free Trade Agreement* ('NAFTA')[125] and *UNIDROIT Principles.* For example, Art. 78 of the *CISG* states that '[i]f a

---

120 Southern Pacific Properties v. Egypt (ICSID Arbitral Tribunal, Case No ARB/84/3, 20 May 1992). See also, Andrew Smolik, 'The Effect of Shari'a on the Dispute Resolution Process Set Forth in the Washington Convention' (2010) 1 *Journal of Dispute Resolution* 151, 172; Florian Grisel, 'The Sources of Foreign Investment Law' in Zachary Douglas, Joost Pauwelyn and Jorge E. Viñuales (eds), *The Foundations of International Investment Law: Bringing Theory into Practice* (Oxford University Press, 2014) 213, 226–227.

121 Marjorie M. Whiteman, *Damages in International Law* (William S. Hein & Company, 1943) 1997. See also R. J. Reynolds Tobacco Company v. The Government of the Islamic Republic of Iran, Iran-US Claims Tribunal, Case No. 35 (145–35–3) (1985) 10 Y.B. Comm. Arb 258; ICC Case No. 6230/1990 (1991) 2(1) *ICC International Court of Arbitration Bulletin* 27; ICC Case No. 6162/1990 (1992) 3(1) ICC *International Court of Arbitration Bulletin* 22. See generally, Brower and Sharpe, above n 104.

122 Gotanda, above n 99, 19. See also Smolik, above n 120.

123 Compania del Desarrollo de Santa Elena v Costa Rica (ICSID Tribunal, Case No ARB/96/1, 17 February 2000) [103].

124 Affolder, above n 105, 91.

125 North American Free Trade Agreement ('NAFTA'), (entered into force on 1 January 1994) <www.nafta-sec-alena.org/Home/Legal-Texts/North-American-Free-Trade-Agreement?mvid=2>.

party fails to pay the price or any other sum that is in arrears, the other party is entitled to interest on it, without prejudice to any claim for damages recoverable under [A]rticle 74.'[126] The next section discusses whether Art. 78 of the *CISG* is compatible with *Shariʿa*.

V *Shariʿa* and international sale of goods contracts

Professor Honnold notes that Art. 78 was introduced because:

> [i]n some legal systems compensation for lost interest is regarded as an aspect of damage assessment; this led to the concern lest laying down rules for damages under Arts. 74 to 77 without providing for interest might be understood as barring the recovery of interest.[127]

Therefore, he argues that Art. 78 overrides domestic law and enables parties to be awarded interest even if the domestic law makes no reference to interest.[128] If Art. 78 is applied in a way that overrides domestic law, then this approach will be incompatible with *Shariʿa* due to the prohibition against *riba*.

Furthermore, as examined further below, the *CISG* Advisory Council Opinion No. 14 addresses this issue and in its black letter rules, recommends that the interest rate stipulated in the domestic law of the creditor's place of business be applied, thus if interest is prohibited then it will not be applied.[129] Two of the recommendations by the *CISG* include Rule 8 which states, '[t]he rate of interest may be determined by the agreement of the parties' and Rule 9 stipulating that 'in the absence of such agreement, the applicable rate of interest is the rate which the court at the creditor's place of business would grant in a similar contract of sale not governed by the *CISG*.' These recommendations will be discussed in more detail later.

The legislative history of Art. 78 shows that there were differences of opinion among member countries at the 1980 Vienna Diplomatic Conference as to whether the rate of interest should be stipulated or not and, due to these

---

126 Also Art. 84(1) of the CISG stipulates that '[i]f the seller is bound to refund the price, he must also pay interest on it, from the date on which the price was paid.' However, this section focuses on Art. 74.

127 John O. Honnold, *Uniform Law for International Sales under the 1980 United Nations Convention* (Wolters Kluwer Law & Business, 4th ed, 2009) 602, 420; Bianca and Bonell note that excluding interest would mean that the question would be determined by domestic law which would lead to uncertainty and divergence between countries as to whether interest should be awarded separately to damages. See C. Massimo Bianca and Michael Joachim Bonell, *Commentary on the International Sales Law: The 1980 Vienna Sales Convention* (Giuffrè, 1987) 569–570.

128 Honnold, above n 127, 420.

129 CISG Advisory Council, CISG Advisory Council Opinion No. 14 – Interest Under Art. 78 CISG (21 and 22 October 2013), Rapporteur: Professor Yesim M. Atamer, <www.CISG.law.pace.edu/CISG/CISG-AC-op14.html> rr 8–9.

differences, it was decided that the rate of interest should not be stipulated.[130] Interestingly, Mr Shafik of Egypt noted that in relation to Art. 78, the *CISG* should provide 'reservations' for countries where interest was forbidden, which would allow the clause to be implemented in a 'different manner.'[131] Such an approach would encourage more countries where interest is forbidden to become signatories, since omitting interest from the *CISG* altogether would be unrealistic, because interest was a 'well-established practice.'[132] Mr Rognlien of Norway also suggested that Arab countries should be accommodated, by adding the phrase 'or any other corresponding fee' after the word interest.[133] Mr Sami of Iraq preferred that 'interest' was not stipulated; however, if this was not possible, countries that did not charge interest should be allowed to enter a reservation in relation to the provision.[134] Mr Ziegel of Canada argued that Arab countries could either omit references to interest, or the *CISG* should make the reference to interest optional, so that countries should be free to 'accept or reject the provisions concerned at the time of accession to the Convention.'[135] However, the *CISG* did not adopt these recommendations for a reservation catering for Muslim countries. Furthermore, to date, only the following Muslim majority countries have acceded to the *CISG*: Albania on 1 June 2010, Egypt on 1 January 1988, Syria on 1 January 1988, Iraq on 1 April 1991, Lebanon on 1 December 2009, Mauritania on 1 September 2000, Bosnia-Herzegovina on 6 March 1992 and recently, Bahrain on 1 October 2014.[136]

Despite the fact the *CISG* mentions interest, there are different views taken by academics, arbitrators and judges, as to how the interest rate should be calculated. Arbitral tribunals will enforce the agreement of the parties if there is an express provision addressing the payment of interest, provided that it does not violate public policy and/or domestic laws on arbitrability and validity (as discussed in the previous chapter).[137] However, if there is no express agreement as

---

130 Bianca and Bonell, above n 127, 569–570; Klaus Peter Berger, 'International Arbitral Practice and the UNIDROIT Principles of International Commercial Contracts' (1998) 46(1) *The American Journal of Comparative Law* 129, 134.

131 1980 Vienna Diplomatic Conference, 34th mtg, Agenda Item 3, (3 April 1980) [10] <http://CISGw3.law.pace.edu/CISG/firstcommittee/Meeting34.html>.

132 Ibid.

133 Ibid., 14.

134 Ibid., 20.

135 Ibid., 23.

136 Hossam A. El-Saghir observes that the Arab community is generally uninformed about the CISG and that academic work/court decisions relating to the CISG in the Arab community are rare and decisions are generally unpublished. For example, Egypt only publishes decisions by the Court of Cassation and Constitutional Court, while published decisions by the lower courts are rare. He also argues that there are inaccuracies in Arts. 25 and 26 of the Arabic translation of the CISG. He notes that Egypt has not applied the CISG in an autonomous way, but instead they only apply Egyptian law parallel to the CISG or ignore the CISG altogether. See El-Saghir, above n 41, 510–511.

137 For example, ICC Case No. 11849/2003 at Pace University Albert H. Kritzer, *CISG Database, Fashion Products Case* (2003) <http://CISGw3.law.pace.edu/cases/031849i1. html>. In this case, interest was awarded to the buyer at a contractually agreed rate. See also

to the rate of interest, some commentators argue that the rate of interest should be determined in accordance with conflict of law rules pursuant to Art. 7(2), because of the view that the rate of interest is an 'external gap' in the *CISG*.[138] Others take the view it is an 'internal gap' or *intra legem* lacuna of the *CISG*, and therefore the tribunal should fill it.[139]

The *CISG* Advisory Council Opinion No. 14 studies the different approaches taken by tribunals. Some commentators argue that the arbitral tribunal should independently determine the rate of interest, taking into consideration the general principles underlying the *CISG*, such as Art. 7(1), which seeks to promote uniformity.[140] This approach is advocated by Professor Honnold, who argues that the rate of interest should be determined in accordance with general principles of the *CISG*, and that this 'has the advantage of promoting the Convention's fundamental purpose of creating a uniform legal regime for international sales and of avoiding some of the complex problems arising from an application of domestic law to the question.'[141] For example, the arbitral tribunal in Vienna in the *Rolled Metal Sheets Case*,[142] determined that the *CISG* was applicable, and even though the *CISG* is silent in regards to the rate of interest, general principles underlying the convention should apply because:

> the immediate recourse to a particular domestic law may lead to results which are incompatible with the principle embodied in Art. 78 of the *CISG*, at least in the cases where the law in question expressly prohibits the payment of interest.[143]

This case seems to take the approach that the prohibition against interest under *Shari'a* is incompatible with the principles underlying the *CISG*.

China International Economic & Trade Arbitration Commission at Pace University Albert H. Kritzer, *CISG Database, Pharmaceutical Products Case* (2000) <http://CISGw3.law. pace.edu/cases/001206c1.html>; In this case, the tribunal determined: "[Buyer] shall pay the interest on the delayed payment based on the 0.45% monthly interest rate agreed by the two parties".

138 Anthony J. McMahon, 'Differentiating Between Internal and External Gaps in the U.N. Convention on Contracts for the International Sale of Goods: A Proposed Method for Determining "Governed by" in the Context of Article 7(2)' (2006) 44 *Columbia Journal of Transnational Law* 992.

139 CISG Advisory Council, CISG Advisory Council Opinion No. 14 – Interest Under Art. 78 CISG (21 and 22 October 2013), Rapporteur: Professor Yesim M. Atamer, <www.CISG. law.pace.edu/CISG/CISG-AC-op14.html> [3.1] – [3.2].

140 Hossam El-Saghir, 'The Interpretation of the CISG in the Arab World' in Olaf Meyer and André Janssen (eds), *CISG Methodology* (Sellier de Gruyter, 2009) 355, 356–357. El-Saghir argues that judges should also review decisions made globally as compiled in international databases such as CLOUT, CISG Database at the University of Pace Law School's Institute of International Commercial Law and UNILEX.

141 Honnold, above n 127, 605, 420.

142 SCH-4366 at Pace University Albert H. Kritzer CISG Database, Rolled Metal Sheets Case (Austria, Arbitral Tribunal Vienna, 15 June 1994) [5.2.2] <http://CISGw3.law.pace.edu/cases/940615a3.html>.

143 Ibid.

Other commentators argue that the tribunal should take a more consistent and predictable approach, by applying one of the following rates: the interest rate of the creditor's place of business, debtor's place of business, currency of the claim or international or regional interest rate such as LIBOR.[144] Alternatively, although contentious, some authors consider that guidance could be drawn from Art. 7.4.9(2) of the *UNIDROIT Principles*, which stipulates that:

> [t]he rate of interest shall be the average bank short-term lending rate to prime borrowers prevailing for the currency of payment at the place for payment, or where no such rate exists at that place, then the same rate in the State of the currency of payment. In the absence of such a rate at either place the rate of interest shall be the appropriate rate fixed by the law of the State of the currency of payment.

The *CISG* Advisory Council also notes that that the most supported view is that the rate of interest is an external gap, which should be 'determined according to domestic law applicable by reference of the conflict of law rules of the forum state.'[145] Those who advocate the conflict of law approach argue that the applicable domestic law should determine the interest rate, because the rate of interest does not fall within the scope of the *CISG*.[146] On the other hand, as discussed earlier, commentators argue that the reason why the rate of interest was not stipulated in the Convention was because it was difficult to agree on a formula, and not because it was outside the scope of the Convention.[147]

Consequently, the *CISG* Advisory Council argues that the determination of the interest rate should not be left to the domestic law as applicable by reference to conflict of law principles, since the outcome will be uncertain because the tribunal could apply the interest rate at the creditor's place of business, debtor's place of business, place of payment, international or domestic interest rate or country of the currency.[148] Therefore it proposes a more predictable approach, and thus the preferable view, according to the *CISG* Advisory Council, is that the law of the state where the creditor has business should be applied to determine

---

144 CISG Advisory Council, CISG Advisory Council Opinion No. 14 – Interest Under Art. 78 CISG (21 and 22 October 2013), Rapporteur: Professor Yesim M. Atamer, <www.CISG.law.pace.edu/CISG/CISG-AC-op14.html> [3.1] – [3.2].

145 Ibid., 3.27.

146 Fritz Enderlein and Dietrich Maskow, *International Sales Law: United Nations Convention on Contracts for the International Sale of Goods: Convention on the Limitation Period in the International Sale of Goods: Commentary* (Oceana, 1992) 312. See also, Affolder, above n 105, 66.

147 Franco Ferrari, 'Uniform Application and Interest Rates Under the 1980 Vienna Sales Convention' (1995) 24(3) *Georgia Journal of International and Comparative Law* 467, 473–478; Berger, above n 130.

148 See discussion of all different outcomes, CISG Advisory Council, CISG Advisory Council Opinion No. 14 – Interest Under Art. 78 CISG (21 and 22 October 2013), Rapporteur: Professor Yesim M. Atamer, <www.CISG.law.pace.edu/CISG/CISG-AC-op14.html> [3.26] – [3.34].

the interest rate. This is because one of the main purposes of an interest claim is to provide compensation for the time value of money to the creditor.[149] Furthermore, the *CISG* Advisory Council believes this approach is similar to that achieved under private international law rules, because it leads to the tribunal making reference to domestic laws to ascertain the interest rate.[150] The *CISG* Advisory Council also notes that out of the 274 decisions surveyed in the Opinion, 103 have either directly or through private international law principles, applied the law of the country where the creditor has business.[151] The *CISG* Advisory Council stipulates:

> [t]he proposed solution might have the negative side effect that the domestic law of the creditor works with a residuary rules which provides for a fixed interest rate that no longer reflects market conditions. Yet whenever the creditor remains under-compensated due to a fixed interest rate, a correction can be achieved through a damages claim based on Art. 74.[152]

The *CISG* Advisory Council recommends that if the domestic law of the creditor does not provide for a rule regarding the default interest rate, or the interest claim is forbidden in the country, then the tribunal should not award interest under Art. 78, and instead, compensate the creditor through Art. 74.[153] Similarly, if compound interest is not permitted under the domestic law of the creditor's place of business, then the creditor cannot claim compound interest under Art. 78, but may be able to claim it as a loss under Art. 74.[154] This approach proposed by the *CISG* Advisory Council Opinion No. 14 aims to provide predictability and uniformity, and was voted on unanimously by the *CISG* Advisory Council.

---

149 CISG Advisory Council, CISG Advisory Council Opinion No. 14 – Interest Under Art. 78 CISG (21 and 22 October 2013), Rapporteur: Professor Yesim M. Atamer, <www.CISG. law.pace.edu/CISG/CISG-AC-op14.html> [3.35].
150 CISG Advisory Council, CISG Advisory Council Opinion No. 14 – Interest Under Art. 78 CISG (21 and 22 October 2013), Rapporteur: Professor Yesim M. Atamer, <www.CISG. law.pace.edu/CISG/CISG-AC-op14.html> [3.37].
151 CISG Advisory Council, CISG Advisory Council Opinion No. 14 – Interest Under Art. 78 CISG (21 and 22 October 2013), Rapporteur: Professor Yesim M. Atamer, <www.CISG. law.pace.edu/CISG/CISG-AC-op14.html> [3.37]. See also, CISG Advisory Council, CISG Advisory Council Opinion No. 14-Addendum Analysis of Case Result of Analysis of 274 Decisions Relating to Art. 78 CISG (21 and 22 October 2013), <www.CISGac.com/ file/repository/CISG_AC_Opinion_14_Decision_Chart_Final.pdf>.
152 CISG Advisory Council, CISG Advisory Council Opinion No. 14 – Interest Under Art. 78 CISG (21 and 22 October 2013), Rapporteur: Professor Yesim M. Atamer, <www.CISG. law.pace.edu/CISG/CISG-AC-op14.html> [3.40].
153 CISG Advisory Council, CISG Advisory Council Opinion No. 14 – Interest Under Art. 78 CISG (21 and 22 October 2013), Rapporteur: Professor Yesim M. Atamer, <www.CISG. law.pace.edu/CISG/CISG-AC-op14.html> [3.40].
154 CISG Advisory Council, CISG Advisory Council Opinion No. 14 – Interest Under Art. 78 CISG (21 and 22 October 2013), Rapporteur: Professor Yesim M. Atamer, <www.CISG. law.pace.edu/CISG/CISG-AC-op14.html> 14.

Alternatively, Sénéchal proposes a slightly different uniform approach, and argues that the award of interest is highly significant, as it ensures that a party is fully compensated.[155] He argues that the calculation of interest should: (1) ensure that the interest awarded reflects what a party would have earned, had it invested its money during the period of time between the date of default and date of award; (2) consistently applies whenever money has been withheld from a claimant, because the charging of interest is standard market practice; (3) reflects market realities, including inflation and market risk premiums; and (4) be awarded at a compounded rate, and on a yearly basis.[156]

Arguably, the *CISG* provides a more practical solution that takes into account the prohibition of *riba*, because if interest or compound interest is not allowed under the creditor's place of business, then interest cannot be claimed and instead, can be claimed as damages under Art. 74 provided the provision's prerequisite are met. A claim for damages is compatible with the concept of *ta'widh* and *gharamah*, as discussed previously. Furthermore, in the event that there is a risk that an arbitral award may not be enforced due to the award of interest, the parties can agree that Art. 78 does not apply to their agreement as per Art. 6 of the *CISG*, which allows deviation from the Convention.[157]

Similarly, commentators argue that the *CISG* and *Shari'a* are compatible because of Islamic principles of good faith, sanctity of contract, specific performance and the recognition of *lex mercatoria*.[158] As discussed at length earlier, most Muslim countries have taken the pragmatic approach by recognising the significance of interest in the modern economy and therefore, the prohibition against interest is not strictly applied. Therefore, the application of Art. 78 of the *CISG* is only problematic if an arbitral award containing interest is enforced in a country where interest is prohibited, such as Iran or Saudi Arabia.[159] As noted earlier, although interest may not be awarded in Qatar, compensation or damages for late payment may be awarded instead. This approach may also be taken in Iran and Saudi Arabia. The issue of enforcement will be examined in more detail in the next chapter.

On the other hand, commentator and academic, Gary Bell, uses the case study of a *murabaha* contract (discussed in Chapter 5) to argue that the *CISG* is not compatible with *Shari'a*, and therefore 'Islamic lawyers would be well advised

---

155 Sénéchal, above n 112, 219.

156 Ibid.

157 T. S. Twibell, 'Implementation of the United Nations Convention on Contracts for the International Sale of Goods (CISG) Under Shari'a Law: Will Article 78 of the CISG Be Enforced When the Forum Is an Islamic State?' (1997) 9 *International Legal Perspectives* 25, 80–81.

158 El-Saghir, above n 41, 515–516; Fatima Akaddaf, 'Application of the United Nations Convention on Contracts for the International Sale of Goods (CISG) to Arab Islamic Countries: Is the CISG Compatible with Islamic Law Principles?' (2001) 13 *Pace International Law Review* 1.

159 El-Saghir, above n 41, 505, 515–516; Akaddaf, above n 158; T. S. Twibell, above n 157, 25; El-Saghir, above n 140.

to exclude the *CISG* when they want their *murabaha* contract to be valid under Islamic law.'[160] Bell argues that the incompatibility stems from the fact that the *murabaha* contract does not allow for interest or uncertainty of price and goods (the principle of *gharar* was discussed in Chapter 5), the concept of good faith under *Shari'a* is wider than that in the *CISG* and finally, non-conformity of goods may result in the contract being rescinded under *Shari'a*.[161]

On the other hand, Akaddaf interprets the 'good faith' requirement in the *CISG* as being compatible with *Shari'a*, because the concept of good faith in the *CISG* 'sometimes acts as a safeguard preventing buyer's speculation at seller's expense by requiring [the] buyer to mitigate losses or by limiting the right to specific performance. Similarly, in the *Shari'a*, there is a presumption of good faith in all transactions.'[162] Akaddaf further argues that the *Shari'a* encourages certainty, prohibits fraudulent dealings and encourages honesty in all transactions. Commentators also observe that this is consistent with the *CISG* notions of good faith as per Art. 7(1) which stipulates that '[i]n the interpretation of this Convention, regard is to be had to its international character and to the need to promote uniformity in its application and the observance of good faith in international trade.' Commentators, such as Koneru, also argue that 'many provisions of the Convention represent "good faith" through its variants, such as "reasonableness" or "fair dealing".'[163] Furthermore, Akaddaf observes that Art. 40 of the *CISG* extends the concept of 'good faith' to the duty to disclose defects in relation to the non-conformity of goods by the seller.[164]

However, as noted earlier, Bell notes that non-conformity of goods in a *murabaha* contract would mean that the entire contract is invalid under *Shari'a* due to the prohibition of *gharar*, whereas, Art. 49(1)(a) of the *CISG* requires a fundamental breach, specifically:

> [t]he buyer may declare the contract avoided (a) if the failure by the seller to perform any of his obligations under the contract or this Convention amounts to a fundamental breach of contract; and (b) in case of non-delivery, if the seller does not deliver the goods within the additional period of time fixed by the buyer in accordance with paragraph (1) of article 47 or declares that he will not deliver within the period so fixed.[165]

160 Gary Bell, 'New Challenges for the Uniformisation of Laws: How the CISG Is Challenged by "Asian Values" and Islamic Law' in Ingeborg Schwenzer and Lisa Spagnolo (eds), *Towards Uniformity: The 2nd Annual MAA Schlechtriem CISG Conference* (Eleven International Publishing, 2011).

161 Ibid., 26–28.

162 Akaddaf, above n 158, 33.

163 Phanesh Koneru, 'The International Interpretation of the UN Convention on Contracts for the International Sale of Goods: An Approach Based on General Principles' (1997) 6 *Minnesota Journal of Global Trade* 105, 139; Akaddaf, above n 158, 32.

164 Ibid., 32–33.

165 Art. 47 (1) of the CISG stipulates that 'The buyer may fix an additional period of time of reasonable length for performance by the seller of his obligations.'

Unlike Akaddaf, Bell highlights one of the main conflicts between *Shari'a* and the *CISG*, which is that in order for a *murabaha* contract to be *Shari'a*-compliant, *gharar* and *riba* should not exist and if it does, as discussed in the previous chapter, the contract will be invalid and non-arbitrable. This applies to any *Shari'a*-compliant financial transaction and not just the *murabaha* contract. According to classical *Shari'a* and AAOIFI Standards on *murabaha*,[166] this is the correct approach; however, the issue that remains is whether an arbitral award will be enforced in a country which strictly applies *Shari'a*. As was discussed in the cases of *Beximco* and *Symphony Gems*, although a *murabaha* contract might not be viewed by some as *Shari'a*-compliant, it may still be enforced if the court of law does not apply *Shari'a* strictly or at all. Therefore, while Bell's argument that the *murabaha* contract conflicts with *CISG* principles may be true in theory, the conflict will only be a practical issue if the *murabaha* contract is governed by *CISG* principles and enforced in a country where: firstly, *Shari'a* strictly applies (i.e., Iran or Saudi Arabia); or secondly, the arbitrator chooses to apply classical *Shari'a* or arbitral law or rules that strictly apply the prohibition of *gharar* and/or *riba*, such as the AAOIFI Standards.

In the event that an arbitrator or court decides to apply *Shari'a*, then the *murabaha* contract will be found to be void if it is found to contain *gharar* and/or *riba*, despite the fact that it might be valid under the principles of the *CISG*. For example, if a *murabaha* contract is subject to the *CISG* and enforcement is sought in Saudi Arabia, then it is possible that the contract may be held void if a Saudi court finds that it contains *gharar* and/or *riba*. This scenario is a possibility because, as will be discussed in the next section, it may be possible for the *CISG* to indirectly apply under Art. 1(1)(b) to a contract between parties based in non-contracting Muslim countries, such as Saudi Arabia.

VI The application of the *CISG* in non-contracting Muslim countries

A conflict between the *CISG* and *Shari'a* may also arise if parties do not stipulate the governing law in their choice of law clause, or if they do not agree to opt out of the interest provision in Art. 78 of the *CISG*. Art. 1 of the *CISG* notes that the Convention applies

> to contracts of sale of goods between parties whose place of business are in different States: (a) when the States are Contracting States; or (b) when the rules of private international law lead to the application of the law of a Contracting State.

This means that the *CISG* can apply to a contract entered by a party from a non-contracting Muslim country, such as Iran or Saudi Arabia, where interest is strictly forbidden. As a general principle, Ferrari notes:

---

166 AAOIFI, above n 10, 221–231.

provided that the parties have not excluded the *CISG* and that no *electio iuris*[167] occurred, the *CISG* should be applied in the courts of Contracting States (provided that the State did not limit the scope of Art. 1(1)(b) by means of an Art. 95 reservation . . . at least to most international sales contracts involving a seller who has its place of business in a Contracting (non-reservatory)[168] State.[169]

Therefore, in a hypothetical scenario where a German seller enters into a contract with a party from Saudi Arabia (a non-Contracting State where interest is forbidden), and the governing law chosen by the parties is German law (and further, parties have not agreed to exclude application of the *CISG*), would the *CISG* apply to the Saudi party if the matter is brought before a German court? Would the *CISG* apply if the matter is brought before a Saudi court? What if the matter is brought before an arbitrator? If the *CISG* applies, would the Saudi party be bound by Art. 78 of the *CISG* which mandates interest? This section attempts to deal with these questions.

The *CISG* will apply under Art. 1(1)(b) of the *CISG*, even if both parties are not from Contracting States, if conflict of law rules of the forum lead to the application of the law of a Contracting State. Even if the approach of the *CISG* Advisory Council Opinion No 14 is followed and the German party is the creditor, then German courts could order the Saudi party to pay interest as per the *CISG* and German law. When a dispute is brought before courts located in Contracting States, such courts are bound to apply the *CISG* because the *CISG* forms part of the applicable domestic law (e.g., part of German law), even if the parties are not from Contracting States.[170]

One solution to this problem could be for both parties to agree to opt out of the *CISG* under Art. 6 which states that: '[t]he parties may exclude the application of this Convention, or subject to Art. 12, derogate from or vary the effect of any of its provisions.' Another solution could be for the parties to agree that they will partially exclude the *CISG* by agreeing that Art. 78 does not apply. In

---

167 'A choice of the law of a specific jurisdiction to govern a legal relationship or the interpretation or enforcement of a legal instrument' See Oxford Reference, 'Electio iuris' (2011) <www.oxfordreference.com/view/10.1093/acref/9780195369380.001.0001/acref-9780195369380-e-604>.

168 A number of countries have made reservations about certain provisions of the CISG. See UNCITRAL, 'Status – United Nations Convention on Contracts for the International Sale of Goods (Vienna, 1980)' (2016) <www.uncitral.org/uncitral/en/uncitral_texts/sale_goods/1980CISG_status.html>.

169 Franco Ferrari, 'The CISG's Sphere of Application: Articles 1–3 and 10' in Franco Ferrari, Harry Flechtner and Ronald Brand (eds), *The Draft Uncitral Digest and Beyond Cases, Analysis and Unresolved Issues in the U.N. Sales Convention: Papers of the Pittsburgh Conference Organized by the Center for International Legal Education (Cile)* (Sweet & Maxwell, 2004) 21, 48.

170 Lisa Spagnolo, 'Iura Novit Curia and the CISG: Resolution of the Faux Procedural Black Hole' in Ingeborg Schwenzer and Lisa Spagnolo (eds), *Towards Uniformity: The 2nd Annual MAA Schlechtriem CISG Conference* (Eleven International Publishing, 2011) 181, 195–196.

the event that parties fail to exclude the application of the *CISG*, or if they do not derogate from Art. 78, the parties could be bound by the *CISG* if the dispute was before a court in a Contracting State because in theory, the court is bound to apply Art. 78.[171]

Alternatively, if the above-mentioned hypothetical dispute between a Saudi party and German party was brought before a Saudi court, then that court would not have to apply the *CISG*, even if it found German law applied, because it is not located in a Contracting State.[172] Furthermore, as discussed earlier, Saudi courts have the discretion to apply *Shari'a* and therefore, they can make the determination that certain provisions in the *CISG* are contrary to Saudi law. This is an issue because countries cannot make reservations in relation to Art. 78 of the *CISG* despite the fact that reservations can be made in relation to other provisions in the *CISG*. It would be interesting to note how Saudi courts would deal with Art. 78 of the *CISG* if a Saudi judge does decide to apply it, or if Saudi Arabia decides to become a Contracting State in the future.[173] Indeed, adoption of the *CISG* in Saudi Arabia would be problematic, particularly since Saudi Arabia would not be at liberty to adapt the *CISG* to exclude Art. 78, because unlike the *UNCITRAL Model Law* adopted by the new *Saudi Arbitration Law 2012*, the *CISG* is a convention. Furthermore, as discussed earlier, no reservation is available in respect of Art. 78.

Furthermore, if the hypothetical dispute between a Saudi and Germany party is resolved through arbitration, the arbitrator is not bound to apply the *CISG*, unless parties have agreed on the *CISG* or the law of a Contracting State as the governing law of the contract. This is due to the concept of party autonomy in arbitration and unlike domestic courts, arbitrators are not bound by the *CISG* or the state's private international law principles.[174] However, the arbitral tribunal may have discretion to apply the *CISG* to the substance of the dispute if the parties have not agreed to a choice of law, when applying conflict of law rules as per Art. 28(2) of the *UNCITRAL Model Law* or an equivalent provision under the applicable law, but this determination must be made in a manner which is consistent with due process and procedural fairness.[175]

---

171 For a discussion on whether courts apply the CISG in practice, see ibid.

172 Ibid., 198.

173 This book does not deal with the intersection between Saudi laws and the CISG. For more information on the compatibility between Saudi laws and the CISG, see Ismaeel Ibrahim Aljeriwi, *The Compatibility of Saudi Domestic Law with the Seller's Obligations Under the Vienna Convention (CISG)* (PhD Thesis, Newcastle University, 2010) <https://theses.ncl.ac.uk/dspace/handle/10443/1044>.

174 Spagnolo, above n 170, 199–200; Andre Janssen and Matthias Spilker, 'The CISG and International Arbitration' in Larry A. DiMatteo (ed), *International Sales Law – a Global Challenge* (Cambridge University Press, 2014) 135, 140.

175 See, e.g., Art. 22.3 London Court of International Arbitration Rules and Art. 21 ICC Arbitration Rules 2012, which stipulate that if the parties have not agreed on the law governing the merits of the dispute, the Arbitral Tribunal may apply laws or rules of law that it considers appropriate. See generally, Spagnolo, above n 170, 200–201; Janssen and Spilker, above n 1174, 140.

There have been many cases where arbitral tribunals have applied the *CISG* as per Art. 1(1)(a),[176] and also where the conflict of law rules have led the tribunal to apply the applicable law of a Contracting State. For example, in a case[177] between a seller from Egypt and a buyer from Morocco,[178] the arbitral tribunal applied the *CISG*, even though Morocco is not a Contracting State. In this case, the seller claimed that the buyer failed to fulfil their contractual obligations in regards the sale of semi-dried dates. The dispute settlement provision stated that the dispute would be settled at the Alexandria Centre for International Arbitration in Egypt, and the seller argued that the *CISG* applied to the dispute. The Panel agreed to apply the *CISG*, despite the fact that the buyer was from Morocco. It did so because Art. 1(1)(b) of the *CISG*, Arts. 10 and 19 of the Egyptian *Civil Code*, and Art. 33(1) of the arbitration rules of the Alexandria Centre for International Arbitration, stipulated that the law of the seat of arbitration governed the proceedings in the absence of a contractual agreement between the parties. This case was criticised by some commentators, such as Al Saghir, who argued that the tribunal applied the *CISG* and the Egyptian *Civil Code* simultaneously, and 'the Panel should have applied the Egyptian law only if both, the CISG provisions and the principles on which the Convention is based fail to resolve the question.'[179] Commentators Dawwas and Shandi also assert that: '[a]s the *CISG* is a *lex specialis* of the international sale of goods, the panel ought to have applied it exclusively and comprehensively. The panel should have excluded the application of Egyptian national law.'[180]

Arbitral tribunals have also applied the *CISG* when the governing law is Iranian law, even though Iran is not a Contracting State and as mentioned previously, prohibits interest. In *Watkins – Johnson v. Islamic Republic of Iran*,[181] a dispute

---

176 See, e.g., ICC Case No. 7531/1994, at Unilex (1994) <www.unilex.info/case.cfm?pid=1 &do=case&id=139&step=FullText>. See also ICC Case No. 7331/1994, at Unilex (1994) <www.unilex.info/case.cfm?pid=1&do=case&id=140&step=FullText>; see also, Court of Arbitration of the ICC Case No. 7153/1992 at Pace University Albert H. Kritzer CISG Database, Hotel Materials Case (1992) <http://CISGw3.law.pace.edu/cases/927153i1. html>.

177 See Alexandria Center for International Arbitration Case Number 6/2003 at Pace University Albert H. Kritzer CISG Database, Semi-Dried Dates Case (2005) <http://CISGw3. law.pace.edu/cases/050116e1.html>.

178 Note that in Morocco, interest is permissible in transactions involving corporations. See generally, Jason Chuah, 'Impact of Islamic Law on Commercial Sale Contracts – a Private International Law Dimension in Europe' (2010) 4 *European Journal of Commercial Contract Law* 191; Akaddaf, above n 158; Mahat Chraibi, 'Morocco-Corporate-Withholding Tax' (2016) *Pricewaterhouse Coopers* <http://taxsummaries.pwc.com/uk/taxsummaries/ wwts.nsf/ID/Morocco-Corporate-Withholding-taxes>; El Ahdab and El Ahdab, above n 59, 485.

179 El-Saghir, above 140, 367–368.

180 Amin Dawwas and Yousef Shandi, 'The Applicability of the CISG to the Arab World' (2011) 16(4) *Uniform Law Review* 813, 832.

181 Watkins-Johnson Co., Watkins-Johnson Ltd. v. Islamic Republic of Iran, Bank Saderat Iran at Albert H. Krtizer, CISG Database, (Iran/U.S. Claims Tribunal, 28 July 1989) <www. unilex.info/case.cfm?pid=1&do=case&id=38&step=FullText>.

arose between a seller from the United States and a buyer from Iran. In this case, the arbitral tribunal considered Art. 88 of the *CISG* in relation to determining that the seller had the right to sell undelivered equipment in order to mitigate damages. The tribunal found that Art. 88(1) of the *CISG* was satisfied because, as stipulated in the article, there had been 'unreasonable delay by the other party in taking possession of the goods . . . [and] reasonable notice of the intention to sell has been given to the other party.' The *CISG* was applied without explanation, even though Iran is not a Contracting State and the governing law of the contract stated

> [t]he Governing law of this contract is the Iranian law. This contract is subject to the Laws of the Imperial Government of Iran and United Sates in every respect if any difference between these two laws the Iranian law will govern.[182]

Some commentators criticise this case, and argue that the case was not in the *CISG's* sphere of application.[183] Commentators argue that the arbitrators in this case not only incorrectly applied the *CISG* as part of *lex mercatoria*,[184] but also applied it before the *CISG* came into effect.[185]

In the event that a court or arbitral tribunal finds that the *CISG* is applicable to a party from a non-contracting Muslim country such as Saudi Arabia or Iran, then a conflict may arise between *Shari'a* and the *CISG*. As discussed previously, the conflict may arise due to the interest provision in Art. 78, or if the contract contains *gharar*. The *CISG* Advisory Council Opinion No. 14 might offer a harmonious solution if the creditor is from Saudi Arabia, because interest would not apply as per Saudi law. This is less clear with reference to Iran due to its interpretation of *Shari'a* which, as discussed earlier, means that Iranian parties can claim interest but are prohibited from paying interest.

However, in the event that the buyer is from Saudi Arabia and the interest rates of the creditor's place of business are applied, the Saudi debtor will be bound by Art. 78 of the *CISG* if the matter goes before a court in a Contracting State. Alternatively, an arbitral tribunal may have the discretion to apply the *CISG* where parties have not agreed on a choice of law of a Contracting State, and may determine that the Saudi party should pay the creditor interest if it chooses to follow the uniform approach suggested by the *CISG* Advisory Council. Similarly, if the *CISG* Advisory Council Opinion No. 14 is followed, parties from countries where compound interest is prohibited may have to pay compound interest if the domestic law of the creditor's place of business stipulates compound interest rates.

---

182 Ibid., 93.
183 Franco Ferrari, *Contracts for the International Sale of Goods Applicability and Applications of the 1980 United Nations Convention* (Martinus Nijhoff Publishers, 2012) 94.
184 Georgios C. Petrochilos, 'Arbitration Conflict of Laws Rules and the 1980 International Sales Convention' (1991) 52 *Revue Hellenique de Droit International* 191.
185 Ferrari, above n 183, 94.

VII Conclusion

This chapter began by analysing the award of interest under both *Shari'a* and contemporary ICA. It argued that lack of clarity in relation to the prohibition of *riba* and its application to the award of interest is further complicated by the inconsistency with which tribunals award interest in contemporary ICA.

Art. 78 of the *CISG* was also analysed in this chapter in relation to and how in certain circumstances, the convention fails to take into consideration *Shari'a*. This book continuously emphasises that *Shari'a* is not a uniform body of codified law. Therefore, depending on the governing law, place of enforcement and the location of the creditor's place of business, the *CISG* may or may not be incompatible with certain interpretations of *Shari'a*. For example, if the *CISG* applies to a *murabaha* contract which is found to contain *gharar* and/or *riba*, then the contract may be enforceable under the *CISG* (unless there is a fundamental breach under Art. 49), but invalid if tribunals or courts apply classical *Shari'a* or *Shari'a* rules as outlined in the AAOIFI Standards or by the Islamic Fiqh Academy in Jeddah.

Alternatively, Egyptian, Syrian or Iraqi law (despite being influenced by *Shari'a*) may be more flexible in their approach, especially since these countries have chosen to become Contracting States. Similarly, the *i-Arbitration Rules* cater for both interest on arbitral awards, and alternative remedies under *Shari'a* as per the agreement of the parties.

If parties do not choose their governing law, or do not agree to opt out of *CISG* provisions, and Art. 1(1)(b) of the *CISG* applies, then a court in a Contracting State will most likely apply the *CISG* as it is a Convention which forms part of the country's domestic law. On the other hand, an arbitral tribunal will have the discretion as to whether or not the *CISG* is applied in such a scenario. Although the *CISG* Advisory Council Opinion No. 14 provides a feasible solution for creditors from countries where *Shari'a* applies, this solution does not cater for debtors from countries such as Saudi Arabia or Iran. Also, it does not cater for debtors from countries where compound interest is prohibited, which, as discussed above, is the majority of Muslim countries. Regardless, this argument assumes that a debtor from a Muslim country will have an issue with the payment of interest.

The failure of the *CISG* to take *Shari'a* into consideration may possibly be one of the reasons why many Muslim countries are not signatories to the *CISG*. In order to increase its international appeal, it is recommended that a provision be included in the *CISG* that takes account of the prohibition against interest, allowing Contracting States to make reservations to the application of Art. 78. As will be discussed in the next chapter, a risk does exist that the award of interest may not be enforced in countries where public policy is based on *Shari'a*.

8 *Shari'a* public policy and the recognition and enforcement of arbitral awards

I Introduction

The public policy exception under Art. V(2)(b) of the *New York Convention* states that an arbitral award may be refused if it would 'be contrary to the public policy' of the country where the arbitral award is enforced. The public policy exception is also noted in Art. 36(1)(b) of the *UNCITRAL Model Law*, which provides that an arbitral award may not be recognised if the enforcement is contrary 'to the public policy' of the respective state. However, international conventions and domestic laws rarely define domestic, international or transnational public policy,[1] which means that national courts are left with the task of ascertaining how the public policy defence applies on a case-by-case basis.

Theoretically, this means that domestic courts in countries where *Shari'a* forms part of the country's constitution or public policy, may take a wide approach to public policy and refuse to enforce arbitral awards that do not comply with *Shari'a*. Practically, however, it is difficult to ascertain whether public policy based on *Shari'a* ('*Shari'a* public policy') may be invoked to deny enforcement of arbitral awards.

This chapter begins by comparing conventional public policy with *Shari'a* public policy. Despite the fact that this book focuses on international commercial arbitration, this chapter provides a comparative review of both international and domestic arbitration cases in order to show when and how *Shari'a* public policy may have an impact upon arbitral awards. Subsequently, the chapter provides a comparative analysis of the six Gulf Cooperative Council (GCC) countries (Saudi Arabia, Kuwait, the United Arab Emirates, Qatar, Bahrain and Oman), as well as Egypt,[2] in order to assess whether *Shari'a* public policy is applied in these jurisdictions to deny enforcement of arbitral awards in practice.

---

1 See generally, Devin Bray and Heather Bray, *International Arbitration and Public Policy* (JurisNet, 2015).
2 The reason why the scope of this chapter is limited to a comparison with the above-mentioned countries is due to the fact that most other jurisdictions have limited or no reported decisions available for the author to rely upon. Furthermore, these jurisdictions are all signatories to the New York Convention which makes the discussion on public policy more relevant.

II The public policy exception in contemporary ICA

Due to the wide ambit of the 'public policy' defence, it is regularly invoked to refuse enforcement of arbitral awards.[3] However, as this section will discuss, courts have indicated that the availability of the public policy defence should not be abused and instead, a narrow approach should be taken when invoking this defence. Since 'public policy' does not have a standard international definition, yet it is a defence provided for under the *New York Convention* and the *UNCITRAL Model Law*, domestic courts take varying approaches when applying the public policy defence. In order to increase awareness of the different approaches taken by national courts, the 2015 report by the IBA Subcommittee on Recognition and Enforcement of Arbitral Awards ('IBA Report') provides reports from 40 jurisdictions.[4]

The IBA Report provides a non-exhaustive list of jurisdictions, which includes civil law jurisdictions that refer to public policy as a fundamental part of the national legal system. Whereas, common law jurisdictions often refer to fundamental values and principles of morality and justice. Common law jurisdictions often cite the case of *Parsons & Whittemore Overseas*[5] in which the U.S. Court of Appeal found that

> [t]he general pro-enforcement bias informing the Convention and explaining its supersession of the Geneva Convention points towards a narrow reading of the public policy defence. Enforcement of foreign arbitral awards may be denied on this basis only where enforcement would violate the forum state's most basic notions of morality and justice.[6]

Furthermore, the IBA Report also refers to some jurisdictions where public policy is given a broader definition.[7] It is interesting to note that while the IBA Report refers to common law and civil law jurisdictions, it does not provide a separate category for countries where public policy is based on *Shariʿa*. For instance, although *Shariʿa* influences the legal systems of Egypt, Pakistan and Indonesia, the IBA Report notes that Egypt falls under the first category (a civil law jurisdiction referring to public policy as part of its legal system), whereas

---

3 Richard Garnett, et al., *A Practical Guide to International Commercial Arbitration* (Oceana Publications, 2000) 109.

4 International Bar Association (IBA) Subcommittee on Recognition and Enforcement of Arbitral Awards, Report on the Public Policy Exception in the New York Convention, (2015) <www.ibanet.org/LPD/Dispute_Resolution_Section/Arbitration/Recogntn_Enfrcemnt_Arbitl_Awrd/publicpolicy15.aspx>.

5 Parsons & Whittemore Overseas 508 F.2d 969, 973 (2d Cir, 1974).

6 Ibid. See also Revere Copper & Brass Inc v Overseas Private Inv Corp 628 F.2d 81, 83 (D.C Cir. 1980): '[T]he federal courts have recognised a strong federal policy in favour of voluntary commercial arbitration. . . . As a result, judicial review of an arbitration award has been narrowly limited.'

7 International Bar Association (IBA) Subcommittee on Recognition and Enforcement of Arbitral Awards, above n 4.

Pakistan and Indonesia fall under the third general category where public policy is given a broad definition.[8] The only mention of *Shariʿa* in the IBA Report is the definition of public policy in the UAE.[9] Under Art. 3 of *the Civil Transactions Law* in the UAE, 'public order'[10] is defined as:

> matters relating to personal status such as marriage, inheritance and lineage, and matters relating to sovereignty, freedom of trade, the circulation of wealth, rules of private ownership and the other rules and foundations upon which society is based, in such manner as not to conflict with the definitive provisions and fundamental principles of the Islamic *Sharia*.[11]

Khatchadourian states that although Qatari law does not define public policy, the meaning is similar to the definition provided under Art. 3 of the *Civil Transactions Law* in the UAE.[12] Therefore, in Qatar, '[d]isputes over contracts considered *Shariʿa* non-compliant, such as loans with excessive interest or aleatory contracts, are considered contrary to public policy.'[13] It is also unclear whether this definition of public policy in the UAE and Qatar relates to domestic public policy or international public policy, although recent case law seems to suggest that courts take a narrow approach to international public policy. For example, in recent court cases in Qatar, two foreign arbitral awards were refused enforcement because the awards were not rendered in the name of His Highness the Emir of Qatar.[14] Subsequently, Qatar changed its approach and on 25 March 2014, the courts reinstated a 2012 ICC decision issued in Doha.[15] It was initially refused

---

8 Ibid.
9 Australia is the only other jurisdiction in the IBA Report that provide a statutory definition for public policy, s 8(7A) of the International Arbitration Act 1974 (Cth) (Australia). See ibid., 2.
10 Public order is the term that the UAE uses for public policy. See ibid., 2.
11 Ibid., 2. See also UAE Civil Transactions Federal Law No. 5 of 1985 [James Whelan (Clifford Chance) trans, The Civil Code <https://lexemiratidotnet.files.wordpress.com/2011/07/uae-civil-code-_english-translation_.pdf>].
12 Minas Khatchadourian, 'The Application of the 1958 New York Convention in Qatar' 1(1) *BCDR International Arbitration Review* 49, 51.
13 Ibid., 52.
14 See Abnaa El Khalaf Company, et al. v. Sayed Aga Jawwed Raza, Qatar Court of Cassation, Petition No. 64/2012, 12 June 2012 (trans, Minas Khatchadourian, Kluwer Law International) (An arbitral award, issued by the Qatar International Center for Conciliation and Arbitration, was set aside because it was not rendered in the name of the Emir); Contracting Co. A v. Sub-Contracting Co. B, Qatar Court of First Instance Ruling, Decision No. 2216 of 2013, 7 December 2013 (In this case, the arbitral award was set aside because it was not rendered in the name of the Emir). See also Anne K Hoffmann, 'Qatari Courts and Foreign Arbitral Awards – The End of the Story?' (2014) *Al Tamimi & Co* <www.tamimi.com/en/magazine/law-update/section-8/may-7/qatari-courts-and-foreign-arbitral-awards-the-end-of-the-story.html>.
15 Qatar No. 1, ABC LLP v. Joint Venture RST and XYZ, Supreme Court of Cassation, Petitions Nos. 45 and 49 of 2014, 25 March 2014 reported in Albert Jan van den Berg (ed), 39 Y.B. Comm. Arb 480–482 (trans, Minas Khatchadourian, Kluwer Law International). See also, Hoffman, above n 14.

enforcement due to being contrary to public policy, as a result of not rendering the award in the name of the Emir. However, in this case, it was noted that foreign arbitral awards should be approached narrowly, and that international public policy did not require the award to be rendered in the name of the Emir.[16]

Although Art. V of the *New York Convention* is unclear on the point, most commentators and court cases have stated that foreign arbitral awards should only be refused on the basis of international public policy, which should be narrower than domestic public policy.[17] For example, in the case of *Eco Swiss China Time Ltd v. Benetton International NV*, the European Court of Justice held that 'it is in the interest of efficient arbitration proceedings that review of arbitration awards should be limited in scope and that annulment of or refusal to recognise an award should be possible only in exceptional circumstances.'[18] Commentators observe that:

> [e]xamples of internationally opprobrious conduct would be where an award was tainted by fraud, corruption, or involved a criminal transaction. Other matters, for example, such as betting or anti-competitive behaviour may be considered improper in certain countries but not others and therefore would not rise to the level of internationally offensive conduct.[19]

As discussed in Chapters 4 and 5, other breaches of public policy may include a breach of procedural fairness or due process, and bias by the arbitrator.[20] However, despite the different approaches taken, the IBA Report shows that most jurisdictions tend to uphold the pro-enforcement bias of the *New York Convention* by taking a narrow approach and applying 'international public policy' standards to foreign arbitral awards.

Some courts have also applied the concept of 'transnational public policy' which has been defined as rules of natural law or universal justice.[21] Junita states that this 'internationalist or delocalised view . . . promote[s] a uniform model norm of the public policy exception . . . through the establishment of transnational public

16 Ibid.
17 Jan Paulsson, 'The New York Convention in International Practice – Problems of Assimilation' in Marc Blessing (ed), *The New York Convention of 1958: A Collection of Reports and Materials Delivered at the ASA Conference held in Zurich on 2 February 1996* (Swiss Arbitration Association, 1996) 113; International Bar Association (IBA) Subcommittee on Recognition and Enforcement of Arbitral Awards, above n 4, 5; United Nations Conference on Trade and Development, Recognition and Enforcement of Arbitral Awards: The New York Convention, UNCTAD/EDM/Misc.232/Add.37 (2003) <http://unctad.org/en/Docs/edmmisc232add37_en.pdf> 38.
18 Eco Swiss China Time Ltd. v. Benetton International NV Case C-126/97 [1999] ECR I-3055, [35].
19 Garnett, et al., above n 3, 109.
20 Ibid., 109.
21 Bray and Bray, above n 1, 25.

policy which sharply departs from domestic public policy.'[22] For example, the IBA Report notes that the concept of transnational public policy has been applied by courts in Switzerland and Lebanon.[23] Furthermore, courts have applied norms stipulated by international arbitration laws, rules and conventions,[24] or:

> mandatory norms which may be imposed on actors in the market either because they have been created by those actors themselves or by civil society at large, or because they have been widely accepted by different societies around the world. These norms aim at being universal. They are the sign of the maturity of the international communities (that of the merchants and that of the civil societies) who know very well that there are limits to their activities.[25]

As is clear from the discussion on *Shari'a* public policy below, the mandatory norms referred to when delineating 'transnational public policy' will be interpreted differently by domestic courts in the context of enforcement of foreign arbitral awards. Additionally, to suggest that there is a 'transnational public policy' based on universal norms which signify a 'mature' international community and 'civil' society, may suggest that those countries which do not accept similar norms are 'uncivilised.' The 2002 'Final International Law Association Report on Public Policy as a Bar to Enforcement of International Arbitral Awards' notes that international public policy differs from transnational public policy, and that the former should be preferred:

> the expression "international public policy" is to be understood in the sense given to it in the field of private international law; namely, that part of the public policy of a State which, if violated, would prevent a party from invoking a foreign law or foreign judgment or foreign award. It is not to be understood, in these Recommendations, as referring to a public policy which is common to many States (which is better referred to as "transnational public policy") or to public policy which is part of public international law.[26]

22 Fifi Junita, 'Public Policy Exception in International Commercial Arbitration – Promoting Uniform Model Norms' (2012) 5(1) *Contemporary Asia Arbitration Journal* 45, 57.
23 International Bar Association (IBA) Subcommittee on Recognition and Enforcement of Arbitral Awards, above n 4, 9–10. See also Martin Hunter and Gui Conde e Silva, 'Transnational Public Policy and Its Application in Investment Arbitration' (2003) 3(3) *The Journal of World Investment* 367. See also, Florentine Sonia Sneij and Ulrich Andreas Zanconato, 'The Role of Shari'a Law and Modern Arbitration Statutes in an Environment of Growing Multilateral Trade: Lessons from Lebanon and Syria' (2015) 12(2) *Transnational Dispute Management* 1, 1–11.
24 Fernando Mantilla-Serrano, 'Towards a Transnational Procedural Public Policy' in Emmanuel Gaillard (ed), *Towards a Uniform International Arbitration Law?* (Juris Publishing, 2005) 163, 168.
25 Catherine Kessedjian, 'Transnational Public Policy' in Albert Jan van den Berg (ed), *International Arbitration 2006: Back to Basics?* (Kluwer Law International, 2007) 857, 861–862.
26 Professor Pierre Mayer, Mr Audley Sheppard and Dr Nagla Nassar, 'Public Policy Exception as Applied by the Courts of the MENA Region' in New Delhi Conference International Law Association, Committee on International Commercial Arbitration (ed), *Final Report on*

Redfern acknowledges that 'transnational public policy' is often an ambiguous concept, and suggests that '[g]eneralized reference by arbitrators to "transnational public policy", without reference to particular national rules and an acceptable choice of law framework for their application, risks appearing an easy way out and a substitute for rigorous analysis.'[27] However, Redfern argues that the role of transnational public policy should be to provide arbitrators with a 'common procedural pattern,' such as the requirement for arbitrators to act in accordance with procedural fairness and due process, which is also contained in most contemporary ICA rules and regulations.[28] Similarly, the IBA Report notes that while differences exist in jurisdictions as to whether they adopt principles of international, transnational or domestic public policy, the purpose of 'making such a distinction is always to narrow down the scope of the public policy which must be considered for assessing whether the enforcement of a foreign award is compatible or not.'[29] Due to the pro-enforcement nature of international arbitration rules, conventions and model laws, transnational public policy should be approached narrowly to increase the likelihood of enforcement.

Generally, public policy is violated on a procedural or substantive basis. For example, as discussed earlier, procedural public policy violations include a breach of due process, the right to be heard, or 'manifest disregard of the law' by the arbitrator.[30] Discussions have taken place as to whether such procedural breaches fall under Art. V(1)(b)[31] and (d)[32] of the *New York Convention*, or may be raised as separate grounds under Art. V(2)(b) on a public policy basis.[33] Other procedural grounds include the violation of equal opportunity to present a case, in regard to which, jurisdictions tend to take a wider or narrower view;[34] fraudulent arbitral awards; arbitral awards obtained through bribery or threats to the arbitrator; and

---

Public Policy as a Bar to Enforcement on International Arbitral Awards (2002), [Recommendation 1(b)]. Reprinted in Pierre Mayer and Audley Sheppard, 'Final ILA Report on Public Policy as a Bar to Enforcement of International Arbitral Awards' (2003) 19(2) *Arbitration International* 246, 250–251.

27 Alan Redfern, 'Comments on Commercial Arbitration and Transnational Public Policy' in Albert Jan van den Berg (ed), *International Arbitration 2006: Back to Basics?* (Kluwer Law International, 2007) 871, 873.

28 Ibid., 875.

29 International Bar Association (IBA) Subcommittee on Recognition and Enforcement of Arbitral Awards, above n 4, 4–5.

30 Garnett, et al., above n 3, 109–111.

31 As noted earlier, Art. V(1)(b) New York Convention provides that an arbitral award may be not be enforced if 'the party against whom the award is invoked was not given proper notice of the appointment of the arbitrator or of the arbitration proceedings or was otherwise unable to present his case.'

32 As noted above, Art. V(1)(d) New York Convention stipulates that 'the composition of the arbitral authority or the arbitral procedure was not in accordance with the agreement of the parties, or, failing such agreement, was not in accordance with the law of the country where the arbitration took place.'

33 International Bar Association (IBA) Subcommittee on Recognition and Enforcement of Arbitral Awards, above n 4, 13.

34 See Chapters 4 and 5. See generally, Mantilla-Serrano, above n 24, 163; Herman Verbist, 'Challenges on Grounds of Due Process Pursuant to Article V(1)(B) of the New York

lack of independence of the arbitrators.[35] Some substantive public policy grounds include: arbitral awards which give effect to illegal activities such as terrorism, drug trafficking, corruption or fraud in international commerce; matters relating to antitrust and competition law; punitive damages; and prohibition of excessive interest and state immunity.[36] This distinction between substantive and procedural public policy is also made in the context of transnational public policy:

> [a]s to the content of substantive transnational public policy, it certainly encompasses the most extreme forms of human conduct that offend public morals. This is a narrow category including prohibitions against activities such as piracy, terrorism, genocide, slavery, smuggling, drug trafficking, bribery and corruption, and paedophilia. In the commercial context substantive transnational public policy may also include the principles of observing obligations ("*pacta sunt servanda*"), the principle of good faith, the prohibition against uncompensated expropriation, the prohibition against discrimination and the protection of those incapable to act.[37]

As will be discussed in more detail in the next section, the *Shari'a* concept of public policy is much wider than the above-mentioned narrow approach taken by most countries.

III Public policy under *Shari'a* and domestic application in GCC and Egypt

As discussed in Chapter 2, the concept of public policy is also recognised under *Shari'a*, and is known as *maslaha* (public interest) and *maqasid al-Shari'a* (higher objectives of *Shari'a*). These two concepts take into consideration the broader social consequences of Islamic law provisions. Classical scholars, such as al-Ghazali, considered *maslaha* a valid concept, if it promoted al-Ghazali's understanding of *maqasid al-Shari'a*. As discussed in Chapter 2 and further as follows, the concept of public policy under *Shari'a* is subjective in nature, since it depends on who is formulating the definition of public policy, and the context in which policy norms are defined. In the context of ICA, contemporary Islamic academics have argued that public policy under *Shari'a* can also be characterised into the categories of procedural and substantive public policy.[38] Procedural public policy under *Shari'a* includes:

   Convention' in Emmanuel Gaillard and Domenico Di Pietro (eds), *Enforcement of Arbitration Agreements and International Arbitral Awards* (Cameron, May 2008) 679, 679.
35 International Bar Association (IBA) Subcommittee on Recognition and Enforcement of Arbitral Awards, above n 4, 14–15.
36 Ibid., 16–17.
37 Bray and Bray, above n 1, 27–28.
38 See generally, Nudrat Majeed, 'Good Faith and Due Process: Lessons from the Shari'ah' (2004) 20(1) *Arbitration International* 97; Samir Saleh, 'The Recognition and Enforcement of Foreign Arbitral Awards in the States of the Arab Middle East' (1985) 1 *Arab Law Quarterly* 19; Mark Wakim, 'Public Policy Concerns Regarding Enforcement of Foreign

1   Equal treatment of the parties[39]
2   Prohibition against the arbitrator making a decision without listening to the plaintiff and defendant[40]
3   Prohibition against an arbitrator making an award without providing parties with the opportunity to submit their case.[41]

Wakim notes that while public policy 'principles are not necessarily found in the *Quran* or *Sunna* . . . they historically constitute the immutable rules of Islamic judicial law.'[42] Yet, as discussed in previous chapters, justice is one of the *maqasid al-Shari'a*, and is prescribed by the Qur'an in numerous verses.[43] The issue, however, is that concepts of 'justice' and 'equality' are subject to a variety of interpretations and as discussed in previous chapters, they are normative values which are often subjective in nature. For example, as noted throughout this book, many contemporary Islamic scholars argue that *Shari'a* rules contrary to notions of justice in the contemporary world should be reinterpreted.[44] Majeed argues that *Shari'a* is consistent with contemporary ICA, because the concepts of due process and *pacta sunt servanda* exist in *Shari'a*.[45] Majeed further states that

> [t]hese principles underpin the approach to dispute resolution as a procedural matter in the *Shari'ah* and have done so from the earliest arbitrations and dispute settlements in Islam to the present day, as well as constituting a critical element in Islamic substantive contract law.[46]

Referring to the concept of *pacta sunt servanda* in *Shari'a*, the following Qur'anic verse is often cited: 'You who believe, fulfil your obligations.'[47] However, the sanctity of contracts needs to be understood in the context of prohibitions under

---

International Arbitral Awards in the Middle East' (2008) 21(1) *New York International Law Review* 1.

39 See Chapter 5 on Evidence and Procedure in Shari'a Arbitration for a comparative discussion on Art. 18 of the UNCITRAL Model Law and Shari'a.

40 Saleh, above n 38, 27.

41 Ibid., 27.

42 Wakim, above n 38, 45.

43 Justice is one of the higher objectives in the Qur'an as stipulated by various verses, such as: 'You who believe, be steadfast in your devotions to God and bear witness impartially: do not let hatred of others lead you away from justice, but adhere to justice, for that is closer to awareness of God.' See, Trans. M. A. S. Abdel Haleem, *The Qur'an* (Oxford University Press, 2004) (Chapter 5, Verse 8). See also Yasir Ibrahim, 'Rashid Rida and Maqasid al-Sharia' (2006) 102/103 *Studia Islamica* 157.

44 For example and as discussed in previous chapters, this includes: Amina Wadud, *Qur'an and Woman* (Oxford University Press, 1999); Fazlur Rahman, *Islam & Modernity: Transformation of an Intellectual Tradition* (The University of Chicago Press, 1982); Khaled Abou El Fadl, *Speaking in God's Name: Islamic Law, Authority and Women* (Oneworld Publications, 2001); Abdullah Saeed, *Reading the Qur'an in the Twenty-First Century: A Contextualist Approach* (Routledge, 2014).

45 Majeed, above n 38, 97–98.

46 Ibid., 98.

47 Haleem, above n 43 (Chapter 5, Verse 1).

Shariʿa, because parties do not have the same autonomy as they would generally have in contemporary ICA.

As Saleh notes,

> [i]t is a fact *[S]hariʿa* law has its set of requisites, abhorrences and ethics which cannot be easily defeated by the agreement of the contracting parties . . . the two restrictive rules of *gharar* . . . and *riba* . . . and public policy as understood in Islam . . . all these have undoubtedly a constraining impact on the concept of freedom of contract with, however, considerable relaxation made possible by contemporary legislation.[48]

While this book does not delve into Islamic contractual law,[49] it does analyse the impact of the prohibition against *riba* and *gharar* on the validity of arbitration agreements and arbitrability (see Chapter 6). Therefore, commentators who argue that *Shariʿa* is compatible with contemporary ICA due to Islamic concepts of due process and *pacta sunt servanda*, need additionally to make clear their understanding of the prohibition of *riba* and *gharar*.

Wakim also observes that '[p]erhaps because of their appeal to universal norms of due process and fairness, Islamic arbitration procedural concerns overlap well with the New York Convention'; however '[w]ith respect to the substantive features of the Islamic concept of public policy, two problems most likely to arise stem from the prohibitions of *riba* and *gharar*.'[50] Nonetheless, as discussed in previous chapters, the prohibition against *riba* and *gharar* is also subject to interpretation, and for this reason, simple interest is considered acceptable in many jurisdictions where *Shariʿa* forms part of the constitution. Similarly, it is important to understand that countries where *Shariʿa* forms part of the national legal system rarely apply *Shariʿa* to refuse enforcement of both domestic and international arbitral awards.

For example, the comparative table (Table 8.1) and comparative graph (Figure 8.1) below provide an overview of foreign and domestic arbitration cases (2004–2015) from Egypt and GCC countries, as reported in Kluwer Arbitration, the IBA Report 2015 and the Summaries of UAE Court Decisions on Arbitrations.[51] It is important to note that while concrete conclusions cannot be made due to the lack of reported decisions available from the region, this section aims

---

48 Emphasis added. Nabil Saleh, 'Forward' in Nayla Comair-Obeid (ed), *The Law of Business Contracts in the Arab Middle East* (Kluwer Law International, 1996) xi–xii.

49 See generally, Nayla Comair-Obeid, *The Law of Business Contracts in the Arab Middle East* (Kluwer Law International, 1996).

50 Wakim, above n 38, 45.

51 Due to the reliability and international reputation of these three sources, this chapter limits its discussion to the cases reported by Kluwer Arbitration, International Bar Association and Graham Lovett, Lara Hammond and Hassan Arab, *Summaries of UAE Courts' Decisions on Arbitration* (ICC Publication, 2013).

Table 8.1 Enforcement of arbitral awards in the GCC and Egypt

GCC Countries and Egypt – Date of accession to NYC (dd/mm/yy)	Number of Cases (2004–2015)	Number of Arbitral Awards Enforced and/or Annulment denied	Enforcement denied and/or annulment accepted (based on Shari'a)	Enforcement denied and/or annulment accepted (non-Shari'a)	Cases where Shari'a considered
UAE[1] (21/08/06)	21	13	0	7	1
Qatar (30/12/02)	8	3[2]	NIL	5[3]	NIL
Oman (25/02/99)	7	4[4]	NIL	3[5]	NIL
Bahrain (6/04/88)	11	7[6]	NIL	4[7]	NIL
Kuwait[8] (28/04/78)	8	5[9]	NIL	3[10]	NIL
Egypt (09/03/59)	47	27[11]	NIL	18[12]	2[13]

1 See Appendix 3 for a list of UAE Table of Enforcement Cases.
2 *Qatar No. 1, ABC LLP v. Joint Venture RST and XYZ,* Supreme Court of Cassation, Petitions Nos. 45 and 49 of 2014, 25 March 2014 reported in Albert Jan van den Berg (ed), 39 Y.B. Comm. Arb 480–482 (Minas Khatchadourian trans, Kluwer Law International); *Parties not indicated,* Court of First Instance of Qatar, Case No. 2768/2012, 24 June 2013, (2015) 7(1) *International Journal of Arab Arbitration.* 47–50; *Parties not indicated,* Court of First Instance of Qatar, Case No. 1413/2007, 26 November 2008, (2009) 1(3) *International Journal of Arab Arbitration,* 249–251.
3 *'R' Company for Trade Projects Management v. Mr. 'J,' Court of Cassation of Qatar,* Petition No. 211 of 2014, 9 December 2014, ITA Board of Reporters, (Minas Khatchadourian trans, Kluwer Law International); *Contracting Co. A v. Sub-Contracting Co. B,* Court of First Instance of Doha, Case No. 2216, 17 December 2013, ITA Board of Reporters, Kluwer Law International; *Abnaa El Khalaf Company et al. v. Sayed Aga Jawwed Raza,* Court of Cassation of Qatar, 12 June 2012, ITA Board of Reporters, (Minas Khatchadourian trans, Kluwer Law International); *Parties Not Indicated,* Case No. 137/CDFI, Court of First Instance of Doha, (2012) 4(2) *International Journal of Arab Arbitration* 87–88; *International Trading and Industrial Investment Co. v. Dyncorp Aerospace Technology,* 763 F. Supp. 2d 12 (D.D.C. 2011).
4 *Parties not indicated,* Supreme Court of Oman, Cassation No. 280/2010, Commercial Circuit, 27 April 2011, (2014) 1(1) *BCDR International Arbitration Review* 149–158; *Parties not indicated,* Court of Appeal, Commercial, 34/2009, 27 April 2009, (2009) 1(3) *International Journal of Arab Arbitration* 245–246; *Parties not indicated,* Court of Cassation, Decision No. 136/2005, 21 December 2005, (2010) 2(4) *International Journal of Arab Arbitration* 101–104; *Parties not indicated,* Court of Appeal of Muscat, Decision No. 628/2013, (2015) 7(1) *International Journal of Arab Arbitration* 43–45.
5 *Parties not indicated,* Court of Cassation, Case No. 174/2005, 31 December 2005, (2011) 3(2) *International Journal of Arab Arbitration,* 77–79; *Company Body Light Industries Limited v. Company Asbagh Sadoline,* High Court in the Sultanate of Oman, 221/2005, 17 October 2005, (2009) 1(1) *International Journal of Arab Arbitration* 417–418. Cf. Abdallah Ben Mohamed Saidi, 'Note – 17 May 2006, High Court' (2009) 1(1) *International Journal of Arab Arbitration* 418–421; *The New Indian Company for Insurance v. The vessel M V IKO and the company Tawel Barwil,* Commercial Circuit, 70/2004, 8 December 2004, (2009) 1(1) *International Journal of Arab Arbitration,* 427–428.

(*Continued*)

Table 8.1 (Continued)

6 *Parties not indicated*, Court of Cassation of Bahrain, Audience No. 108/2012, 21 January 2013, (2014) 6(3) *International Journal of Arab Arbitration* 13–16; *Parties not indicated*, Court of Cassation of Bahrain (Second Circuit), Challenge No. 259/2009, 4 May 2010, (2011) 3(4) *International Journal of Arab Arbitration*, 29–33; *Establishment v. Limited Liability Company*, Court of Cassation of Bahrain, Fourth High Civil Court, Case No. 02/2009/9679/9, 10 February 2010 and Court of Cassation of Bahrain, Third High Civil Court, Appeal No. 03/2010/540/9, 24 November 2010 and Court of Cassation of Bahrain, First Court of Cassation, Cassation No. 746 for the Year 2010, 12 March 2012 (2013) 38 Y.B. Comm. Arb 574–576; *Parties Not Indicated*, Supreme Court, Case No. 241/2008, 17 November 2008, (2011) 3(2) *International Journal of Arab Arbitration* 36–37; *Parties Not Indicated*, Supreme Court, Case No. 75/2007, 7 January 2008, (2011) 3 (2)) *International Journal of Arab Arbitration* 33–35; *Parties not indicated*, Court of Cassation, 328/2005, 30 January 2006, (2010) 2(2) *International Journal of Arab Arbitration* 112–114; *Parties not indicated*, Court of Cassation, 165/2005, 3 October 2005, (2009) 1(3) *International Journal of Arab Arbitration* 65–67.
7 *Parties not indicated*, Court of Cassation of Bahrain, Challenge No. 101 of 2010, 2 April 2012, (2013) 5(3) *International Journal of Arab Arbitration*, 37–39; *Parties not indicated*, Court of Cassation of Bahrain, 156/2004, 4 July 2005, 1(4) *International Journal of Arab Arbitration* 139–140; *Parties not indicated*, Court of Cassation of Bahrain, 305/2004, 9 May 2005, (2009) 1(4) *International Journal of Arab Arbitration* 137–138; *Parties not indicated*, Court of Cassation of Bahrain, 78/2003, 16 February 2004, (2010) 2(1) *International Journal of Arab Arbitration* 105–106.
8 See also Saad Badah, 'The Enforcement of Foreign Arbitral Awards in the GCC Countries: Focus on Kuwait' (2014) 3(1) *International Law Research* 24.
9 *Parties not indicated*, Court of Cassation (Second Commercial Circuit) Case No. 47/2008, 4 January 2009, (2011) 3(2) *International Journal of Arab Arbitration*, 57–59; *Parties not indicated*, Court of First Instance, 28 December 2008, (2010) 2(4) *International Journal of Arab Arbitration* 81–82; *Parties not indicated*, Court of Cassation (Commercial), 668/2006, 10 February 2008, (2009) 1(3) *International Journal of Arab Arbitration* 171–173; *Parties not indicated*, Court of Appeals (First Judicial Arbitral Tribunal, 20 December 2006, (2010) 2(2) *International Journal of Arab Arbitration* 145–147; *Parties not indicated*, Court of Cassation (Commercial Circuit) 671/2004, 23 November 2006, (2009) 1(2) *International Journal of Arab Arbitration*, 168–174.
10 *Parties Not Indicated*, Court of Appeal of Kuwait (Judicial Arbitration Tribunal), Request for Arbitration No. 16/2001, 8 May 2008, (2009) 1(4) *International Journal of Arab Arbitration* 173–178; *Company for International Investment v. holding company 'Al Bab,'* Court of Cassation, (2nd Commercial Circuit) 773/2006, 6 April 2008, (2009) 1(1) *International Journal of Arab Arbitration* 269–271; *Parties Not Indicated*, Court of Cassation – Civil Circuit, 511/2005, 13 February 2006, (2010) 2(3) *International Journal of Arab Arbitration* 139–141. See also Mohamed Al Tuwayjri, 'Note – 13 February 2006, Court of Cassation – Civil Circuit,' (2010) 2(3) *International Journal of Arab Arbitration*, 142–147.
11 *Parties not indicated*, Court of Appeal of Cairo, Case No. 23/128, 4 August 2014, (2015) 7(1) *International Journal of Arab Arbitration* 19–21; *Parties not indicated*, Court of Appeal of Cairo, Case No. 48/130, 2 June 2014, 6(4) *International Journal of Arab Arbitration* 23–28; *Parties not indicated*, Court of Appeal of Cairo, Case No. 13/128, 20 April 2014, 7(1) *International Journal of Arab Arbitration* 22–28; *Parties not indicated*, Court of Appeal of Cairo, Arbitration Case No. 32/128j, 6 June 2012, (2013) 5(2) *International Journal of Arab Arbitration* 11–14; *Parties not indicated*, Court of Appeal of Cairo, Case No. 38/128J, 8 January 2012, 4(4) *International Journal of Arab Arbitration* 29–32; *Parties not indicated*, Court of Appeal of Cairo, Case No. 43/128j, 2 November 2011, (2012) 4(3) *International Journal of Arab Arbitration*, 54–56; *Parties not indicated*, Court of Appeal of Cairo, Case No. 4/128N, 7 September 2011, (2013) 5(1) *International Journal of Arab Arbitration* 37–38; *Parties not indicated*, Court of Appeal of Cairo, Case No. 59/125 (2012) 4(2) *International Journal of Arab Arbitration* 74–76; *Parties not indicated*, Court of Appeal of Cairo (Seventh Circuit), Commercial Arbitration No. 70/123j, 9 March 2011, 3(4) *International Journal of Arab Arbitration* 35–41; *Parties not indicated*, Court of Appeal of Cairo, Case No. 10/127j, 4 January 2011, (2012) 4(1) *International Journal of Arab Arbitration* 21–26; *Sobhy Hussein Ahmed (Contractor) v. Cooperative*

Association of Construction and Housing for the employees of a petroleum company 'Suez Gulf' (Owner), Cairo Court of Appeal, 7th Commercial Circuit, 102/123, 9 June 2009, (2009) 3(1) *International Journal of Arab Arbitration* 71–74; *Parties not indicated*, Cairo Court of Appeals (Seventh Commercial Circuit) 112/124, 5 May 2009, (2010) 2(10) *International Journal of Arab Arbitration* 109–112; *Parties not indicated*, Cairo Court of Appeals, Seventh Commercial Circuit, 29/125, 29/125, 5 May 2009, (2010) 2(1) *International Journal of Arab Arbitration* 120–122; *Parties not indicated*, Cairo Court of Appeal, Seventh Commercial Division, 55/122, 7 April 2009, (2009) 1(4) *International Journal of Arab Arbitration* 141–142; *Mr. Muhammad Aly Muhammad Muhammad el Bari in his capacity as the legal representative of the company Brother for Import Export and supply v. Mr. Thai Jin Yang, president of the South Korean company Hano Acorporish*, Court of Appeal (7th Economic Circuit) 23/125, 2 July 2008, (2009) 1(2) *International Journal of Arab Arbitration* 113–117; *Parties not indicated*, Court of Cassation, 13 February 2014, Case No 7595/81; *Mr. Mounir Ghabour Hannah v. American International Group (AIG)*, Cairo Court of Appeals, 62nd Circuit, Commercial, 70/123, 7 May 2008, (2009) 1(1) *International Journal of Arab Arbitration* 183–189; *Parties not indicated*, Supreme Court, Commercial Division, 9736/65, 11 March 2008, (2009) 1(4) *International Journal of Arab Arbitration* 143–144; *Parties not indicated*, Supreme Court, Commercial Division, 730/76, 8 February 2008, (2009) 1(4) *International Journal of Arab Arbitration* 150–157 and Cairo Court of Appeal (Commercial Court) No. 91, 26 April 2006, Case No 49/133; *Lieutenant, President of the Board of the Cooperative association for the lieutenants of the Armed Forces v. Mr. Kamal Abdel Aziz el Zouhayri*, Cairo Court of Appeals, 7th Economic Circuit, 71/123, 5 February 2008, (2009) 1(1) *International Journal of Arab Arbitration* 248–252; *Parties not indicated*, Supreme Court of Cassation, Commercial Division, 2010/64, 22 January 2008, 1(4) *International Journal of Arab Arbitration*, 145–147; *Horus for Shipping and Navigation Company v. Ergo Shipping S.A., Court of Appeals*, Circuit 91, Commercial, 92/123, 16 January 2008, (2009) 1(2) *International Journal of Arab Arbitration* 125–132; *Karim Abou Youssef, Amal Tourism Complex Co. v. Ministry of Tourism, Court of Cassation*, 4721/73, 27 December 2007, *ITA Board of Reporters*, (Kluwer Law International); *Saudi-Egyptian company for Touristic Development v. Meridian S.A.*, Cairo Court of Appeal, 7th Economic Circuit, 123/119, 3 April 2007, (2009) 1(2) *International Journal of Arab Arbitration* 141–148; *Parties not indicated*, Court of Appeal – Cairo – Seventh Commercial Circuit, 119/124, 2 February 2010, 2(3) *International Journal of Arab Arbitration* 114–119. See also *Parties not indicated* Cairo Court of Appeal, Commercial Circuit No 7, Cases No 35, 41, 44, 45/129, 5 February 2013; Cairo Court of Appeal, Commercial Circuit No.8, 15 February 2015 – recourse against Exequatur Order No 18/126; Cairo Court of Appeal, Commercial Circuit No 7, 7 April 2013; Cases No 20, 64/128 and 16,20, 47/129 as reported in Ismail Selim, *Report on Egyptian Public Policy as a Ground for Annulment and/or Refusal of Enforcement of Arbitral Awards*, (2015) < www.ibanet.org/LPD/Dispute_Resolution_Section/Arbitra tion/Recogntn_Enfrcemnt_Arbitl_Awrd/publicpolicy15.aspx >.

12 *Parties not indicated*, Cairo Court of Appeal – Seventh Commercial Circuit, 33/124j; 30/124j; 33/123j, 2 February 2010, (2011) 3(1) *International Journal of Arab Arbitration* 65–67; *Parties not indicated*, Court of Cassation – Civil and Commercial Circuit, 98/79j, 24 December 2009, (2011) 3(1) *International Journal of Arab Arbitration* 68–70; *Parties not indicated*, Cairo Court of Appeal, Eighth Circuit, Commercial, 75/125, 18 May 2009, (2010) 2(1) *International Journal of Arab Arbitration* 136–138; *Parties not indicated*, Cairo Court of Appeal – Eighth Commercial Circuit, 28 February 2009, (2010) 2(4) *International Journal of Arab Arbitration* 67–70; *Parties not indicated*, Cairo Court of Appeals (Seventh Commercial Circuit) 114/124, 2 December 2008, (2010) 2(1) *International Journal of Arab Arbitration* 126–127; *Parties not indicated*, Cairo Court of Appeals (62nd Circuit, Commercial) 462/2005, 7 May 2008, (2009) 1(1) *International Journal of Arab Arbitration* 204–208; *Mr. Eid Muhammad Eid Ibrahim, Mr. Ossama Muhammad Eid Ibrahim v. Mr. Himam Sayed Othman Sanad, Mr. Ahmad Abdel Al Farhat Hmad and others*, Cairo Court of Appeals, 7th Circuit, Economy, 140/124, 6 May 2008, (2009) 1(2) *International Journal of Arab Arbitration* 209–212; *Customs Authority v. Islamic company for imports and exports*, Cairo Court of Appeals, 8th Circuit, 91 Commercial, 102/124, 22 April 2008, (2009) 1(1) *International Journal of Arab Arbitration* 190–193; *Miss Fatima Muhammad Metwaly v. Mr. Muhammad Salah el Dine Muhammad Metwali, Miss Wafak Hanem Muhammad Metwali and others*, Cairo Court of Appeals, 62nd Circuit, Commercial, 29/2004,

(*Continued*)

Table 8.1 (Continued)

6 March 2008, (2009) 1(1) *International Journal of Arab Arbitration* 180–182; *Mr. Korni Muhammad Farjani, Mr. Hussein Ali Farjani and others v. Mr. Muhammad Abdel Raouf Muhammad el Wahesh, Mr. Jamal Fawzi Ali el Wahesh and others*, Cairo Court of Appeals, 91st Circuit, Commercial, 21/124, 13 February 2008, (2009) 1(1) *International Journal of Arab Arbitration* 237–242; *Mr. Muhammad Abdel Kawi Ahmad Mokbel, Mr. Ahmad Abdel Kawi Ahmad Mokbel and others v. Mr. Adel Abdel Majid Abdel Latif, Mr. Muhammad Mahmoud Metwali and others*, Cairo Court of Appeals, Jizza Department, 91st Circuit, Commercial, 110/124, 2 February 2008, (2009) 1(1) *International Journal of Arab Arbitration* 195–198; *Mrs. Fayqa Mahmoud Al-Dasouki Zaqzaq v. Mr. Ahmad Fouad Ali Ahmad Ali, Mr. Yusri Mahmoud Saadedine Ahmad and others*, Cairo Court of Appeals, Department of Giza, Circuit (91), Commercial, 37/123, 16 January 2008, (2009) 1(2) *International Journal of Arab Arbitration* 133–140; *Alexandria for Soaps and Oils v. Alexandria for Navigation Procurements (Amoun Procurement for Navigation)*, Court of Cassation, Commercial Circuit, 607/63, 27 March 2007, 1(1) *International Journal of Arab Arbitration* 213–216; *Rila Netex for touristic town v. Agro Trade Company for reclamation of lands*, Court of Cassation, Commercial Circuit, 10635/1976, 27 February 2007, 1(2) *International Journal of Arab Arbitration* 93–96; *Mr. Wael Ali Moussa, Mrs. Fatima Muhammad Sleiman and others v. Dr. Kamal el Dine Abdel Rahman Darwish, Dr. Oueiss Ali el Jabali*, Cairo court of Appeals, Jizza Circuit, 91st Commercial Division, 23/2005, 1 October 2005, (2009) 1(1) *International Journal of Arab Arbitration* 199–203; *Parties not indicated*, Court of Cassation – Commercial Circuit, 2414/72, 22 March 2005, (2010) 2(3) *International Journal of Arab Arbitration* 97–99; See also cases reported in ibid: Cairo Court of Appeal, Commercial Circuit No.91, 27 April 2005, Case No. 95/120; Cairo Court of Appeal, Commercial Circuit, No. 91, 29 January 2006, Cases No. 13 et 14/121. Cairo Court of Appeal, Commercial Circuit No. 91 30 May 2006 No. 43 et 89/122; Cairo Court of Appeal, Economic Circuit No. 7, 2 July 2007 No.68/123; Court of Cassation, Commercial and Economic Circuit, 8 October 2013, Challenge No. 9882/80.

13 *Shari'a* was not explicitly mentioned; partial annulment of excessive interest aspect of the arbitral award. See discussion as follows.

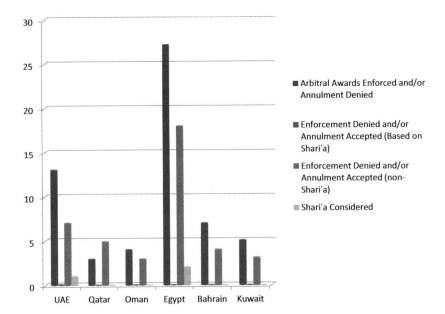

Figure 8.1 Enforcement of arbitral awards in the GCC and Egypt

to highlight common themes from those international and domestic arbitration cases which are available from reputable sources.

By way of illustration, in the UAE, only one case (out of the 21 cases considered in this chapter) applies *Shari'a* public policy in a domestic arbitration relating to an insurance claim between two natural persons.[52] Therefore, the one case that considered *Shari'a* was not in the context of international commercial arbitration. This is despite the fact that, as mentioned above, Arts. 2 and 3 of the *UAE Civil Transactions* law refer to *Shari'a* as forming part of UAE's public policy. The UAE courts also take a narrow approach to international public policy as opposed to domestic public policy, in order to uphold a pro-arbitration attitude and attract international business to the country.[53] For example, there is the UAE case of *Airmech Dubai LLC v. Maxtel International LLC*,[54] where the Petitioner argued that the arbitral award contained interest and was contrary to *Shari'a*. This argument was rejected by the UAE Court of Cassation. The Court held that UAE Civil Procedure Codes which limit interest rates do not apply to foreign arbitral awards, because the UAE is a signatory to the *New York Convention*. It was also noted that UAE law only prohibited interest between natural persons.[55] This case further ruled:

> Article 238 of the Civil Procedure Code provides that international conventions that have become enforceable in the UAE by virtue of their ratification shall apply to disputes concerning the enforcement of foreign court decisions and arbitral awards as domestic law.[56]

The significance of enforcing foreign arbitral awards due to the *New York Convention* was also emphasised in *United Arab Emirates No. 1, Shipowners v. Charterers*.[57] In this particular case, the UAE Court of First Instance enforced two arbitral awards issued by the London Maritime Arbitrators Association on the basis that the *New York Convention* had been adopted by the UAE. The Court also ruled that it does not reconsider the merits of foreign arbitral awards.[58]

---

52 Parties Not Indicated, Dubai Court of Cassation, 146/2008, 9 November 2008 reported in (2010) 2(3) *International Journal of Arab Arbitration* 240; Hassan Arab and Laila El Shentenawi, *The UAE Country Report* (2015) <www.ibanet.org/LPD/Dispute_Resolution_Sec tion/Arbitration/Recogntn_Enfrcemnt_Arbitl_Awrd/publicpolicy15.aspx> 94–96.

53 Ibid., 6.

54 Court of Cassation of Dubai, Appeal No. 132 of 2012, 18 September 2012 reported in (2013) 5(1) *International Journal of Arab Arbitration*, 52 and Graham Lovett, Lara Hammond and Hassan Arab, *Summaries of UAE Courts' Decisions on Arbitration* (ICC Publication, 2013) 123–124.

55 Ibid.

56 Ibid.

57 United Arab Emirates No. 1, Shipowners v. Charterers, Court of First Instance, Fujairah, 27 April 2010 (2011) 36 Y.B. Comm. Arb 353.

58 Ibid.

Similarly, Egypt generally takes a pro-enforcement attitude towards foreign arbitral awards, due to the ratification of the New York Convention, which overrides its domestic law.[59] The Egyptian Court of Cassation ruled:

> If Egypt has joined the New York [C]onvention related to the recognition and enforcement of foreign awards of 1958 with a presidential decree n°171 of 1959 rendered on 2 February 1959, then it becomes an enforceable legislation as of 8 June 1959 and is considered as one of the laws of the State even if it contradicts national arbitration laws.[60]

Only two Egyptian cases (out of the 47 reported cases noted in this chapter) consider *Shari'a* generally when discussing the award of interest. For example, in *Andritz v. National Cement Co,*[61] National Cement Company ('the Respondent') sought annulment of the ICC arbitral award rendered in 1999, which required it to reimburse Andritz ('the Plaintiff') for letters of guarantees which the Plaintiff claimed had not been properly executed. The reimbursement included the value of the letters of guarantee, and interest which was calculated in accordance with the LIBOR plus 3% per annum from 7 April 1998 until the date of payment.[62] Although *Shari'a* was not mentioned in the judgement, the Court of Cassation overturned the Court of Appeal's decision to annul the entire arbitral award, and noted that the excessive interest rate aspect of the arbitral award could be annulled, but that the remainder of the award enforced. This was because the total interest awarded exceeded the maximum rate of 7% as per Art. 227 of the Civil Code. Commenting on the case of *Andritz v. National Cement Co*, Wahab observes that the 7% cap only applies if Egyptian law is the applicable law, and under Egyptian domestic public policy, as opposed to international or transnational public policy, since:

> while under Islamic law payment of interest is prohibited and considered a principle of public policy, the Egyptian rule restricting interest to 7% or less . . . is considered a domestic mandatory rule. Thus, it should not be

59 Amr Elatter, *Enforcement of International Arbitration Awards: A Comparative Study Between Egypt, USA, and the Gulf Cooperation Council Countries* (Lambert Academic Publishing, 2013) 53–55.
60 Egypt for Foreign Trade v. R.D. Harbottles (Mercantile) Case No. 64/2010, Court of Cassation, Commercial Circuit, 22 January 2008, 1(1) *International Journal of Arab Arbitration* 174.
61 Case No. 810/71, Supreme Court of Cassation, Commercial and Civil Division, 25 January 2008 reported in (2009) 1(4) *International Journal of Arab Arbitration* 148 and Ismail Selim, *Report on Egyptian Public Policy as a Ground for Annulment and/or Refusal of Enforcement of Arbitral Awards* (2015) <www.ibanet.org/LPD/Dispute_Resolution_Sec tion/Arbitration/Recogntn_Enfrcemnt_Arbitl_Awrd/publicpolicy15.aspx>.
62 Shalakany Law Office, 'Interest Rates and Arbitral Awards: Issues of Public Policy' (30 October 2008) <www.internationallawoffice.com/Newsletters/Arbitration-ADR/Egypt/Shala kany-Law-Office/Interest-Rates-and-Arbitral-Awards-Issues-of-Public-Policy?redir=1>.

applicable in transnational transactions where the applicable law is a foreign law. On such account, it is hoped that in future rulings Egyptian courts will acknowledge the domestic nature of the interest rate cap, as its elevation to a public policy principle in the context of private international law cannot be justified.[63]

Similarly, in another case, the Egyptian Court of Cassation partially annulled the interest aspect of the arbitral award, because the late payment interest rate was awarded at the rate of the Egyptian Central Bank, as opposed to the maximum rate under the *Egyptian Civil Code*.[64] Therefore, these two cases indicate that arbitral awards consisting of simple interest at the maximum rate of 7% are enforceable, and in the event that the interest rate exceeds the simple interest rate of 7%, Egyptian courts have the discretion to either sever the excessive interest (in which case the application of *Shari'a* may be considered), or enforce the arbitral award inclusive of the excessive interest (in which case *Shari'a* is ignored).[65] The latter approach is used for foreign arbitral awards due to Egypt's general pro-enforcement attitude. Selim notes that Egyptian public policy:

neither refers to Islamic *Shari'a* nor to international public policy. Indeed, since the middle of the twentieth century, Egyptian law and jurisprudence have adopted the well-known dual approach by distinguishing between a domestic conception of public policy and an international one pertinent to conflict of laws and extendable, mutatis mutandis, to recognition and enforcement of foreign judgements and foreign and international arbitral awards.[66]

However, despite the recent pro-enforcement attitude of many Muslim countries, many commentators have a cynical view of enforcement of foreign arbitration awards in these countries. This is due to historical non-enforcement of foreign arbitral awards on grounds that generally do not confirm to international practice,[67] or even more recent cases, such as arbitral awards which were not rendered in the name of the Emir in Qatar (as discussed above),[68] or real estate

63 Ibid.
64 Court of Cassation, Commercial Circuit, 22 March 2011, Challenge No. 12790/75 reported in Selim, Report on Egyptian Public Policy, above n 61.
65 Ibid., 4. Egypt also distinguishes between international public policy and domestic public policy.
66 Ismail Selim, 'Public Policy Exception as Applied by the Courts of the MENA Region' in United Nations Commission on International Trade Law (ed), *Second Conference for a Euro-Mediterranean Community of International Arbitration*, Cairo, 12 November 2015 (UNCITRAL, 2015) 32.
67 Arthur Gemmell, 'Commercial Arbitration in the Middle East' (2006) 5 *Santa Clara Journal of International Law* 169, 188.
68 Abnaa El Khalaf Company, et al. v. Sayed Aga Jawwed Raza, Qatar Court of Cassation, Petition No. 64/2012, 12 June 2012 (trans, Minas Khatchadourian, Kluwer Law International); Contracting Co. A v. Sub-Contracting Co. B, Qatar Court of First Instance Ruling, Decision No. 2216 of 2013, 7 December 2013.

disputes in the UAE.[69] The lack of enforcement is concerning as it ultimately defeats the objective of the *New York Convention* and in turn, the arbitration processes itself.[70] However, as noted earlier and as indicated by Table 8.1 and Figure 8.1, if recent trends noted in the reported cases discussed in this chapter accurately reflect reality, then one can conclude that the above-mentioned jurisdictions are beginning to respect the enforcement of foreign arbitral awards. Nevertheless, the situation is more complex in Saudi Arabia, as will be discussed in more detail as follows.

IV Saudi Arabia

Saudi Arabia acceded to the *New York Convention* on 19 April 1994. Saudi Arabia entered into a reciprocity reservation limiting the obligations of recognition and enforcement of arbitral awards to countries that are also signatories of the *New York Convention*.[71] It is also a signatory to the following conventions:

- Arab Convention on the Enforcement of Foreign Judgements and Arbitral Awards ('*Arab League Convention*');
- Riyadh Convention on Judicial Cooperation;
- The Amman Arab Convention on Commercial Arbitration;
- The Convention on the Settlement of Investment Disputes between States and Nationals of other States.[72]

As well as being signatory to these conventions, Saudi Arabia has also been a party to a number of ICC Disputes.[73] Yet, it has the reputation of being a jurisdiction in which it is extremely difficult to enforce foreign arbitral awards.[74] Baamir

---

69 *Parties Not Indicated*, Court of Cassation of Dubai, Case No. 320 of 2013, 22 June 2014, reported in (2015) 7(1) *International Journal of Arab Arbitration* 81 (Enforcement denied because Art. 3 of Law No. 13 of 2008 regulating the Interim Real Estate Register in the UAE provides that sales or transfers will be void if not recorded with the Register. Therefore, the matter is against public policy and the arbitral award is invalid/not enforced).

70 Shaistah Akhtar, 'Arbitration in the Islamic Middle East: Challenges and the Way Ahead' (2008) *International Comparative Legal Guides* <http://www.iclg.co.uk/index. php?area=4&show_chapter=2201&ifocus=1&kh_publications_id=83> 11.

71 New York Arbitration Convention, *The New York Arbitration Convention on the Recognition and Enforcement of Foreign Arbitral Awards 10 June 1958* <www.newyorkconvention.org/countries>.

72 Jean-Benoît Zegers, 'Recognition and Enforcement of Foreign Arbitral Awards in Saudi Arabia' (2014) 1(1) *BCDR International Arbitration Review* 69, 75–77.

73 International Chamber of Commerce, '2008 Statistical Report' (2009) 20(1) *ICC International Commercial Arbitration Bulletin* 5.

74 See generally, Kristin Roy, 'The New York Convention and Saudi Arabia: Can a Country Use the Public Policy Defense to Refuse Enforcement of Non-Domestic Arbitral Awards?' (1994) 18 *Fordham International Law Journal* 920; see also, Wakim, above n 38; Thomas Carbonneau, 'The Ballad of Transborder Arbitration' (2002) 56(4) *University of Miami Law Review* 773, 794.

notes that 'Saudi courts might enforce foreign arbitral awards or judgments on the basis of reciprocity; however, the application of this concept is still a matter of theoretical argument.'[75] One of the reasons for this may be because public policy in Saudi Arabia is based on customs and morals derived from *Shari'a*.[76]

Furthermore, as discussed in previous chapters, although judges have the discretion to apply any of the four schools of thought within *Shari'a*, the majority of judges in Saudi courts tend to apply the Hanbali school of law, which can often lead to a narrow interpretation of *Shari'a*.[77] That said, judges have the discretion to reject a narrow interpretation of *Shari'a*, such as the view that only men can act as arbitrators. Harb and Leventhal note that

> [t]he new arbitration [L]aw represents a moderni[s]ation of the arbitral regime in the Kingdom of Saudi Arabia while remaining in the context of the Hanbali madhhab of Islamic fiqh . . . [n]onetheless, the new Law represents a more liberal approach to arbitration . . . the new Saudi arbitration Law embodies several "arbitration-friendly" principles of the UNICTRAL Model Law such as the competence-competence and separability, harmonising the Hanbali-based law with international tenets of arbitration law.[78]

On the other hand, Roy argues:

> [a]s Saudi Arabian law and policy is diametrically opposed to the rules and laws of many member nations, Saudi Arabian courts may find it easy to reject non-domestic arbitral awards pursuant to *New York Convention* Article V(2)(B). In essence, Saudi Arabia may not be required to enforce any more non-domestic arbitral awards than it did prior to its 1994 accession to the *New York Convention*.[79]

Although Roy's paper precedes the introduction of the recent 2012/2013 arbitration reforms in Saudi Arabia, the difficulty of enforcing foreign arbitral awards in Saudi Arabia is also noted in the 2014 IBA Arbitration Guide, in which Zezers and Elzorkany observe that '[n]otwithstanding that KSA [Kingdom of Saudi Arabia] acceded to the *New York Convention*, awards rendered outside KSA are still notoriously difficult to enforce in KSA.'[80]

---

75 Abdulrahman Yahya Baamir, *Saudi Law and Judicial Practice in Commercial and Banking Arbitration* (PhD Thesis, Brunel University, 2008).

76 Ibid., 180.

77 Dr. Abdullah F. Ansary, 'A Brief Overview of the Saudi Arabian Legal System' (2015) <www.nyulawglobal.org/globalex/Saudi_Arabia1.html>.

78 Jean-Pierre Harb and Alexander G. Leventhal, 'The New Saudi Arbitration Law: Modernization to the Tune of Shari'a' (2013) 30 *Journal of International Arbitration* 113, 129.

79 Roy, above n 74, 954.

80 Jean-Benoît Zegers and Omar Elzorkany, *Kingdom of Saudi Arabia, International Bar Association* (2014) <www.ibanet.org/Article/Detail.aspx?ArticleUid=a646cf32-0ad8-4666-876b-c3d045028e64> 5.

As discussed in Chapter 2, Saudi Arabia recently introduced the new *Saudi Enforcement Law 2013*, which replaces Art. 13(g) of the *Board of Grievances Law* (1 October 2007).[81] This new law establishes an independent enforcement court as part of the Royal Order issued in 2015, which overhauled the previous judicial system and established a court system.[82] Under the previous system, Art. 20 of the Implementing Regulations of the old *Saudi Arbitration Law 1983* gave the Board of Grievances power to ratify the arbitral award, by stating that 'the arbitrator's award shall be applicable when it is final by order of the entity which is primarily competent to look into the dispute.'[83] This meant that the Board of Grievances considered objections raised by any party in relation to the arbitral award, as well as dealing with general commercial law matters. In the event that the arbitral award was found to be against public policy or *Shariʿa*, and the country where the arbitral award was issued did not accord reciprocal treatment of judgements of Saudi courts, the Board of Grievances could refuse to enforce the foreign arbitral award.[84] As will be discussed in further detail, in some cases the Board of Grievances reconsidered the merits of the arbitral award, despite the fact that in 1985, the President of the Board of Grievances issued a Board Circular noting that the Board would not reconsider or review the subject matter of the arbitral award.[85]

On the other hand, the new *Saudi Enforcement Law 2013* establishes independent enforcement judges, who will deal solely with the enforcement of arbitration awards.[86] Theoretically, under Art. 11 of the new *Saudi Enforcement Law 2013*, the courts are not to reconsider the merits of the dispute. Art. 11 stipulates the following:

a) Kingdom Courts are not authorised to discuss any dispute already ordered or adjudged, providing that any such discussion shall be restricted to foreign court who takes decision or judgement, as per international jurisdiction rules applicable by their laws.

81 Jean-Benoît Zegers, 'National Report for Saudi Arabia (2013)' in Jan Paulsson and Lise Bosman (eds), *ICCA International Handbook on Commercial Arbitration* (Kluwer Law International, Supplement No. 75, July 2013, 1984) 1, 77.

82 Ansary, above n 77.

83 Saud Al-Ammari and Timothy Martin, 'Arbitration in the Kingdom of Saudi Arabia' (2014) 30(2) *Arbitration International* 387, 401. The power to enforce foreign judgements was also decreed by the Board of Grievances, Royal Decree Number M/51, 10 May 1982.

84 Art. 6 of Rules of Civil Procedure (Saudi Arabia), Board of Grievances, Council of Ministers Resolution Number 190, 20 June 1989 cited in Alexander Kritzalis, 'Saudi Arabia' in Dennis Campbell (ed.), *International Execution Against Judgment Debtors Vol. 2* (Sweet & Maxwell, 1993) SAU-6.

85 Circular Number 7 of the President of the Board of Grievances, 5 May 1985 cited in ibid., SAU-8.

86 Jones Day, 'The New Enforcement Law of Saudi Arabia: An Additional Step Toward a Harmonized Arbitration Regime' (September 2013) <www.jonesday.com/the-new-enforcement-law-of-saudi-arabia-an-additional-step-toward-a-harmonized-arbitration-regime-09-04-2013/>.

[In respect of enforcement of the decision or judgement, it is required that]:

b) Parties of any adjudged lawsuit are summoned to attend, are represented lawfully, and were provided necessary time to provide their defense.
c) Judgement or order becomes final according to regulations of issuing court.
d) Judgement or order doesn't conflict with any other judgement or order issued for the same subject from any other competent judicial authority in the Kingdom.
e) Judgement or order doesn't violate public laws applicable in the Kingdom.[87]

Nevertheless, many commentators argue that despite the new *Saudi Enforcement Law 2013*, in practice, '[f]oreign awards may be subjected to a *de novo* review by the Saudi court of competent jurisdiction, which will also apply Saudi law to the substance of the dispute and perhaps review factual determinations before enforcement is possible.'[88] Law firm, Jones Day, also argues that the new *Saudi Enforcement Law 2013* 'in theory, guarantee[s] that the merits of the dispute will not be revisited. However, it remains to be seen what effect these provisions will have in practice.'[89]

Enforcement can also be refused under Art. 11 of the Saudi Enforcement Law if the arbitral award is against public policy in Saudi Arabia, and Art. 50(2) stipulates that the court can set aside an arbitral award if it is found to contravene 'the provisions of the *Sharia* Law, or the Kingdom's public policy.' In regards to enforcement, Art. 55 of the new *Saudi Arbitration Law 2012* further states that an arbitral award shall not violate the provisions of '*Shari'a* and general regulation in the Kingdom.' Nonetheless with reference to interest, Art. 55 of the New Law notes that it is possible to sever the non *Shari'a*-compliant part of the arbitral award (such as the award of interest), and thus enforce the remainder of the award. As noted in the previous chapter, interest or *riba* is forbidden under *Shari'a* and Saudi law, and only damages in the nature of compensation for losses arising from late/non-payment (as discussed in Chapter 7) can be awarded. Historically, Saudi courts have been inconsistent in their approach to arbitral awards with an interest component. In some cases, the interest aspect of the award has been severed and the remainder of the award has been enforced. In other cases, the entire arbitral award has been refused enforcement. The two approaches are discussed below.

A *Non-enforcement of arbitral awards containing interest*

In the highly publicised case of *Jadawel International v. Emaar Properties PJSC*, a dispute arose in 2006 between the Saudi company ('Jadawel') and the UAE

---

87 Royal Decree No. M/53 (legislation date 3 July 2012, published in the official Saudi Gazette (Um Al-Qura) on 31 August 2012 and came into effect on 27 February 2013).
88 Zegers and Elzorkany, above n 80, 5.
89 Jones Day, above n 86.

company ('Emaar') in regards to a conditional joint venture in Saudi Arabia.[90] Jadawel claimed that Emaar had breached the joint venture by agreeing to conduct business with another company.[91] Emaar argued that the joint venture agreement was conditional upon approval from its board of directors and relevant UAE authorities.[92] In 2008, Jadawel issued arbitration proceedings with the ICC, and an arbitral tribunal (consisting of three Saudi arbitrators) found the joint venture agreement to be ineffective, and ordered legal costs against Jadawel.[93] Jadawel filed an appeal against the arbitral award before the Board of Grievances in Saudi Arabia. In an unexpected decision, the Board refused to enforce the foreign arbitral award, and conducted a re-examination of the merits of the award, including an assessment of whether the award complied with *Shariʿa*.[94] On April 2009, the Second Commercial Court of the Board of Grievances overturned the ICC Award, and Emaar was ordered to pay US$228,000 in damages, and ordered to deliver 18.61 million shares to Jadawel inclusive of profit earned from the shares since the date of signing the joint venture agreement on 28 December 2003.[95] According to Emaar's 2009 annual report, they were also ordered to pay the arbitrator's fee, being Saudi Arabian Riyal ('SAR') 45,000. Emaar filed an appeal on 26 August 2009 with the Appellant Chamber for commercial cases requesting the enforcement of the original arbitral award, and a dismissal of the Board of Grievances' judgement. The parties decided to enter terms of settlement and on 26 December 2010, the Court of Appeal of the Board of Grievances in Riyadh issued a judgement confirming the terms, which revoked the conditional joint venture agreement and withdrew all other claims that the parties had made against each other.[96]

This case was significant for a number of reasons. Firstly, it shows the reluctance of Saudi courts to enforce foreign judgements, despite being a signatory to international conventions such as the *New York Convention* (as discussed earlier) during the proceedings of the case. Secondly, the case is indicative of the fact that Saudi courts have, in the past, reconsidered the merits of foreign arbitral awards, which is not only contrary to international practice, but also increases the risk

---

90 Zegers, above n 81, 21.
91 Ibid., 21; Association for International Arbitration, 'International Commercial Arbitration in the Deserts of Arabia' (2009) 2 <www.arbitration-adr.org/documents/?i=62>.
92 Emaar Properties PJSC, 'Emaar Annual Report 2009' (2009) <www.emaar.com/en/investor-relations/annual-reports/Downloads/2009%20Annual%20Report.pdf>
93 Ibid.
94 Ibid.
95 Ibid.; see also Global Arbitration Review, 'Saudi Court Rewrites Arbitration Award' (2009) <http://globalarbitrationreview.com/news/article/15257/saudi-court-rewrites-arbitration-award>.
     Global Arbitration Review, 'Dubai Company Defeats US$1.2 Billion Claim' (2008) <http://globalarbitrationreview.com/news/article/14827/dubai-company-defeats-us12-billion-claim/>.
96 Emaar Properties PJSC and Its Subsidiaries, '13th Annual General Meeting: Directors' Report and Consolidated Financial Statements' (2010) <www.euroland.com/pdf/AE-EMAAR/AR_ENG_2010.pdf>.

of non-enforcement of foreign arbitral awards. Third, since Saudi courts do not publish judicial reasoning on publicly accessible sources, there is no transparency and understanding of the reasons behind the refusal to enforce arbitral awards. For example, it is unclear why the Board of Grievances, in the case of *Jadawel*, decided to reverse the ICC decision. Although some commentators have argued that the decision was reversed on *Shariʿa* grounds,[97] the reasoning behind the case is not publicly accessible, and thus the specific grounds upon which the arbitral award was refused enforcement remain unclear. If the issue was that the arbitral award consisted of interest, then the Board of Grievances could have severed the interest aspect and simply enforced the remainder of the arbitral award. However, the fact that the entire decision was reversed attracted much criticism from international experts.[98]

Zeger also reports an arbitration case from 2004 where a Saudi and German party were involved in arbitration proceedings under the ICC rules.[99] The three-member arbitral tribunal in London ordered the Saudi party to pay the costs of arbitration from the date of the final award (31 January 2004), which included the payment of interest at the rate of 6%. When the German party tried to enforce the award in Saudi Arabia, the arbitral award was initially rejected on the basis that the Saudi court at first instance incorrectly believed that the German party would not reciprocate the enforcement of a Saudi award in its jurisdiction. On appeal the Appellate Court of the Board of Grievances rejected the grounds that there was an absence of reciprocity, and asked the lower court to make a new finding. The lower court then rejected the entire arbitral award on the basis that it contained an order to pay interest.[100] The fact that the court at first instance did not understand that both Germany and Saudi Arabia were signatories to the *New York Convention* shows a lack of understanding among certain judges in Saudi Arabia as to how the convention operates. Although the Appellate Court of the Board of Grievances realised that the arbitral award could not be rejected on the grounds of reciprocity, this ultimately did not matter, since the lower court found the arbitral award to be inconsistent with *Shariʿa* due to the provision of interest.

---

97 Jones Day, above n 86.
98 Association for International Arbitration, 'International Commercial Arbitration in the Deserts of Arabia' (2009) 2 <www.arbitration-adr.org/documents/?i=62>; Seema Bono, 'Middle East and North Africa Overview' (2015) *International Arbitration 2015* <www.iclg.co.uk/practice-areas/international-arbitration-/international-arbitration-2015/13-middle-east-and-north-africa-overview>; Jones Day, above n 86; Herbert Smith Freehills LLP, 'Saudi Arabian Court Overturns ICC Award' (2009) <www.lexology.com/library/detail.aspx?g=26515e46-a971-496b-82c7-da73e837e496>; Global Arbitration Review, 'Saudi Court Rewrites Arbitration Award' (2009) <http://globalarbitration review.com/news/article/15257/saudi-court-rewrites-arbitration-award>.

Global Arbitration Review, 'Dubai Company Defeats US$1.2 Billion Claim' (2008) <http://globalarbitrationreview.com/news/article/14827/dubai-company-defeats-us12-billion-claim/>.

99 Zegers, above n 81, 12.
100 Ibid., 12.

It is unclear why the lower court did not simply sever the interest aspect of the arbitral award and instead, rejected enforcement of the arbitral award altogether.

This inconsistency also exists in the area of domestic banking disputes in Saudi Arabia. For example, Baamir notes a dispute between a Saudi bank and businessman where they entered into a loan agreement in 1985, and consequently a dispute arose because the businessman refused to repay his debt to the bank.[101] The parties agreed to resolve their dispute subject to the ICC Arbitration rules with the Jeddah Chamber of Commerce and Industry. The arbitral tribunal determined that the businessman was in default, and the Saudi bank had the right to receive interest pursuant to the loan agreement between the parties. This decision was based on the fact that, under *Shariʿa* law, contractual obligations should be upheld (due to the concept of *pacta sunt servanda* as discussed previously).[102] This decision by the arbitral tribunal is an example of an approach which justifies the award of interest on the basis that *Shariʿa* requires parties to respect their contractual obligations. This is despite the fact that, as discussed earlier, the principle of *pacta sunt servanda* is only upheld provided that the contract does not violate *Shariʿa* rules, such as the prohibition against *riba* and *gharar*. Regardless of the tribunal's decision, when the Saudi bank tried to enforce the arbitral award, the Board of Grievances severed the interest part of the arbitral award and enforced the remainder of the award.[103] However, Baamir notes that in many arbitration cases, the Board of Grievances does not enforce the arbitral award, which means that the parties must begin a new claim before an alternative body, such as the Committee for the Settlement of Commercial Disputes.[104]

Baamir states that because the Board of Grievances generally considers the banking industry non-compliant with *Shariʿa* due to the industry being based on interest, it follows, therefore, that many arbitration agreements and arbitral awards are rendered void due to the contractual arrangements based on interest.[105] Therefore, banks in Saudi Arabia resolve matters through the Committee for the Settlement of Banking Disputes, which is a body that is more lenient in the provision of interest, as opposed to judicial bodies in Saudi Arabia. Similarly, Baamir argues that in international banking disputes where at least one of the parties is a foreign party, the first preference of parties is to arbitrate in jurisdictions other than Saudi Arabia, due to the Saudi courts' strict adherence to *Shariʿa*.[106]

101 Abdulrahman Yahya Baamir, *Shari'a Law in Commercial and Banking Arbitration: Law and Practice in Saudi Arabia* (Ashgate, 2010) 171.
102 Ibid., 171.
103 Ibid. The Board of Grievances also gave the parties the option of referring the dispute to the Committee for the Settlement of Commercial Disputes.
104 Ibid., 171–174.
105 Ibid.
106 Ibid., 174.

B *Partial enforcement of arbitral awards inclusive of interest*

Despite decisions where judicial courts in Saudi Arabia have completely refused enforcement of arbitral awards due to the provision of interest, there have also been a number of cases where the interest aspect of the arbitral award has simply been severed. For example, in a 1977 case, a Saudi and Bahraini party entered into a sales contract found to be void by a Bahraini court.[107] The Bahraini party was awarded the purchase price resulting from a void sale contract, as well as legal fees and interest accruing from the date of judgement. When the Bahraini party tried to enforce the judgement in Saudi Arabia, the Board of Grievances allowed the enforcement as per the *Arab League Convention*. However, the interest aspect of the arbitral award was severed due to non-compliance with *Shari'a*. This was an important decision, as the Board of Grievances was able to recognise the foreign judgement and simply sever the interest aspect of the award.[108]

Baamir does mention a case where an arbitral award (inclusive of interest) was made in Bahrain, but the interest aspect of the award was refused enforcement in Saudi Arabia, and the losing party ultimately paid the principal amount of money without interest.[109] Similarly, Shareef reports that an Egyptian judgement was brought before the Board of Grievances in Jeddah, and was only partially enforced because the statutory interest aspect of the award was severed, due to non-compliance with *Shari'a*.[110]

The historical inconsistency with which Saudi courts have dealt with interest in arbitral awards leads one to speculate whether non-compliance with *Shari'a* is the reason for refusal of enforcement of the above arbitral awards, or whether the Saudi courts are simply hesitant to enforce any foreign arbitral awards. If foreign arbitral awards from 1977 were enforced and the interest aspect of the arbitral award was severed, then why were arbitral awards from 2004 to 2006 refused enforcement all together? It is important to address such inconsistency, because it can often be viewed by foreign parties as indicative of possible bias towards local parties. For example, commentators often warn against bias in contemporary ICA because, as Paulsson observes generally, the 'temptation to favour the national party is very often present in full force.'[111] Consequently, this is also one of the reasons why parties may choose not to arbitrate on Saudi Arabia, as they may view it as a jurisdiction which is not neutral.

The partial enforcement of arbitral awards is consistent with Art. 55 of the New Law and therefore, it should be expected that the Saudi courts will partially enforce arbitral awards by severing the interest component of the arbitral award and upholding the remainder. Although partial enforcement is not mentioned in

---

107 Kritzalis, above n 84, SAU 20.
108 Ibid., SAU 20.
109 Baamir, above n 101, 167.
110 Nais Al-Shareef, *Enforcement of Foreign Arbitral Awards in Saudi Arabia* (PhD Thesis, Dundee University, 2000) 193.
111 Paulsson, above n 17, 116.

the *New York Convention* in the context of public policy, partial enforcement is noted in Art. V(1)(c) of the *New York Convention* if:

> [t]he award deals with a difference not contemplated by or not falling within the terms of the submission to arbitration, or it contains decisions on matters beyond the scope of the submission to arbitration, provided that, if the decisions on matters submitted to arbitration can be separated from those not so submitted, that part of the award which contains decisions on matters submitted to arbitration may be recognized and enforced.

Interestingly, in some cases partial enforcement as expressed in the above Art. V(1) (c) has been extended to awards which would be denied enforcement due to public policy in secular countries, such as Austria. For example, in *Buyer (Austria) v. Seller (Serbia and Montenegro)*,[112] the Supreme Court in Austria held that the interest rate was excessive and contrary to Austrian public policy and therefore, the interest aspect of the arbitral award was severed.[113] Born argues that:

> [t]he same rule permitting partial recognition is nonetheless more generally-applicable under Article V's other exceptions, even in the absence of express language like that in Article V(1)(c). That is the conclusion of numerous recognition decisions, with no apparent contrary reported precedent. Indeed, there is a substantial argument that the Convention not only permits, but also requires, recognition and enforcement of separable, valid portions of an award.[114]

Although partially severing interest from the arbitral award is better than refusing enforcement completely, the refusal to award interest by Saudi courts is still inconsistent with international norms, because most domestic courts will award interest (especially in cases where the governing law is not Saudi law or *Shari'a*), and is also detrimental for parties that are otherwise entitled to large sums of interest. Further, Saudi courts have, in the past, reconsidered the merits of arbitration disputes (as discussed earlier in the case of *Jadawel v. Emaar*), despite the fact that the Board of Grievances issued a Board Circular in 1985 stating that the subject matter of arbitral awards would not be reviewed.[115]

Consequently, many foreign parties try to avoid enforcement in Saudi Arabia, and do not apply Saudi law to their arbitration agreements because, by avoiding Saudi law, 'there are no impediments to the enforcement of interest and other

---

112 Buyer (Austria) v. Seller (Serbia and Montenegro), [Supreme Court of Austria] 3 Ob 221/ 04b, 26 January 2005.
113 See also Martin King and Ian Meredith, 'Partial Enforcement of International Arbitration Awards' (2010) 26(3) *Arbitration International* 381.
114 Gary Born, *International Commercial Arbitration* (Kluwer Law International, 2nd ed, 2014) 3434.
115 Kritzalis, above n 84, SAU-8.

prohibited or disputed sale contracts.'[116] For this reason, Baamir suggests that parties should have well-drafted agreements which avoid Saudi Arabia as a place of enforcement.[117]

C Saudi cases reported by Kluwer arbitration

Kluwer Arbitration reports four Saudi cases (discussed below) dealing with the enforcement of arbitral awards or arbitration agreements, and of these four cases, three have applied *Shari'a*. However, since the reported judgements are not comprehensive, it is difficult to draw precise conclusions. For example, in one Saudi case,[118] the court found that the matter should be resolved through arbitration. One of the factors considered was that the parties were Muslim and therefore, the courts should refer the matter to arbitration as per agreement. The reasoning of the case, as reported in Kluwer, does not indicate why being Muslim was considered to be a factor. One can assume that it is because arbitration or conciliation is the recommended method of dispute resolution for Muslims, but the decision is still vague, in that it does not explain the reasoning or the implications for parties that are not Muslim.

In another case,[119] the arbitrator sat on the same board of directors as one of the parties to the arbitration. The Court indicated that, under *Shari'a*, an arbitrator or judge is considered biased if they are related to the parties. However, it held that sitting on the same board of directors as one of the parties was not enough to show that the arbitrator was biased. Again, the reasoning of the case, as provided in Kluwer, is unclear and it may be that the Court found that whilst the arbitrator was on the same board as one of the parties, nothing on the evidence indicated that the arbitrator had acted in an impartial way. The court reasoned:

> article 10 of the arbitration law states that challenges to arbitrators cannot be decided unless there are brought on the same grounds as challenges to judges, and that *Shari'a* Law insists on challenging only for valid reasons. . . . And whereas the circuit court was informed of the grounds for the challenge and having applied *Shari'a Law* to it, it has found that a judge may be challenged on the grounds that he committed a crime. As stated in Islamic doctrine, and according to Dr. Wahbe Al-Zheily, a judge accused by one of the parties of partiality towards another should resign as a judge cannot rule on a case that involves a parent or a sibling or children. . . . This was stated

116 Baamir, above n 101, 173.
117 Ibid., 174.
118 Parties Not Indicated, Board of Grievances of Saudi Arabia, undated 2014, (2015) 7(1) *International Journal of Arab Arbitration* 91.
119 Parties Not Indicated, Board of Grievances of Saudi Arabia, undated 2012, (2014) 6(2) *International Journal of Arab Arbitration* 29. Initially, this case was heard before the commercial circuit, Parties not indicated, Court of Grievance – Commercial Circuit, undated, (2010) 2(3) *International Journal of Arab Arbitration* 203.

in the book of El-Magny for Ibn Kodama and Bedaya Almogtahed for Ibn Rashed and others.[120]

In another case,[121] *Shariʿa* applied to the arbitration and the arbitral award was found to comply with *Shariʿa* principles. The court also strictly decided that no additional money could be awarded as compensation because:

> As for the compensation claim for the delay in the payment of the dues, it is legally known that the fixed dues consist of a debt owing against the debtor and no additional amount should be added to the debt in consideration of the extension of the time limit because it is a usury prohibited under Islamic *Shariʿa*.
>
> Since the Circuit did not find any impediment to the enforcement of the award under Islamic *Shariʿa*, it decides the rejection of the objection and orders the enforcement of the arbitral award in accordance with the provision of Article 20 of the Arbitration Rules.[122]

The previous cases indicate that *Shariʿa* is considered in arbitration matters. It is unclear whether it is considered by courts in foreign arbitral awards in practice, despite the power under legislation to do so, and the exact sources on which the judges are relying are unclear. For example, in the cases mentioned above,[123] Saudi judges refer to the rules of impartiality under *Shariʿa* and cite Al Muqni' which is a book on *Shariʿa* written by the classical Hanafi scholar, Ibn Qudamah (d. 1224). The judge also cites *Bidayat al-Mujtahid* (the Distinguished Jurist's Primer),[124] which is a general book on *Shariʿa* jurisprudence written by Ibn Rushd (d. 1198). The issue with referring to these books with regard to the rules of arbitration, such as the impartiality of judges and arbitrators, is that the books only provide general commentary on *Shariʿa*. For example, in Ibn Rushd's book, the Distinguished Jurist's Primer, a chapter is dedicated to judgements (in Arabic: *aqdiya*). The chapter states that under *Shariʿa*, a judge[125] must be

120 Parties Not Indicated, Board of Grievances of Saudi Arabia, undated 2012, (2014) 6(2) *International Journal of Arab Arbitration* 29. Initially, this case was heard before the commercial circuit, Parties Not Indicated, Court of Grievance – Commercial Circuit, undated, (2010) 2(3) *International Journal of Arab Arbitration* 203.

121 Parties Not Indicated, Board of Grievances of Saudi Arabia, 1767/2/J, 21 February 2004 (2010) 2(1) *International Journal of Arab Arbitration* 203.

122 Parties Not Indicated, Board of Grievances of Saudi Arabia, 1767/2/J, 21 February 2004 (2010) 2(1) *International Journal of Arab Arbitration* 203, 208 (emphasis added).

123 Parties Not Indicated, Board of Grievances of Saudi Arabia, undated 2012, (2014) 6(2) *International Journal of Arab Arbitration* 29 and Parties Not Indicated, Board of Grievances of Saudi Arabia, undated, (2010) 2(3) *International Journal of Arab Arbitration* 203.

124 Ibn Rushd, (trans, Professor Imran Nyazee), *The Distinguished Jurist's Primer (Bidayat Al-Mujtahid)* (Garnet Publishing, 2000).

125 As discussed in earlier chapters, arbitrators and judges have the same qualifications under Shariʿa.

impartial, free (not a slave), male, intelligent, Muslim and sane.[126] As discussed in Chapter 4, Saudi Arabia has recently appointed a female arbitrator, which means that classical *Shari'a* books are not always relied upon. Furthermore, due to the general commentary provided on *Shari'a*, classical scholars such as Ibn Rushd do not discuss the laws of impartiality in detail.

Consequently, it is difficult to rely on classical scholars to resolve the contemporary issue of whether an arbitrator (who is also a member of the same board as one of the parties) is impartial. The situation is further complicated due to the lack of publicly accessible judicial precedent in Saudi Arabia. Thus, when determining *Shari'a* matters, Saudi judges do not rely on codified *Shari'a*. Instead they depend on various books by classical Islamic scholars, contemporary Islamic expert witnesses, as well as the Qur'an and hadith. Dr. Abdullah F. Ansary states that:

> To learn the law of Saudi Arabia, one turns first to the '*fiqh*', Islamic Law. In other words, one turns not to State legislation or court precedents but to the opinions, the '*ijtihad*,' of religious-legal scholars from both the past and the present who, by their piety and learning, have become qualified to interpret the scriptural sources and to derive laws therefrom. Most of the Islamic law applied today, according to the recognized Islamic schools of law, can be found in books of '*fiqh*' that were written by Muslim scholars (*ulama*) over a period of nearly fourteen centuries. Judges in Saudi Arabia consult these books (especially those considered to be the primary sources in each Islamic school of law) in order to formulate their rulings.[127]

One of the reasons why *Shari'a* has not been codified is because various Islamic scholars fear that codification will erode the traditional approach of relying on Islamic sources such as the Qur'an, hadith and the views articulated by classical Islamic scholars from the Hanafi, Maliki, Shafii or Hanbali schools of thought.[128] However, a codification could always refer to the preferred school of thought and for this reason, as discussed in Chapter 2, Saudi Arabia has been in the process of discussing the codification of *Shari'a* since 2014, although to date, no such codification of *Shari'a* is publicly accessible. The lack of codification makes it extremely difficult for foreign lawyers to understand whether and how *Shari'a* will be applied to foreign arbitral awards. Therefore, codification of *Shari'a* in Saudi Arabia may have two consequences. Firstly, if the interpretation is based on a rigid and textual interpretation of *Shari'a*, this will impact on Saudi Arabia's recent attempt to modernise their arbitration law in order to attract foreign investors, and be more involved in contemporary ICA. On the other hand, if the codification clarifies the minimal impact of classical *Shari'a* on ICA, and takes a pro-enforcement approach in accordance with contemporary ICA norms, this will mutually benefit Saudi Arabia and foreign parties. Secondly and similarly,

126 Ibn Rushd, above n 124, 553–554.
127 Ansary, above n 77.
128 Ibid.

given the fact that Saudi Arabia does not have a judicial system which makes its decisions publicly available and binding, and due to the international nature of arbitration, arbitration case law in Saudi Arabia should be reported on international databases. In fact, apart from the handful of cases listed previously, there are no detailed cases published by Kluwer Arbitration which discuss the enforcement of foreign arbitral awards or how *Shariʿa* provisions of the new arbitration law will apply. Gemmell observes that:

> [o]ne need not be a lyrical optimist to be sanguine about the future prospects for commercial arbitration in the Islamic Middle East. Currently, the 'developed' world needs Middle Eastern oil and the prospect of international 'arm twisting' are unlikely. However, the day will inevitably come when mutual commercial interests will intertwine and become so interdependent that international private law and Islamic law will stand where neither dominates the other; this day will be predicated on mutual respect and understanding for each body of law, including its historical foundations and modern application.

In order to achieve the objective of mutual understanding between contemporary ICA and *Shariʿa*, Saudi Arabia has attempted to modernise its arbitration law by modelling arbitral law in accordance with the *UNCITRAL Model Law*. However, unless the *Shariʿa* aspect of the new arbitration law is clarified, foreign parties will remain uncertain about the enforcement status of foreign arbitral awards, and the consequences of selecting Saudi arbitration law as the applicable law.[129]

V Conclusion

Shariʿa public policy is based on religious concepts which are based on traditional sources and that are wider in nature by comparison with contemporary and conventional public policy. Although *Shariʿa* public policy is recognised in GCC countries, such as Qatar and the UAE, it is rarely applied in practice. Case law from Egypt and GCC countries suggests that the region is beginning to endorse a pro-enforcement attitude, by applying the narrower concept of international public policy when considering the enforcement of foreign arbitral awards. This is also suggested by the recent case in Qatar in which an ICC decision in 2012 was initially refused enforcement due to being contrary to public policy, as a result of not rendered the award in the name of the Emir. However, the decision was later overturned and the arbitral award was reinstated on 25 March 2014.

On the other hand, *Shariʿa* is applied in Saudi Arabia, but there are limited arbitration cases with detailed judicial reasoning made available to the public. For

---

129 See also John Balouziyeh, 'Saudi Arabia's New Arbitration Law Sees More Investors Opting for Arbitration in Saudi Arabia' (2013) <http://kluwerarbitrationblog.com/2013/05/29/saudi-arabias-new-arbitration-law-sees-more-investors-opting-for-arbitration-in-saudi-arabia/>.

this reason, it is unclear whether the recent arbitration reform in Saudi Arabia will enable it to become a pro-arbitration jurisdiction. *Shari'a* is clearly articulated as a consideration under Art. 55 of the New Arbitration Law, and Art. 11 of the new *Saudi Enforcement Law 2013*. If the role of *Shari'a* in arbitration matters is not clarified, foreign parties will be hesitant in selecting Saudi Arabia as the *lex arbitri* and, if possible, will try to avoid enforcement in the jurisdiction. Further, the recent ICC statistics note that Saudi Arabia was never selected by parties themselves as a place for arbitration (between the years 2008 and 2014), but instead was only fixed by the courts on one occasion in 2014.[130]

It is recommended that *Shari'a*'s influence on arbitration matters be further clarified in the GCC and Saudi Arabia, and case law with detailed judicial reasoning be made readily available to the public, in order to increase transparency for international parties. Consequently, this will increase the level of predictability and consistency for parties that wish to enforce their arbitral awards in countries where *Shari'a* forms part of the country's public policy.

---

130 International Chamber of Commerce, '2014 Statistical Report' (2015) *ICC International Commercial Arbitration Bulletin* 5.

9 Reform proposals, further research and conclusion

I Reform proposals – towards harmonisation or unification?

This book argues that contemporary ICA and *Shari'a* can harmoniously co-exist if: firstly, there is mutual respect and recognition between the two systems; and secondly, *Shari'a* is developed as a comprehensive legal framework that governs arbitration proceedings. Proposed here are important components of the *Shari'a*-compliant legal framework, which would be predictable, effective and harmonious with contemporary ICA. Born states that one of the main reasons for the development of a legal framework for contemporary ICA is to facilitate 'international trade and investment by providing a stable, predictable and effective legal framework in which these commercial activities may be conducted.'[1]

With similar objectives in mind, this book argues for the development of *Shari'a*-compliant arbitral rules and guidelines, and to include a reservation within the *CISG*, in order to achieve the overarching objective of harmonisation, as opposed to uniformity, between contemporary ICA and *Shari'a*. Furthermore, this book argues that *Shari'a* is open to multiple interpretations due to *Shari'a*-based legal theories, such as *maqasid al-Shari'a*, *maslaha*, and *ijtihad*. Consequently, the concept of party autonomy in contemporary ICA, as well as a contextual approach to *Shari'a*, are two fundamental concepts which can contribute towards legal harmonisation between the two systems.

As noted in Chapters 1 and 2, due to the advent of globalisation, the international community is moving towards legal harmonisation, and resolving international commercial disputes through international arbitration, as opposed to domestic litigation.[2] This has led to spaces for effective international dispute resolution, and has encouraged states to establish an international and national legal environment that supports arbitration.[3] It is therefore important that international and national approaches to arbitration co-exist harmoniously.

1 Gary Born, *International Commercial Arbitration* (Kluwer Law International, 2nd ed, 2014).
2 Charles Brower and Jeremy Sharpe, 'International Arbitration and the Islamic World: The Third Phase' (2003) 97 *The American Society of International Law* 643.
3 Ibid.

However, Andenas, Andersen and Ashcroft argue that legal harmonisation should not simply be viewed through the lens of globalisation, and that the theory of harmonisation is a broader conceptual framework permeating both public and private law, as well as other disciplines such as sociology, political theory and international relations.[4] They broadly define harmonisation as 'the basic notion of the bringing together of legal ideas to allow a functioning in unison.'[5] Zeller makes an important distinction between harmonisation and unification by arguing that 'harmoni[s]ation is a process of making rules similar, whereas unification aims at the sameness of rules.'[6] Soni contends that harmonisation can be distinguished from the unification of laws because the latter 'means implementation of homogenous set of laws that are assigned by international organizations and embraced by separate states.'[7] On the other hand, 'instead of adopting a single set of laws, harmoni[s]ation involves comprehensive vehicles by which divergence in laws prevailing in heterogeneous countries are reconciled.'[8] This definition of harmonisation could also apply to independent nation states and parties who do not share the same secular approach to ICA, and wish to apply *Shari'a* to arbitration in a way that is consistent with the regulatory framework of contemporary ICA.

Consequently, this book proposes reforms aspiring towards 'harmonisation,' as opposed to 'unification,' between contemporary ICA system and *Shari'a*. One of the reasons why these reforms are proposed is to increase efficiency by promoting legal certainty, stability and consistency through harmonising international commercial laws.[9] Differences between legal systems, such as the civil and common laws,[10] are often addressed when the topic of harmonising arbitration law is discussed; however, harmonisation with *Shari'a* is rarely analysed in detail.[11] Waincymer notes that '[i]t is important to acknowledge that a comparison between

---

4 Mads Andenas, Camilla Baasch Andersen and Ross Ashcroft, 'Towards a Theory of Harmonisation' in Mads Andenas and Camilla Baasch Andersen (eds), *Theory and Practice of Harmonisation* (Edward Elgar, 2011) 572, 574–575.
5 Ibid., 577.
6 Puja Soni, *The Benefits of Uniformity in International Commercial Law with Special Reference to the United Nations Convention on Contracts for the International Sale of Goods* (1980) Electronic Library Convention on Contracts for the International Sale of Goods <http://cisgw3.law.pace.edu/cisg/biblio/soni.html> 10.
7 Ibid., 10.
8 Ibid.
9 Richard Garnett, 'International Arbitration Law: Progress Towards Harmonisation' (2002) 3 *Melbourne Journal of International Law* 400–401.
10 Jeffrey Waincymer, *Procedure and Evidence in International Arbitration* (Kluwer Law International, 2012) 37.
11 Ayad attempts to harmonise all three systems of law. See Mary Ayad, 'Harmonisation of International Commercial Arbitration Law and Sharia: The Case of Pacta Sunt Servanda vs Ordre Public: The Use of Ijtihad to Achieve Higher Award Enforcement' (2009) 6 *Macquarie Journal of Business Law* 93; Mary Ayad, 'Towards a Truly Harmonised International Commercial And Investment Arbitration Law Code (Hicialc): Enforcing Mena-Foreign Investor Arbitrations via a Single Regulatory Framework: A New Map for a New Landscape' (2010) 7 *Macquarie Journal of Business Law* 285.

civil and common law traditions is also incomplete in failing to give appropriate deference to the values and practices of Asian and Middle Eastern systems.'[12]

The distinction between harmonisation and unification is important because as Bourdieu observes, certain approaches may be viewed as:

> a quasi-mechanical effect of the intensification and accelerating of circulation and exchange, leading to an ecumenical reconciliation of all cultural traditions, or as an effect of imperialism exercised by a few great industrial powers capable of exporting and imposing, on a universal scale, not only their products but also their style of life.[13]

However, from an Asia-Pacific perspective, some authors take the view that the unified international approach to arbitration is compatible with all cultures, and in fact enhances foreign investment and business:

> [t]his Western influence on international arbitration culture in Asia should not be seen as a negative. To the contrary, it could be considered as having helped to attract foreign investment in certain Asian economies, particularly in public interest areas of infrastructure, resources and utilities, and assisted local businesses in their exporting activities by making them savvier and more attractive to foreign business partners . . . [w]hile modern international arbitration had its origins in the West, its growth and global utilization are detaching it (or perhaps have now detached it) from those origins, making it too difficult to link arbitration – in its current form – to any one tradition or region. It is not a form of clandestine Western imperialism but an integral part of the universal modernisation process, which serves to facilitate trade and commerce.[14]

Conversely, Sornarajah argues that developing countries must accept contemporary ICA in order to attract foreign investment, and that international law is in fact 'a system that is weighted in favour of the capital exporting States.'[15] Although Sornarajah analyses systemic bias in the context of arbitral awards and assesses whether developed States are preferred (or 'capital exporting States'), the argument of systemic bias may also be applied to the legal framework of contemporary ICA, including institutional rules, conventions and model laws such as the *UNCITRAL Model Law*. Waincymer also notes that:

---

12 Waincymer, above n 10, 43.
13 Yves Dezalay and Bryant Garth, *Dealing in Virtue: International Commercial Arbitration and the Construction of a Transnational Legal Order* (The University of Chicago Press, 1996) vii.
14 Simon Greenberg, Christopher Kee and Romesh Weeramantry, *International Commercial Arbitration: An Asia-Pacific Perspective* (Cambridge University Press, 2010) 51.
15 Muthucumaraswamy Sornarajah, 'The Climate of International Arbitration' (1991) 8(2) *Journal of International Arbitration* 47.

[p]rejudices in terms of intelligence and sophistication between first world and third world parties be particularly problematic. Neutrality is challenged when arbitrators are aligned to one party only from a socio-economic perspective. Western adjudicators treating a third world legal system as primitive is a particularly sobering aspect of such cultural perspectives.[16]

This book discusses the problematic consequences resulting from viewing *Shari'a* as a body of law that is too unsophisticated to apply to contemporary ICA. In the context of the *CISG*, Bell argues 'Islamic law poses great challenges to the movement to create uniform laws for international commerce, and that comparative legal scholarship should take Islamic law into account and look beyond civil and common law approaches and rules.'[17] Similarly, in relation to the *CISG* and developing countries where *Shari'a* applies, the Pakistani representative, Mr Mehdi, made the following comment at the 12th Plenary meeting on 11 April 1980:

> [t]he importance of the Convention which had been adopted could not be denied, but it should be noted that, although some of Pakistan's views had been taken into account, the views of the third world countries had not always been given sufficient consideration, although harmony between them and the other nations was a prerequisite for any progress.[18]

As discussed in Chapter 1, one of the main questions posed in this book is whether *Shari'a* is harmonious with contemporary ICA, given that the latter consists of international rules, guidelines and conventions which have been developed by Western-based institutions in the 20th and 21st centuries. This book does not completely accept the argument made by Greenberg, Kee and Weeramantry, which is that contemporary ICA is inherently universal and compatible with all cultures. Instead, it argues that the contemporary ICA system and *Shari'a* (as a body of law which is not codified) are currently not harmonious, because they are not 'functioning in unison'[19] to achieve the goals of legal certainty, predictability and stability. For example, if *Shari'a* is not codified (Chapter 2), then secular jurisdictions, such as England, may not recognise *Shari'a* as a body of law capable of governing arbitration effectively and comprehensively (Chapter 3).

---

16 Waincymer, above n 10, 45–46.
17 Gary Bell, 'New Challenges for the Uniformisation of Laws: How the CISG Is Challenged by "Asian Values" and Islamic Law' in Ingeborg Schwenzer and Lisa Spagnolo (eds), *Towards Uniformity: The 2nd Annual MAA Schlechtriem CISG Conference* (Eleven International Publishing, 2011) 11.
18 United Nations Conference for Contracts on the International Sale of goods, Summary Records of the Plenary Meetings, 11th Plenary Meeting on 10 April 1980, Un Doc. A/Conf.97/SR.11. <www.CISG.law.pace.edu/CISG/plenarycommittee/summary12.html>.
19 Mads Andenas, Camilla Baasch Andersen and Ross Ashcroft, 'Towards a Theory of Harmonisation' in Mads Andenas and Camilla Baasch Andersen (eds), *Theory and Practice of Harmonisation* (Edward Elgar, 2011) 572, 577.

Similarly, as discussed in Chapter 4, the classical interpretation of *Shariʿa* may lead to results which are contrary to international (or transnational) public policy or domestic public policy in secular jurisdictions. An example of this is allowing parties to choose gender and/or to specify religion when appointing arbitrator/s. Chapter 5 further analyses current attempts by institutions such as the AIAC, to create *Shariʿa*-compliant arbitration rules (i.e., the *i-Arbitration Rules*). It argues that such rules require further reform, in order to create a more effective system of evidence and procedure consistent with international rules and guidelines. As summarised further below, Chapters 6, 7 and 8 examine the prohibition against *riba* and *gharar*, and its impact on arbitrability, validity of arbitration agreements, arbitral awards and enforceability in contemporary ICA. Therefore, the reforms proposed in this book address how *Shariʿa* and contemporary ICA can co-exist effectively, and thus harmoniously. The discussion in Chapters 6–8 will be explored further as follows.

II Scope and objectives of proposed reforms – *Shariʿa* compliancy or commercial pragmatism?

It is important to note that the objective of the current *i-Arbitration Rules* developed by the AIAC is not strict *Shariʿa* compliance, but to cater for both the international and *Shariʿa* market.[20] According to Rajoo:

> KLRCA seeks to augment its already established and internationally recognised commercial arbitration services by making them accessible to parties utilising Islamic banking in their business. This is achievable in part thanks to the existing Islamic finance expertise and industry present in Malaysia. The [i]-Arbitration Rules build on existing *UNCITRAL Model Law* principles by adding scope for determination of issues relating to Shariʿa principles through reference to the relevant Shariʿa council or expert taking into account the characteristics of the transaction involved and the will of the parties . . . [t]he IICRA, by contrast, provides a forum for arbitration of disputes wholly in accordance with Shariʿa law.[21]

This book argues that while the IICRA rules may be *Shariʿa*-compliant, they are not effective and comprehensive arbitral rules suited to contemporary ICA. Regarding rules developed by the AIAC, commentators such as Oseni argue that the *i-Arbitration Rules* 'may look like the Islamic model since . . . there is direct mention of Islamic banking and finance services but the substance is largely questionable when considered under the classical Islamic models.'[22] Therefore,

---

20 Datuk Sundra Rajoo, 'KLRCA's New i-Arbitration Rules: Islamic Finance in the Global Commercial Arena' (2014) 6(2) *International Journal of Arab Arbitration* 16–17.

21 Ibid., 16–17.

22 Umar Oseni, 'Islamic Banking and Finance Disputes: Between the Classical and Modern Mechanisms of Dispute Resolution' in Adnan Trakic and Hanifah Haydar Ali Tajuddin

contrary to the approach taken by the AIAC and the IICRA, the proposed reforms in this book aim to improve upon such rules in order to result in a comprehensive body of arbitration rules that are both *Shari'a*-compliant, and which are capable of harmoniously coexisting with contemporary ICA. Unlike Oseni who refers to classical *Shari'a*, this book argues for the recognition and development of a contextual interpretation of *Shari'a* that provides greater flexibility, rather than a literalist and monolithic approach to *Shari'a* (Chapter 2). Furthermore, as noted previously, the proposed reforms in this book aspire to harmonisation as opposed to unification, because this book argues that mutual respect and recognition between *Shari'a* and contemporary ICA is fundamental to harmony. Consequently, the following sections summarise the proposals for reform contained in this book. The aim is to achieve the above-mentioned dual objectives of being *Shari'a*-compliant, as well as legal harmonisation, including: (1) reform of current *Shari'a*-compliant arbitral rules; (2) the development of possible international *Shari'a* guidelines; and (3) reform of the *CISG*. These three proposals are discussed in more detail as follows.

III Reforming *Shari'a*-compliant arbitral rules

As mentioned earlier, one of the main arguments of this book is that the codification of *Shari'a* will result in an effective, predictable and stable regulatory regime harmonious with contemporary ICA. Therefore, this book analyses the existing codified arbitral rules, and argues that they require further reform. For example, this book proposes reforms to the *i-Arbitration Rules*, which are preferred over the *IICRA Rules* for reasons mentioned in this book (Chapters 4–7) and summarised further below. The *i-Arbitration Rules* are also preferred over the AAOFI Guidelines, because the latter simply contains a brief 'arbitration standard' referring to general arbitration under *Shari'a*, and the standard is vague and ill defined. The following sections summarise and elaborate on the recommendations made in preceding chapters in relation to existing arbitral rules.

A Proposal 1: remove pre-requisites of religion and/or gender

As discussed in Chapter 4, section 8 of the *AAOIFI Standard* No. 32 encourages the appointment of Muslims as arbitrators. Although this requirement is not a strict one, Chapter 4 argues that religion and gender should not be stipulated in arbitral rules, in order to be consistent with international notions of neutrality and non-discrimination. Therefore, the recommended approach is the one taken by the *IICRA Rules* and the *i-Arbitration Rules*, which do not stipulate pre-requisites of religion and/or gender. Further, this recommendation is also *Shari'a*-compliant under the views of Hanafi scholars, and/or if parties or

---

(eds), *Islamic Banking and Finance: Principles, Instruments and Operations* (The Malaysian Current Law Journal, 2016) 18.

institutions choose to follow a contextual interpretation of *Shariʿa*, which recognises contemporary norms of justice and equality.

B   *Proposal 2: comprehensive procedural guidelines regulating* Shariʿa *experts*

Chapter 5 argues that applying classical *Shariʿa* to evidence and procedural matters can lead to results that are not harmonious with contemporary ICA. Instead, this book proposes a contextual interpretation of *Shariʿa* by applying *usul-ul fiqh* principles. Furthermore, if contemporary notions of fairness, equality and justice are viewed as being *maqasid al-Shariʿa* (higher objectives of *Shariʿa*) and major *Shariʿa* prohibitions (such as *riba* and *gharar*) are avoided, then the development of evidence and procedural rules can lead to *Shariʿa compliance*. However, due to the subjective nature of *Shariʿa*, this chapter examines procedures through which *Shariʿa* matters can be referred to experts.

Therefore, Chapter 5 critically analyses evidentiary procedures as stipulated in the *IICRA Rules* and *i-Arbitration Rules*. It proposes the development of existing *i-Arbitration Rules* and the appointment of an expert under the *i-Arbitration Rules*, as opposed to relying on party-appointed witnesses or the expertise of arbitral tribunals as per *IICRA Rules*. This is because the procedure outlined by the *IICRA Rules* limits parties to the IICRA *Shariʿa* board, or simply relies on the arbitral tribunal's expertise, which is better suited to domestic disputes in the UAE, rather than international commercial disputes which are often more complex.

This chapter also notes that the *i-Arbitration Rules* should be further developed by incorporating some of the *IBA Rules* and Art. 29 of the *UNCITRAL Rules 2010*, which provide a more comprehensive procedure for appointment of experts by the arbitral tribunal. Therefore, the *i-Arbitration Rules* should be reformed, or independent guidelines developed, in order to include procedures regarding the submission of a statement of independence and impartiality by *Shariʿa* expert/s, and the preparation of an expert report outlining the *Shariʿa* expert's qualifications, as well as the methodology and reasoning utilised by the expert when providing evidence. The *i-Arbitration Rules* should also contain a provision in which parties are given the right to interrogate experts, as stipulated in Art. 6.5 of the *IBA Rules* and Art. 26(2) of the *UNCITRAL Model Law*.

C   *Proposal 3: interest on arbitral awards*

If the *AAOIFI Standards* are used to determine whether interest can be awarded on arbitral awards (Chapter 6), this may result in a conflict between the *i-Arbitration Rules* and the *AAOIFI Standards* in the event that they are applied concurrently. As discussed in Chapter 6, the *AAOIFI Standards* allow for late payment charges to be channelled to charities, but do not stipulate a provision on compensation or *taʾwidh*, due to the view that it may contain interest. The *AAOIFI Standard* on arbitration can be reformed to include special provisions on the calculation of interest on arbitral awards specifically. This could include a provision which either accepts both *gharamah* and *ta'widh*,[23] or which clarifies its own position on *Shari'a*-compliant remedies.

On the other hand, the *IICRA Rules* do not specify an approach in relation to the calculation of interest on arbitral awards at all. Therefore, the *i-Arbitration Rules* provide the most comprehensive approach with reference to the calculation of interest, and unlike the *AAOIFI Standards*, the rule is specifically concerned with arbitral awards. However, as discussed in Chapter 6, the *i-Arbitration Rules* also include a provision under Rule 12(8)(b), allowing the arbitral tribunal to award interest when calculating the arbitral award. From a *Shari'a* perspective, the fact that the *i-Arbitration Rules* include the discretion to award interest could defeat the purpose of *Shari'a*-compliant arbitration rules. This is because if parties wish to have interest calculated, they can make necessary amendments to *Shari'a*-compliant arbitral rules to include such a provision, or opt for the *UNCITRAL Rules 2010* instead. One of the main differences between the *UNCITRAL Rules 2010* and *Shari'a*-compliant arbitration rules is the prohibition of *riba* and/or *gharar*. Therefore, as discussed previously, in order to provide a set of rules catering for Muslims and the Islamic finance market, such rules should comply with *Shari'a* and co-exist harmoniously with contemporary ICA.

Consequently, this book proposes that the award of interest should not be stipulated, in order to maintain the distinct *Shari'a*-compliant nature of these rules. Furthermore, although the lack of interest being awarded may impact on claimants in arbitral proceedings, it has no effect on the enforceability of the arbitral award, as long as it is consistent with the agreement of the parties. If parties do not wish to subject themselves to *Shari'a*-compliant rules, or have a different understanding of '*Shari'a*-compliancy,' they can choose not to select such rules, and this may be more often the case where one of the parties is not Muslim and/or the two Muslim parties each have a different understanding of *Shari'a*. Another option could be the development of independent guidelines in addition to the concepts of *gharamah* and *ta'widh* regarding the calculation of remedies in a *Shari'a*-compliant manner. However, the discussion of a broader set of international *Shari'a*-compliant remedies, which caters for the different schools of thought and interpretations in *Shari'a*, is beyond the scope of this book, and requires further research.

IV Development of *Shari'a*-compliant guidelines

A Proposal 4: clarify the impact of Shari'a on arbitration agreements and arbitrability

As discussed in Chapter 6, the issue of arbitrability and validity of arbitration agreements is more complex in *Shari'a*, as opposed to contemporary ICA, due

---

23 Shari'a-compliant remedies as noted in the i-Arbitration Rules and expanded on in more detail in Chapter 6.

to the additional prohibitions of *gharar* and *riba*. One of the reasons why the *i-Arbitration Rules* do not stipulate the impact of *Shari'a* on arbitration agreements and arbitrability is noted by director of the AIAC, Professor Sundra Rajoo, who states that the *i-Arbitration Rules*:

> maintain the commercial nature of parties' business, however, by limiting the involvement of the relevant *Shari'a* council or expert to the point of *Shari'a* law referred, and allowing the remainder of the dispute to be resolved on a commercial basis according to the governing legal principles agreed upon. By way of example, a dispute may be separated into contractual issues and financial issues, with the financial issues determined according to *Shari'a* law while the contractual issues are determined according to the agreed governing law, whether that be English, New York or Bahrain law, as the case may be. This allows parties to protect the *Shari'a* integrity of their transactions without losing access to international commercial dispute resolution mechanisms and standards enjoyed by commercial entities around the world.[24]

The question of arbitrability and validity of arbitration agreements is typically determined according to the governing law agreed upon by the parties and the public policy of the country where the arbitral award is enforced or arbitration agreement is challenged. However, as noted in Chapter 6, the domestic laws of countries, such as the UAE and Saudi Arabia, do not provide clarity on what constitutes *riba* and *gharar*, and case law is not easily accessible in these countries. As discussed in Chapter 8, it is also clear that most countries, such as the UAE, only apply domestic public policy, including the non-arbitrability of matters involving *riba*, to domestic arbitration, and not to international arbitration.

On the other hand, in Saudi Arabia, *Shari'a* is a paramount consideration in the country's public policy (domestic and international), and the new *Saudi Arbitration laws* with respect to arbitration. Therefore, the prohibition of *riba* and *gharar* is most likely to apply in the context of arbitrability in international transactions. However, it is unclear exactly how Saudi courts will apply the *Shari'a* prohibitions when determining arbitrability and validity of arbitration agreements. This is because Saudi law does not clearly stipulate its interpretation of the prohibition of *riba* and *gharar*, or how it applies to contemporary contracts and arbitration agreements. Furthermore, as mentioned earlier, case law, which might assist in explaining this, is not readily accessible in the country.

Consequently, if the question of arbitrability is determined by the governing law of countries where *Shari'a* applies and is paramount, such as Saudi Arabia, then the prohibition against *riba* and *gharar* may be applied to arbitration agreements involving international transactions. Due to the lack of clear guidelines in relation to what constitutes *riba* and *gharar*, and because Islamic experts interpret these prohibitions in different ways, this could lead to inconsistency and lack of predictability for the parties concerned.

---

24 Rajoo, above n 20, 17.

One possible solution could be the adoption of *AAOIFI Standards* as part of Saudi law, and for these standards to also be used by arbitral tribunals, experts or courts, in order to ascertain whether financial agreements are *Shari'a*-compliant, and thus arbitrable. As discussed in previous chapters, the AAOIFI provides *Shari'a*-compliant standards in relation to various Islamic finance products to promote a standardised approach among international Islamic finance institutions. Use of the *AAOIFI Standards* for this purpose would also benefit from its further reform and development of the current Arbitration Standard 32 of the *AAOIFI Standards*, to include a provision specifying the impact of *riba* and/ or *gharar* on arbitrability and arbitration agreements. The standard could note that if the subject matter is consistent with *AAOIFI Standards* on Islamic finance agreements, the matter will be arbitrable. In the event that the subject matter contains *riba* and/or *gharar* (as defined by the *AAOIFI Standards*) and the agreement does not comply with *Shari'a*, the matter should be non-arbitrable, and consequently, the award should be subject to being set aside by a court.

Furthermore, if parties wish to conduct their arbitration in a *Shari'a*-compliant manner, and if they accept the AAOFI's interpretation of the *Shari'a*, parties can specify in their arbitration clause that their arbitration be subject to the *i-Arbitration Rules* and the *AAOIFI Standards* (in relation to matters of arbitrability and validity). This would provide predictability and consistency in regard to the impact of *Shari'a* on arbitration agreements and arbitrability. It may also increase chances of the arbitration being *Shari'a*-compliant and therefore, enforceable in countries such as Saudi Arabia.

However, there may be parties, tribunals, experts or judicial officers within Saudi courts who do not agree with the interpretation of *Shari'a* as stipulated in the *AAOIFI Standards*. As discussed in Chapter 5, the *Shari'a* standards established by the AAOIFI are not accepted and followed by all Islamic law experts, which is why it is important for the arbitral tribunal to consult the parties before determining which *Shari'a* expert/s are to be selected.

Alternatively, although a detailed discussion is beyond the ambit of this book, this issue could be dealt with through the development of international *Shari'a* guidelines similar to the *UNCITRAL Model Law* or *IBA Rules*, which parties could choose to agree upon if they find certain governing laws unclear, such as Saudi and UAE arbitration laws. Furthermore, as noted previously, if parties do not want to adhere to a strict *Shari'a*-compliant set of arbitration rules, they can choose to apply the *i-Arbitration Rules* in their current form, and choose a more predictable governing law, as opposed to Saudi law or UAE law, to govern contractual issues such as arbitrability.

In relation to enforceability in Saudi Arabia, the Saudi laws should clarify the approach that Saudi courts will take regarding *riba* and *gharar*, and their impact on arbitration agreements, by reforming their current laws, or publishing their own *Shari'a* guidelines. As noted above, this clarification is extremely important, considering the lack of judicial precedent or publicly accessible Saudi case law. Such guidelines would also need to clarify: (1) the extent to which *Shari'a* will apply to international arbitral awards, considering the prohibition against *riba* and *gharar*; and (2) how *Shari'a* will apply if Saudi law is chosen by parties to be the governing law in relation to the determination of substantive matters, such as arbitrability. Although the Saudi government has noted in the past that it will codify *Shari'a*, to date this has not been done in a comprehensive manner. As discussed in previous chapters, the codification of *Shari'a* could lead to certainty, if *Shari'a* is applied in a way which is harmonious with contemporary ICA standards. Alternatively, if a textual and rigid application of *Shari'a* is codified, then this may dissuade foreign parties and investors from engaging with Saudi parties, selecting Saudi laws, or enforcing awards in the jurisdiction.

B Proposal 5: clarify the impact of Shari'a on arbitral awards

Similar to the issue of arbitrability, Chapters 7 and 8 note the lack of clarity in relation to the impact of *Shari'a* on arbitral awards. Although simple interest may be awarded according to the domestic law of most countries discussed in Chapter 7, Saudi law does not clarify whether interest or alternative principles, such as *gharamah* and *ta'widh*, can be awarded on arbitral awards. In fact, there have been ICC decisions where simple interest was awarded by the tribunal, despite the applicability of Saudi law, which prohibits *riba* due to the application of *Shari'a*.[25] Consequently, Saudi arbitration law also needs to clarify the impact of *Shari'a* on arbitral awards, through reform of the current law or by publishing *Shari'a* guidelines clarifying how compensation should be calculated, and whether simple interest can be awarded.

As noted in Chapter 7, the prohibition of *riba* also needs to be clarified in relation to the enforcement of foreign arbitral awards which include interest. It is unclear whether Saudi courts will sever the interest aspect of the award and enforce the remainder of the arbitral award, or whether the entire arbitral award will be void due to the provision of interest. Additionally, if Saudi courts do not recognise alternative forms of compensation, such as *gharamah* and *ta'widh*, then arbitration conducted in accordance with the *i-Arbitration Rules* may not be enforced in Saudi Arabia. This may be the case if the concept of compensation or *ta'widh* is viewed as violating *Shari'a* by being characterised as a legal mechanism awarding interest under the guise of compensation.

Therefore, countries such as Saudi Arabia and Iran, where *Shari'a* may be applied in a strict manner, should develop guidelines clarifying the extent to which *Shari'a* will apply to arbitrability and arbitral awards. This would inform arbitral tribunals, such as ICC tribunals, how Saudi law should be applied when determining issues of arbitrability and calculating arbitral awards. Further, it would provide parties who choose Saudi law as the governing law with clarity and predictability in relation to the impact of *Shari'a* regarding arbitrability of matters, and the calculation of arbitral awards. Similar benefits will arise from such clarifications in other jurisdictions where there is strict application of Sharia, such

---

25 ICC Case No. 7063 (1996) 22 Yearbook Commercial Arbitration 87, 90; ICC Case No. 8677 (2009) 1(4) *International Journal of Arab Arbitration 333*, 41.

as Iran. Finally, such guidelines could also clarify the extent to which public policy based on *Shari'a* will be applied at the enforcement stage. In particular, the guidelines should explain whether international arbitral awards will be enforced, if the subject matter contains *riba* and/or *gharar*, or if the arbitral award contains *riba* as defined by the specific jurisdiction. The harmonisation of contemporary ICA and *Shari'a* requires predictability, transparency and consistency regarding the applicability of *Shari'a*. Therefore, even if certain conflicts arise between the two systems, such as the award of interest, parties will have further clarity as to the consequences of choosing Saudi law as the governing law, or enforcing arbitral awards in Saudi Arabia.

C Proposal 6 – reform of the CISG

The final reform proposed refers to Art. 78 of the *CISG*, which makes provision for the payment of interest. As argued in Chapter 7, despite the interest provision in the *CISG*, *Shari'a* and contemporary ICA can still co-exist harmoniously because countries can choose not to be signatories to the Convention. In fact, most Muslim countries are not signatories to the *CISG*, except for certain Middle Eastern states such as Egypt, Syria, Lebanon and Bahrain. However, Chapter 7 notes that in certain circumstances, the *CISG* may apply to a party from a non-signatory Muslim country, although these circumstances may be narrow due to the concept of party autonomy in arbitration, it is still possible. If the *CISG* applies, the arbitral tribunal may decide to apply interest rates from the creditor's place of business pursuant to Art. 78 *CISG*. A further issue may also arise if the creditor's place of business allows for compound interest because, as discussed in Chapter 6, the legal systems of most Muslim countries only make provision for simple interest.

Thus, the award of interest under the *CISG* might create tension between *Shari'a* and contemporary ICA in limited specific situations, depending on the governing law, the creditor's place of business and place of enforcement, or if one of the parties follows a textual interpretation of *Shari'a* which prohibits all forms of interest. This book proposes that one possible solution to decrease the probability of interest applying, while not altogether eliminating the possibility, is if Contracting States are provided with the flexibility to make a reservation in relation to Art. 78. This would also increase the international appeal of the *CISG*, by ensuring that it caters for alternative systems, such as *Shari'a*, and therefore assist in achieving the goal of mutual respect and recognition between the two systems.

V Conclusion

This book argues that *Shari'a* can effectively apply to and harmoniously exist with contemporary ICA if: firstly, *Shari'a* laws and *Sharia*-compliant arbitration rules codified and further developed; and secondly, if there is mutual respect and recognition between *Shari'a* and contemporary ICA. It also proposes reforms that attempt to reduce possible conflicts between the two systems. One of the findings of this research is that the two systems can exist in harmony, despite the possible conflicts outlined in this book, because of party autonomy, which is one of the fundamental principles of contemporary ICA. Garnett notes that

> [w]hile the process of harmonisation has been challenged by some scholars on the ground that it is insensitive to cultural and economic diversity, such concerns have had little impact in the area of international commercial arbitration where . . . the philosophy of party autonomy is deeply entrenched.[26]

Further, the fact that *Shari'a* is subject to multiple interpretations has the following implications. On the one hand, it means that *Shari'a* cannot effectively apply to arbitration as an uncodified body of law; therefore, its application can lead to uncertainty and lack of predictability for parties and tribunals and courts involved in the arbitration (Chapter 3). On the other hand, the variety of interpretations suggests that parties are not confined to classical *Shari'a*, and have the autonomy to agree to alternative interpretations. Such alternative interpretations can be further developed through reformative *usul-ul fiqh* principles and *maqasid al Shari'a*, the existence of which therefore provides *Shari'a* with the flexibility to harmonise with contemporary ICA. However, this book does recognise that due to the limited case law and publicly available arbitral decisions, the findings of this research are limited to theoretical discussions on the compatibility between the two systems, as well as practical reforms through which *Shari'a*-compliant rules can be further developed.

In summary, this book argues that in order for *Shari'a* to effectively apply to and harmoniously exist with contemporary ICA, its multiple interpretations and applications need to be understood (Chapter 2). *Shari'a* should be recognised by secular courts (Chapter 3), and parties that choose *Shari'a* must understand the consequences of stipulating qualifications of arbitrators based on gender and/ or religion (Chapter 4). Evidence and procedural rules must be comprehensively developed (Chapter 5). Furthermore, the prohibition of *riba* and *gharar* and its impact on arbitration agreements should be clarified in countries where public policy is based on *Shari'a* (Chapter 6). Allowance for the prohibition against *riba* should be considered by international conventions such as the *CISG* (Chapter 7). Finally, countries where *Shari'a* influences public policy should clarify the extent to which arbitral awards containing *riba* will or will not be enforced (Chapter 8).

Therefore, in order for *Shari'a* to be an internationally enforceable and effective body of law, which can co-exist harmoniously with contemporary ICA, the following needs to occur in order to achieve mutual respect and recognition between the two systems:

1   *Shari'a*-compliant arbitration rules already in existence need to be comprehensively developed. The proposals for reform include the development of

---

26 Garnett, above n 9, 401.

the existing *i-Arbitration Rules*, and further research into a possible *Shari'a*-compliant international model law that countries, such as Saudi Arabia, can adopt in order to clarify their stance on matters such as the impact of *riba* and *gharar* on arbitrability and arbitral awards. Further, countries such as Saudi Arabia need to clarify the impact of *Shari'a*, by further reforming their existing arbitration laws, or through the development of codified Shari'a rules and/or guidelines.

2   Courts in secular countries (such as the United Kingdom), and international conventions (such as the *CISG*), should cater for and recognise *Shari'a*.

The above-mentioned reforms will contribute towards mutual respect and recognition between contemporary ICA and *Shari'a*. The reforms will ensure that contemporary ICA is truly 'international' by catering for global cultural and religious needs, and the proposals may also encourage more Muslim countries to ratify international conventions and adopt international model laws. Due to the recent growth of the Islamic finance industry, and the increase in demand for *Shari'a*-compliant rules and *Shari'a* qualified arbitrators, the proposed reforms will also increase competition and contribute towards international economic well-being.

Bibliography

A Articles/books/reports/working papers/theses

(AAOIFI), Accounting and Auditing Organization for Islamic Financial Institutions, *Shari'ah Standards* (Dar Al Maiman, 2015)

Abu Sadah, Muhammad, *International Contracting and Commercial Arbitration: An Analysis of the Doctrine of Harmonisation and Regionalism with Special Reference to the Middle East Region* (PhD thesis, Cardiff University, 2006)

Abu Sadah, Muhammad, 'Philosophical Basis of the Legal Theory Underlying International Commercial Arbitration in the Middle East Region' (2009) 8(2) *Journal of International Trade Law and Policy* 137

Abu Sadah, Muhammad, 'International Arbitration Contract Principles: Analysis of Middle East Perceptions' (2010) 9(2) *Journal of International Trade Law and Policy* 148

Abuhimed, Fahad Ahmed Mohammed, *The Rules of Procedure of Commercial Arbitration in the Kingdom of Saudi Arabia (Comparative Study)* (PhD thesis, The University of Hull, 2006)

Abu-Nimer, Mohammed, 'A Framework for Nonviolence and Peacebuilding in Islam' (2000–2001) 15 *Journal of Law & Religion* 217, 247

Academy, Islamic Development Bank and Islamic Fiqh, *Resolutions and Recommendations of the Council of the Islamic Fiqh Academy 1985–2000* (Islamic Research and Training Institute, 2000)

Ad-Darir, As-Siddiq Muhammad Al-Amin, *Gharar: Impact on Contracts in Islamic Fiqh* (Al Baraka Banking Group, 2012)

Affolder, Natasha, 'Awarding Compound Interest in International Arbitration' (2001) 12(1) *American Review of International Arbitration* 45

Ahdab, Abdel Hamid El and Jalal El Ahdab, *Arbitration with the Arab Countries* (Kluwer Law International, 2011)

Ahmed, Habib and Nourah Mohammad Aleshaikh, 'Debate on Tawarruq: Historical Discourse and Current Rulings' (2014) 28(3) *Arab Law Quarterly* 278

Ainley, Michael, et al., 'Islamic Finance in the UK: Regulation and Challenges' (Report, Financial Services Authority, 2007)

Akaddaf, Fatima, 'Application of the United Nations Convention on Contracts for the International Sale of Goods (CISG) to Arab Islamic Countries: Is the CISG Compatible with Islamic Law Principles?' (2001) 13 *Pace International Law Review* 1

Al Jarba, Mohammed, *Commercial Arbitration in Islamic Jurisprudence: A Study of Its Role in the Saudi Arabian Context* (PhD Thesis, Aberystwyth University, 2001)

Al Awabdeh, Mohamed, *History and Prospect of Islamic Criminal Law with Respect to the Human Rights* (PhD thesis, The Humboldt University of Berlin, 2005)

Al-Ammari, Saud and Timothy Martin, 'Arbitration in the Kingdom of Saudi Arabia' (2014) 30(2) *Arbitration International* 387

Alassaf, Abdullah and Bruno Zeller, 'The Legal Procedures of Saudi Arbitration Regulations 1983 and 1985' (2010) 7 *Macquarie Journal of Business Law* 170

Al-Atawneh, Muhammad, *Wahhabi Islam Facing the Challenges of Modernity* (Brill, 2010)

Al-Fadhel, Faisal, 'Respect for Party Autonomy Under Current Saudi Arbitration Law' (2009) 23(1) *Arab Law Quarterly* 31–57

Ali, Ahmed, *Al-Qur'an: A Contemporary Translation* (Princeton University Press, 1988)

Ali, Syed Nazim, *Islamic Finance: Current Legal and Regulatory Issues* (Islamic Legal Studies Program Harvard, 2005)

Ali, Abd Al-Rahman Ibn Al-Jawzi (trans, Abdullah Bin Hamid, *The Attributes of God* (Amal Press, 2016)

Aljazy, Omar, 'Arbitrability in Islamic Law' (2000) 16 *The Lebanese Review of Arbitration* 1

Aljazy, Omar, 'Jurisdiction of Arbitral Tribunals in Islamic Law (Shari'a)' in Miguel Ángel Fernández-Ballesteros and David Arias (eds), *Liber Amicorum Bernardo Cremades* (Wolters Kluwer España; La Ley, 2010)

Aljeriwi, Ismaeel Ibrahim, *The Compatibility of Saudi Domestic Law with the Seller's Obligations Under the Vienna Convention (CISG)* (PhD Thesis, Newcastle University, 2010) <https://theses.ncl.ac.uk/dspace/handle/10443/1044>

Al-Nasair, Mohamed and Ilias Bantekas, 'Nullity and Jurisdictional Excess as Grounds for Non-Enforcement of Foreign Awards in Bahrain and the UAE' (2013) 30 *Journal of International Arbitration* 283

Alrajhi, Abdulmajed, 'Islamic Finance Arbitration: Is It Possible for Non-Muslims to Arbitrate Islamic Financial Disputes?' (2015) 12(4) *Transnational Dispute Management* 1

Al-Ramahi, Aseel, 'Sulh: A Crucial Part of Islamic Arbitration' (Working Paper # 12, London School of Economics and Political Science, 2008)

Alrifai, Tariq, *Islamic Finance and the New Financial System: An Ethical Approach to Preventing Future Financial Crises* (Wiley, 2015)

Al-Shamsi, Jasim Salim, 'Restricting Resorting to [Civil] Laws in Contract [Disputes] and Accepting the Arbitration of Shari'ah Boards Instead' (The 5th Annual Shari'ah Supervisory Boards Conference for Islamic Financial Institutions, Bahrain, 19–20 November 2005)

Al-Shareef, Nais, *Enforcement of Foreign Arbitral Awards in Saudi Arabia* (PhD Thesis, Dundee University, 2000)

Al-Shatibi, Ibrahim ibn Musa Abu Ishaq, *Al Muwafaqat fi Usul al-Shari'a (The Reconciliation of the Fundamentals of Islamic Law)* (Garnet Publisher, 2015)

al-Shatibi, Ibrahim ibn Musa Abu Ishaq, *The Reconciliation of the Fundamentals of Islamic Law Volume II* (trans, Imran Ahsan Khan Nyazee, Garnet Publisher, 2015) [trans of: *Al Muwafaqat fi Usul al-Shari'a* (first published 1884)]

Al-Subaihi, Abdulrahman A., *International Commercial Arbitration in Islamic Law, Saudi Law and the Model Law* (PhD thesis, The University of Birmingham, 2004)

Al-Zuhayli, Muhammad, *Maqasid al-Shari'ah: Asas li huquq al-insan, Kitab al-Ummah*, Series No. 87 (Doha: Ministry of Awqaf and Islamic Affairs of Qatar, 2003)

Amin, Sayed Hassan, 'Banking and Finance Based on Islamic Principles- Law and Practice in Modern Iran' (1989) 9(1) *Islamic & Comparative Law Quarterly* 1

Amin, Sayed Hassan, *Islamic Law in the Contemporary World* (Vahid Publications, 1985)

Andenas, Mads, Camilla Baasch Andersen and Ross Ashcroft, 'Towards a Theory of Harmonisation' in Mads Andenas and Camilla Baasch Andersen (eds), *Theory and Practice of Harmonisation* (Edward Elgar, 2011) 572

Anderson, Scott, 'Forthcoming Changes in the *Shari'ah* Compliance Regime for Islamic Finance' (2010) 35 *The Yale Journal of International Law* 237

An-Na'im, Abdullahi, *Islam and Human Rights* (Ashgate Publishing 2010)

Ansell, Meredith O. and Ibrahim Massaud al-Arif, *The Libyan Civil Code: An English Translation and a Comparison with the Egyptian Civil Code* (The Oleander Press, 1971)

Arfazadeh, Homayoon, 'A Practitioner's Approach to Interest Claims Under Sharia Law in International Arbitration' in Filip De Ly and Laurent Levy (eds), *Interest, Auxiliary and Alternative Remedies in International Arbitration* (International Chamber of Commerce, 2008)

Asad, Muhammad, *The Message of the Qur'an* (Gibraltar, 1980)

Ashford, Peter, *Handbook on International Commercial Arbitration* (JuristNet, LLC, 2nd ed, 2014)

Auda, Jasser, *Maqasid al-Shari'ah as Philosophy of Islamic Law: A Systems Approach* (The International Institute of Islamic Thought, 2007)

Ayad, Mary, 'Harmonisation of International Commercial Arbitration Law and Sharia: The Case of Pacta Sunt Servanda vs Ordre Public: The Use of Ijtihad to Achieve Higher Award Enforcement' (2009) 6 *Macquarie Journal of Business Law* 93

Ayad, Mary, 'Towards a Truly Harmonised International Commercial and Investment Arbitration Law Code (Hicialc): Enforcing Mena-Foreign Investor Arbitrations via a Single Regulatory Framework: A New Map for a New Landscape' (2010) 7 *Macquarie Journal of Business Law* 285

Ayad, Mary Boulos, *A Proposal to Guide Future Draft Art: Provisions for a Model Harmonised International Commercial Law Code (HICALC) in the Middle East and North African or a Uniform Arab Arbitration Law* (PhD thesis, Macquarie University, 2012)

Ayub, Muhammad, *Understanding Islamic Finance* (Wiley, 2007)

Baamir, Abdulrahman Yahya, 'Saudi Arabia' in Gordon Blanke and Habib Al Mulla (eds), *Arbitration in the MENA* (Juris Publishing, 2016)

Baamir, Abdulrahman Yahya, *Shari'a Law in Commercial and Banking Arbitration: Law and Practice in Saudi Arabia* (Ashgate, 2010)

Baamir, Abdulrahman Yahya, *Saudi Law and Judicial Practice in Commercial and Banking Arbitration* (PhD Thesis, Brunel University, 2008)

Badah, Saad, 'The Enforcement of Foreign Arbitral Awards in the GCC Countries: Focus on Kuwait' (2014) 3(1) *International Law Research* 24

Badawy, Tarek, 'The General Principles of Islamic Law as the Law Governing Investment Disputes in the Middle East' (2012) 29(3) *Journal of International Arbitration* 255

Balz, Kilian, 'Islamic Law as Governing Law under the Rome Convention: Universalist Lex Mercatoria v. Regional Unification of Law' (2001) 6 *Uniform Law Review* 37

Balz, Kilian, *Sharia Risk? How Islamic Finance Has Transformed Islamic Contract Law* (Islamic Legal Studies Program Harvard Law School, 2008)

Balz, Kilian, 'Islamic Financing Transactions in European Courts' in S. Nazim Ali (ed), *Islamic Finance: Current Legal and Regulatory Issues* (Islamic Legal Studies Program, Harvard Law School, 2005)

Bantekas, Ilias, 'Arbitrability in Finance and Banking' in Ilias Bantekas, Loukas Mistelis and Stavros Brekoulakis (eds), *Arbitrability: International & Comparative Perspectives* (Kluwer Law International, 2009) 291

Bantekas, Ilias, 'The Foundations of Arbitrability in International Commercial Arbitration' (2008) 27 *Australian Year Book of International Law* 193

Barraclough, Andrew and Jeffrey Waincymer, 'Mandatory Rules of Law in International Commercial Arbitration' (2005) 6 *Melbourne Journal of International Law* 205

Bauer, Karen, 'Debates on Women's Status as Judges and Witnesses in Post-Formative Islamic Law' (2010) 130(1) *Journal of the American Oriental Society* 1

Bell, Gary, 'New Challenges for the Uniformisation of Laws: How the CISG Is Challenged by "Asian Values" and Islamic Law' in Ingeborg Schwenzer and Lisa Spagnolo (eds), *Towards Uniformity: The 2nd Annual MAA Schlechtriem CISG Conference* (Eleven International Publishing, 2011)

Belohlavek, Alexander J., Filip Cerny and Nadeada Rozehnalova, *Czech (& Central European) Yearbook of Arbitration 2013- Borders of Procedural and Substantive Law in Arbitral Proceedings* (Juris Publishing, 2013)

Berger, Klaus Peter, 'International Arbitral Practice and the UNIDROIT Principles of International Commercial Contracts' (1998) 46(1) *The American Journal of Comparative Law* 129

Bernini, Giorgio, 'The Parties' Right to Choose Their Arbitrator and the Prohibition Against Discrimination: An Unstable Balance. A Comment on the Judgments in *Jivraj v. Hashwani*' (2013) 24 *American Review of International Arbitration* 27

Bhatti, Maria, 'Taxation of Islamic Finance Products' (2015) 20(2) *Deakin Law Review* 264

Bhatti, Maria and Ishaq Bhatti, 'Development of Legal Issues of Corporate Governance for Islamic Banking' in Mohamed Ariff and Munawar Iqbal (eds), *The Foundations of Islamic Banking: Theory, Practice and Education* (Edward Elgar Publishing Ltd., 2011) 87

Bin Zaid, Abdulaziz Mohammed A., *The Recognition and Enforcement of Foreign Commercial Arbitral Awards in Saudi Arabia: Comparative Study with Australia* (PhD Thesis, University of Wollongong, 2013)

Black, Ann, 'Alternative Dispute Resolution in Brunei Darussalam: The Blending of Imported and Traditional Processes' (2001) 13(2) *Bond Law Review* 305–334

Blackaby, Nigel, Constantine Partasides, Alan Redfern and Martin Hunter, *Redfern and Hunter on International Arbitration* (Oxford University Press, 5th ed, 2009)

Blanke, Gordon and Habib Al Mulla, *Arbitration in the MENA Legislation* (Juris Publishing, 2016)

Blessing, Marc, 'The Law Applicable to the Arbitration Clause and Arbitrability' in A. J. van den Berg (ed), *Improving the Efficiency of Arbitration Agreements and Awards: 40 Years of Application of New York Convention* (Kluwer Law International, 1999)

Bonell, C. Massimo Bianca and Michael Joachim, *Commentary on the International Sales Law: the 1980 Vienna Sales Convention* (Giuffrè, 1987)

Born, Gary, *International Commercial Arbitration* (Kluwer Law International, 2nd ed, 2014)

Boshoff, Leon, 'Saudi Arabia: Arbitration vs Litigation' (1985) 1 *Arab Law Quarterly* 299

Branson, David J. and Jr. Richard E. Wallace, 'Awarding Interest in International Commercial Arbitration: Establishing a Uniform Approach' (1988) 28 *Virginia Journal of International Law* 919

Bray, Devin and Heather Bray, *International Arbitration and Public Policy* (JurisNet, 2015)

Brekoulakis, Stavros, 'Arbitrability- Persisting Misconceptions and New Areas of Concern' in Loukas Mistelis and Stavros Brekoulakis (eds), *Arbitrability: International & Comparative Perspectives* (Kluwer Law International, 2009)

Brekoulakis, Stavros, 'Systemic Bias and the Institution of International Arbitration: A New Approach to Arbitral Decision-Making' (2013) 4(3) *Journal of International Dispute Settlement* 553

Briggs, Adrian, *Agreements on Jurisdiction and Choice of Law* (Oxford Private International Law Series, 2008)

Brower, Charles and Jeremy Sharpe, 'Awards of Compound Interest in International Arbitration: The Aminoil Non-Precedent' (2006) 3(5) *Transnational Dispute Management* 155

Brower, Charles and Jeremy Sharpe, 'International Arbitration and the Islamic World: The Third Phase' (2003) 97 *The American Society of International Law* 643

Brown, Jonathan, *Misquoting Muhammad: The Challenge and Choices of Interpreting the Prophet's Legacy* (OneWorld, 2015)

Carbonneau, Thomas, 'The Ballad of Transborder Arbitration' (2002) 56(4) *University of Miami Law Review* 773

Chern, Cyril, *The Law of Construction Disputes* (Informa Law, 2010)

Chuah, Jason, 'Islamic Principles Governing International Trade Financing Instruments: A Study of the Morabaha in English Law' (2006) 27(1) *Northwestern Journal of International Law & Business* 137

Chuah, Jason, 'Impact of Islamic Law on Commercial Sale Contracts- a Private International Law Dimension in Europe' (2010) 4 *European Journal of Commercial Contract Law* 191

Cipras, Tomas, *Financial and Insurance Formulas* (Springer Verlag, 2010)

Colon, Julio, 'Choice of Law and Islamic Finance' (2011) 46 *Texas International Law Journal* 411

Comair-Obeid, Nayla, *The Law of Business Contracts in the Arab Middle East* (Kluwer Law International, 1996)

Cotterrell, Roger, 'Law and Culture: Inside and Beyond the Nation State' (Research Paper No 4, Queen Mary University of London of Law Legal Studies, 2009)

Cotterrell, Roger, *Law, Culture and Society: Legal Ideas in the Mirror of Social Theory* (Routledge, 2006)

Croff, Carlo, 'The Applicable Law in an International Commercial Arbitration: Is It Still a Conflict of Laws Problem?' (1982) 16(4) *The International Lawyer* 613

Dar, Humayon and Umar Moghul, *The Chancellor Guide to the Legal and Sharia Aspects of Islamic Finance* (Harriman House, 2010)

Daradkeh, Lafi, 'Commercial Arbitration under Investment Treaties and Contracts: Its Importance and Danger in the Arab World' (2013) 27 *Arab Law Quarterly* 393

Dasteel, Jeff, 'Arbitration Agreements That Discriminate in the Selection and Appointment of Arbitrators' (2012) 11(4) *Richmond Journal of Global Law & Business* 383

Dawwas, Amin and Yousef Shandi, 'The Applicability of the CISG to the Arab World' (2011) 16(4) *Uniform Law Review* 813

Derains, Yves and Laurent Lévy, *Is Arbitration Only as Good as the Arbitrator? Status, Powers and Role of the Arbitrator* (International Chamber of Commerce, 2011)

Dessemontet, François, 'Emerging Issues in International Arbitration: The Application of Soft Law, Halakha and Sharia by International Arbitral Tribunals' (2012) 23 *American Review of International Arbitration* 545

Dezalay, Yves and Bryant Garth, *Dealing in Virtue: International Commercial Arbitration and the Construction of a Transnational Legal Order* (The University of Chicago Press, 1996)

D'Silva, Magdalene, 'Dealing in Power: Gatekeepers in Arbitrator Appointment in International Commercial Arbitration' (2014) 5(3) *Journal of International Dispute Settlement* 605

Dupuy, Pierre-Marie, 'Unification Rather Than Fragmentation of International Law? The Case of International Investment Law and Human Rights Law' in Pierre-Marie Depuy, Francesco Francioni and Ernst Ulrich Petersmann (eds), *Human Rights in International Investment Law and Arbitration* (Oxford University Press, 2009)

E. Maret, Rebecca, 'Mind the Gap: The Equality Bill and Sharia Arbitration in the United Kingdom' (2013) 36(1) *Boston College International and Comparative Law Review* 255

Eijk, Esther van, 'Sharia and National Law in Saudi Arabia' in Jan Michiel Otto (ed), *Sharia Incorporated* (Leiden University Press, 2010)

Eisenberg, David and Craig Nethercott, *Islamic Finance: Law and Practice* (Oxford University Press, 2012)

Elatter, Amr, *Enforcement of International Arbitration Awards: A Comparative Study Between Egypt, USA, and the Gulf Cooperation Council Countries* (Lambert Academic Publishing, 2013)

El-Kosheri, Ahmed S. and Karim Y. Youssef, 'The Independence of International Arbitrators: An Arbitrator's Perspective' (2007) *Special Supplement of the ICC Intl. Court of Arb. Bull: Independence of Arbitrators* 43

El-Saghir, Hossam A., 'The Interpretation of the CISG in the Arab World' in Andre Janssen and Olaf Meyer (eds), *CISG Methodology* (Sellier European Law Publishers, 2009) 355

El-Saghir, Hossam A., 'The CISG in Islamic Countries- the Case of Egypt' in Larry A. DiMatteo (ed), *International Sales Law- a Global Challenge* (Cambridge University Press, 2014) 505

El-Saghir, Hossam, 'The Interpretation of the CISG in the Arab World' in Olaf Meyer and André Janssen (eds), *CISG Methodology* (Sellier de Gruyter, 2009) 355

Elsaman, Radwa, 'Factors to Be Considered Before Arbitrating in the Arab Middle East: Examples of Religious and Legislative Constraints' (2011) 1(2) *International Commercial Arbitration Brief* 8

Emaar Properties PJSC, 'Emaar Annual Report 2008' (2008) <www.emaar.com/ Emaar.Upload/EMR-SINGAPORE-EN-US/CMS/annual_report_2008.pdf>

Emaar Properties PJSC and Its Subsidiaries, '13th Annual General Meeting: Directors' Report and Consolidated Financial Statements' (2010) <www.euroland.com/ pdf/AE-EMAAR/AR_ENG_2010.pdf>

Emaar Properties PJSC, 'Emaar Annual Report 2009' (2009) <www.emaar.com/en/ investor-relations/annual-reports/Downloads/2009%20Annual%20Report.pdf>

Enderlein, Fritz and Dietrich Maskow, *International Sales Law: United Nations Convention on Contracts for the International Sale of Goods: Convention on the Limitation Period in the International Sale of Goods: Commentary* (Oceana, 1992)

Engle, Rachel, 'Party Autonomy in International Arbitration: Where Uniformity Gives Way to Predictability' (2002) 15 *The Transnational Lawyer* 323

Ernst & Young, *World Islamic Banking Competitiveness Report 2016* (2016) <www.ey.com/Publication/vwLUAssets/ey-world-islamic-banking-competitiveness-report-2016/$FILE/ey-world-islamic-banking-competitiveness-report-2016.pdf>

Fadel, Mohammad, 'Two Women, One Man: Knowledge, Power, and Gender in Medieval Sunni Legal Thought' (1997) 29 *International Journal of Middle East Studies* 185

Fadl, Khaled Abou El, *Speaking in God's Name: Islamic Law, Authority and Women* (Oneworld Publications, 2001)

Fadl, Khaled Abou El, 'Islam and the Challenge of Democracy' (2003) *Boston Review* (online) <http://bostonreview.net/archives/BR28.2/abou.html>

Farook, Sayd and Mohammad Omar Farooq, 'Shari'ah Governance, Expertise and Profession: Educational Challenges in Islamic Finance' (2013) 5(1) *ISRA International Journal of Islamic Finance* 137

Fealy, Greg and Virginia Hooker (eds), *Voices of Islam in Southeast Asia: A Contemporary Sourcebook* (Institute of Southeast Asian Studies, 2006)

Ferrari, Franco, *Contracts for the International Sale of Goods Applicability and Applications of the 1980 United Nations Convention* (Martinus Nijhoff Publishers, 2012)

Ferrari, Franco, 'The CISG's Sphere of Application: Articles 1–3 and 10' in Franco Ferrari, Harry Flechtner and Ronald Brand (eds), *The Draft Uncitral Digest and Beyond Cases, Analysis and Unresolved Issues in the U.N. Sales Convention: Papers of the Pittsburgh Conference Organized by the Center for International Legal Education (Cile)* (Sweet & Maxwell, 2004) 21

Ferrari, Franco, 'Uniform Application and Interest Rates Under the 1980 Vienna Sales Convention' (1995) 24(3) *Georgia Journal of International and Comparative Law* 467

Flannery, Robert Merkin and Flannery Louis, *Arbitration Act 1996* (Informa Law, 5th ed, 2014)

Fraser, Henry S., 'Sketch of the History of International Arbitration' (1926) 11(2) *Cornell Law Review* 179

Fry, James, 'Islamic Law and the Iran-United States Claims Tribunal: The Primacy of International Law over Municipal Law' (2002) 18(2) *Arbitration International* 105

Gaillard, Emmanuel and John Savage, *Fouchard Gaillard Goldman on International Commercial Arbitration* (Kluwer Law International, 1999)

Gamal, Mahmoud El, *Islamic Finance: Law, Economics and Practice* (Cambridge University Press, 2006)

Gamal, Mahmoud El, *A Basic Guide to Contemporary Islamic Banking and Finance* (Rice University, 2000)

Garner, James, 'A Critical Perspective on the Principles of Islamic Finance Focusing' (2013) 1(1) *Leeds Journal of Law and Criminology* 69

Garnett, Richard, 'International Arbitration Law: Progress Towards Harmonisation' (2002) 3 *Melbourne Journal of International Law*

Garnett, Richard, et al., *A Practical Guide to International Commercial Arbitration* (Oceana Publications, 2000)

Gemmell, Arthur, 'Commercial Arbitration in the Middle East' (2006) 5 *Santa Clara Journal of International Law* 169

Giardina, Andrea, 'Issues of Applicable Law and Uniform Law on Interest: Basic Distinctions in National and International Practice' in Filip De Ly and Laurent Levy (eds), *Interests, Auxiliary and Alternative Remedies in International Arbitration* (Dossiers, ICC Institute of World Business Law, 2008) 131

Gotanda, John, 'Awarding Interest in International Arbitration' (1996) 90 *The American Journal of International Law* 40

Gotanda, John, 'A Study of Interest' (Working Paper No 83, Villanova University School of Law, 2007) 1

Grais, Wafik and Matteo Pellegrini, 'Corporate Governance in Institutions Offering Islamic Financial Services- Issues and Options' (Working Paper 4052, World Bank Policy Research, 2006)

Greenberg, Simon, Christopher Kee and Romesh Weeramantry, *International Commercial Arbitration: An Asia-Pacific Perspective* (Cambridge University Press, 2010)

Greenwood, Lucy and C. Mark Baker, 'Is the Balance Getting Better? An Update on the Issue of Gender Diversity in International Arbitration' (2015) 31(3) *Arbitration International* 413

Grisel, Florian, 'The Sources of Foreign Investment Law' in Zachary Douglas, Joost Pauwelyn and Jorge E. Viñuales (eds), *The Foundations of International Investment Law: Bringing Theory into Practice* (Oxford University Press, 2014) 213, 226–227

Haddad, Jane Smith and Yvonne Yazbeck, *The Oxford Handbook of American Islam* (Oxford University Press, 2014)

Hadfield, Gillian, 'The Public and the Private in the Provision of Law for Global Transactions' in Volkmar Gessner (ed), *Contractual Certainty in International Trade – Empirical Studies and Theoretical Debates on Institutional Support for Global Economic Exchanges* (Hart Publishing, 2009) 239

Haleem, Muhammad Abdel, *Criminal Justice in Islam: Judicial Procedure in the Shari'ah* (I. B. Tauris, 2003)

Haleem, Muhammad Abdel, (trans), *The Qur'an* (Oxford University Press, 2004)

Hallaq, Wael, *An Introduction to Islamic Law* (Cambridge University Press, 2009)

Hallaq, Wael, *A History of Islamic Legal Theories: An Introduction to Sunnī Uṣūl Al-Fiqh* (Cambridge University Press, 1997)

Hallaq, Wael, *The Impossible State* (Columbia University Press, 2013)

Hallaq, Wael, 'Was the Gate of Ijtihad Closed?' (1984) 16(1) *International Journal of Middle East Studies* 3

Hallaq, Wael, *Shari'a: Theory, Practice, Transformations* (Cambridge University Press, 2009)

Hammoud, Lara and Sami Houerbi, 'ICC Arbitration in the Arab World' (2008) 25(2) *Journal of International Arbitration* 231

Hamza, Hichem, 'Sharia Governance in Islamic Banks: Effectiveness and Supervision Model' (2013) 6(3) *International Journal of Islamic and Middle Eastern Finance and Management* 226

Hanefeld, Inka, 'Arbitration in Banking and Finance' (2013) 9 *NYU Journal of Law and Business* 917

Hanotiau, Bernard and Oliver Caprasse, 'Public Policy in International Commercial Arbitration' in Emmanuel Gaillard and Domenico Di Pietro (eds), *Enforcement of Arbitration Agreements and International Arbitral Awards: The New York Convention in Practice* (Cameron, May 2008)

Harb, Jean-Pierre and Alexander G. Leventhal, 'The New Saudi Arbitration Law: Modernization to the Tune of Shari'a' (2013) 30 *Journal of International Arbitration* 113

Haron, Sudin and Wan Nursofiza Wan Azmi, *Islamic Finance and Banking System: Philosophies, Principles and Practices* (McGraw-Hill Education, 2009)

Harter-Uibopuu, Kaja, 'Anthropological and Historical Foundations: Ancient Greek Approaches Toward Alternative Dispute Resolution' (2002) 10 *Williamette Journal of International Law & Dispute Resolution* 47

Hasan, Zulkifi and Mehmet Asutay, 'An Analysis of the Courts' Decisions on Islamic Finance Disputes' (2011) 3(2) *ISRA International Journal of Islamic Finance*

Hasan, Zulkifi and Mehmet Asutay, 'An Analysis of the Courts' Decisions on Islamic Finance Disputes' (2011) 3(2) *ISRA International Journal of Islamic Finance* 41

Hasan, Aznan, 'An Introduction to Collective *Ijtihad* (*Ijtihad Jama'i*): Concept and Applications' (2003) 20(2) *The American Journal of Islamic Social Sciences* 26

Hassan, Kabir and Mervyn Lewis, *Handbook of Islamic Banking* (Edward Elgar Publishing, 2007)

Hassan, Tariq, 'International Arbitration in Pakistan: A Developing Country Perspective' (2002) 19(6) *Journal of International Arbitration* 591

Hassan, Kabir, Rasem Kayed and Umar Aimhanosi Oseni, *Introduction to Islamic Banking & Finance: Principles and Practice* (Pearson, 2013)

Hassim, Eeqbal, *Origins of Salafism in Indonesia: A Preliminary Insight* (Lambert Academic Publishing, 2010)

Haykel, Bernard, 'On the Nature of Salafi Thought and Action' in Roel Meijer (ed), *Global Salafism: Islam's New Religious Movement* (Columbia University Press, 2009)

Hejailan, Salah Al, 'The New Saudi Arbitration Act: A Comprehensive and Article by Article Review' (2012) 4 *International Journal of Arab Arbitration* 15

Holtzmann, Howard and Joseph Neuhaus, *A Guide to the UNCITRAL Model Law on International Commercial Arbitration: Legislative History and Commentary* (Kluwer Law International, 1989)

Honnold, John O., *Uniform Law for International Sales Under the 1980 United Nations Convention* (Wolters Kluwer Law & Business 4th ed, 2009)

Hook, Maria, 'Arbitration Agreements and Anational Law: A Question of Intent?' (2011) 28 *Journal of International Arbitration* 175

Hoover, Jon, *Ibn Taymiyya's Theodicy of Perpetual Optimism* (Brill, 2007)

Hourani, Albert, *A History of the Arab Peoples* (Faber and Faber, 2005)

Hunter, Martin and Volker Triebel, 'Awarding Interest in International Arbitration' (1980) 6(1) *Journal of International Arbitration* 7

Huntington, Samuel P., *The Clash of Civilizations and the Remaking of World Order* (Simon & Schuster, 1996)

Hussain, Jamila, 'The Shariah – Ignore It? Reform It? Or Learn to Live with It?' (2006) 8 *University of Technology Sydney Law Review* 87

Hussain, Jamila, *Islam: Its Law and Society* (The Federation Press, 3rd ed, 2011)

Hwang, Michael and Katie Chung, 'Defining the Indefinable: Practical Problems of Confidentiality in Arbitration' (2009) 26(5) *Journal of International Arbitration* 609

Hwang, Michael, 'Commercial Courts and International Arbitration- Competitors or Partners?' (2015) 31(2) *Arbitration International* 193

Ibn al-Arabi, Abu Bakr *Ahkam Al-Quran* (Dar al-Kitab al-Arabi, 2008)

Ibrahim, Yasir, 'Rashid Rida and Maqasid al-Sharia' (2006) 102/103 *Studia Islamica* 157

ICC Commission Report: Financial Institutions and International Arbitration (2016) <www.iccwbo.org/Training-and-Events/All-events/Events/2016/ICC-Commission-Report-Financial-Institutions-and-International-Arbitration/>

Idid, Dato' Syed Ahmad and Umar A. Oseni, 'Appointing a Non-Muslim as Arbitrator in Tahkim Proceedings: Polemics, Perceptions and Possibilities' (2014) 5 *Malayan Law Journal Articles* 1

International Chamber of Commerce, '2008 Statistical Report' (2009) 20(1) *ICC International Commercial Arbitration Bulletin*

International Chamber of Commerce, '2009 Statistical Report' (2010) 21(1) *ICC International Commercial Arbitration Bulletin*

International Chamber of Commerce, '2010 Statistical Report' (2011) 22(1) *ICC International Commercial Arbitration Bulletin*

International Chamber of Commerce, '2011 Statistical Report' (2012) 23(1) *ICC International Commercial Arbitration Bulletin*

International Chamber of Commerce, '2012 Statistical Report' (2013) 24(1) *ICC International Commercial Arbitration Bulletin*

International Chamber of Commerce, '2013 Statistical Report' (2014) 25(1) *ICC International Commercial Arbitration Bulletin*

International Chamber of Commerce, '2014 Statistical Report' (2015) *ICC International Commercial Arbitration Bulletin*

International Monetary Fund Report, *Islamic Finance: Opportunities, Challenges and Policy Options* (2015) <www.imf.org/external/pubs/ft/sdn/2015/sdn1505.pdf>

International Bar Association (IBA) Subcommittee on Recognition and Enforcement of Arbitral Awards, *Report on the Public Policy Exception in the New York Convention*, (2015) <www.ibanet.org/LPD/Dispute_Resolution_Section/Arbitration/Recogntn_Enfrcemnt_Arbitl_Awrd/publicpolicy15.aspx>

Isaacs, Nathan, 'Two Views of Commercial Arbitration' (1927) 40 *Harvard Law Review* 929

Ismail, Mohamed, *International Investment Arbitration* (Taylor and Francis, 2013)

Janssen, Andre and Matthias Spilker, 'The CISG and International Arbitration' in Larry A. DiMatteo (ed), *International Sales Law- a Global Challenge* (Cambridge University Press, 2014)

Jokisch, Benjamin, *Islamic Imperial Law: Harun-al-Rashid's Codification Project* (Walter de Gruyter GmbH & Co, 2007)

Junita, Fifi, 'Public Policy Exception in International Commercial Arbitration – Promoting Uniform Model Norms' (2012) 5(1) *Contemporary Asia Arbitration Journal* 45

Junius, Andreas, 'Islamic Finance: Issues Surrounding Islamic Finance as a Choice of Law Under German Conflict of Laws Principles' (2006) 7 *Chicago Journal of International Law* 537

Kamali, Mohammad Hashim, '*Maqasid al-Shari'ah* and *Ijtihad* as Instruments of Civilisational Renewal: A Methodological Perspective' (2011) 2(2) *Islam and Civilisational Renewal* 245

Kamali, Mohammad Hashim, *Shari'ah Law: An Introduction* (Oneworld Publications, 2008)

Kamali, Mohammad Hashim, *Principles of Islamic Jurisprudence* (The Islamic Texts Society, 1991)

Kantor, Mark, 'A Code of Conduct for Party-Appointed Experts in International Arbitration- Can One Be Found?' (2010) 26(3) *Arbitration International* 323

Karl, David, 'Islamic Law in Saudi Arabia: What Foreign Attorneys Should Know' (1991) 25 *George Washington Journal of International Law and Economics* 131

Kessedjian, Catherine, 'Transnational Public Policy' in Albert Jan van den Berg (ed), *International Arbitration 2006: Back to Basics?* (Kluwer Law International, 2007) 857

Khalil, Emad H. and Abdulkader Thomas, 'Interest in Islamic Economics: Understanding Riba' in *The Modern Debate over Riba in Egypt* (Routledge, 2006)

Khalil, Emad H. and Abdulkader Thomas, 'The Modern Debate over Riba in Egypt' in AbdulKader Thomas (ed), *Interest in Islamic Economics: Understanding Riba* (Routledge, 2006)

Khalil, Emad H. and Abdulkader Thomas, 'The Modern Debate over Riba in Egypt' in Abdulkader Thomas (ed), *Interest in Islamic Economics: Understanding Riba* (Routledge, 2006) 69

Khalil, Emad H., 'Interest in Islamic Economics: Understanding Riba' in *Interest in Islamic Economics: Understanding Riba* (Routledge, 2006)

Khan, Salman, 'The Role of Shari'a Advisement in an Islamic Financial Institution' in Humayon Dar and Umar Moghul (eds), *The Chancellor Guide to the Legal and Sharia Aspects of Islamic Finance* (Harriman House, 2010)

Khatchadourian, Minas, 'The Application of the 1958 New York Convention in Qatar' 1(1) *BCDR International Arbitration Review* 49

King, Henry and Marc Leforestier, 'Arbitration in Ancient Greece' (1994) 49(3) *Dispute Resolution Journal* 38

King, Martin and Ian Meredith, 'Partial Enforcement of International Arbitration Awards' (2010) 26(3) *Arbitration International* 381

Koneru, Phanesh, 'The International Interpretation of the UN Convention on Contracts for the International Sale of Goods: An Approach Based on General Principles' (1997) 6 *Minnesota Journal of Global Trade* 105, 139

Kouris, Steven, 'Confidentiality: Is International Arbitration Losing One of Its Major Benefits' (2005) 22(2) *Journal of International Arbitration* 127

Kritzalis, Alexander, 'Saudi Arabia' in Dennis Campbell (ed), *International Execution Against Judgment Debtors Vol. 2* (Sweet & Maxwell, 1993) SAU 20

Kutty, Faisal, 'The Shari'a Factor in International Commercial Arbitration' (2006) 28 *Loyola of Los Angeles International and Comparative Law Review* 565

Laldin, Dr. Mohamad Akram, Dr. Mohamed Fairooz Abdul Khir and Nusaibah Mohd Parid, 'Fatwas in Islamic Banking: A Comparative Study Between Malaysia and Gulf Cooperation Council (GCC) Countries' (2012) Research Paper 31 *International Shari'ah Research Academy for Islamic Finance* 1

Laldin, Mohamad Akram, 'Shari'ah- Non-compliance Risk' in Rifaat Ahmed Abdel Karim and Simon Archer (eds), *Islamic Finance the New Regulatory Challenge* (John Wiley & Sons Singapore, 2013)

Lalive, Pierre, 'On the Neutrality of the Arbitrator and of the Place of Arbitration' in Eugene Bucher and Claude Reymond (eds), *Swiss Essays on International Arbitration* (Schulthess, 1984)

Lee, Ilhyung, 'Practice and Predicament: The Nationality of the International Arbitrator (With Survey Results)' (2007) 31(3) *Fordham International Law Journal* 603

Levi-Tawil, Elana, 'East Meets West: Introducing Sharia into the Rules Governing International Arbitrations at the BCDR-AAA' (2011) 12 *Cardozo Journal of Conflict Resolution* 609

Lew, Julian, Loukas Mistelis and Stefan Michael Kröll, *Comparative International Commercial Arbitration* (Kluwer Law International, 2003)

Lewis, Mervyn and Latifa Algaoud, *Islamic Banking* (Edward Elgar, 2001)

Lezzar, Nasr Eddine, 'Algeria' in Lise Bosman (ed), *Arbitration in Africa: A Practitioner's Guide* (Kluwer Law International, 2013) 277

Livingstone, Mia Louise, 'Party Autonomy in International Commercial Arbitration: Popular Fallacy or Proven Fact?' (2008) 25(5) *Journal of International Arbitration* 529

Long, David, 'The Board of Grievances in Saudi Arabia' (1973) 27(1) *Middle East Journal* 71

Lovett, Graham, Lara Hammond and Hassan Arab, *Summaries of UAE Courts' Decisions on Arbitration* (ICC Publication, 2013)

Luttrell, Sam, *Bias Challenges in International Commercial Arbitration: The Need for a "Real Danger" Test* (Kluwer Law International, 2009)

Luttrell, Sam, 'Choosing Dubai: A Comparative Study of Arbitration Under the UAE Federal Code of Civil Procedure and the Arbitration Law of the DIFC' (2008) 9(3) *Business Law International* 254

Luttrell, Sam, 'Australia Adopts the "Real Danger" Test for Arbitrator Bias' (2010) 26(4) *Arbitration International* 625

Lynch, Katherine, *The Forces of Economic Globalization: Challenges to the Regime of International Commercial Arbitration* (Kluwer Law International, 2003)

Maita, Aida, 'Arbitration of Islamic Financial Disputes' (2014) 20 *Annual Survey of International & Comparative Law* 35

Majeed, Nudrat, 'Investor-State Disputes and International Law: From the Far Side' (2004) 98 *American Society of International Law Proceedings* 30

Majeed, Nudrat, 'Good Faith and Due Process: Lessons from the Shari'ah' (2004) 20(1) *Arbitration International* 97

Majid, Saleh Majid and Faris, 'Application of Islamic Law in the Middle East – Interest and Islamic Banking' (2003) 20(1) *International Construction Law Review* 177

Malintoppi, Loretta, 'Independence, Impartiality, and Duty of Disclosure of Arbitrators' in Peter Muchlinski, Federico Ortino and Christoph Schreuer (eds), *Oxford Handbook of International Investment Law* (Oxford University Press, 2008) 789

Mallat, Chibli, *Introduction to Middle Eastern Law* (Oxford University Press, 2007)

Mann, F. A., 'Compound Interest as an Item of Damage in International Law' (1987) 21(3) *UC Davis School of Law Review* 577

Mantica, Margit, 'Arbitration in Ancient Egypt' (1957) 12 *Arbitration Journal* 155

Mantilla-Serrano, Fernando, 'Towards a Transnational Procedural Public Policy' in Emmanuel Gaillard (ed), *Towards a Uniform International Arbitration Law?* (Juris Publishing, 2005)

Matthaei, Louise E., 'The Place of Arbitration and Mediation in Ancient Systems of International Ethics' (1908) 2(4) *The Classical Quarterly* 241

Mayer, Pierre and Audley Sheppard, 'Final ILA Report on Public Policy as a Bar to Enforcement of International Arbitral Awards' (2003) 19(2) *Arbitration International* 246

Mayer, Professor Pierre, Mr. Audley Sheppard and Dr. Nagla Nassar, 'Public Policy Exception as Applied by the Courts of the MENA Region' in New Delhi Conference International Law Association, Committee on International Commercial Arbitration (ed), *Final Report on Public Policy as a Bar to Enforcement on International Arbitral Awards* (International Law Association, 2002)

McFarland, Robert L., 'Are Religious Arbitration Panels Incompatible with Law? Examining "Overlapping Jurisdictions" in Private Law' (2013) 4 *Faulkner Law Review* 367

McMahon, Anthony J., 'Differentiating Between Internal and External Gaps in the U.N. Convention on Contracts for the International Sale of Goods: A Proposed Method for Determining "Governed by" in the Context of Article 7(2)' (2006) 44 *Columbia Journal of Transnational Law* 992

Merdad, Hesham, Kabir Hassan and Yasser Alhenawi, 'Islamic Versus Conventional Mutual Funds Performance in Saudi Arabia: A Case Study' (2010) 23(2) *Journal of King Abdulaziz University: Islamic Economics* 157

Merkin, Robert and Louis Flannery, *Arbitration Act 1996* (Informa Law, 5th ed, 2014)

Merkin, Rob, 'The Rome I Regulation and Reinsurance' (2009) 5 *Journal of Private International Law* 69

Mews, Constant J. and Ibrahim Abraham, 'Usury and Just Compensation: Religious and Financial Ethics in Historical Perspective' (2007) 72(1) *Journal of Business Ethics*

Mistelis, Loukas, *Arbitrability- International and Comparative Perspectives* (Kluwer Law International, 2009)

Mistelis, Loukas, 'Delocalization and Its Relevance in Post-Award Review' (Queen Mary University of London, School of Law Legal Studies Research Paper No. 144/ 2013, 2013)

Mistelis, Loukas and Stavros Brekoulakis (eds), 'Reality Test: Current State of Affairs in Theory and Practice Relating to "Lex Arbitri"' (2006) 17(2) *American Review of International Arbitration* 155

Mohamad, Tun Abdul Hamid and Adnan Takic, 'Enforceability of Islamic Financial Contracts in Secular Jurisdictions: Malaysian Law as the Law of Reference and Malaysian Courts as the Forum for Settlement of Disputes' (ISRA Research Paper No. 33, 2012)

Mohtashami, Reza, et al., 'United Arab Emirates' in International Bar Association (ed), *Arbitration – Country Guides* (International Bar Association, 2013)

Morse, Professor C. G. J., Professor David McClean and Lord Collins of Mapesbury, *Dicey, Morris and Collins on the Conflict of Laws* (Sweet & Maxwell, 15th ed, 2012)

Mourre, Alexis, 'Are Unilateral Appointments Defensible? On Jan Paulsson's Moral Hazard in International Arbitration' in Stefan Michael Kröll, et al. (eds), *International Arbitration and International Commercial Law: Synergy, Convergence and Evolution* (Kluwer Law International, 2011) 381

Muscati, Sina Ali, 'Late Payment in Islamic Finance' (2006) 6 *UCLA Journal of Islamic and Near Eastern Law* 47

Mustafa, Abdul-Rahman, *On Taqlīd: Ibn al Qayyim's Critique of Authority in Islamic Law* (Oxford University Press, 2013)

Mustill, Michael and Stewart Boyd, *Commercial Arbitration* (Butterworths, 2nd ed, 1989)

Mustill, Sir Michael and Stewart Boyd, *Commercial Arbitration: 2001 Companion Volume to the Second Edition* (Butterworths, 2001)

Mustill, M. J., 'Foreword: Sources for the History of Arbitration' (1998) 14(3) *Arbitration International* 235

Nasr, Seyyed Hossein, *The Heart of Islam* (HarperCollins, 2004)

Nasr Seyyed Hossein, trans, *The Study Quran: A New Translation and Commentary* (HarperCollins Publishers, 2015)

Nassif, Karim, 'Arbitrability Under UAE Law' (2013) 5(1) *International Journal of Arab Arbitration* 5

Nathan, K. V. S. K., 'Who Is Afraid of Sharia? Islamic Law and International Commercial Arbitration' (1993) 59(2) *Arbitration: The Journal of the Chartered Institute of Arbitrators Arbitration*

Nesheiwat, Faris and Ali Al-Khasawneh, 'The 2012 Saudi Arbitration Law: A Comparative Examination of the Law and Its Effect on Arbitration in Saudi Arabia' (2015) 13(2) *Santa Clara Journal of International Law* 444

O'Malley, Nathan D., *Rules of Evidence in International Arbitration: An Annotated Guide* (Routledge, 2012)

Oseni, Umar, 'Islamic Banking and Finance Disputes: Between the Classical and Modern Mechanisms of Dispute Resolution' in Adnan Trakic and Hanifah Haydar Ali Tajuddin (eds), *Islamic Banking and Finance: Principles, Instruments and Operations* (The Malaysian Current Law Journal, 2016)

Oseni, Umar, 'Shari'ah Court-Annexed Dispute Resolution of Three Commonwealth Countries- a Literature Review' (2015) 26(2) *International Journal of Conflict Management* 214

Oseni, Umar and Abu Umar Faruq Ahmad, 'Blazing the Trail: The Institutional Framework for Dispute Resolution in Malaysia's Islamic Finance Industry' (2012) 4(2) *ISRA International Journal of Islamic Finance* 159

Othman, Aida, ' "And Amicable Settlement Is Best": Sulh and Dispute Resolution in Islamic Law' (2007) 21(1) *Arab Law Quarterly* 64–90

Park, William, *Arbitration of International Business Disputes: Studies in Law and Practice* (Oxford University Press, 2nd ed, 2012)

Park, William, 'Arbitrator Bias' (2015) *Transnational Dispute Management* 1

Park, William, 'Neutrality, Predictability and Economic Cooperation' (1995) 12 *Journal of International Arbitration* 99

Paulsson, Jan, 'The New York Convention in International Practice- Problems of Assimilation' in Marc Blessing (ed), *The New York Convention of 1958: A Collection of Reports and Materials Delivered at the ASA Conference Held in Zurich on 2 February 1996* (Swiss Arbitration Association, 1996)

Peters, Rudolph, *Crime and Punishment in Islamic Law* (Cambridge University Press, 2005)

Petrochilos, Georgios, *Procedural Law in International Arbitration* (Oxford University Press, 2004)

Petrochilos, Georgios C., 'Arbitration Conflict of Laws Rules and the 1980 International Sales Convention' (1991) 52 *Revue Hellenique de Droit International* 191

Poudret, Jean-François and Sébastien Besson, *Comparative Law of International Arbitration* (Sweet & Maxwell, 2nd ed, 2007)

Price, Richard and Essam Al Tamimi, *United Arab Emirates Court of Cassation Judgements: 1998–2003* (Brill, Arab & Islamic Law Series, 2005)

Pryles, Michael, 'Limits to Party Autonomy in Arbitral Procedure' (2007) 24(3) *Journal of International Arbitration* 327

Pryles, Michael, 'Application of the Lex Mercatoria in International Commercial Arbitration' (2008) 31 *UNSW Law Journal* 319

Rahman, Fazlur, 'Riba and Interest' (1964) 3 *Islamic Studies* 1

Rahman, Fazlur, *Islam & Modernity: Transformation of an Intellectual Tradition* (The University of Chicago Press, 1982)

Rajoo, Datuk Sundra, 'KLRCA's New i-Arbitration Rules: Islamic Finance in the Global Commercial Arena' (2014) 6(2) *International Journal of Arab Arbitration*

Ramadan, Tariq, 'Ijtihad and Maslaha: The Foundations of Governance' in M. A. Muqtedar Khan (ed), *Islamic Democratic Discourse: Theory, Debates, and Philosophical Perspectives* (Lexington Books, 2006) 3

Rau, Alan Scott, 'The Culture of American Arbitration and the Lessons of ADR' (2005) 40(3) *Texas International Law Journal* 449

Redfern, Alan, et al., *Redfern and Hunter on International Arbitration* (Oxford University Press, 5th ed, 2009)

Redfern, Alan, 'Comments on Commercial Arbitration and Transnational Public Policy' in Albert Jan van den Berg (ed), *International Arbitration 2006: Back to Basics?* (Kluwer Law International, 2007) 871

Rehman, Scheherazade, 'Globalization of Islamic Finance Law' (2008) 25(4) *Wisconsin International Law Journal* 625

Reiss, Maria, 'The Materialization of Legal Pluralism in Britain: Why Shari'a Council Decisions Should Be Non-Binding' (2009) 26 *Arizona Journal of International and Comparative Law* 739

Renner, Moritz, 'Private Justice, Public Policy: The Constitutionalization of International Commercial Arbitration' in Walter Mattlie and Thomas Dietz (eds), *International Arbitration and Global Governance: Contending Theories and Evidence* (Oxford University Press, 2014) 117

Rizwan, Saad, 'Forseeable Issues and Hard Questions: The Implications of U.S. Courts Recognizing and Enforcing Foreign Arbitral Awards Applying Islamic Law Under the New York Convention' (2013) 98(2) *Cornell Law Review* 493

Roebuck, Derek, *Ancient Greek Arbitration* (The Arbitration Press, 2001)

Roebuck, Derek, 'Sources for the History of Arbitration: A Bibliographical Introduction' (1998) 14(3) *Arbitration International* 237

Roy, Kristin, 'The New York Convention and Saudi Arabia: Can a Country Use the Public Policy Defense to Refuse Enforcement of Non-Domestic Arbitral Awards?' (1994) 18 *Fordham International Law Journal* 920

Rubins, Jack Coe Jr. and Rubins Noah, 'Regulatory Expropriation and the Tecmed Case: Context and Contributions' in Todd Weiler (ed), *International Investment Law and Arbitration: Leading Cases from the ICSID, NAFTA, Bilateral Treaties and Customary International Law* (Cameron, May 2005) 597

Rühl, Giesela, 'Party Autonomy in the Private International Law of Contracts – Transatlantic Convergence and Economic Efficiency' in Eckart Gottschalk, et al. (eds), *Conflict of Laws in a Globalized World* (Cambridge University Press, 2007) 153

Rushd, Ibn and Professor Imran Nyazee, trans, *The Distinguished Jurist's Primer (Bidayat Al-Mujtahid)* (Garnet Publishing, 2000)

Saeed, Abdullah, *Islamic Banking and Interest* (Brill, 1996)

Saeed, Abdullah, *Reading the Qur'an in the Twenty-First Century: A Contextualist Approach* (Routledge, 2014)

Saeed, Abdullah, '*Ijtihad* and Innovation in Neo-Modernist Islamic Thought in Indonesia' (1997) 8(3) *Islam and Christian-Muslim Relations* 279

Saeed, Abdullah, *The Qur'an: An Introduction* (Routledge, 2008)

Saeed, Abdullah, 'The Moral Context of the Prohibition of Riba' (1995) 12 *The American Journal of Islamic Social Sciences* 496

Said, Edward, 'The Clash of Ignorance' (2001) 273(12) *The Nation* 11

Saleh, Nabil, *Unlawful Gain and Legitimate Profit in Islamic Law: Riba, Gharar and Islamic Banking* (Cambridge University Press, 1986)

Saleh, Samir, *Commercial Arbitration in the Arab Middle East: Shari'a, Syria, Lebanon and Egypt* (Hart Publishing, 2006)

Saleh, Samir, 'The Recognition and Enforcement of Foreign Arbitral Awards in the States of the Arab Middle East' (1985) 1 *Arab Law Quarterly* 19

Saleh, Nabil, 'Forward' in Nayla Comair-Obeid (ed), *The Law of Business Contracts in the Arab Middle East* (Kluwer Law International, 1996) xi–xii

Sarea, Adel Mohammed and Mustafa Mohd Haefah, 'Adoption of AAOIFI Accounting Standards by Islamic Banks of Bahrain' (2013) 11(2) *Journal of Financial Reporting and Accounting* 131

Schacht, Joseph, *An Introduction to Islamic Law* (Oxford University Press, 1964)

Schultz, Thomas, 'Human Rights: A Speed Bump for Arbitral Procedures? An Exploration of Safeguards in the Acceleration of Justice' (2006) 9(1) *International Arbitration Law Review* 8

Sénéchal, Thierry, 'Present-Day Valuation in International Arbitration: A Conceptual Framework for Awarding Interest' in Filip De Ly and Laurent Levy (eds), *Interests, Auxiliary and Alternative Remedies in International Arbitration* (Dossiers, ICC Institute of World Business Law, 2008) 219

Sfeir, George, 'The Saudi Approach to Law Reform' (1988) 36(4) *The American Journal of Comparative Law* 729

Shaharuddin, Amir, 'The Bay al Inah Controversy in Malaysian Islamic Banking' (2012) 26 *Arab Law Quarterly* 499

Shahri, Nima Nasrollahi and Amir Hossein Tanhayi, 'An Introduction to Alternative Dispute Settlement in the Iranian Legal System: Reconciliation of Shari'a Law with Arbitration as a Modern Institution' (2015) 12(2) *Transnational Dispute Management* 1

Shalakany, Amr A., 'Arbitration and the Third World: A Plea for Reassessing Bias Under the Specter of Neoliberalism' (2000) 41(2) *Harvard International Law Journal* 419

Shehabi, Faris, 'Resolving Shariah Disputes- Navigating the Governing Law' (2015) 12(2) *Transnational Dispute Management* 1

Silva, Martin Hunter and Gui Conde E., 'Transnational Public Policy and Its Application in Investment Arbitration' (2003) 3(3) *The Journal of World Investment* 367

Singh, Nagendra, 'The Machinery and Method for Conduct of Inter-State Relations in Ancient India' in Yôrām Dinšṭein and Mala Tabory (eds), *International Law at a Time of Perplexity: Essays in Honour of Shabtai Rosenne* (Martinus Nijhoff Publishers, 1989) 845

Smolik, Andrew, 'The Effect of Shari'a on the Dispute Resolution Process Set Forth in the Washington Convention' (2010) 1 *Journal of Dispute Resolution* 151

Sneij, Florentine Sonia and Ulrich Andreas Zanconato, 'The Role of *Shari'a* Law and Modern Arbitration Statutes in an Environment of Growing Multilateral Trade: Lessons from Lebanon and Syria' (2015) 12(2) *Transnational Dispute Management*

Soni, Puja, *The Benefits of Uniformity in International Commercial Law with Special Reference to the United Nations Convention on Contracts for the International Sale of Goods* (Electronic Library Convention on Contracts for the International Sale of Goods, 1980) <http://cisgw3.law.pace.edu/cisg/biblio/soni.html>

Sornarajah, Muthucumaraswamy, 'The Climate of International Arbitration' (1991) 8(2) *Journal of International Arbitration* 47

Spagnolo, Lisa, '*Iura Novit Curia* and the CISG: Resolution of the Faux Procedural Black Hole' in Ingeborg Schwenzer and Lisa Spagnolo (eds), *Towards Uniformity: The 2nd Annual MAA Schlechtriem CISG Conference* (Eleven International Publishing, 2011) 181

Sturges, Wesley A., 'Arbitration – What Is It?' (1960) 35 *New York University Law Review* 1031

Susskind, Anne, 'Shari'ah Law Sits Easily with Arbitration' (2011) 49(11) *Law Society Journal* 26

Swaylim, Dr. Sami ibn Ibrahim al, *Tawarruq Banking Products* (Organization of the Islamic Conference- The International Islamic Fiqh Academy, 2009)

Tamimi, Hind, 'Interest Under the UAE Law as Applied by the Courts in Abu Dhabi' (2002) 17(1) *Arab Law Quarterly* 50

Taniguchi, Yasuhei, 'Is There a Growing International Arbitration Culture? An Observation from Asia' in Albert Jan van den Berg (ed), *International Dispute Resolution: Towards an International Arbitration Culture* (Kluwer Law International, 1998) 31

Tannous, Sami and Seema Bono, 'International Arbitration 2016: United Arab Emirates' in Steven Finizio and Charlie Caher (eds), *International Comparative Legal Guide to International Arbitration 2016* (Global Legal Group, 2016) 464.

Tarin, Shaheer, 'An Analysis of the Influence of Islamic Law on Saudi Arabia's Arbitration and Dispute Resolution Practices' (2015) 26 *American Review of International Arbitration* 131

Thomas, AbdulKader, *Interest in Islamic Economics: Understanding Riba* (Routledge, 2006)

Thomson Reuters, Islamic Corporation for the Development of the Private Sector (ICD)- *Islamic Finance Development Report 2015: Global Transformation* (2015) <www.zawya.com/mena/en/ifg-publications/241115073158K/>

Trakman, Leon E., 'Confidentiality in International Commercial Arbitration' (2002) 18(1) *Arbitration International* 1

Twibell, T. S., 'Implementation of the United Nations Convention on Contracts for the International Sale of Goods (CISG) Under Shari'a Law: Will Article 78 of the CISG Be Enforced When the Forum Is an Islamic State?' (1997) 9 *International Legal Perspectives* 25

Unal, Murat, *The Small World of Islamic Finance: Shariah Scholars and Governance- A Network Analytic Perspective* (Funds@Work, 2011).

Usmani, Muhammad Taqi, *An Introduction to Islamic Finance* (Kluwer Law International, 2002)

Veeder, V. V., 'Arbitral Discrimination Under English and EU Law' in Yves Derains and Laurent Lévy (eds), *Is Arbitration only as Good as the Arbitrator? Status, Powers and Role of the Arbitrator* (International Chamber of Commerce, 2011) 91

Verbist, Herman, 'Challenges on Grounds of Due Process Pursuant to Article V(1)(B) of the New York Convention' in Emmanuel Gaillard and Domenico Di Pietro (eds), *Enforcement of Arbitration Agreements and International Arbitral Awards* (Cameron, May 2008)

Vissier, Hans, *Islamic Finance: Principles and Practice* (Edward Elgar Publishing Limited, 2nd ed, 2013)

Vogel, Frank, *Islamic Law and Legal System: Studies of Saudi Arabia* (Brill, 2000)

Vogel, Frank and Samuel Hayes, *Islamic Law and Finance: Religion, Risk and Return* (Kluwer Law International, 1998)

Wadud, Amina, *Qur'an and Woman: Rereading the Sacred Text from a Woman's Perspective* (Oxford University Press, 1999)

Wadud, Amina, *Inside the Gender Jihad: Women's Reform in Islam* (Oneworld Publications, 2006)

Waincymer, Jeffrey, *Procedure and Evidence in International Arbitration* (Kluwer Law International, 2012)

Wakim, Mark, 'Public Policy Concerns Regarding Enforcement of Foreign International Arbitral Awards in the Middle East' (2008) 21(1) *New York International Law Review* 1

Wallgren-Lindholm, Carita, '*Ad hoc* Arbitration vs Institutional Arbitration' in Giuditta Cordero-Moss (ed), *International Commercial Arbitration: Different Forms and Their Features* (Cambridge University Press, 2013)

Wallgren-Lindholm, Carita '*Ad hoc* Arbitration vs Institutional Arbitration' in Giuditta Cordero-Moss (ed), *International Commercial Arbitration: Different Forms and Their Features* (Cambridge University Press, 2013), 61–81

Warde, Ibrahim, *Islamic Finance in the Global Economy* (Edinburgh University Press, 2000)

Weiss, Bernard G., *The Spirit of Islamic Law* (University of Georgia Press, 1998)

Westermann, W. L., 'Interstate Arbitration in Antiquity' (1907) 2(5) *The Classical Journal* 197

White, Andrew, 'Dispute Resolution and Specialized ADR for Islamic Finance' in David Eisenberg and Craig Nethercott (eds), *Islamic Finance: Law and Practice* (Oxford University Press, 2012) 306

White, Andrew and Chen Mee King, 'Legal Risk Exposure in Islamic Finance' in Simon Archer and Rifaat Ahmed Abdel Karim (eds), *Islamic Finance: The New Regulatory Challenge* (John Wiley & Sons 2013)

Whiteman, Marjorie M., *Damages in International Law* (William S. Hein & Company, 1943)

Wiley, Kit, 'Human Rights, *Sharia* Law and the Western Concept of Democracy' in David Claydon (ed), *Islam, Human Rights and Public Policy* (Acorn Press, 2009)

Wilson, Rodney, *Legal, Regulatory and Governance Issues in Islamic Finance* (Edinburgh University Press, 2012)

Yaacob, Hakimah, 'Towards Our Own *Lex Mercatoria*: A Need for Legal Consensus in Islamic Finance' (2014) 22 *Pertanika Journal of Social Sciences and Humanities* 257

Yang, Inae, '*Nurdin Jivraj v. Sadruddin Hashwani*: The English Court of Appeal Erects a Regulatory Barrier to the Appointment of Arbitrators in the Name of Anti-Discrimination' (2011) 28(3) *Journal of International Arbitration* 243

Yuksel, Edip, Layth Saleh al-Shaiban and Martha Schulte-Nafeh, *Quran: A Reformist Translation* (Brainbow Press, 2007)

Yusuf, Hamza, *Shaykh Murabtal Haaj's Fatwa on Following One of the Four Accepted Madhhabs* <http://shaykhhamza.com/transcript/Fatwa-on-Following-a-Madhab>

Zahraa, Mahdi and Nora Abdul Hak, 'Tahkim (arbitration) in Islamic law Within the Context of Family Law Disputes' (2006) 20(1) *Arab Law Quarterly* 2

Závodná, Martina, *The European Convention on Human Rights and Arbitration* (Diploma, Masaryk University, 2013/2014)

Zegers, Jean-Benoit, 'Recognition and Enforcement of Foreign Arbitral Awards in Saudi Arabia' (2014) 1(1) *BCDR International Arbitration Review* 69

Zegers, Jean-Benoît, 'National Report for Saudi Arabia (2013)' in Jan Paulsson and Lise Bosman (eds), *ICCA International Handbook on Commercial Arbitration* (Kluwer Law International, Supplement No. 75, July 2013, 1984) 1

B Cases

1 Arbitral awards

A1, India v B1 LLC, UAE and B2 SAL (2010) 2(3) *International Journal of Arab Arbitration* 270

Alexandria Center for International Arbitration Case Number 6/2003 at Pace University Albert H. Kritzer *CISG* Database, *Semi-Dried Dates Case* (2005) <http://CISGw3.law.pace.edu/cases/050116e1.html>

Arbitration Tribunal: Award in the Matter of an Arbitration Between BP Exploration Co. (Libya) v Libyan Arab Republic (1979) 53 ILR 297

Case No. 5505 of 1987, Preliminary Award, Mozambique Buyer v Netherlands Seller (1988) XIII Y.B. Comm. Arb 110

China International Economic & Trade Arbitration Commission at Pace University Albert H. Kritzer, *CISG* Database, *Pharmaceutical Products Case* (2000) <http://CISGw3.law.pace.edu/cases/001206c1.html>

Grove-Skanska v. Lockheed Aircraft Int'l AG, ICC Case No. 3903 (1981), unreported, cited and reported in David J. Branson and Jr Richard E. Wallace, 'Awarding Interest in International Commercial Arbitration: Establishing a Uniform Approach' (1988) 28 *Virginia Journal of International Law* 919, 933–937

ICC Case No. 11849/2003 at Pace University Albert H. Kritzer, *CISG* Database, *Fashion Products Case* (2003) <http://CISGw3.law.pace.edu/cases/031849i1.html>

ICC Case No. 4606 (1987), unreported, cited and reported in David J. Branson and Jr. Richard E. Wallace, 'Awarding Interest in International Commercial Arbitration: Establishing a Uniform Approach' (1988) 28 *Virginia Journal of International Law* 919

ICC Case No. 5082/1980 (2004) 15(1) ICC *International Court of Arbitration Bulletin* 63

ICC Case No. 5277/1987 (1988) 13 Y.B. Comm. Arb 80

lCC Case No. 5835 (1999) 10(2) ICC *International Court of Arbitration Bulletin* 33

ICC Case No. 6162/1990 (1992) 3(1) *ICC International Court of Arbitration Bulletin* 22

ICC Case No. 6230/1990 (1991) 2(1) *ICC International Court of Arbitration Bulletin* 27

ICC Case No. 7063 (1996) 22 Y.B. Comm. Arb 87

ICC Case No. 7153/1992 at Pace University Albert H. Kritzer *CISG* Database, *Hotel Materials Case* (1992) <http://CISGw3.law.pace.edu/cases/927153i1.html>

ICC Case No. 7263 (2004) 15 ICC *International Court of Arbitration Bulletin* 71

ICC Case No. 7331/1994, at Unilex (1994) <www.unilex.info/case.cfm?pid=1&do=case&id=140&step=FullText>

ICC Case No. 7373 (Final Award) (2004) 15(1) *ICC International Court of Arbitration Bulletin* 72

ICC Case No. 7531/1994, at Unilex (1994) <www.unilex.info/case.cfm?pid=1&do=case&id=139&step=FullText>

ICC Case No. 8677 (2009) 1(4) *International Journal of Arab Arbitration* 333

InterMaritime Management SA (Switzerland) v. Russin & Vecchi (U.S.) 22 Y.B. Comm. Arb 789, 798 (1997)

Aryeh v. Iran, Iran-US CTR, Award No. 581=842/843/844-1 (22 May 1997)

Iran-US CTR, Case No. 35 (145-35-3) (1985) 10 *Yearbook Commercial Arbitration* 258

Iran-US CTR, *McCollough & Company, Inc. v. Ministry of Post, Telegraph and Telephone* (1986) 11 IRAN-U.S. Claims Tribunal Report

Islamic Republic of Iran v. United States of America, Decision, IUSCT Case No. A19 (DEC 65-A19-FT) (1988) 13 Y.B. Comm. Arb 258

Kuwait and the American Independent Oil Company (Aminoil) (1982) 21 ILM 976

Libyan American Oil Co. v. the Government of the Libyan Arab Republic (1981) 20 ILM 1

Petroleum Development (Trucial Coast) Ltd. v. Sheikh of Abu Dhabi (1952) 19 Int'l & Comp. L.Q. 247; 18 ILR 144

Pipeline Contractor v. Oil Company, Final Award (1989) 14 Y.B. Comm. Arb 47

R.J. Reynolds Tobacco Company v. The Government of the Islamic Republic of Iran, Iran-US Claims Tribunal, IUSCT Case No. 35 (145-35-3) (1985) 10 *Yearbook Commercial Arbitration* 258

Ruler of Qatar v. International Marine Oil Company Ltd. (1953) 20 ILR 534

Saudi Arabia v. Arabian American Oil Company (Aramco) (1958) 27 ILR 117

SCH-4366 at Pace University Albert H. Kritzer *CISG* Database, *Rolled Metal Sheets Case* (Austria, Arbitral Tribunal Vienna, 15 June 1994) <http://CISGw3.law.pace.edu/cases/940615a3.html>

Starrett Housing Corp. v. Iran [1987] 16 Iran-U.S. C.T.R (Iran-US Claims Tribunal) 269 <http://translex.uni-koeln.de/232100>

Syrian State Trading Org v. Ghanaian State Enterprise, ICC Case No. 4237 (1985) 10 Y.B. Comm. Arb 52

Texas Overseas Petroleum Co. [TOPCO] v. Libyan Arab Republic (1978) 17 ILM 1

Watkins-Johnson Co., Watkins-Johnson Ltd. v. Islamic Republic of Iran, Bank Saderat Iran at Albert H. Krtizer, *CISG* Database, (Iran/U.S. Claims Tribunal, 28 July 1989) www.unilex.info/case.cfm?pid=1&do=case&id=38&step=FullText

2 Bahrain

Establishment v. Limited Liability Company, Court of Cassation of Bahrain, Fourth High Civil Court, Case No. 02/2009/9679/9, 10 February 2010

Court of Cassation of Bahrain, Third High Civil Court, Appeal No. 03/2010/540/9, 24 November 2010

Court of Cassation of Bahrain, First Court of Cassation, Cassation No. 746 (2010) 12 March 2012 (2013) 38 *Yearbook Commercial Arbitration* 574

Parties Not Indicated, Court of Cassation of Bahrain (Second Circuit), Challenge No. 259/2009, 4 May 2010, (2011) 3(4) *International Journal of Arab Arbitration,* 29

Parties Not Indicated, Court of Cassation of Bahrain, 156/2004, 4 July 2005, 1(4) *International Journal of Arab Arbitration* 139

Parties Not Indicated, Court of Cassation of Bahrain, 305/2004, 9 May 2005, (2009) 1(4) *International Journal of Arab Arbitration* 137

Parties Not Indicated, Court of Cassation of Bahrain, 78/2003, 16 February 2004, (2010) 2(1) *International Journal of Arab Arbitration* 105

Parties Not Indicated, Court of Cassation of Bahrain, Audience No. 108/2012, 21 January 2013, (2014) 6(3) *International Journal of Arab Arbitration* 13

Parties Not Indicated, Court of Cassation of Bahrain, Challenge No. 101 of 2010, 2 April 2012, (2013) 5(3) *International Journal of Arab Arbitration,* 37

Parties Not Indicated, Court of Cassation, 165/2005, 3 October 2005, (2009) 1(3) *International Journal of Arab Arbitration* 65

Parties Not Indicated, Court of Cassation, 328/2005, 30 January 2006, (2010) 2(2) *International Journal of Arab Arbitration* 112

Parties Not Indicated, Supreme Court, Case No. 241/2008, 17 November 2008, (2011) 3(2) *International Journal of Arab Arbitration* 36

Parties Not Indicated, Supreme Court, Case No. 75/2007, 7 January 2008, (2011) 3(2) *International Journal of Arab Arbitration* 33

3 Egypt

Alexandria for Soaps and Oils v. Alexandria for Navigation Procurements (Amoun Procurement for Navigation), Court of Cassation, Commercial Circuit, 607/63, 27 March 2007, 1(1) *International Journal of Arab Arbitration* 213

Andritz v. National Cement Co, Case No. 810/71, Supreme Court of Cassation, Commercial and Civil Division, 25 January 2008 reported in (2009) 1(4) *International Journal of Arab Arbitration* 148

Cairo Court of Appeal, Commercial Circuit No.91, 27 April 2005, Case No. 95/120

Cairo Court of Appeal, Commercial Circuit, No. 91, 29 January 2006, Cases No. 13 et 14/121

Cairo Court of Appeal, Commercial Circuit No. 91 30 May 2006 No. 43 et 89/122

Cairo Court of Appeal, Economic Circuit No. 7, 2 July 2007 No.68/123

Court of Cassation, Commercial and Economic Circuit, 8 October 2013, Challenge No. 9882/80

Customs Authority v. Islamic Company for Imports and Exports, Cairo Court of Appeals, 8th Circuit, 91 Commercial, 102/124, 22 April 2008, (2009) 1(1) *International Journal of Arab Arbitration* 190

Egypt for Foreign Trade v. R.D. Harbottles (Mercantile) Case No. 64/2010, Court of Cassation, Commercial Circuit, 22 January 2008, 1(1) *International Journal of Arab Arbitration* 174

Horus for Shipping and Navigation Company v. Ergo Shipping S.A., *Court of Appeals*, Circuit 91, Commercial, 92/123, 16 January 2008, (2009) 1(2) *International Journal of Arab Arbitration* 125–132

Karim Abou Youssef, Amal Tourism Complex Co. v. Ministry of Tourism, Court of Cassation, 4721/73, 27 December 2007, *ITA Board of Reporters* (Kluwer Law International)

Lieutenant, President of the Board of the Cooperative Association for the Lieutenants of the Armed Forces v. Mr. Kamal Abdel Aziz el Zouhayri, Cairo Court of Appeals, 7th Economic Circuit, 71/123, 5 February 2008, (2009) 1(1) *International Journal of Arab Arbitration* 248

Miss Fatima Muhammad Metwaly v. Mr. Muhammad Salah el Dine Muhammad Metwali, Miss Wafak Hanem Muhammad Metwali and Others, Cairo Court of Appeals, 62nd Circuit, Commercial, 29/2004, 6 March 2008, (2009) 1(1) *International Journal of Arab Arbitration* 180

Mr. Eid Muhammad Eid Ibrahim, Mr. Ossama Muhammad Eid Ibrahim v. Mr. Himam Sayed Othman Sanad, Mr. Ahmad Abdel Al Farhat Hmad and Others, Cairo Court of Appeals, 7th Circuit, Economy, 140/124, 6 May 2008, (2009) 1(2) *International Journal of Arab Arbitration* 209

Mr. Korni Muhammad Farjani, Mr. Hussein Ali Farjani and Others v. Mr. Muhammad Abdel Raouf Muhammad el Wahesh, Mr. Jamal Fawzi Ali el Wahesh and Others, Cairo Court of Appeals, 91st Circuit, Commercial, 21/124, 13 February 2008, (2009) 1(1) *International Journal of Arab Arbitration* 237

Mr. Mounir Ghabour Hannah v. American International Group (AIG), Cairo Court of Appeals, 62nd Circuit, Commercial, 70/123, 7 May 2008, (2009) 1(1) *International Journal of Arab Arbitration* 183

Mr. Muhammad Abdel Kawi Ahmad Mokbel, Mr. Ahmad Abdel Kawi Ahmad Mokbel and Others v. Mr. Adel Abdel Majid Abdel Latif, Mr. Muhammad Mahmoud Metwali and Others, Cairo Court of Appeals, Jizza Department, 91st Circuit, Commercial,

110/124, 2 February 2008, (2009) 1(1) *International Journal of Arab Arbitration* 195

Mr. Muhammad Aly Muhammad Muhammad el Bari in His Capacity as the Legal Representative of the Company Brother for Import Export and Supply v. Mr. Thai Jin Yang, President of the South Korean Company Hano Acorporish, Court of Appeal (7th Economic Circuit) 23/125, 2 July 2008, (2009) 1(2) *International Journal of Arab Arbitration* 113

Mr. Wael Ali Moussa, Mrs. Fatima Muhammad Sleiman and Others v. Dr. Kamal el Dine Abdel Rahman Darwish, Dr. Oueiss Ali el Jabali, Cairo Court of Appeals, Jizza Circuit, 91st Commercial Division, 23/2005, 1 October 2005, (2009) 1(1) *International Journal of Arab Arbitration* 199

Mrs. Fayqa Mahmoud Al-Dasouki Zaqzaq v. Mr. Ahmad Fouad Ali Ahmad Ali, Mr. Yusri Mahmoud Saadedine Ahmad and Others, Cairo Court of Appeals, Department of Giza, Circuit (91), Commercial, 37/123, 16 January 2008, (2009) 1(2) *International Journal of Arab Arbitration* 133

Parties Not Indicated Cairo Court of Appeal, Commercial Circuit No 7, Cases No 35, 41, 44, 45/129, 5 February 2013

Parties Not Indicated, Cairo Court of Appeal – Eighth Commercial Circuit, 28 February 2009, (2010) 2(4) *International Journal of Arab Arbitration* 67

Parties Not Indicated, Cairo Court of Appeal – Seventh Commercial Circuit, 33/124j; 30/124j; 33/123j, 2 February 2010, (2011) 3(1) *International Journal of Arab Arbitration* 65–67

Parties Not Indicated, Cairo Court of Appeal, Commercial Circuit No.8, 15 February 2015- Recourse Against Exequatur Order No 18/126; Cairo Court of Appeal, Commercial Circuit No 7, 7 April 2013; Cases No 20, 64/128 and 16,20, 47/129

Parties Not Indicated, Cairo Court of Appeal, Eighth Circuit, Commercial, 75/125, 18 May 2009, (2010) 2(1) *International Journal of Arab Arbitration* 136

Parties Not Indicated, Cairo Court of Appeal, Seventh Commercial Division, 55/122, 7 April 2009, (2009) 1(4) *International Journal of Arab Arbitration* 141

Parties Not Indicated, Cairo Court of Appeals (62nd Circuit, Commercial) 462/2005, 7 May 2008, (2009) 1(1) *International Journal of Arab Arbitration* 204

Parties Not Indicated, Cairo Court of Appeals (Seventh Commercial Circuit) 114/124, 2 December 2008, (2010) 2(1) *International Journal of Arab Arbitration* 126

Parties Not Indicated, Cairo Court of Appeals (Seventh Commercial Circuit) 112/124, 5 May 2009, (2010) 2(10) *International Journal of Arab Arbitration* 109

Parties Not Indicated, Cairo Court of Appeals, Seventh Commercial Circuit, 29/125, 29/125, 5 May 2009, (2010) 2(1) *International Journal of Arab Arbitration* 120

Parties Not Indicated, Court of Appeal – Cairo – Seventh Commercial Circuit, 119/124, 2 February 2010, 2(3) *International Journal of Arab Arbitration* 114

Parties Not Indicated, Court of Appeal of Cairo (Seventh Circuit), Commercial Arbitration No. 70/123j, 9 March 2011, 3(4) *International Journal of Arab Arbitration* 35

Parties Not Indicated, Court of Appeal of Cairo, Arbitration Case No. 32/128j, 6 June 2012, (2013) 5(2) *International Journal of Arab Arbitration* 11

Parties Not Indicated, Court of Appeal of Cairo, Case No. 10/127j, 4 January 2011, (2012) 4(1) *International Journal of Arab Arbitration* 21

Parties Not Indicated, Court of Appeal of Cairo, Case No. 13/128, 20 April 2014, 7(1) *International Journal of Arab Arbitration* 22

Parties Not Indicated, Court of Appeal of Cairo, Case No. 23/128, 4 August 2014, (2015) 7(1) *International Journal of Arab Arbitration* 19

Parties Not Indicated, Court of Appeal of Cairo, Case No. 38/128J, 8 January 2012, 4(4) *International Journal of Arab Arbitration* 29

Parties Not Indicated, Court of Appeal of Cairo, Case No. 4/128N, 7 September 2011, (2013) 5(1) *International Journal of Arab Arbitration* 37

Parties Not Indicated, Court of Appeal of Cairo, Case No. 43/128j, 2 November 2011, (2012) 4(3) *International Journal of Arab Arbitration*, 54

Parties Not Indicated, Court of Appeal of Cairo, Case No. 48/130, 2 June 2014, 6(4) *International Journal of Arab Arbitration* 23–28

Parties Not Indicated, Court of Appeal of Cairo, Case No. 59/125 (2012) 4(2) *International Journal of Arab Arbitration* 74

Parties Not Indicated, Court of Cassation – Civil and Commercial Circuit, 98/79j, 24 December 2009, (2011) 3(1) *International Journal of Arab Arbitration* 68

Parties Not Indicated, Court of Cassation – Commercial Circuit, 2414/72, 22 March 2005, (2010) 2(3) *International Journal of Arab Arbitration* 97

Parties Not Indicated, Court of Cassation, 13 February 2014, Case No 7595/81

Parties Not Indicated, Supreme Court of Cassation, Commercial Division, 2010/64, 22 January 2008, 1(4) *International Journal of Arab Arbitration*, 145

Parties Not Indicated, Supreme Court, Commercial Division, 730/76, 8 February 2008, (2009) 1(4) *International Journal of Arab Arbitration* 150–157 and Cairo Court of Appeal (Commercial Court) No. 91, 26 April 2006, Case No 49/133

Parties Not Indicated, Supreme Court, Commercial Division, 9736/65, 11 March 2008, (2009) 1(4) *International Journal of Arab Arbitration* 143

Rila Netex for Touristic Town v. Agro Trade Company for Reclamation of Lands, Court of Cassation, Commercial Circuit, 10635/1976, 27 February 2007, 1(2) *International Journal of Arab Arbitration* 93

Saudi-Egyptian Company for Touristic Development v. Meridian S.A., Cairo Court of Appeal, 7th Economic Circuit, 123/119, 3 April 2007, (2009) 1(2) *International Journal of Arab Arbitration* 141

Sobhy Hussein Ahmed (Contractor) v. Cooperative Association of Construction and Housing for the Employees of a Petroleum Company "Suez Gulf" (Owner), Cairo Court of Appeal, 7th Commercial Circuit, 102/123, 9 June 2009, (2009) 3(1) *International Journal of Arab Arbitration* 71

4 India

International Investor KCSC v. Sanghi Polyesters Ltd./Civil Revision Petition Nos 331 and 1441 of 2002 (1) ALT 364; [2003] 43 SCL 271 AP (Andhra High Court) <http://indiankanoon.org/doc/1639330/>

5 Kuwait

Company for International Investment v. Holding Company "Al Bab", Court of Cassation, (2nd Commercial Circuit) 773/2006, 6 April 2008, (2009) 1(1) *International Journal of Arab Arbitration* 269

Parties Not Indicated, Court of Appeal of Kuwait (Judicial Arbitration Tribunal), Request for Arbitration No. 16/2001, 8 May 2008, (2009) 1(4) *International Journal of Arab Arbitration* 173

Parties Not Indicated, Court of Appeals (First Judicial Arbitral Tribunal, 20 December 2006, (2010) 2(2) *International Journal of Arab Arbitration* 145

Parties Not Indicated, Court of Cassation – Civil Circuit, 511/2005, 13 February 2006, (2010) 2(3) *International Journal of Arab Arbitration* 139

Parties Not Indicated, Court of Cassation (Commercial Circuit) 671/2004, 23 November 2006, (2009) 1(2) *International Journal of Arab Arbitration*, 168

Parties Not Indicated, Court of Cassation (Commercial), 668/2006, 10 February 2008, (2009) 1(3) *International Journal of Arab Arbitration* 171

Parties Not Indicated, Court of Cassation (Second Commercial Circuit) Case No. 47/2008, 4 January 2009, (2011) 3(2) *International Journal of Arab Arbitration*, 57

Parties Not Indicated, Court of First Instance, 28 December 2008, (2010) 2(4) *International Journal of Arab Arbitration* 81

6 Malaysia

Affin Bank Berhad v. Marilyn Ho Siok Lin [2006] 7 MLJ 249
Malayan Banking Bhd v. Ya'kup Oje & Anor [2007] 5 CLJ 311
Mohd Alias Ibrahim v. RHB Bank BHD & Anor [2011] 4 CLJ 654 (25 April 2011) (High Court Malaya)

7 Oman

Company Body Light Industries Limited v. Company Asbagh Sadoline, High Court in the Sultanate of Oman, 221/2005, 17 October 2005, (2009) 1(1) *International Journal of Arab Arbitration* 417

Parties Not Indicated, Court of Appeal of Muscat, Decision No. 628/2013, (2015) 7(1) *International Journal of Arab Arbitration* 43

Parties Not Indicated, Court of Appeal, Commercial, 34/2009, 27 April 2009, (2009) 1(3) *International Journal of Arab Arbitration* 245

Parties Not Indicated, Court of Cassation, Case No. 174/2005, 31 December 2005, (2011) 3(2) *International Journal of Arab Arbitration* 77

Parties Not Indicated, Court of Cassation, Decision No. 136/2005, 21 December 2005, (2010) 2(4) *International Journal of Arab Arbitration* 101

Parties Not Indicated, Supreme Court of Oman, Cassation No. 280/2010, Commercial Circuit, 27 April 2011, (2014) 1(1) *BCDR International Arbitration Review* 149

The New Indian Company for Insurance v. The Vessel M V IKO and the Company Tawel Barwil, Commercial Circuit, 70/2004, 8 December 2004, (2009) 1(1) *International Journal of Arab Arbitration* 427

8 Qatar

Abnaa El Khalaf Company et al. v. Sayed Aga Jawwed Raza, Court of Cassation of Qatar, 12 June 2012, ITA Board of Reporters, (Minas Khatchadourian trans, Kluwer Law International)

Contracting Co. A v. Sub-Contracting Co. B, Court of First Instance of Doha, Case No. 2216, 17 December 2013, ITA Board of Reporters, Kluwer Law International

International Trading and Industrial Investment Co. v. Dyncorp Aerospace Technology, 763 F. Supp. 2d 12 (D.D.C. 2011)

Parties Not Indicated, Case No. 137/CDFI, Court of First Instance of Doha (2012) 4(2) *International Journal of Arab Arbitration* 87

Parties Not Indicated, Court of First Instance of Qatar, Case No. 2768/2012, 24 June 2013, (2015) 7(1) International Journal of Arab Arbitration 47

Parties Not Indicated, Court of First Instance of Qatar, Case No. 1413/2007, 26 November 2008, (2009) 1(3) *International Journal of Arab Arbitration* 249

Qatar No. 1, ABC LLP v. Joint Venture RST and XYZ, Supreme Court of Cassation, Petitions Nos. 45 and 49 of 2014, 25 March 2014 reported in Albert Jan van den Berg (ed), 39 *Yearbook Commercial Arbitration* 480–482 (Minas Khatchadourian trans, Kluwer Law International)

"R" Company for Trade Projects Management v. Mr. "J", Court of Cassation of Qatar, Petition No. 211 of 2014, 9 December 2014, ITA Board of Reporters, (Minas Khatchadourian trans, Kluwer Law International)

9 Saudi Arabia

Midland International Trade Services Ltd. v. Al Sudairy (1990) *Financial Times*

Parties Not Indicated, Board of Grievances of Saudi Arabia, 1767/2/J, 21 February 2004 (2010) 2(1) *International Journal of Arab Arbitration* 203

Parties Not Indicated, Court of Grievance- Commercial Circuit, undated, (2010) 2(3) *International Journal of Arab Arbitration* 203

Parties Not Indicated, Board of Grievances of Saudi Arabia, undated 2012, (2014) 6(2) *International Journal of Arab Arbitration* 29

Parties Not Indicated, Board of Grievances of Saudi Arabia, undated 2014, (2015) 7(1) *International Journal of Arab Arbitration* 91

Parties Not Indicated, Ruling No. 189/T/4 of 1427 AH 2007

10 Switzerland

ATF 112 Ia 166, 22 July 1986 (Swiss Federal Tribunal)

ATF 117 Ia 166, 30 April 1991 (Swiss Federal Tribunal)

A v. Union des associations europeennes de football (UEFA) (Swiss Federal Tribunal), 11 June 2001, (2001) 3 *ASA Bulletin* 566

11 United Arab Emirates

Airmech Dubai LLC v. Maxtel International LLC, Dubai Court of Cassation of Dubai, Appeal No. 132 of 2012, 18 September 2012 (2013) 5(1) *International Journal of Arab Arbitration* 52

Baiti Real Estate Development v. Dynasty Zarooni Inc, Dubai Court of Cassation, Appeal No. 180 of 2011, 12 February 2012 (2013) 5(1) *International Journal of Arab Arbitration* 50

Construction Company International (C.C.I.) v. The Government of the Democratic Republic of Sudan, Dubai Court of Cassation of Dubai, No. 156/2013 Civil, 18 August 2013 (2014) 1(1) *BCDR International Arbitration Review* 137

Explosivos Alaveses SA (Spain) v. United Management Chile Limited, Dubai Court of Cassation of Abu Dhabi, Cassation No. 679/2010 Commercial, 16 June 2011 (2014) 1(1), *BCDR International Arbitration Review* 125

Federal Supreme Court- Petition No. 831 of the 25th Judicial Year and Petition No. 67 of the 26th Judicial Year issued on 23 May 2004 cited in Graham Lovett, Lara Hammond and Hassan Arab, *Summaries of UAE Courts' Decisions on Arbitration*. (ICC Publication, 2013) 57

Parties Not Indicated, Abu Dhabi, Dubai Court of Cassation, *Case No. 2847/2013* [2014] 6(4) *International Journal of Arab Arbitration* 49

Parties Not Indicated, Abu Dhabi, Federal High Court, *Case No. 891/27*, 17 June 2006 (2009) 1(1) *International Journal of Arab Arbitration* 516

Parties Not Indicated, Abu Dhabi, Federal Supreme Court, 10 October 2006 (2010) 2(4) *International Journal of Arab Arbitration* 117

Parties Not Indicated, Abu Dhabi, Federal Supreme Court, *Case No.* 245/20, 7 May 2000 cited in Hind Tamimi, 'Interest under the UAE Law as Applied by the Courts in Abu Dhabi' (2002) 17(1) *Arab Law Quarterly* 50, 52

Parties Not Indicated, Abu Dhabi, High Federal Court, 56/27, 12 May 2006 (2009) 1(1) *International Journal of Arab Arbitration* 511

Parties Not Indicated, Court of Cassation – Dubai, 240/2007, 13 January 2008 (2010) 2(3) *International Journal of Arab Arbitration* 238

Parties Not Indicated, Court of Cassation of Abu Dhabi, Case No. 2847/2013, 12 February 2014 (2014) 6(4) *International Journal of Arab Arbitration* 49

Parties Not Indicated, Court of Cassation of Dubai, 146/2008, 9 November 2008 (2010) 2(3) *International Journal of Arab Arbitration* 240; Graham Lovett, Lara Hammond and Hassan Arab, *Summaries of UAE Courts' Decisions on Arbitration*. (ICC Publication, 2013), 96

Parties Not Indicated, Court of Cassation of Dubai, 218/2006, 17 October 2006 (2009) 1(3) *International Journal of Arab Arbitration* 139

Parties Not Indicated, Court of Cassation of Dubai, 351/2005, 1 July 2006 (2009) 1(4) *International Journal of Arab Arbitration* 159

Parties Not Indicated, Court of Cassation of Dubai, *Case No. 320 of 2013*, 22 June 2014 (2015) 7(1) *International Journal of Arab Arbitration* 81

Parties Not Indicated, Court of Cassation of Dubai, Civil Challenge No. 103 of 2011 (2012) 4(2) *International Journal of Arab Arbitration* 111

Parties Not Indicated, Court of Cassation of Dubai, Civil Challenge, *Case No. 265/ 2007*, 3 February 2008 (2010) 2(1) *International Journal of Arab Arbitration* 245

Parties Not Indicated, Court of Cassation of Dubai, Commercial Chamber, Dubai, 268/2007, 19 February 2008 (2010) 2(1) *International Journal of Arab Arbitration* 231

Parties Not Indicated, Court of Cassation of Dubai, Petition No. 132 of 2012, 22 February 2012 [Graham Lovett, Lara Hammond and Hassan Arab, *Summaries of UAE Courts' Decisions on Arbitration* (ICC Publication, 2013), 124]

Parties Not Indicated, Court of Cassation of Dubai, Petition No. 280/2008, 22 September 2009

Parties Not Indicated, Court of Cassation of Dubai, Recourse No. 222/2005, 22 January 2006 (2009) 1(4) *International Journal of Arab Arbitration* 164

Parties Not Indicated, Court of First Instance of Dubai, Case No. 688 of 2014, 17 September 2014 (2015) 7(1) *International Journal of Arab Arbitration* 86

Parties Not Indicated, Dubai Court of Cassation, Petition No. 14 of 2012, 16 September 2012 as cited in Graham Lovett, Lara Hammond and Hassan Arab, *Summaries of UAE Courts' Decisions on Arbitration.* (ICC Publication, 2013), 122–123
Parties Not Indicated, Federal High Court, Abu Dhabi, 676/2009, 18 October 2009 (2010) 2(2) *International Journal of Arab Arbitration* 225
Parties Not Indicated, Federal Supreme Court, Abu Dhabi, 10 October 2006, (2010) 2(4) *International Journal of Arab Arbitration* 117
United Arab Emirates No. 1, Shipowners v. Charterers, Court of First Instance, Fujairah, 27 April 2010 (2011) 36 Y.B. Comm. Arb 353

12 United Kingdom

Al Bassam v. Al Bassam [2002] EWHC 2281
AT&T Corporation and another v. Saudi Cable [2000] 2 Lloyd's Rep 127
C v. D [2007] EWCA Civ 1282
Deutsche Schachtbau- und Tiefbohrgesellschaft mbH v. Ras Al Khaimah National Oil Co and another appeal [1987] 2 All ER 769
Deutsche Schachtbau-und Tiefbohr GmbH v. Ras al Khaimah National Oil Co & Shell International Petroleum Co Ltd.; sub nom Deutsche Schachtbau-und Tiefbohrgesellschaft mbH v. Ras Al Khaimah National Oil Co [1990] 1 AC 295
Glencore International AG v. Metro Trading International Inc [2001] All ER (Comm) 103
Halpern v. Halpern [2007] EWCA Civ 291; [2008] Q.B. 195
Islamic Investment Company of the Gulf (Bahamas) Ltd. v. Symphony Gems NV (unreported, Queens Bench Division, Commercial Court, 13 February 2002)
Jivraj v. Hashwani (2010) EWCA (Civ) 712
Jivraj v. Hashwani [2009] EWHC 1364
Mousaka Inc v. Golden Seagull Maritime Inc [2002] 1 All ER 726
Musawi v. RE International (UK) Ltd. & Ords [2007] EWHC 2981
Petroleum Development (Trucial Coast) Ltd. v. Sheikh of Abu Dhabi (1951) 19 ILR 144
Porter v. Magill [2002] AC 357
re The Owners of the Steamship Catalina and The Owners of the Motor Vessel Norma [1938] 61 Lloyd's Rep. 360
Regina v. Gough [1993] AC 646
Sanghi Polyesters Ltd. (India) v. The International Investor KCSC (Kuwait) [2000] 1 Lloyd's Rep 480
Shamil Bank of Bahrain v. Beximco Pharm. Ltd. [2004] EWCA Civ 19
Soleimany v. Soleimany [1999] QB 785

13 United States of America

Hays v. Hays, 23 Wend. 363 (N.Y. Sup. Ct. 1840)
International Standard Electric Corporation ('ISEC') v. Bridas Sociedad Anonima Petrolera,
Indus Y. Commercial 745 F Supp 172 (SDNY, 1990)
International Trading and Industrial Investment Co. v. Dyncorp Aerospace Technology, 763 F. Supp. 2d 12 (D.D.C. 2011)
Martin v. Vansant, 99 Wash. 106, 117 (Wash. 1917)
Mitsubishi Motors Corporation v. Soler Chrysler-Plymouth Inc 723 F.2d 155, 164 (1st Cir, 1983)

National Group for Communications and Computers Ltd., Plaintiff, v. Lucent Technologies International Inc. 331 F. Supp. 2d 290 (D.N.J, 2004)

Parsons & Whittemore Overseas Co. v. Societe Generale de l'Industrie due Papier (RAKTA) 508 F.2d 969, 975–76 (2nd Cir, 1974)

Revere Copper & Brass Inc v. Overseas Private Inv Corp 628 F.2d 81, 83 (D.C Cir. 1980)

Saudi Basic Industries Corporation ('SABIC') v. Mobile Yanbu Petrochemical Co 866 A.2d 1 (Del, 2005)

14 *Other*

Appellate Body Report, *Canada-Continued Suspension of Obligations in the EC-Hormones Dispute*, WT/DS321/AB/R (16 October 2008)

Atlantic Triton Co v. People's Republic of Guinea (ICSID Arbitral Tribunal, Case No. ARB/84/1, 21 April 1986)

Compania del Desarrollo de Santa Elena v. Costa Rica (ICSID Tribunal, Case No ARB/96/1, 17 February 2000)

Desert Lines Project L.L.C. v. The Republic of Yemen Award (ICSID Case Arbitral Tribunal, Case No. Arb/05/17, 6 February 2008)

Eco Swiss China Time Ltd. v. Benetton International NV Case C-126/97 [1999] ECR I-3055

Factory at Chorzow (Germany v. Poland) [1927] PCIJ (ser A) No 9 (July 26)

R v. Suisse (1987) Eur Comm HR 30 *Yearbook of European Convention Human Rights* 36 as cited in Herman Verbist, 'Challenges on Grounds of Due Process Pursuant to Article V(1)(B) of the New York Convention' in Emmanuel Gaillard and Domenico Di Pietro (eds), *Enforcement of Arbitration Agreements and International Arbitral Awards* (Cameron, May, 2008) 679, 690

Southern Pacific Properties v. Egypt (ICSID Arbitral Tribunal, Case No ARB/84/3, 20 May 1992)

C Legislation and regulations

1 *Australia*

International Arbitration Act 1974 (Cth)

2 *Egypt*

Constitution of the Arab Republic of Egypt (Amended 2014) [Egyptian Government trans, <www.sis.gov.eg/Newvr/Dustor-en001.pdf>]

Egyptian Civil Code 1948 (World Intellectual Property Organisation, <www.wipo.int/wipolex/en/text.jsp?file_id=205494> [University of Minnesota Human Rights Library trans, <http://www1.umn.edu/humanrts/research/Egypt/Civil%20Law.pdf>.]

3 *Germany*

German Civil Procedure Code [Trans-Lex, 'The New German Arbitration Law-(English Translation' <www.trans-lex.org/600550>)

4 Kuwait

Code of Civil and Commercial Procedure No. 38 of 1980 (Kuwait) [trans (1989) 4(1) *Arab Law Quarterly* 25]

Kuwaiti Trade Law No. 68 of 1980 ('*Kuwaiti Commercial Code*') (World Intellectual Property Organisation, <www.wipo.int/wipolex/en/details.jsp?id=7582> [Siham Barakat, Research Fellow, Australian Council for Educational Research, trans]

Kuwaiti Constitution 1962 (reinstated 1992) [World Intellectual Property trans, <www.wipo.int/edocs/lexdocs/laws/en/kw/kw004en.pdf>]

5 Italy

Italian Code of Civil Procedure (Title VIII of Book IV of the Italian Code of Civil Procedure)' <www.jus.uio.no/lm/italy.arbitration/806.html>

6 Iran

Civil Code of Islamic Republic of Iran [M.A.R Taleghani trans, *The Civil Code of Iran*] (Rothman, 1995)

Constitution of the Islamic Republic of Iran 1979 (as last amended on July 28, 1989) [World Intellectual Property Organisation trans <www.wipo.int/wipolex/en/details.jsp?id=7697>]

7 Iraq

Iraqi Civil Code 1951 (United Nations Refugee Agency Refworld trans, <www.refworld.org/docid/55002ec24.html>)

8 Jordan

Jordanian Civil Code 1976 World Intellectual Property Organisation, <www.wipo.int/wipolex/en/text.jsp?file_id=227215> [Siham Barakat, Research Fellow, Australian Council for Educational Research, trans]

9 Malaysia

Central Bank Act 1958 (replaced by Central Bank Act 2009)
Central Bank Act 2009

10 Netherlands

Code of Civil Procedure in Netherlands [Dutch Civil Law, 'Code of Civil Procedures' <www.dutchcivillaw.com/civilprocedureleg.htm>]

11 Oman

Commercial Code of 1990 (Oman) Omani government trans, <www.oman.om/wps/wcm/connect/7b72e2d8-ba8e-48d4-b44e-c7c3570b639b/OMAN+I+COMMERCIAL+law1.pdf?MOD=AJPERES>

12 Pakistan

Constitution of the Islamic Republic of Pakistani (International Labour Organisation, www.ilo.org/dyn/natlex/natlex4.detail?p_lang=en&p_isn=33863)

13 Saudi Arabia

Basic Law of Governance (promulgated by the Royal Decree No. A/90 (1992) (Royal Embassy of Saudi Arabia Washington, DC trans, <www.saudiembassy.net/about/country-information/laws/The_Basic_Law_Of_Governance.aspx>)

Gas Concession Agreement Between the Kingdom of Saudi Arabia and Lukoil Overseas (Umm Alqura Gazette No. 3990/4 May 2004) as cited in Ilias Bantekas, 'Arbitrability in Finance and Banking' in Loukas Mistelis and Stavros Brekoulakis (eds), *Arbitrability: International & Comparative Perspectives* (Kluwer Law International, 2009) 291, 309

Old Implementation Rules 1985, Resolution No. 7/2021/M (legislation dated 27 May 1985)

Old Saudi Arbitration Law 1983, Royal Decree No. M/46 [legislation dated 25 April 1983, replaced by *Saudi Arbitration Law 2012*]

Saudi Arbitration Law 2012, Royal Decree No. M/34 [legislation dated 16 April 2012, published in the official Saudi Gazette (Um Al-Qura) on 8 June 2012 and came into effect on 9 July 2012]

Saudi Enforcement Law 2013, Royal Decree No. M/34 [legislation date 16 April 2012, published in the official Saudi Gazette (Um Al-Qura) on 8 June 2012 and came into effect on 9 July 2012]

14 Syria

Syrian Civil Code 1949 (World Intellectual Property Organisation, www.wipo.int/wipolex/en/details.jsp?id=10917) [Siham Barakat, Research Fellow, Australian Council for Educational Research, trans]

15 United Arab Emirates (UAE)

Commercial Transactions Law (UAE) 1993 [Dawoud S. El Alami trans, *The Law of Commercial Procedure of the United Arab Emirates* (Graham & Trotman, 1994)]

Federal Law No. 3 of 1987 ('Federal Penal Code') (UAE) [Al Mubasheri, Advocates & Legal Consultancy trans]

Federal Law No. 5 of 1985 [*James Whelan* (Clifford Chance) trans, *The Civil Code* <https://lexemiratidotnet.files.wordpress.com/2011/07/uae-civil-code-_english-translation_.pdf>]

Federal Law No 11 of 1992 (UAE) translated in Gordon Blanke and Habib Al Mulla, *Arbitration in the MENA Legislation* (Juris Publishing, 2016)

UAE Constitution (The Federal National Council Standing Orders trans, 1997)

16 United Kingdom

Arbitration and Mediation Services (Equality) Bill [HL] 2014–15 (11 June 2014) <http://services.parliament.uk/bills/2014-15/arbitrationandmediationservices equality/stages.html>

English Arbitration Act 1996
Equality Act 2010

17 United States of America

New Jersey Statutes Annotated (N.J. Stat. Ann.) (revised 2015)
New York City Administrative Code (N.Y.C. Admin. Code) (*current through local law 2016/104, enacted 31 August 2016*)
Pennsylvania Human Relations Act, 43 Pa. Stat. Ann. §§ 951 to 963 <www.phrc. pa.gov/Resources/Law-and-Legal/Pages/The-Pennsylvania-Human-Relations-Act.aspx#.WGQ8b1V96Uk>

D International instruments

1 International conventions and other similar instruments

European Convention on International Commercial Arbitration, opened for signature 21 April 1961, 484 UNTS 364 (entered into force 7 January 1964)
New York Arbitration Convention, *The New York Arbitration Convention on the Recognition and Enforcement of Foreign Arbitral Awards* opened for signature 19 June 1958, 330 UNTS 38 (entered into force 7 June 1959)
North American Free Trade Agreement ('NAFTA'), (entered into force on 1 January 1994), <www.nafta-sec-alena.org/Home/Legal-Texts/North-American-Free-Trade-Agreement?mvid=2>
Organisation of Islamic Cooperation, *The Cairo Declaration of Human Rights* <www. oic-oci.org/english/article/human.htm>
United Nations Convention on Contracts for the International Sale of Goods, opened for signature 11 April 1980, 1489 UNTS 3 (entered into force 1 January 1988)

2 Model laws

UNCITRAL Model Law on International Commercial Arbitration, adopted 11 December 1985, as amended 7 July 2006

3 Arbitration rules

Arbitration Rules of the Singapore International Arbitration Centre (6th edition), effective 1 August 2016
Hong Kong International Arbitration Centre Administered Arbitration Rules, effective 1 September 2008
International Chamber of Commerce Rules of Arbitration, effective 1 January 2012
IICRA, *Chart and Arbitration and Reconciliation Procedures*, effective 25 February 2007 <iicra.com/admin/download.php?file_name=arb.pdf&content_type=>
International Centre for Dispute Resolution, *International Dispute Resolution Procedures (Including Mediation and Arbitration Rules (effective 1 June 2014)* <www. adr.org/aaa/ShowProperty?nodeId=/UCM/ADRSTAGE2020868&revision=lat latestrelea>

Kuala Lumpur Regional Centre for Arbitration, *KLRCA Arbitration Rules 2012*,' in force on 20 September 2012, <https://lbrcdn.net/cdn/files/gar/articles/KLRCA_i-Arbitration_Rules.pdf>

Kuala Lumpur Regional Centre for Arbitration, *KLRCA Arbitration Rules*, revised 2013 <http://klrca.org/rules/arbitration/>

London Court of International Arbitration, *LCIA Arbitration Rules 2014*, effective 1 October 2014

Saudi Centre for Commercial Arbitration Rules 2016, effective May 2016 <http://sadr.org/en/adr-services-2/arbitration-2/rules/>

Swiss Rules of International Arbitration, effective June 2012

UNCITRAL Arbitration Rules 2010, adopted 1976 and revised 2010

World Intellectual Property Organisation, *World Intellectual Property Organisation Arbitration Rules*, effective 1 June 2014

4 Other soft law instruments

Chartered Institute of Arbitrators, *Protocol for the Use of Party-Appointed Expert Witnesses in International Arbitration*, adopted September 2007

Dubai International Financial Centre Courts, *Enforcement Guidelines*, dated 3 January 2016

International Bar Association, *Guidelines on Conflict of Interest in International Arbitration*, adopted 23 October 2014

International Bar Association, *International Bar Association Rules on the Taking of Evidence in International Arbitration 2010*, adopted 29 May 2010

International Institute for the Unification of Private Law ('*UNIDROIT*'), *UNDROIT Principles of International Commercial Contracts 2010* <www.unidroit.org/instruments/commercial-contracts/unidroit-principles-2010>

Lex Mercatoria Database, *Principles of European Contract Law* (2002) <www.jus.uio.no/lm/eu.contract.principles.parts.1.to.3.2002/>

Regulation (EC) No 593/2008 of the European Parliament and of the Council of 17 June 2008 on the Law Applicable to Contractual Obligations (Rome I) [2008] OJ L 177/6 E. CISG Advisory Council Opinions, Parliamentary Documents, Conference Papers, Websites, Blogs & Other Materials

(AAOIFI), Accounting and Auding Organization for Islamic Financial Institution, *AAOIFI: What We Do* (2016) <http://aaoifi.com/?lang=en>

Abbas, Mohammed, 'Shortage of Scholars Troubles Islamic Banking' (2008) *The New York Times* <www.nytimes.com/2008/01/22/business/worldbusiness/22iht-bank.4.9412578.html?_r=0&pagewanted=print>

Akhtar, Shaistah, 'Arbitration in the Islamic Middle East: Challenges and the Way Ahead' (2008) *International Comparative Legal Guides* 11 <www.iclg.co.uk/index.php?area=4&show_chapter=2201&ifocus=1&kh_publications_id=83>

Al Shamsi, Jasim Salim, 'Restricting Resorting to [Civil] Laws in Contract [Disputes] and Accepting the Arbitration of Shari'ah Boards Instead' (The 5th Annual Shari'ah Supervisory Boards Conference for Islamic Financial Institutions, Bahrain, 19–20 November 2005)

Asian International Arbitration Centre, 'AIAC Arbitration Rules (Revised 2018)' (2018) <www.aiac.world/Arbitration-i-Arbitration/>

Al Tuwayjri, Mohamed, 'Note – 13 February 2006, Court of Cassation – Civil Circuit,' (2010) 2(3) *International Journal of Arab Arbitration*, 142

Almulhim, Mulhim Hamad, 'The First Female Arbitrator in Saudi Arabia,' *Kluwer Arbitration Blog* (Jeddah) (29 August 2016) <http://kluwerarbitrationblog.com/2016/08/29/the-first-female-arbitrator-in-saudi-arabia/>

Ansary, Dr. Abdullah F., 'A Brief Overview of the Saudi Arabian Legal System' (2015) <www.nyulawglobal.org/globalex/Saudi_Arabia1.html>

Arab, Hassan and Laila El Shentenawi, *The UAE Country Report* (2015) <www.ibanet.org/LPD/Dispute_Resolution_Section/Arbitration/Recogntn_Enfrcemnt_Arbitl_Awrd/publicpolicy15.aspx>

Arbitration, Association for International, 'International Commercial Arbitration in the Deserts of Arabia' (2009) 2 <www.arbitration-adr.org/documents/?i=62>

Ashurst, *English Court of Appeal Decision: Impact on Institutional Arbitration Clauses* <www.ashurst.com/publication-item.aspx?id_Content=5436>

Asian International Arbitration Centre, *i-Arbitration* <www.aiac.world/Arbitration-i-Arbitration/>

Asian International Arbitration Centre, *Frequently Asked Questions* (2018) <https://aiac.world/wp-content/i-arbitration/rules_iarb_en/PDF-Flip/PDF.pdf>

Balouziyeh, John, 'Saudi Arabia's New Arbitration Law Sees More Investors Opting for Arbitration in Saudi Arabia' (2013) <http://kluwerarbitrationblog.com/2013/05/29/saudi-arabias-new-arbitration-law-sees-more-investors-opting-for-arbitration-in-saudi-arabia/>

Bank, Al Rayan, *About us* <www.alrayanbank.co.uk/useful-info-tools/about-us/>

Bank, Islamic Development, 'Modes of Finance' (2014) <www.isdb.org/mof/index.html#p=2>

Baz, Abdul-'Aziz ibn 'Abdullah ibn, 'Fatwas of Ibn Baz, Volume 3' <www.alifta.com/Search/ResultDetails.aspx?languagename=en&lang=en&view=result&fatwaNum=&FatwaNumID=&ID=218&searchScope=14&SearchScopeLevels1=&SearchScopeLevels2=&highLight=1&SearchType=exact&SearchMoesar=false&bookID=&LeftVal=0&RightVal=0&simple=&SearchCriteria=allwords&PagePath=&siteSection=1&searchkeyword=119111109101110032100114105118105110103#firstKeyWordFound>

BBC News, 'Egypt referendum: "98% back new constitution",' *BBC* (online), (19 January 2014) <www.bbc.com/news/world-middle-east-25796110>

'Bill Stages – *Arbitration and Mediation Services (Equality) Bill*' [HL] 2014–15 (11 June 2014) <http://services.parliament.uk/bills/2014-15/arbitrationandmediationservicesequality/stages.html>

Blanke, Gordon, 'Public Policy in the UAE: Has the Unruly Horse Turned into a Camel?' *Kluwer Arbitration Blog* (14 October 2012) <http://kluwerarbitrationblog.com/blog/2012/10/14/public-policy-in-the-uae-has-the-unruly-horse-turned-into-a-camel/>

Bono, Seema, 'Middle East and North Africa Overview' (2015) *International Arbitration 2015* <www.iclg.co.uk/practice-areas/international-arbitration-/international-arbitration-2015/13-middle-east-and-north-africa-overview>

Campbell, Fiona, 'Arbitrability of Disputes: Issues of Arbitrability and Public Policy in the UAE' *Al Tamimi & Co* (May 2014) <www.tamimi.com/en/magazine/law-update/section-8/may-7/arbitrability-of-disputes-issues-of-arbitrability-and-public-policy-in-the-uae.html>

Chraibi, Mahat, 'Morocco- Corporate- Withholding Tax' (2016) Pricewaterhouse Coopers <http://taxsummaries.pwc.com/uk/taxsummaries/wwts.nsf/ID/Morocco-Corporate-Withholding-taxes>

CISG Advisory Council, *CISG Advisory Council Opinion No. 14- Interest Under Article 78 CISG* (21 and 22 October 2013), Rapporteur: Professor Yesim M. Atamer, <www.CISG.law.pace.edu/CISG/CISG-AC-op14.html>

Clyde & Co, 'Insurance and Reinsurance in Saudi Arabia' (2015) <www.clydeco. com/uploads/Files/CC007080_PLG_KSA_Brochure_ME_V4_11-03-15.pdf>

Craig Tevendale, '*Jivraj*- It's Back and This Time It's at the European Commission' (28 September 2012) *Kluwer Arbitration Blog* <http://kluwerarbitrationblog. com/2012/09/28/jivraj-its-back-and-this-time-its-at-the-european-commission/>

Dehais, Fahad Al, 'Saudi Arabia' (20 April 2016), *Global Arbitration Review* (online) <http://globalarbitrationreview.com/chapter/1036981/saudi-arabia>

Dhimmi (2016) Oxford University Press <www.oxfordislamicstudies.com/article/ opr/t125/e536>

'Dispute Resolution: The Final Piece of the Puzzle,' *Islamic Finance News* [Supplements] (7 November 2012) *Expanded Academic ASAP*

Dubai International Arbitration Centre, 'Arbitration in the UAE' <www.diac.ae/ idias/rules/uae/>

Dubai International Finance Centre, 'DIFC Authority Releases Updated Version of Guide to Islamic Finance' *Dubai International Finance Centre* (online) (20 July 2009) <www.difc.ae/news/difc-authority-releases-updated-version-guide-islamic-finance>

Ethiopia, United Nations, 'Universal Declaration of Human Rights Signatories' (2014) <http://unethiopia.org/universal-declaration-of-human-rights-signatories/>

European Commission, *Trade in Goods with Saudi Arabia* (2016) <http://trade. ec.europa.eu/doclib/docs/2006/september/tradoc_113442.pdf>

European Commission, *Trade in Goods with United Arab Emirates* (2016) <http:// trade.ec.europa.eu/doclib/docs/2006/september/tradoc_113458.pdf>

Gamal, Mahmoud El, 'An Economic Explication of the Prohibition of Gharar in Classical Islamic Jurisprudence' (Paper presented at the 4th International Conference on Islamic Economics, Leicester, 13–15 August 2000) <www.ruf.rice.edu/ ~elgamal/files/gharar.pdf>

Global Arbitration Review, 'Dubai Company defeats US$1.2 Billion Claim' (2008) <http://globalarbitrationreview.com/news/article/14827/dubai-company-defeats-us12-billion-claim/>

Global Arbitration Review, 'KLRCA to Unveil Islamic Arbitration Rules,' *Global Arbitration Review* (online) (17 September 2009) <http://globalarbitrationre view.com/article/1031606/klrca-to-unveil-islamic-arbitration-rules>

Global Arbitration Review, 'Saudi Court Rewrites Arbitration Award' (2009) <http:// globalarbitrationreview.com/news/article/15257/saudi-court-rewrites-arbitra tion-award>

Hadd (Oxford University Press, 2016) <www.oxfordislamicstudies.com/article/opr/ t125/e757>

Hadith:

Book 24, Hadith No. 3587, *Sunan Abi Dawud* <http://sunnah.com/abudawud/ 25/24>

Book 31, Hadith No. 12, *Muwatta Malik* <http://sunnah.com/urn/413240>

Sunnah, *Riba* <http://sunnah.com/search/?q=riba>

Vol. 3, Book 12, Hadith 1229; Vol. 3, Book 12, Hadith No. 2194; Vol. 5, Book 44, Hadith No. 4522; Book 31, Hadith No. 1, *Sunna* <http://sunnah.com/ search/?q=gharar>

Vol. 3, Book 12, Hadith No. 1230, *Jami' at-Tirmidhi* <http://sunnah.com/tirmidhi/14/30>

Vol. 3, Book 12, Hadith No. 2195, *Sunan Ibn Majah* <http://sunnah.com/urn/1265140>

Vol. 3, Book 13, Hadith No. 1352, *Jami' at-Tirmidhi* <http://sunnah.com/tirmidhi/15>

Vol. 3, Book 35, Hadith No. 445, *Sahih al-Bukhari* <http://sunnah.com/bukhari/35/5>

Vol. 3, Book 41, Hadith No. 585, *Sahih al-Bukhari* <http://sunnah.com/bukhari/43/16>

Vol. 4, Book 56, Hadith No. 760, *Sahih Bukhari* <www.sahih-bukhari.com/Pages/Bukhari_4_56.php>

Vol. 40, Hadith No. 28, *Hadith Nawawi* <http://sunnah.com/nawawi40/28>

Vol. 40, Hadith No. 32, Hadith Nawawi <http://sunnah.com/nawawi40>

Vol. 5, Book 57, Hadith No. 3, *Sahih al-Bukhari* <www.sahih-bukhari.com/Pages/Bukhari_5_57.php>

Halim, Ruba Abdel, 'DIAC Discusses the Launch of an Islamic Arbitration Window' *Zawya* (online) (8 February 2016) <www.zawya.com/story/DIAC_discusses_the_launch_of_an_Islamic_Arbitration_Window-ZAWYA20160208120400/>

Harb, Jean-Pierre, Fahad Habib and Sheila Shadmand, 'The New Saudi Arbitration Law' (2012) *Jones Day Publications* <www.jonesday.com/new_saudi_arbitration_law/>

Hashemi, Nader and Emran Qureshi, *Human Rights* (Oxford University Press, 2016) <www.oxfordislamicstudies.com/article/opr/t236/e0325>

Herbert Smith Freehills LLP, 'Saudi Arabian Court Overturns ICC Award' (2009) <www.lexology.com/library/detail.aspx?g=26515e46-a971-496b-82c7-da73e837e496>

Hoffmann, Anne K., 'Qatari Courts and Foreign Arbitral Awards- the End of the Story?' (2014) *Al Tamimi & Co* <www.tamimi.com/en/magazine/law-update/section-8/may-7/qatari-courts-and-foreign-arbitral-awards-the-end-of-the-story.html>

Human Rights Watch, 'Arbitrary Detention and Unfair Trials in the Deficient Criminal Justice System of Saudi Arabia' (2010) 20 *Precarious Justice* 91 <www.hrw.org/reports/2008/saudijustice0308/saudijustice0308web.pdf>

Ibn Qudama, Muwaffaq al-Din (Oxford University Press, 2016) <www.oxfordislamicstudies.com/article/opr/t125/e953>

Ijtihad (Oxford University Press, 2016) <www.oxfordislamicstudies.com/article/opr/t236/e0354>

International Islamic Centre for Reconciliation and Arbitration ('IICRA'), *Establishment* (30 January 2013) <http://iicra.com/en/misc_pages/detail/4c855d3580>

International Islamic Centre for Reconciliation and Arbitration ('IICRA'), *Who We Are* (30 January 2013) <http://iicra.com/en/misc_pages/detail/4c76b6d187>

International Islamic Mediation and Arbitration Centre, *IMAC: About Us* <www.arabcci.org/IMAC_aboutus.htm>

International *Shari'ah* Research Academic for Islamic Finance, *Fatwa in Islamic Finance* <http://ifikr.isra.my/documents/10180/16168/blp-isra%20sep%20bulletin%20Tawarruq.pdf>

Interview with Faris Shehabi, Former Head of Legal Services, Kuala Lumpur Regional Centre of Arbitration (Phone Interview, 15 May 2005)

Isik, Ilhan and Taobo Zheng, *Ratification of International Human Rights Treaties – Saudi Kingdom* (2010) University of Minnesota Human Rights Library <http://hrlibrary.umn.edu/research/ratification-saudikingdom.html>

Islamic Banking Department of State Bank of Pakistan, 'Fit & Proper Criteria for Appointment of Shariah Advisors' (2004) <www.sbp.org.pk/ibd/2004/f%20&%20p%20test%20for%20sa.pdf>

Islamic Banking Department of State Bank of Pakistan, *Essentials of Islamic Modes of Financing* (5 October 2015) State Bank of Pakistan <www.sbp.org.pk/press/2004/Islamic_modes.pdf>

Jones Day, 'Kuala Lumpur Regional Center for Arbitration Rebrands as Asian International Arbitration Centre,' Jones Day, February 2018 <www.jonesday.com/Kuala-Lumpur-Regional-Centre-for-Arbitration-Rebrands-as-Asian-International-Arbitration-Centre-02-14-2018/?RSS=true>

Jones Day, 'The New Saudi Arbitration Law' (September 2012) <www.jonesday.com/new_saudi_arbitration_law/>

Jones Day, 'The New Enforcement Law of Saudi Arabia: An Additional Step Toward a Harmonized Arbitration Regime' (September 2013) <www.jonesday.com/the-new-enforcement-law-of-saudi-arabia-an-additional-step-toward-a-harmonized-arbitration-regime-09-04-2013/>

Kalicki, Jean, 'Social Media and Arbitration Conflicts of Interest: A Challenge for the 21st Century' on *Kluwer Arbitration Blog* (23 April 2012) <http://kluwerarbitrationblog.com/2012/04/23/social-media-and-arbitration-conflicts-of-interest-a-challenge-for-the-21st-century>

Khan, Fouzia, '37 Women Complete Arbitration Course,' *Arab News* (Jeddah) (31 May 2013) <www.arabnews.com/news/453495>

Klötzel, Dr. Thomas R, 'Keynote Address' (Speech delivered at the i-Arbitration Conference,

Kuala Lumpur Regional Centre for Arbitration, (8 May 2015) <https://youtu.be/SgzpDNDQ-cc?list=PLkdbSlXVnul0p1b_AjhF8GwGa_ddKRTuZ>

Lawrence, Jonathan, Peter Morton and Hussain Khan, 'Resolving Islamic Finance Disputes' *K & L Gates* (online) (23 September 2013) <www.klgates.com/files/...d738.../Dispute_Resolution_in_Islamic_Finance.pdf>

Malaysia, Bank Negara, 'Malaysia: Central Bank of, Shariah Resolutions in Islamic Finance' (2010) <www.bnm.gov.my/microsites/financial/pdf/resolutions/shariah_resolutions_2nd_edition_EN.pdf>

Malaysia, Bank Negara, 'Guidelines on the Governance of Shariah Committee for the Islamic Financial Institutions' <www.bnm.gov.my/guidelines/01_banking/04_prudential_stds/23_gps.pdf>

Malaysia, Bank Negara, 'Shariah Governance Framework' (2010) <www.bnm.gov.my/guidelines/05_shariah02_Shariah_Governance_Framework_20101026.pdf>

Malaysia, Securities Commission, 'Resolutions of the Securities Commission Shariah Advisory Council' (2004) <www.sc.com.my/wp-content/uploads/eng/html/icm/Resolutions_SAC_2ndedition.pdf>

Malaysia, Securities Commission, 'Resolutions of the Shariah Advisory Council of the Securities Commission Malaysia' (2012–2014) <www.sc.com.my/wp-content/uploads/eng/html/icm/Resolution_SAC_2012-2014.pdf>

Ministerial Decision 151/2002, Ministry of Commerce and Industry, 'Specifying the Interest in Consideration of a Loan or Commercial Debt' (Sultanate of Oman [Said Al Shahry Law Office and Richards Butler Law Firm, trans])

Muhammad Ibn Abd al-Wahhab (Oxford University Press, 2016) <www.oxfordislamicstudies.com/article/opr/t125/e916?_hi=0&_pos=16>

Muslim World League Islamic Fiqh Council, *Resolutions of Islamic Fiqh Council* <http://themwl.org/downloads/Resolutions-of-Islamic-Fiqh-Council-2.pdf>

Oxford Reference, 'Electio iuris' (2011) <www.oxfordreference.com/view/10.1093/acref/9780195369380.001.0001/acref-9780195369380-e-604>

Pew Research Center, *The Future of World Religions: Population Growth Projections, 2010–2050*, (2015) <www.pewforum.org/files/2015/03/PF_15.04.02_Projec tionsFullReport.pdf>

Practical Law, 'KLRCA Publishes New Rules' *Practical Law: A Thomson Reuters Legal Solution* (online) (30 October 2013) <http://us.practicallaw.com/2-547-2965?q=&qp=&qo=&qe=>

Qa'ud, Abdullah ibn, et al., 'Hadith Mutawatir and Hadith-ul-Ahad, Fatwa no. 4696' <www.alifta.com/Search/ResultDetails.aspx?languagename=en&lang=en&view=result&fatwaNum=&FatwaNumID=&ID=1245&searchScope=7&SearchScope Levels1=&SearchSSearchScop2=&highLight=1&SearchType=exact&Search Moesar=false&bookID=&LeftVal=0&RightVal=0&simple=&SearchCriteria=allwords &PagePath=&siteSection=1&searchkeywsea=119111109101110>

Qanun (Oxford University Press, 2016) <www.oxfordislamicstudies.com/article/opr/t125/e1917>

Qatar International Court and Dispute Resolution Centre, *The Qatar Financial Centre Civil and Commercial Court Regulations and Procedural Rules* (2010) <www.qicdrc.com.qa/sites/default/files/s3/wysiwyg/qfc_civil_and_commercial_court_regulations_date_of_issuance_15_december_2010_0.pdf>

Saidi, Abdallah Ben Mohamed, 'Note – 17 May 2006, High Court' (2009) 1(1) *International Journal of Arab Arbitration* 418

Saleh, Alex and Riza Ismail, 'The Choice of Law and Dispute Settlement Resolution in Islamic Cross Border Finance Transactions' *Islamic Finance News* (online) (25 May 2011) <http://islamicfinancenews.com/news/choice-law-and-dispute-settlement-resolution-islamic-cross-border-finance-transactions>

Saudi Centre for Commercial Arbitration, *About SCCA* <http://sadr.org/en/about-2/organization>

Sachs, Klaus and Nils Schmidt-Ahrendts, 'Experts: Neutrals or Advocates' (2010) *International Council for Commercial Arbitration Conference 2010*

Sefrioui, Kamal, 'Qatar' (2015) *The International Comparative Legal Guide to International Arbitration 2015* <www.iclg.co.uk/practice-areas/international-arbitration-/international-arbitration-2015/qatar#chaptercontent13>

Sefioui, Kamal, 'Qatar' (2016) *International Comparative Legal Guide to International Arbitration 2016* <www.iclg.co.uk/practice-areas/international-arbitration-/international-arbitration-2016/qatar#chaptercontent13>

Selim, Ismail, *Report on Egyptian Public Policy as a Ground for Annulment and/or Refusal of Enforcement of Arbitral Awards* (2015) <www.ibanet.org/LPD/Dis pute_Resolution_Section/Arbitration/Recogntn_Enfrcemnt_Arbitl_Awrd/pub licpolicy15.aspx>

Selim, Ismail, 'Public Policy Exception as Applied by the Courts of the MENA Region' in United Nations Commission on International Trade Law (ed), *Second Conference for a Euro-Mediterranean Community of International Arbitration, Cairo*, 12 November 2015 (UNCITRAL, 2015).

Shalakany Law Office, 'Interest Rates and Arbitral Awards: Issues of Public Policy' (30 October 2008) <www.internationallawoffice.com/Newsletters/Arbitration-

ADR/Egypt/Shalakany-Law-Office/Interest-Rates-and-Arbitral-Awards-Issues-of-Public-Policy?redir=1>

Shii Islam (Oxford University Press, 2016) <www.oxfordislamicstudies.com/article/opr/t125/e2189?_hi=26&_pos=238#>

Standard & Poor's Ratings Services: McGraw Hill Financial, *Islamic Finance Outlook 2016 Edition* (2016) <www.spratings.com/documents/20184/86966/Islamic_Finance_Outlook_2016_v2/4d9d6fd9-3b11-4ae2-9168-13ee2543b73b>

Sunni Islam (Oxford University Press, 2016) <www.oxfordislamicstudies.com/article/opr/t125/e2280?_hi=2&_pos=2>

Tamimi, Esaam Al, 'Sharia Law and Its Application to International Arbitration' (April 2012) 248 *Al Tamimi & Co- Law Update*

Tamimi, Essam Al, 'Arbitrators Dealing with Real Estate Property Disputes – Is It a Matter of Public Policy?' (2014) <www.tamimi.com/en/magazine/law-update/section-8/june-6/arbitrators-dealing-with-real-estate-property-disputes-is-it-a-matter-of-public-policy.html>

Tan, Vineeta, 'World Nations Turn to Islamic Arbitration Services as Shariah Finance Goes International' *Islamic Finance News* (online) (29 June 2016) <http://islamicfinancenews.com/news/world-nations-turn-islamic-arbitration-services-shariah-finance-goes-international-0>

Taqi al-Din Ahmad Ibn Taymiyyah (Oxford University Press, 2016) <www.oxfordislamicstudies.com/article/opr/t125/e959>

The International Swaps and Derivatives Association, '2013 ISDA Arbitration Guide' <https://www2.isda.org/attachment/==/ISDA_Arbitration_Guide_Final_09.09.13.pdf>

The Panel of Recognised International Market Experts in Finance <www.primefinancedisputes>

The Peninsula Qatar, 'Qatar International Court Plans Expansion' *The Peninsula Qatar* (online) (4 July 2012) <www.thepeninsulaqatar.com/news/qatar/199730/qatar-international-court-plans-expansion>

Thomsons Reuters Zawya, 'The Sharjah International Commercial Arbitration Centre Approves the Operational Plan for 2016 and its List of Arbitrators' *Zawya* (online) (19 January 2016) <www.zawya.com/story/The_Sharjah_International_Commercial_Arbitration_Centre_approves_the_Operational_Plan_for_2016_and_its_List_of_Arbitrators-ZAWYA20160119135617/>

[UN] Secretary General: Possible Features of a Model Law on International Commercial Arbitration' UN Doc A/CN.9/207 (14 May 1981) XII *UNCITRAL Yearbook* 78

'Islamic Arbitration: A Healthy Debate' *Islamic Finance News* (online) (6 February 2013) <http://islamicfinancenews.com/news/islamic-arbitration-healthy-debate>

UNCITRAL, 'Status- United Nations Convention on Contracts for the International Sale of Goods (Vienna, 1980)' (2016) <www.uncitral.org/uncitral/en/uncitral_texts/sale_goods/1980CISG_status.html>

United Kingdom, *Parliamentary Debates*, House of Lords (19 October 2012) Column 1683, (*Baroness Cox*) <www.publications.parliament.uk/pa/ld201213/ldhansrd/text/121019-0001.htm#12101923000438>

United Nations Conference for Contracts on the International Sale of Goods, Summary Records of the Plenary Meetings, 11th Plenary Meeting on 10 April 1980,

Un Doc. A/Conf.97/SR.11 <www.*CISG*.law.pace.edu/*CISG*/plenarycommittee/ summary12.html>

United Nations Conference on Trade and Development, *Recognition and Enforcement of Arbitral Awards: The New York Convention*, UNCTAD/EDM/Misc.232/ Add.37 (2003) <http://unctad.org/en/Docs/edmmisc232add37_en.pdf>

United Nations, 65th Meeting of the Third Committee, General Assembly UN Doc A/C.3/39/SR.65 at 95 (1984)

United States Census Bureau, *U.S. Trade in Goods with Saudi Arabia* (2016) <www. census.gov/foreign-trade/balance/c5170.html>

United States Census Bureau, U.S. Trade in Goods with United Arab Emirates (2016) <www.census.gov/foreign-trade/balance/c5200.html>

Vienna Diplomatic Conference 1980, 34th mtg, (3 April 1980) <http://*CISG*w3.law. pace.edu/*CISG*/firstcommittee/Meeting34.html>

Zawya, Thomson Reuters, 'Shariah Scholars' <www.zawya.com/shariahscholars/ sch_profile.cfm?scholarid=9>

Zawya, Thomsons Reuters, 'The Sharjah International Commercial Arbitration Centre approves the Operational Plan for 2016 and its List of Arbitrators' (2016) <www.zawya.com/story/The_Sharjah_International_Commercial_Arbitration_ Centre_approves_the_Operational_Plan_for_2016_and_its_List_of_Arbitrators- ZAWYA20160119135617/>

Zegers, Jean-Benoît and Omar Elzorkany, *Kingdom of Saudi Arabia* (International Bar Association, 2014) www.ibanet.org/Article/Detail.aspx?ArticleUid=a646cf32- 0ad8-4666-876b-c3d045028e64

Index

Page numbers in *italic* indicate a figure and page numbers in **bold** indicate a table on the corresponding page.